THE EMERGENCE OF
GERMAN IDEALISM

**STUDIES IN PHILOSOPHY
AND THE HISTORY OF PHILOSOPHY**

General Editor: Jude P. Dougherty

Studies in Philosophy
and the History of Philosophy   Volume 34

The Emergence of German Idealism

Edited by Michael Baur and
Daniel O. Dahlstrom

THE CATHOLIC UNIVERSITY OF AMERICA PRESS
Washington, D.C.

Copyright © 1999
The Catholic University of America Press
All rights reserved
Printed in the United States of America

The paper used in this publication meets the minimum requirements of American National Standards for Information Science—Permanence of Paper for Printed Library materials, ANSI Z39.48-1984.
∞

LIBRARY OF CONGRESS CATALOGING-IN-PUBLICATION DATA
    The emergence of German idealism / edited by Michael Baur and Daniel O. Dahlstrom.
        p. cm. — (Studies in philosophy and the history of philosophy ; v. 34)
    Includes bibliographical references and index.
    1. Idealism, German. I. Baur, Michael. II. Dahlstrom, Daniel O. III. Series.
    B21.S78 vol. 34 1999
    [B2849.I3]
    141'.0943—dc21
    98-30101
    ISBN 978-0-8132-3050-4 (pbk)

Contents

Introduction   1

I. THE UNITY OF KANT'S PHILOSOPHY

1. DANIEL O. DAHLSTROM, The Unity of Kant's Critical Philosophy   13

II. THE CRITICAL RECEPTION OF THE CRITICAL PHILOSOPHY: REINHOLD AND THE SKEPTICS

2. ALEXANDER VON SCHÖNBORN, Karl Leonhard Reinhold: "... Endeavoring to keep up the pace *mit unserem zeitalter*"   33
3. MICHAEL BAUR, The Role of Skepticism in the Emergence of German Idealism   63

III. ABSTRACT REALISM AND THE PRIMACY OF THE PRACTICAL: ESSAYS ON FICHTE

4. DANIEL BREAZEALE, Fichte's Abstract Realism   95
5. KARL AMERIKS, Fichte's Appeal Today: The Hidden Primacy of the Practical   116

IV. THE AESTHETIC TURN: ESSAYS ON SCHILLER, HÖLDERLIN, AND THE ROMANTICS

6. JOHN MCCUMBER, Schiller, Hegel, and the Aesthetics of German Idealism   133
7. KARSTEN HARRIES, The Epochal Threshold and the Classical Ideal: Hölderlin contra Hegel   147
8. KENNETH L. SCHMITZ, The Idealism of the German Romantics   176

V. THE MORAL BEGINNINGS: SCHELLING AND HEGEL ON THE KANTIAN POSTULATES

9. KLAUS DÜSING, The Reception of Kant's Doctrine of Postulates in Schelling's and Hegel's Early Philosophical Projects   201

VI. LIBERATING THE ABSOLUTE FROM TRANSCENDENTAL PHILOSOPHY: ESSAYS ON SCHELLING

10. HANS MICHAEL BAUMGARTNER, The Unconditioned in Knowing: I—Identity—Freedom   241
11. XAVIER TILLIETTE, The Problem of Metaphysics   251

VII. CONTRADICTION AND CONTINUITY: ESSAYS ON HEGEL'S DEVELOPMENT

12. MEROLD WESTPHAL, *Von Hegel bis Hegel:* Reflections on "The Earliest System-Programme of German Idealism"   269
13. MARTIN J. DE NYS, Hegel on Absolute Knowing   288

APPENDIX ONE. The Earliest System-Programme of German Idealism (1796 or 1797)   309

APPENDIX TWO. Chronology of a Selection of Some Central Works in the Historical Transition from Transcendental Philosophy to German Idealism: 1781–1807   311

List of Contributors   315
Bibliography   319
Name Index   331

THE EMERGENCE OF
GERMAN IDEALISM

Introduction
MICHAEL BAUR AND DANIEL O. DAHLSTROM

Immanuel Kant's "critical philosophy," as he himself characterizes it, is rightly renowned for its criticism of the metaphysical pretensions of reason unaided by experience. In the *Critique of Pure Reason,* Kant goes to considerable lengths to disestablish the sort of speculative metaphysics that is erected on the premise that the human mind can have a clear and distinct, that is to say, a purely intellectual, nonsensory insight into the natures and causes of things. Yet, remarkably, within a generation, Kant's own efforts give way to one putatively new system of speculative metaphysics after the other, each claiming to complete his project by, among other things, applying the principles of the critical philosophy to that philosophy itself. Part of the reason for this development can be found in Kant's own thinking. For by no means does his skepticism about speculative metaphysics extend to all forms of a priori knowledge or to all nonempirical principles of human experience. His critical philosophy is, again in his own terms, also a "transcendental philosophy," one aimed at determining the principles that render a particular region of human endeavor—knowing, acting, enjoying—possible. In the minds of Kant's prominent critics, however, the task of identifying and recursively demonstrating these transcendental principles and their unity requires reintroducing speculative metaphysics or something closely akin to it. A redefined metaphysics accordingly takes shape in a German idealism that, nevertheless, sees its speculations, in the manner just described, as a consequence of Kant's transcendental philosophy.

The preceding account of German idealism's development from its Kantian roots is, of necessity, highly abbreviated and, it must be confessed, a bit presumptuous. For, in truth, the exceedingly complex story of the critical yet speculative reaction to Kant's philosophy from 1786 to 1807 (from the publication of Reinhold's *Letters on the Kantian Philosophy* to the publication of Hegel's *Phenomenology of Spirit*) has never been fully told and, indeed, with good reason since it is a story replete with the thrusts, parries, and counterthrusts of a variety of thinkers, some of whom historians have largely forgotten or neglected, with their own developing and often divergent views on the prospects of philosophy after Kant. As a consequence, suitably informed accounts and philosophically reasoned assessments of the thought that led to the emergence of German idealism from Kant's transcendental philosophy have been in short supply. The present volume cannot remedy this lack, but it is an attempt to contribute to an understanding of some of the major factors and considerations that led to or attended the metaphysical speculations of German philosophers after Kant. In addition to ten new essays on the emergence of German idealism, the present volume contains translations of three significant German and French investigations of post-Kantian thought, hitherto unavailable in English.

Before turning to the post-Kantian thinkers themselves, however, it may prove useful to review the parameters of Kant's transcendental philosophy and, in particular, given subsequent concerns about the purported lack of unity to Kant's philosophy and about the inadequacy of its foundation, to consider how Kant himself construed the unity of his philosophy. This issue is the subject of the opening essay, "The Unity of Kant's Critical Philosophy" by Daniel O. Dahlstrom. Taking his cues from the three questions in which, in Kant's view, all the interests of reason come together ("What can I know? What should I do? What may I hope for?"), Dahlstrom surveys the basic arguments and conclusions of Kant's critical writings. The aim of the survey is to indicate in what sense Kant believed himself to have found in the principle of purposiveness, as elaborated in the *Critique of Judgment*, a principle capable of mediating between the principles governing the theoretical order of science and the practical order of freedom, in short, the principles of nature and of morality, demonstrated in the *Critique of Pure Reason* and the *Critique of Practical Reason*, respectively.

Among the handful of thinkers who figured prominently in the early reception of Kant's critical philosophy, arguably none is more central than the intriguing ex-priest and Freemason from Vienna, Karl Leonhard Reinhold. Probably no work, for example, is more responsible for instilling and spreading not only interest in Kant's philosophy but also the need for critical engagement with it than Reinhold's *Briefe über die Kantische Philosophie* of 1786–1787. Yet, until recently, Reinhold's role in the emergence of German idealism has been largely ignored. In his essay "Karl Leonard Reinhold: '. . . Endeavoring to keep up the pace *mit unserem Zeitalter,*'" Alexander von Schönborn takes some important steps toward rectifying this situation by demonstrating how profoundly Reinhold's program of *Elementarphilosophie,* conceived as an attempt to complete the critical philosophy by grounding it in a single first principle, shapes the philosophical projects of the post-Kantian idealists. But Schönborn also dispels the neo-Kantian myth, concocted on the basis of this influence, that Reinhold is significant only as a harbinger of "the fall into metaphysical mysticism." In addition to tracing the several changes Reinhold made to his system within the general ambit of German idealism, Schönborn also recounts how Reinhold's turn to realism and concern with the philosophy of language provoked an intemperate reaction by Fichte, Schelling, and Hegel that consisted in caricature rather than careful consideration of Reinhold's reasoning. The result was yet another myth, the neo-Hegelian myth that Reinhold's significance lay merely in being a popularizer of philosophy and that, like the public, he lacked the autonomy of thought requisite of a serious philosopher. In the course of demolishing this myth and reviewing the development of Reinhold's thought, Schönborn demonstrates that Reinhold is not merely the initiator and knowledgeable reformer of much that is present in post-Kantian philosophical systems, but also a profound critic of them, someone both ready and able to move beyond them.

The importance of Reinhold for the early reception of Kant's philosophy is further corroborated by the next essay in the volume, "The Role of Skepticism in the Emergence of German Idealism" by Michael Baur. In this essay Baur seeks to dispel the popular myth that the post-Kantian German idealists were uncritical speculative metaphysicians with little concern for the skeptical problems that had first aroused Kant from his dogmatic slumber. In fact, the development of thought from Kant to Hegel is best described, Baur argues, not as a repudiation or mitigation of skepticism, but rather as a radicalization and deepening of it. The radicalization of skepticism, however, does not mark a departure from systematic philosophy. The movement from Kant to Hegel is paralleled by the emergence of the insight that systematic philosophy can respond adequately to skepticism only by demonstrating the fundamental identity-in-difference between skepticism and itself. Baur substantiates these claims by tracing some of the crucial steps taken on the intellectual journey from Kant to Hegel, for example: the early skeptical attacks upon Kant's philosophy; Reinhold's attempt to salvage transcendental philosophy by reformulating it as a descriptive philosophy of consciousness; G. E. Schulze's skeptical assault on Reinhold's attempt and on the idea of transcendental philosophy in general; Fichte's creative appropriation of Schulze's critique; and finally, Hegel's transformation of the Fichtean strategy and mediated return to the starting point of this process of skeptical awakening: David Hume.

Fichte's philosophy, in particular, his unique brand of realism and the primacy he accords the practical, is the subject of the next two essays. In "Fichte's Abstract Realism," Daniel Breazeale addresses the seeming contradiction between Fichte's claim concerning the allegedly absolute character of the self and Fichte's apparent admission that there is an external "check" upon this very same self. Breazeale's resolution of the difficulty emphasizes both the absoluteness of the self and the irreducibility of the "check" to the activity of the self. The label of "abstract realism" appropriately captures both sides of the Fichtean position: Fichte is a "realist" since the self's other is ultimately irreducible to the activity of the self; however, this realism is abstract, since it does not entail the actual existence of any particular object outside of the self. That is, Fichte's realism does not imply the givenness of any particular object to the self, but only the (practical) givenness of a task, namely, the self's infinite task of undertaking a determination within itself. For Breazeale, it would be accurate to describe the Fichtean self as a living contradiction. In order for the self to be conscious of its own finitude (and thus in order for it to be a self at all), the self must recognize some limit upon itself. However, if the limit is a limit for the self (as it must be), then the self automatically transcends the limit in the very act of acknowledging it. Hence, the self is simultaneously both limited and unlimited. Breazeale unpacks the various ways in which the self can be said to experience the "check" by which it recognizes its own limitedness: as "feeling" on an immediate and abstract level; as the "summons" of another free being within the richer context of intersubjectivity; or (on an existential and philosophical level) as an "affront" to a proudly idealistic self that would deny its dependence on all givenness or contingency.

In his essay "Fichte's Appeal Today: The Hidden Primacy of the Practical," Karl Ameriks contends that the radical nature and the limitations of Fichte's doctrine of the primacy of the practical have not been adequately appreciated, even by Fichte's most ardent contemporary admirers. Unlike Kant, Fichte held that no theoretical philosophy whatsoever, not even a critical metaphysics of transcendental idealism, is capable of rescuing our ordinary belief in our inner freedom. Fichte accordingly argued that pure practical reason must be methodologically prior to theoretical reason; only our prior commitment to freedom can save both the existence of a world beyond mere representations and the claims of the moral law upon us (neither of which theoretical philosophy would be able to deliver in any case). Ameriks argues that Fichte's radicalized assertion of the primacy of the practical is problematic in several respects, accounting for the endeavor, undertaken by contemporary followers of Fichte, to provide a nonpractical, "neutralized" demonstration of the absoluteness of subjectivity. According to Ameriks, such strategies are ultimately inconsistent with Fichte's own argumentation, and they fail to address the latent ambiguities and difficulties of the Fichtean position. Until Fichte scholars give greater attention to these problems, it will not be possible, Ameriks concludes, to appreciate the full significance of Fichte's doctrine of the primacy of the practical.

The aesthetic turn in post-Kantian thinking takes center stage in the next collection of essays as the import of the work of Schiller, Hölderlin, and the romantics for the development of German idealism is addressed. In "Schiller and the Aesthetics of German Idealism," John McCumber aims to articulate the "middle term" by which we might understand how Schiller's aesthetics and ethics can be integrated with the metaphysics of German idealism. As Hegel notes, Schiller is to be praised for his intuition that the relation between sense and intellect is not one of indifference or domination, but one of harmony and accord. But unlike Hegel, Schiller holds that it is aesthetics, and not philosophy, that shows us how to achieve a proper harmony between intellect and sense. Furthermore, Schiller's aesthetic theory depends on an acceptance of the Kantian thing-in-itself. Thus it is not clear how Schiller's aesthetics can be integrated with the metaphysics of German idealism, which requires no thing-in-itself. Even more problematically, it is not clear why the elimination of the thing-in-itself from German idealistic metaphysics does not lead to the view that truth consists in the domination of reason over sense (as it does in Fichte). According to McCumber, Schiller himself suggests answers to these puzzles. For Schiller, sensible matter can be reconciled with reason and morality because it prefigures both. Thus, in a sense, Schiller does reject the thing-in-itself. Conversely, Hegel does not reject the thing-in-itself per se, but only the view that the thing-in-itself is an indeterminable "something" beyond experience. That is, Hegel understands the real as necessarily embodied. Since language for Hegel is the most perfect material embodiment of the intelligible, his metaphysics is perhaps best understood as linguistic metaphysics. As McCumber shows, our understanding of Hegel and Schiller in relation to one another enriches the meaning of both.

Another poet who figured prominently in the emergence of German idealism is the friend and classmate of Hegel and Schelling in the *Tübinger Stift*, Johann Christian Friederich Hölderlin. However, while acknowledging Hölderlin's importance to the genesis of German idealism (as evidenced by consideration of the fragment "The Earliest System-Programme of German Idealism"), Karsten Harries argues that German idealism could develop as it did only because Hegel and Schelling were able to leave their former friend behind, rejecting his elevation of aesthetic intuition above theory and the attendant suggestion that philosophy is subordinate to poetry. Harries demonstrates how Hölderlin wrestles in his poetry with the question of the contrasting import of Greek and Christian conceptions of divinity, a theme of great significance to the young idealists. Yet, as Harries points out, Hölderlin could not reconcile himself, as could Hegel, to the loss of the perfect mediation of sense and spirit ("paradigms of beauty") characteristic of Greek art and religion. As a result, according to Harries, Hölderlin calls for the poet—not a philosopher, but a new embodiment of Christ and Greek gods—to assume "the essential task of mediating between the Highest and the people." From the point of view of an older Hegel, Hölderlin becomes the "beautiful soul" with an adolescent nostalgia for a world that is no more, indulging in a melancholy typical of neoclassicism. But Harries also shows how Hölderlin's more tragic understanding of history prevents him from following Hegel's reconciliatory *Aufhebung* of history. In a concluding segment, Harries comments on Hölderlin's poem *Patmos*, in order to demonstrate how the poet balances "the eschatological understanding of history common to both pietism and Hegel with a Sophoclean openness to the abyss."

If the work of Schiller and Hölderlin cannot be ignored in any attempt to understand the development of post-Kantian philosophy, neither can that of the German romantics: A. W. Schlegel and his brother Friedrich, Ludwig Tieck, Karl Wilhelm Ferdinand Solger, Novalis, and Wilhelm Heinrich Wackenroder. Yet, as Kenneth Schmitz shows in his essay "The Idealism of the German Romantics," the relationship is thornier since, among other things, it concerns the relation, sometimes critical, sometimes sympathetic, not of a single writer, but of an entire literary movement to the newly developing philosophical tradition. "There is no typical romantic," as Schmitz puts it, any more than there is a typical philosopher or even a typical idealist philosopher. Nevertheless, Schmitz demonstrates four post-Kantian themes in which romanticism and metaphysical idealism fruitfully intersect: first, the organic wholeness of nature, expressed in the German conception of *Geist*; second, the understanding of human subjectivity as a free but nonetheless natural part of that whole; third, an aesthetic and creative imagination as the power behind that freedom, a power that fuses the real with the ideal; and fourth, a critical attitude that takes its bearings from the oneness of all things, both real and ideal. In regard to this last point, Schmitz discusses how the metaphysics of creativity, embraced by the romantics and formulated by the idealists, differs from traditional metaphysics. The difference, he maintains, lies in the new metaphysics' incorporation of infinitude into its concept of *Geist,* and, in conclusion, Schmitz explains how, in the wake of Kant's critical philosophy, this incorporation became credible to romantics and idealists alike.

The development of the thought of Schelling and Hegel is the general theme of the last five essays of the volume, the first of which demonstrates the distinctively moral beginning of that development, evidenced by the contrasting ways in which Kant's doctrine of postulates figures in Schelling's and Hegel's early metaphysical projects.

Although Kant rejected the proofs presented by speculative metaphysics for the existence of an immortal soul, freedom, and God, these "ideas of reason," as he calls them, resurface as postulates of pure practical (moral) reason. In other words, these metaphysical ideas have a proper place for Kant and that place is ethics. According to Klaus Düsing, Schelling's and Hegel's criticisms of Kant's foundational principles take place only in the wake of their response to the latter's doctrine of postulates. Hence, in order to appreciate their criticisms and the idealist metaphysics generated by them, it is necessary first to understand "The Reception of Kant's Doctrine of Postulates in Schelling's and Hegel's Early Philosophical Projects," the subject and title of Düsing's essay. This essay recounts in detail the different ways in which Schelling and Hegel critically appropriate Kant's doctrine of postulates and idea of the highest good in the course of elaborating their diverse ethical theories. Düsing shows how both Schelling's and Hegel's reconstructions of the doctrine of postulates were shaped by, among other things, a dissatisfaction with the way the doctrine had been transformed and put to use in the theologies of professors at Tübingen. More importantly, Düsing demonstrates how the German idealists, taking to heart the ethical place accorded to metaphysical ideas by Kant, attempt in their early projects to establish metaphysics on an ethical foundation.

In his essay "The Unconditioned in Knowing: I—Identity—Freedom" Hans Michael Baumgartner sets out to show how, from its inception, Schelling's philosophy is not so much a transcendental philosophy as it is a sustained attempt, using the concepts and argumentative strategies of transcendental philosophy, "to do justice to the conception of the absolute in the theoretical-philosophical realm." The absolute I, available only through an intellectual intuition, is more fundamental than the sort of finite knowing and self-consciousness that generally frame the efforts of transcendental philosophy. At the same time, Baumgartner argues, this absolute I has a teleologically moral function in Schelling's thought that binds "philosophy and the historical process together" in a manner that once again decisively departs from the parameters of the transcendental philosophy of his predecessors.

If Schelling breaks with transcendental philosophy in its Kantian and Fichtean senses, Xavier Tilliette shows that transcendental philosophy, in turn, casts a long shadow on Schelling's attempts to construct a metaphysics of the absolute, the content of which is freedom. Tilliette sketches how Schelling repeatedly wrestled with "The Problem of Metaphysics" (the title of Tilliette's piece) not only after Kant and Fichte but after Spinoza as well. The young Schelling moved, as Tilliette recounts, from the Fichtean-transcendental completion of philosophy in practical philosophy through several versions of philosophical systems to the subsumption of theoretical philosophy by a philosophy of nature in which the "metaphysical impulse" is generally diminished. At this juncture, as Tilliette puts it, "the serene and peaceful descriptions of *Hen Kai Pan* leave no room for the transcendental, and testify to a truce in Schelling's restless thought." Nonetheless, Tilliette points out, the term "metaphysics" recurs in Schelling's maturer stages of thought, albeit principally as an honorific title for "either the theory of potencies or, possible, positive philosophy, which in the last analysis resolves itself into the philosophy of religion."

In his essay "*Von Hegel bis Hegel:* Reflections on the 'Earliest System-Programme of German Idealism,'" Merold Westphal examines the "Earliest System-Programme of German Idealism" and its meaning for our understanding of Hegel in particular and German idealism in general. Three "un-Hegelian" themes stand out in the "Earliest System-Programme": the primacy of practical reason, the irrationality of the state, and the primacy of the aesthetic. These themes bear witness to Hegel's early affirmation of a moral-religious-ethical form of community that could provide a meaningful link to what is eternal, notwithstanding the irrational politics of the mechanized modern state. By contrast, the mature Hegel affirmed the primacy and autonomy of theory as the fundamental means for achieving contact with an ultimate source of meaning. In sketching the basic trajectory of Hegel's career, Westphal shows how, in many ways, Hegel's development mirrors the development of German idealism itself, of which Hegel is so often seen to be the culmination. Undoubtedly, Hegel's self-transformation from young *Volkserzieher* to mature philosopher is deeply rooted in his own sense of disillusionment and resignation. However, this explanation may not sufficiently account for Hegel's later turn to philosophical speculation. And if that is the case, Westphal suggests, then perhaps there is more to be learned from Hegel and German idealism.

In "Hegel on Absolute Knowing," Martin De Nys offers three general and interrelated observations that collectively illuminate Hegel's development, his relation to Kant, and the meaning of his absolute idealism. First, De Nys shows how Hegel's early moral and religious thought aimed to preserve yet transcend the limiting dichotomies and distinctions of Kantian thought. In this early period, the concept of "love" emerged as paradigmatic for Hegel's understanding of how moral autonomy might be reconciled with receptivity to otherness. Secondly, De Nys explains how the account of apperception in the First *Critique* both presupposes and problematizes Kant's own sharp distinction between the receptivity of sensible intuition and the spontaneity of the understanding. Finally, De Nys shows how Hegel's account of absolute knowing settles the problems that Hegel had left unresolved in the 1790s, and reenacts, in a deliberate and self-conscious way, Kant's simultaneous preserving and canceling of the dichotomy between spontaneity and receptivity. Hegel's doctrine of "absolute knowing" is thus surprisingly Kantian in its own way.

At the very beginning of the movement known as German idealism, Hegel and his schoolmates at the *Tübinger Stift* struggled to understand and actualize the hidden possibilities of Kant's philosophy. This struggle is documented in the "Earliest System-Programme of German Idealism," a fragment written down in Hegel's hand, but the authorship of which has been a source of considerable controversy. Düsing concludes his study by arguing for Hegel's authorship of the "Earliest System-Programme," based in part on the way in which the doctrine of postulates surfaces in that fragment; Westphal, too, accepts the contention that Hegel is its author. Tilliette, on the other hand, affirms Schelling's authorship, while Harries cites reasons to see the stamp of Hölderlin's thought in the work. A new translation of this important fragment is contained as an Appendix to the present volume.

PART I
THE UNITY OF KANT'S PHILOSOPHY

1   The Unity of Kant's Critical Philosophy
DANIEL O. DAHLSTROM

Apart from the trivial senses of having been written by the same individual, in the same language, and with the same general style and structure, at the same place (Konigsberg), and during roughly the same period (the Enlightenment), there is considerable controversy as to the extent to which some sort of underlying unity may be ascribed to the doctrines elaborated in Kant's three *Critiques*. There are those who, like the great German idealists and materialists (I am thinking of Fichte, Schelling, Hegel, and Marx, respectively) seem certain that they have found the key to such a unity, but at the cost of erecting and thereby transforming the insights of Kant's critical philosophy into a kind of absolute science. Others—for example, those of a more Aristotelian or of a more positivist stripe—are just as convinced that, in the wake of Kant's defense of mechanical explanations in natural science and his deconstruction of traditional metaphysics, Kant's talk of morality and aesthetics, teleology and religion, is simply inconsistent and purely apologetic. Still others, not unsympathetic to Kant's philosophical project, look outside his critical works to his essays on history and politics in order to uncover the underlying unity of his thought.[1] Each of these interpretations heeds Kant's own remark to the effect that it is possible to understand a thinker or writer better than the thinker or writer himself does. The aim of the following paper is, however, more modest, though no less daunting and controversial. The aim is to try to understand how Kant himself, at least at a certain point, namely, at the end of the critical decade of the 1780s, perceived the unity of his system. But before turn-

---

1. For Yovel, the reintegration of a concept of rational history (based upon Kant's short essays on historical subjects) into Kant's system reveals a "historical antinomy" within that system; for Velkley, Kant's critique of metaphysics has "a practical aim" and the unity of the system lies in "the end of reason," the supremacy of its own legislation; see Yirimiahu Yovel, *Kant and the Philosophy of History* (Princeton, N.J.: Princeton University Press, 1980), pp. 271ff., and Richard L. Velkley, *Freedom and the End of Reason: On the Moral Foundation of Kant's Critical Philosophy* (Chicago and London: University of Chicago Press, 1989), pp. 164ff.

ing to this task, it may be useful to indicate some reasons why there might be something to be gained by such an undertaking.

A great part of our lives is dominated by the juggernaut of science and technology. In contrast to those living in centuries past, we look to the institution of science and not to religion in matters concerning the truth about nature in general. Increasingly science uncovers how nature at microscopic and macroscopic levels, in our genetic makeup and in various ecosystems, decisively influences our lives and well-being. Not unconnected to this march of science, everyday our lives seem to become a little more dependent upon a thick web of technologies—for example, technologies of energy, production, medicine, communication, and defense.

At the same time, we have a keen sense of the limits of science and technology, namely, the dense reality and inscrutable fates of individuals. Science is, for the most part, concerned with individual phenomena only as confirming or disconfirming instances of theories always developed at some level of generality. When an individual supposed to be in a particular species or class exhibits anomalous or aberrant behavior, this is of interest to the scientist, but only as the promise of a new classification, the determination of a new type. Individuals have an undeniable place within technologies but only as interchangeable parts. Technologies are typically constructed for human beings in general, or for communities, or even for types of individuals (e.g., the handicapped), but not for individuals as such. There are, to be sure, important exceptions to this rule (notable in the application of some medical technologies such as prosthetic surgery). Nevertheless, social and economic constraints require that technologies aim principally for a common, not an individual, good.

Perhaps, then, it is not so strange that our culture at least to some extent sets limits on science and technology. However, setting these limits is due to more than just the fact that science and technology, however beneficial they are for individuals, inevitably construe individuals in terms of generalities. Our moral and legal traditions positively affirm the radical integrity and significance of the individual, ascribing the person distinctive rights and responsibilities. Despite the overwhelming evidence of physiology and marketing research, and even despite the increasing appeal to the psychiatrist's testimony, courts still purport to judge people on the basis of the intentions and degree of freedom discernible in their decisions and actions. We hold ourselves, lovers, friends, and family accountable even if we are also able to forgive ourselves and them. But both holding accountable and forgiving ourselves and others makes sense only if there is something that is supposed to be done and only if we are free to do what we are supposed to do.

We seem, in effect, to live in two incompatible worlds. There is the world of science that explains how things in nature in general come about, and thus how generic things can be made to come about. The world of science holds great, indeed, undoubtedly the best promise of mastering nature or—if the idea of such promise is an overly and dangerously pretentious dream—at least of maximizing our place in nature. Yet it seems just as surely to be ultimately in mortal conflict with any notion of human freedom. The world of morality and religion, on the other hand, insists that we are free, free to accomplish what does not exist but ought to. The world of morality and religion, moreover, holds out to us a promise incontestably greater than that of science, namely, the promise of final justice and an immortal destiny.

If this scenario rings true at all for our contemporary culture, then Immanuel Kant is very much our contemporary. For Kant, more than any other philosopher, suspends human existence between the claims of science and those of morality. The problem of the unity of his critical philosophy is nothing less than the problem of the unity of our culture, our contemporary existence. In order to appreciate Kant's own solution to this problem, however, it is first necessary to see how he formulates the problem. This task, as already noted, is quite formidable since it requires an overview of, at the very least, his three *Critiques.* Moreover, in addition to the substantive question of the unity to the contents of the three *Critiques,* there is the historical fact that, if there is such a unity, it was a developing one. For, in the first place, there is no reason to think that Kant envisioned a system in the form of the three *Critiques* when he penned the final lines to the *Critique of Pure Reason,* published in 1781. The *Critique of Practical Reason* did not take shape until about the time he was revising the First *Critique,* six years later. More significantly, in the First *Critique* he denies the very possibility of a critique of taste, basing his denial on the fact that rules or criteria for evaluating the beautiful are merely empirical. It is accordingly somewhat surprising that, in a letter to Reinhold dated December 28, 1787, he writes that he is at work on a critique of taste and has discovered "another type of a priori principles." Moreover, within the following two years the critique of taste becomes only the first half of the eventual *Critique of Judgment,* as the principles of the latter are extended to teleological as well as to aesthetic judgments.

Nevertheless, once the Third *Critique* was completed, Kant proceeded to give his readers some important clues regarding the unity of the critical system. Each of his *Critiques*—together with the "fourth critique," *Religion within the Limits of Reason Alone*—can be viewed as providing an answer to one of the three questions that, in his view, every philosopher, worthy of the name, should address:

What can I know?
What should I do?
What may I hope for?

In what follows, as a means of stating the problem and addressing the unity of Kant's critical philosophy on its own terms, the arguments and conclusions of each of Kant's three *Critiques* are summed up as an answer respectively to one of these three questions.

1. *"What can I know?"* In 1781, at the age of fifty-seven and after a decade of relative quiet for so prolific a philosophical writer, Kant published the *Critique of Pure Reason*. There, countering what he considered a skeptical challenge to the legitimacy of pure and applied mathematics as well as the legitimacy of a theoretical science of nature, Kant set out to demonstrate what makes these disciplines possible. Boldly proposing that space and time are forms of human sensibility and that the fundamental concepts of theoretical knowledge can be derived from the logic of human understanding, Kant explained how arithmetic, geometry, and chronometry are intuitively necessary; how scientists, carpenters, and engineers can successfully apply the ideal character of mathematics to the real world; and how everything studied by the natural sciences is linked together—at least at a certain level—in a chain of causal mechanisms.

Kant's explanation was novel because, unlike his more rationalist predecessors, he grounded the pretensions of mathematics and physics to universality and necessity not in some grand metaphysical scheme of God and nature, but rather in an analysis of human subjectivity, specifically, the cognitive capacities of the human subject, construed as the conditions of any possible experience. This new sort of grounding (he called it "transcendental") distinguished him from the likes of Leibniz and Wolff in other ways as well. From the fact that human cognitive capacities—basically, the understanding and the imagination—are finite, he drew the inference that the validity of mathematics and theoretical natural science is inherently linked and thereby also limited to the phenomenal world, that is to say, to the world as it appears or insofar as it can be experienced. At the same time, this combined justification and limitation of science implied the illegitimacy of the speculative science known as "metaphysics," with its claims to know or to be able to demonstrate the nature of things-in-themselves beyond the phenomenal order. From the theoretical point of view of legitimate sciences, the traditional themes of speculative metaphysics—for example, an immaterial and potentially immortal soul, spatial or temporal beginnings or ends of the universe, freedom, and a first cause or supreme being—are, in Kant's technical jargon, simply ideas, empty concepts referring to what lies beyond any possible experience. These ideas are generated by a pretension of pure reason to make theoretical claims about objects solely on the basis of its otherwise quite legitimate capacity to make and determine valid inferences a priori. Hence, Kant's masterpiece, the *Critique of Pure Reason*, gets its title from its demonstration that such ideas as those of the soul, the beginning of time, and God, as products of pure reason, are neither verifiable nor falsifiable.

At the same time, Kant labors to show how these ideas are perfectly natural, inevitable, and useful, even "indispensable." They serve to remind science at each stage of its development that the greatest possible unity (homogeneity, specificity, and continuity) in its researches always lies ahead of it.[2] These ideas have no transcendental use, that is to say, they provide us with no knowledge of objects, but they have an immanent, heuristic use. They constitute the indispensable, but usually tacit, assumption of all empirical research, namely, that nature as it is actually experienced conforms to our attempts to understand it in a logically coherent manner. There is, moreover, another purpose that, in Kant's eyes, is served by his critique of the ideas of pure reason. By showing that the idea of God can be neither proven nor disproven, he claims to have freed religion from speculation and thereby removed any possibility of an atheistic objection to it.[3]

In the *Critique of Pure Reason*, then, the truncated answer to the question "What can I know?" is that *I can know the truth of claims made in the theoretical disciplines of pure and applied mathematics and physics, but I cannot know the truth of claims made by speculative metaphysics.*

2. *"What should I do?"* With the publication of the *Critique of Pure Reason*, however, Kant's critical activity was only beginning. That immortality, freedom, and God, as ideas and thus neither provable nor disprovable, cannot themselves be matters of knowledge, leaves open the possibility that they are matters of faith.[4] Yet, if it is not possible on the basis of theoretical or speculative reason to determine the truth about these

2. Immanuel Kant, *Kritik der reinen Vernunft*, ed. Raymund Schmidt (Hamburg: Meiner, 1971), pp. B378–89, B670–73, B685f. All references to the *Kritik der reinen Vernunft* (*Critique of Pure Reason*) are cited with the abbreviation 'KrV,' followed by the page numbers of the 1781 or 1787 editions, indicated in the customary manner by the letters 'A' and 'B' respectively.

3. Immanuel Kant, *Kants handschriftlicher Nachlaß*, volume 10 in *Kants gesammelte Schriften*, volume 23 (Berlin: de Gruyter, 1955), p. 59.

4. KrV Bxxx.

ideas, why should we believe in them? Kant's answer to this question is given in his Second *Critique,* the *Critique of Practical Reason,* published in 1788. Unlike the First *Critique,* the *Critique of Practical Reason* is concerned with reason not as a capacity to know (*Erkenntnisvermögen*), but as a capacity to determine the will (*Begehrungsvermögen*).[5] The "will" here signifies something quite private and intimate, the interior of a person's desires, intentions, and choices, regardless of whether they are realized or not. If or—better—to the extent that someone's choices are in fact determined by a principle issuing from his or her reason alone and not by anything given, that is to say, not by any combination of physiological and psychological conditioning, then that person is self-determining or free.

The moral law, Kant argues, is just such a principle. In other words, by formulating the moral law, Kant is answering the question "What should I do?," but this answer is at the same time an acknowledgment of the possibility of freedom. To be sure, how a free will is possible remains for Kant "a problem that human reason cannot resolve"; freedom is, as he puts it, an "inscrutable" fact.[6] Nevertheless, what I should do is act in such a way that what motivates me personally could at the same time serve as a law for everyone or, what for Kant amounts to the same thing, I should treat humanity, in myself and others, always as the purpose of my actions, always as an end and never merely as a means. The universality of the moral law in the first formulation and the reference to humanity in the second formulation testify to an ideal that is not given in experience. Instead, this ideal, a world in which we treat each other with mutual respect as persons and not things, a world in which our wills are not so much subject to nature as nature is subject to our wills, can only be an imperative of reason, a law it imposes on itself.[7]

The moral law, so construed, does not tell us to be happy; a conception of happiness is always a product of experience, inevitably based upon some mix of physiological makeup, psychological factors, and so-

5. Immanuel Kant, *Kritik der praktischen Vernunft* in *Kants Werke,* volume 5 (Berlin: de Gruyter, 1968), pp. 15f, 44f. (hereafter = 'KpV'). Not to be overlooked, however, is the fact that Kant indicates the relation between his theoretical and practical philosophy already at the conclusion to the *Critique of Pure Reason* in the three sections of the "Canon of Pure Reason" in the doctrine of method at the end of the book.

6. KpV 72; Immanuel Kant, *Kritik der Unteilskraft* in *Kants Werke,* volume 5 (Berlin: de Gruyter, 1968), pp. 457, 468 (hereafter = 'KU'); *Religion innerhalb der Grenzen der bloßen Vernunft* in *Kants Werke,* volume 6 (Berlin: de Gruyter, 1968), pp. 21, 24, 43 (hereafter = 'Religion').

7. KpV 30f, 44. Of course, it is questionable whether this ideal is not in some sense given in experience or, even if it is, whether it cannot be the product of some sort of physiological and/or psychological factors. If Kant's appeal to a spontaneity in human beings is itself ultimately no more than a postulate, then the integrity of the moral philosophy seems to be severely undermined.

cial conditioning. Insofar as choices are motivated by such a conception, they are not free choices. Nor can a conception of happiness, properly speaking, serve as a basis for morality with a pretense to more than a merely relative or conditional validity. There is a notorious difference of opinion among individuals and cultures as to what happiness is. But, on Kant's analysis, instead of instructing us to be happy or to maximize our happiness, the moral law demands categorically—with no "ifs, ands, and buts"—that we act in such a way as to be worthy of happiness, without promise of the same.[8] The moral law is not about what is or will be, but about what ought to be, or, as Kant also puts it, virtue and happiness are two completely different things.[9] In other words, questions of morality, of what I should do, are not questions of happiness, nor is there anything in the moral law that ensures our happiness if our actions are in fact determined by what the moral law dictates.

However, while not promising happiness and not being able to guarantee the realization of what ought to be, the concept of moral law presupposes at least that it is possible, more or less, to carry out its imperatives. ("If I *should,* then I *can.*") Our understanding of what is right and wrong enjoins us to act a certain way, regardless of the consequences and regardless of whether or not we in fact do so, but it also postulates that we are free to act this way and that the natural order can be morally transformed. But to suppose such a compatibility between morality and nature is tantamount to postulating that nature itself is the work of an intelligent being, God. "It is morally necessary," as Kant puts it, "to assume the existence of God."[10] Or else we must "regard moral laws as empty fantasies."[11]

There exists some controversy among Kant scholars as to the exact force of this moral necessity to postulate God's existence.[12] The difficulty is that, on the one hand, Kant clearly states that someone unconvinced of God's existence cannot on that account consider himself excused from the demands of the moral law.[13] In Kant's view, atheists and agnostics are, no less than believers, bound to the moral law. On the other hand, Kant just as clearly affirms that "morality leads unavoidably to religion, by virtue of which it expands to the idea of a powerful, moral lawgiver outside the human being, in whose will there is that final purpose

8. KrV B834.   9. KpV 112.
10. KpV 115, 124ff.   11. KrV B839.
12. Allen Wood, *Kant's Moral Religion* (Ithaca, N.Y.: Cornell University Press, 1970), pp. 26–30; L. W. Beck, *A Commentary on Kant's "Critique of Practical Reason"* (Chicago: University of Chicago Press, 1960), pp. 235f.; Yovel, *Kant and the Philosophy of History,* pp. 41–80; Niels Otto Schroll-Fleischer, *Der Gottesgedanke in der Philosophie Kants* (Odense, Denmark: Odense University Press, 1981), pp. 137–49.
13. KU 450f.

(of the creation of the world), which at the same time can and should be the final purpose of the human being."[14]

The fact that Kant reformulated this issue of the relation between morality and religious belief so many times and in so many ways suggests that, if he was not himself unsure about it, he was at least aware that it presented a potential difficulty to his readers. His official view seems to be that the relation between morality and religious belief presents no problem as long as we keep distinct what the moral law tells us we ought to do and what implications we can theoretically draw from the fact that there is such a moral imperative.[15] From a purely practical point of view, moral obligations need not, indeed, cannot, be based upon religious beliefs about Providence or about future rewards and punishment. Such beliefs subvert the freedom of the action, substituting happiness for worthiness of happiness as the motive of the action. As Kant puts it in his lectures on moral philosophy, "the human being can hope to be happy, yet that must not move him, but rather only console him."[16] Indeed, Kant claims that if we could arrive at knowledge of God's existence, "all morality would dissipate" and images of reward and punishment would take the place of genuinely moral motivation.[17] At the same time, from a theoretical point of view, having accepted moral obligations on their own merits, it is possible, even inevitable, that we ask what is implied by carrying out moral imperatives. The worthiness to be happy implies the possibility of happiness, and the demand for a moral order implies that the natural order is in fact amenable to moral transformation.

In this way, according to Kant, it is the concept of the moral law that gives us reason to believe that we are free and that there is an intelligible author of nature. Despite the "infinite chasm" between what we can know and what we should do, between a science that supposes that everything in nature is determined and a morality that supposes the freedom and autonomy of persons, the conclusions of the *Critique of Pure Reason* and those of the *Critique of Practical Reason* are not only consistent, but complementary.[18] While neither provable nor disprovable by science, the theoretically empty, but noncontradictory, ideas of freedom and divinity acquire what positive content they have from the implications of

---

14. *Religion* 6.
15. KrV B833. Whether bad faith in this respect can be avoided is, of course, another question altogether.
16. Immanuel Kant, *Kants Vorlesungen*, volume 4 in *Kants gesammelte Schriften*, volume 27 (Berlin: de Gruyter, 1974), p. 284.
17. Immanuel Kant, *Kants Vorlesungen*, volume 5 in *Kants gesammelte Schriften*, volume 28 (Berlin: de Gruyter, 1972), pp. 1083f.
18. KpV 48ff.; at KpV 54f. Kant says that a practical, not a theoretical, aim lies behind the dissatisfaction with the application of causality to objects of experience alone.

adherence to the moral law.[19] For we cannot seriously entertain acting morally without "postulating" that we are free, responsible agents and that nature is ultimately not hostile to morality, in other words, without postulating that nature is the work of an intelligent, benevolent creator. In Kant's technical jargon the ideas of freedom and divinity are "postulates," propositions that we can theoretically entertain but not prove and yet at the same time propositions that are inseparably connected to an a priori, unconditionally valid law: the moral law.[20] As postulates, they in no way expand the scope of our knowledge about the nature of things; there is no theoretical knowledge of the existence of freedom, immortality, or a benevolent creator, but a purely rational belief in them is implied by the moral law.[21]

Nevertheless, even if we are persuaded to allow Kant the consistency and complementarity of these conclusions to his first two *Critiques* (that is to say, his theoretical and practical philosophy, or, as it might be expressed today, his philosophy of science and his moral philosophy), we must concede that that consistency and complementarity have been purchased at the cost of ascribing any *theoretical* or *practical* (moral) unity to the critical philosophy, and thereby to the conception of human subjectivity lying at the basis of Kant's entire project.[22] By distinguishing between the world as it appears and the world as it may be in itself, Kant effectively secures both science's theoretical determinations and morality's free choices, but only at the expense of suspending the human individual eerily on a tightrope of faith between these two realms. Insofar as I consider myself under the lens of science, my existence is fully determined by the state of my body in nature. Yet, at the same time, the moral traditions of my culture, my interpersonal relations, and ultimately my conscience tell me that I have to act as a responsible agent, treating others not as things to be used, but as themselves persons, fellow responsible agents. In other words, without knowing how this is possible, I must be able by acting morally to have an effect on the natural order that, in the eyes of science, is completely determined.[23] Nature must at least afford us a way of thinking about it that conforms to moral imperatives. Of course, Kant's argument is that, if I recognize the necessity and validity of this moral law, then I do not know but have reason to believe in Providence, a divine order providing for the ultimate harmony of nature and

---

19. KpV 136; KrV B835f. 20. KpV 122, 124, 132.
21. KpV 142–46.

22. This consideration suggests affinities with Heidegger's transcendental efforts in *Sein und Zeit* to unpack what "to be" means in the case of human existence in a way that is both pretheoretical and not beholden to some moral aim.

23. It would be useful, at this juncture, to consider Kant's notion of respect, the "pineal gland" of his moral philosophy.

morality. Note, however, that this faith is a faith based upon practical reason or morality. If you will permit me to indulge a metaphor, that tightrope of faith, on which we are suspended between nature and freedom, science and morality, seems to be secured only on one side.

3. *"What may I hope for?"* In the third and final installment of his critical philosophy, the *Critique of Judgment,* published in 1790, Kant addresses these very concerns.[24] As the title suggests, there is a parallel between this *Critique* and its predecessors. In the First *Critique* Kant inquires into the a priori principles of knowing and finds such principles in the imagination and understanding. In the Second *Critique* he searches for an a priori principle of desire and motivation and locates the source of such a principle—the moral law—in pure practical reason. Similarly, in the *Critique of Judgment,* Kant inquires whether there is an a priori principle of our feelings, specifically, our feelings of pleasure and displeasure, and he uncovers such a principle in the power of judgment. The identification of this a priori principle of judgment completes the critical philosophy in more than one sense. Not only is it the third and final transcendental principle within the critical philosophy, but it is also the basis for any "transition" (*Übergang*) between the other two principles or, in short, between nature and freedom (morality).[25]

That transcendental principle of judgment is the principle of purposiveness. In both Introductions to the *Critique of Judgment* Kant establishes this principle in general before turning to specific types of purposiveness. His argument for this principle, which may seem strange to those who think of Kant as a proponent of Newtonian mechanics, is based upon a consideration of what is presupposed by empirical research on nature or what he also calls "reflective judgment" on nature as it is experienced. The First *Critique* has already established that nature in general is a network of causal mechanisms. But actual research on nature presupposes far more than that. Inasmuch as it begins with particular facts or data that present themselves, the researcher reflects on them, comparing them among themselves or with his own capacity to apprehend them, in order to locate some general principles or order in terms of which those facts can be understood.[26] (What is being described here as research that begins with particular data is, in Kant's technical jargon, the work of "reflective judgment.") Research tacitly presupposes that such common principles can be found throughout nature and across

---

24. KU 175f.
25. See the Appendix at the end of this paper.
26. What is described here is the work of reflective judgment; see KU 179ff.; see also Klaus Düsing, *Die Teleologie in Kants Weltbegriff,* 2d ed. (Bonn: Bouvier, 1986), pp. 51–65.

diverse species, that there is some sort of continuity from one domain to the next, and that nature—not only in regard to its very general, theoretical laws, but also in regard to more specific, empirical laws—allows for endless specification. In short, the scientist researching nature presupposes that nature specifies itself in a way that conforms with the scientist's own methods and ways of studying nature.[27] "Thus," as Kant puts it,

> [reflective] judgment must assume for its own use as a principle a priori that what is contingent, as far as human insight is concerned, in the particular (empirical) laws of nature contains a lawlike unity . . . that for us, to be sure, cannot be grounded, but is thinkable. . . . This transcendental concept of a purposiveness of nature is, then, neither a concept of nature nor a concept of freedom, since it attributes nothing at all to the object (of nature), but only represents the sole way we have to proceed in reflection on objects of nature in regard to a thoroughgoing, coherent experience.[28]

In order to research nature or, in Kant's terminology, in order to be able to reflect on the specific data and facts of nature in the hope of finding some general order among them, we have to presume that nature will cooperate, that it is somehow attuned to this process. Kant labels this principle of purposiveness "the technology [or art] of nature," namely, the presumption that nature has some underlying purpose, a conception unifying it at every level and in every part of it, including that part known as "human nature" and that activity known as "scientific research."[29] In short, research demands that nature be construed as though it were a work of technology or art.

The scientist's need to presume nature's purposiveness, its basic conformity to the scientist's own aims, amounts to investigating the particular laws of nature *as if* some sort of intellect—quite unlike our own intellect—had imparted those laws. The presupposition that there is an intelligible order to the phenomena investigated implies the *idea* of an intellect, a divine or divinelike intellect, as the basis of that order. Setting it off against our own discursive intellects, Kant calls it the "intuitive intellect" (or "understanding," given that the German *Verstand* is the translation for *intellectus*). This idea of an intuitive intellect, based as it is upon science's need to presume the purposiveness of nature, in no way, of course, provides a proof of God's existence. However, it does provide

---

27. Immanuel kant, *Kants handschriftlicher Nachlaß*, volume 7 in *Kants gesammelte Schriften*, volume 20 (Berlin: de Gruyter, 1942), p. 215; KU 410f.
28. KU 183f.
29. Immanuel Kant, *Erste Einleitung in die Kritik der Urteilskraft*, ed. Gerhard Lehmann, second edition (Hamburg: Meiner, 1970), pp. 11f., 26; KU 410f.

some more positive content to the idea and additional reason to believe in God's existence.[30]

Yet what does this principle of purposiveness have to do with pleasure? Recall that in Kant's scheme of the systematic unity of his critical philosophy he construes the principle of purposiveness as an a priori principle neither of knowing nor of willing, but of the feelings of pleasure and displeasure, and that as such it is supposed to make possible the transition between those other principles of the system or, in short, between nature and freedom. In order to explain how the presumption of nature's purposiveness is an a priori principle of our feelings of pleasure and displeasure, Kant first points out that the successful resolution of research is as much dependent upon nature's cooperation as it is upon our own research schemes. When research succeeds, it is accompanied not simply by the joy of discovery and accomplishment, but, more importantly, by a more resilient kind of pleasure, the pleasure of wonder or amazement (*Bewunderung*) in having our expectations confirmed and the aims of our research (more or less) realized. This distinctive pleasure (reminiscent of θαυμάζειν, for both Plato and Aristotle the source of philosophy itself)[31] thus presupposes the principle of purposiveness.[32] We are delighted and amazed that nature, despite its immense diversity, to some degree conforms and discloses itself to our capacity to grasp it. (Kant concedes that in the ordinary course of studying nature the pleasure we take in being able to grasp nature gradually becomes so mixed with the mere knowledge of nature that it may no longer be particularly noticeable.) Nevertheless, not only is empirical research possible only on the supposition that nature will comply with the researcher's efforts to come to grips with nature, but this compliance itself is the source of a distinctive kind of pleasure.

There are, in addition, two different kinds of purposiveness, two distinctive ways in which nature presents itself to us, that we cannot judge otherwise than as if nature acted according to a purpose and that, when we make these judgments, produce (respectively) a distinctive kind of pleasure in us. The two parts of the *Critique of Judgment*, the critique of aesthetic judgment and the critique of teleological judgment, are devoted respectively to these two kinds of purposiveness. When we come across

---

30. KU 180f., 406. It bears noting, especially in view of the essays assembled here, that the notion of an intuitive intellect or understanding is a favorite theme of Hegel's interpretation of Kant. From his earliest to his latest published remarks on Kant's philosophy, Hegel repeatedly takes up the theme of intuitive understanding in a positive way. Unlike Kant, he does not construe it as a mere idea of reflective judgment, but as an approximation of a genuine human cognitive capability.
31. Cf. *Theatetus* 155d and *Metaphysics* 1.2.982b12f.
32. KU 187.

some beautiful form in nature, for example, a sunset or a waterfall, its beauty is quite independent of whether we scientifically understand it or whether it promotes our moral character or whether it gratifies some physiological craving. In fact, natural beauties do not seem to serve any purpose at all and yet we cannot help but judge them as if they were the fulfillment of some purpose.

Aesthetic judgments are not cognitive judgments and the purposiveness involved in experiences of the beautiful is strictly "subjective." For Kant, beauty is not simply in the eye of the beholder, but it is also not an objective property of things. Rather, it is a property of the forms of certain things in relation to the human subject, forms that put the mind's ability to imagine and to understand in a kind of free play that is irreducible to a single image or concept. Thus, while the disinterested pleasure we take in beauty does not involve any extension of our knowledge of nature, it is still a pleasure intrinsically involved with our cognitive capacities and specifically with their enhancement, short of cognitive closure or resolution. Hence, on Kant's account, natural beauty, no less than scientific research, points to the technology or artistry of nature. In his own words,

the self-sufficient natural beauty uncovers for us a technology of nature which represents nature as a system according to laws, the principle of which we do not encounter in the entire capacity of our understanding, namely, the principle of a purposiveness with respect to our power of judgment. . . . It, thus, to be sure, does not actually extend our knowledge of objects of nature, but it nevertheless does extend our concept of nature as a mere mechanism to the concept of it as art.[33]

In the beautiful and in the sublime Kant finds a subjective basis for a "transition" from the realm of nature to that of morality. While it is necessary, on Kant's analysis, to understand that neither a genuine judgment that something is beautiful nor a feeling that something is sublime is motivated by moral interests any more than it is by the interests of science or sensuality, he also recognizes that both the beautiful and the sublime are "purposeful in relation to moral feeling."[34] "The beautiful," he notes, "prepares us to love something, even nature itself, disinterestedly; the sublime to prize it even against our (sensuous) interest."[35] Beauty, for Kant, is a "symbol of morality," presenting an analogy to morality that is itself universally respected due to the fact that, in a moral judgment, the will is free in its conformity to laws dictated by reason.[36] Given this analogy, Kant concludes, the appreciation of beauty "makes

33. KU 246.
34. KU 267.
35. Ibid.
36. KU 351ff.

possible the transition from the allurements of the senses to the habitual moral interest without too violent a step."[37]

There are also things in nature that we have to judge as having a purpose and not simply, like the beautiful, in relation to us, but as it were objectively. Moreover, they are things that, no less than beauties in nature, are sources of wonder and amazement for us. While we generally and legitimately explain things and events in nature mechanically, that is, in terms of their antecedent conditions, we also repeatedly come across phenomena for which that mechanical sort of explanation does not appear to suffice. It is absurd, Kant claims, for us to hope that a Newton could emerge who might be able to explain the generation of a blade of grass according to natural laws, without recourse to some notion of purpose.[38] Organic beings, in Kant's view, are the only sort of things in nature that must be regarded as its purposes and that justify the introduction of teleology into natural science.[39] The general principle of the purposiveness of nature is validated by the fact that empirical research (reflection on nature) takes place and by the fact that this is conceivable to us only on the assumption that nature is so structured that it cooperates with that research. The research itself may, however, result only in mechanical explanations of natural phenomena. On the other hand, while it is made possible and even prepared by that general transcendental principle of purposiveness, the principle of organic or objective purposiveness is occasioned and justified for reflective judgment by the appearance of (the fact that there are) organic entities. Rather than being the product of an assemblage of parts or antecedent conditions, the unity of an organism first makes the constitution and reciprocal relations of its parts necessary. The idea of the efficacy of this unity can only be explained by us as a purpose.

On Kant's analysis, then, both the beautiful and the organic can only be judged on the basis, respectively, of subjective and objective purposiveness. As in the case of empirical research in general, we cannot help but relate to certain things and events in nature otherwise than as if they correspond to some purpose, some conception of their outcomes. That is to say, even though we are unable in an absolute sense to say what the purposes of these natural forms and formations are, we are compelled to think of them as if they existed to serve some purpose—and that is precisely what it means to say that they are "purposive." This way of relating, moreover, brings a distinctive kind of pleasure, the pleasure of wonder, along with it. Yet, even if all this is granted, what precisely does it have

---

37. KU 354.
39. KU 375f.

38. KU 400.

to do with the unity of the critical philosophy, with the transition from nature to freedom, indeed, with the question "What may I hope for?"

In order to answer these questions, it is necessary first to remind ourselves that the principle of purposiveness remains regulative, not constitutive, for Kant. The need to presuppose a concept of a purpose for empirical research, for appreciation of the beautiful, and for understanding organic life is ultimately based not on knowledge that there are such purposes, but on the finitude of the human knower. At the same time, however, the purposiveness of beautiful forms and organic beings illustrates how it is possible to conceive of the unity of nature and freedom, the realms of science and morality. They demonstrate that postulating God's existence, as the source of the compatibility of our natural selves and our moral vocations, is not an empty demand of practical (moral) reason.

Culture itself is defined by Kant as nature's ultimate purpose, "ultimate" because culture is what disciplines and shapes our desires "to make us receptive to purposes higher than nature itself can provide."[40] At the center of this cultural process is, along with science, fine art (*schöne Kunst*) because its pleasures can be shared universally and because it brings a society a certain refinement, a kind of training for the moral rule of reason. Note that fine art contributes to culture not by preaching moral lessons but by promoting a certain disposition, a disposition that suspends a purely physiological relation to nature.

Perhaps now it is possible to appreciate why Kant believed that he had elaborated in the *Critique of Judgment* a principle mediating between the other two *Critiques*. The principle of purposiveness provides a basis for a connection between the theoretical order of science and the practical order of morality, between nature and freedom. This principle is itself neither theoretical nor practical but rather aesthetic (in a broad sense of the term, as he puts it in the unpublished first Introduction to the *Critique of Judgment*). The principle does not by itself provide us with knowledge of the nature of things; it does not tell us what we ought to do. But it does explain the distinctive pleasure of wonder and amazement that accompanies scientific research, the experience of beauty, the attempt to understand organic beings, and—even though they have been mentioned here only in passing—the achievements of art and culture. Above all, it is this purposiveness and the pleasures it provides that give us hope.

The unity of Kant's critical philosophy is thus contained in his answer to the question "What may we hope for?" According to Kant, we have reason to hope, and not merely to believe, that there is some unity and

40. KU 431–435.

purpose to human life, that there is some underlying purpose unifying the nature studied by science and the freedom postulated by morality. The reasons for this hope are the fact that scientific research on nature takes place at all and the fact that there are natural beauties and organic beings, facts that are only explicable to us on the assumption that nature acts according to a purpose.

Appendix

Kant's three *Critiques* are, by his own account, supposed to determine the a priori principles of three faculties of the mind: cognition, feelings of pleasure and displeasure, and desire.[41] However, each *Critique* locates its transcendental principle (lawlikeness, purposiveness, final purpose) in a distinctive *cognitive* capacity (understanding, judgment, reason) and with respect to a specific application (nature, art, freedom). What follows is Kant's own "table" or "overview of all major faculties according to their systematic unity." I have numbered the faculties in order to compare them briefly with the questions animating the three *Critiques*.

Faculties of the Mind altogether	*Cognitive Faculties*	*A Priori Principles*	*Application To*
1. Cognition	Understanding	Lawlikeness	Nature
2. Feeling of Pleasure & Displeasure	Judgment	Purposiveness	Art
3. Desire	Reason	Final Purpose	Freedom

While Kant addresses all three questions in each *Critique* to some extent, each *Critique* (along with the *Religion within the Limits of Reason Alone* in the case of the Third *Critique*) can be regarded as an attempt to answer principally one of three questions:

1. *Critique of Pure Reason* (1781, 1787): What can I know?
3. *Critique of Practical Reason* (1788): What should I do?
2. *Critique of Judgment* (1790) and *Religion within the Limits of Reason Alone* (1793): What may I hope for?

According to this "overview," the answers to the questions "What can I know?" and "What should I do?" are at extremes, though, of course, the two *Critiques* dealing with these questions chronologically precede the

---

41. This threefold structure, articulated by Mendelssohn and Tetens in the 1770s, has obvious affinities with the Platonic conception of the soul, as Robert Sokolowski reminded me. I am also grateful to Richard Kennington for his line of questioning, challenging the trenchancy of the restrictions placed by Kant upon the notions of purposiveness and history within the critical philosophy.

Critique of Judgment. Yet it should be noted that Kant calls the critique of aesthetic judgment "the propadeutic of all philosophy."[42] In his Logic lectures, Kant adds a fourth question, to which the other three refer: "What is the human being?"[43]

42. KU 194.
43. Immanuel Kant, *Logik* in *Kants Werke*, volume 9 (Berlin: de Gruyter, 1968), p. 25.

PART II

THE CRITICAL RECEPTION OF THE CRITICAL PHILOSOPHY: REINHOLD AND THE SKEPTICS

2   Karl Leonhard Reinhold: "... Endeavoring to keep up the pace *mit unserem zeitalter*"[1]

ALEXANDER VON SCHÖNBORN

Some readers of this volume will undoubtedly greet this title with the question "Karl Leonhard who?" Others will recall Reinhold as a popularizer of Kant and/or as someone who played a role in Fichte's formulation of his *Wissenschaftslehre* and/or as someone dismissed by Hegel in his *Differenzschrift* as a prime example of that eclectic and syncretistic "unphilosophy" which he calls "popular philosophy" or, as we might put it today, "pop philosophy."[2] Many of us thus know relatively little about Reinhold's work. Indeed, when the first volume of his correspondence appeared, a little over a decade ago, the publication was announced and reviewed by the *Frankfurter Allgemeine Zeitung* under the heading "Letters of a Forgotten Philosopher."[3]

Nor is this lack of familiarity easily remedied by consulting a text summarizing the history of philosophy. When, for example, we turn to F. Copleston's still widely used *A History of Philosophy*, we find a single sentence in the text, noting that, prior to Fichte, Reinhold "had already demanded that the Kantian criticism should be turned into a system, that is to say, that it should be derived systematically from one fundamental principle." An appended footnote adds that Reinhold "accepted and defended the philosophy of Fichte" from about 1797. "But he was a restless spirit, and after a few years he turned to other lines of thought."[4]

---

1. This citation is taken from a letter, dated November 5, 1786, to Reinhold from his former teacher, Don Paulus Pepermann, who is quoting an earlier, no longer extant letter by Reinhold. See *Karl Leonhard Reinhold Korrespondenzausgabe der österreichischen Akademie der Wissenschaften*, ed. Reinhard Lauth, Eberhard Heller, and Kurt Hiller (Stuttgart-Bad Cannstatt: Friedrich Frommann Verlag Günther Holzboog, 1983), p. 160.
2. G. W. F. Hegel, *Differenz des Fichte'schen und Schelling'schen Systems der Philosophie* (Hamburg: Felix Meiner Verlag, 1962), pp. 110–12.
3. *Frankfurter Allgemeine Zeitung*, no. 141 (June 22, 1983), p. 10.
4. Frederick Copleston, S.J., *A History of Philosophy*, 9 vols. (New York: Doubleday, 1985), 7.33.

Given this situation, it strikes me as important to say something about the reasons for Reinhold's being a "forgotten philosopher" before turning to the development of his views and their role in the emergence of German idealism. For, as will become apparent, a preliminary ground-clearing is necessary—a testimonial, if you will, to the need for this volume. Put differently, I hope to undo, at least, the forgetting of this forgetting of Reinhold.

Now in philosophy, as elsewhere, the decision to read a piece of work is frequently based on a recommendation by someone whose judgment is respected. Heeding the recommendation is more likely when the recommending philosopher is not only competent but unusually gifted and especially known for speaking her or his mind in a critical and forthright manner. It is most likely when several such individuals concur, especially if they are known to disagree strongly with each other on most methodological and substantive issues. If one were to compile a short list of individuals fitting these standards during Reinhold's lifetime, one would have to include Fichte, Garve, Herder, Jacobi, Kant, Maimon, and Schopenhauer. Each of these bestowed his highest praise on the quality of Reinhold's philosophic work.

For instance, in a letter to Reinhold in 1794, Fichte characterized him as "the most acute thinker of his time"[5] and, later that year, went on to claim in print that "after the genial spirit of Kant no greater gift could be given to philosophy than through the systematic spirit of Reinhold."[6] Garve wrote Reinhold in 1789: "With entire conviction do I recognize you among our younger philosophers as the one who combines the greatest acumen and the strictest precision in concepts with the most consummate use of his language."[7] When, on the basis of his *Briefe über die Kantische Philosophie,* Reinhold was being considered for the position of extraordinary professor at the University of Jena, Herder's recommendation—in spite of Reinhold's subject matter and effusive praise of Kant—was "positive without qualification."[8] After reading the major por-

---

5. Johann Gottlieb Fichte, letter to Reinhold, dated March 1, 1794, in Ernst Reinhold, *Karl Leonhard Reinhold's Leben und litterarisches Wirken, nebst einer Auswahl von Briefen Kant's, Fichte's, Jacobi's und andrer philosophirender Zeitgenossen an ihn* (Jena: Friedrich Frommann, 1825), p. 168.

6. Johann Gottlieb Fichte, *Ueber den Begriff der Wissenschaftslehre oder der sogenannten Philosophie, als Einladungsschrift zu seinen Vorlesungen über diese Wissenschaft* (Weimar: Verlag des Industrie-Comptoirs, 1794), p. vi.

7. Christian Garve, letter to Reinhold, dated August 14, 1789, in Reinhold, *Leben und litterarisches Wirken*, p. 346.

8. Johann Gottfried Herder, cited in Kurt Röttgers, "Die Kritik der reinen Vernunft und K. L. Reinhold. Fallstudie zur Theoriepragmatik in Schulbildungsprozessen," in *Akten des 4. internationalen Kant-Kongresses Mainz. 6.–10. April 1974, Teil II. 2: Sektionen*, ed. Gerhard Funke (Berlin: Walter de Gruyter, 1974), p. 798.

tion of Reinhold's *Versuch einer neuen Theorie des menschlichen Vorstellungsvermögens*, Jacobi wrote to him in 1790:

> As far as I have read, I find the treatment exemplary. Only the most tenacious industry, combined with the rarest clarity of mind and an energy of thought straining always to the same degree—never too much and never too little, only a spirit who, wholly in possession of itself, composes its powers as it will, could have produced such a masterpiece.[9]

Kant, after reading the *Briefe*, wrote to Reinhold in appreciation, noting that "Nothing can surpass them in elegance coupled with profundity,"[10] and, in the following year, published the same praise at greater length in the concluding pages of his essay "On the Use of Teleological Principles in Philosophy." Maimon wrote to Kant that Reinhold "is the one whom, after you, I most esteem because of his unusual acuity."[11] Schopenhauer, in 1813, sent Reinhold a copy of his dissertation, noting in his cover letter that he did so "in the admiration owed the man who through the first recognition and the spreading of the immortal doctrines of Kant acquired enduring merit and who demonstrated, afterwards as well, the purest love and striving for the truth, suborning all other motives, more than anyone else."[12]

These encomia, which could easily be multiplied, strongly suggest the need for an explanation for Reinhold's neglect. This explanation is not hard to find once the problem has been recognized. It consists in two myths with ideological content that have dominated the writing of the pertinent history of philosophy. One of these myths is the neo-Kantian, the other is the Hegelian/neo-Hegelian.

In his works following the initial *Briefe* of 1786–1787, Reinhold began insisting that, while Kant had come up with the right conclusions, their foundations remained inadequate and that what was consequently required was a reconstruction of the critical philosophy so as to complete it *a parte ante* by grounding it in a single first principle.[13] Since some

---

9. Friedrich Heinrich Jacobi, letter to Reinhold, dated February 11, 1790, in Reinhold, *Leben und litterarisches Wirken*, pp. 227–28.
10. Immanuel Kant, letter to Reinhold, dated December 18, 1787, in Reinhold, *Leben und litterarisches Wirken*, p. 127.
11. Salomon Maimon, lettter to Kant, dated September 20, 1791, in *Kant's gesammelte Schriften*, Prussian Academy of Sciences edition, 24 vols. (Berlin: Walter de Gruyter, 1922), 11.285 (Vol. 2 of Correspondence).
12. Arthur Schopenhauer, letter to Reinhold, dated 1813, cited in Alfred Klemmt, *Karl Leonhard Reinholds Elementarphilosophie: Eine Studie über den Ursprung des spekulativen deutschen Idealismus* (Hamburg: Verlag von Felix Meiner, 1958), p. 589.
13. See, e.g., Karl Leonhard Reinhold, *Beyträge zur Berichtigung bisheriger Missverständnisse der Philosophen*, 2 vols. (Jena: Johann Michael Mauke, 1790), 1.265, 273, and *Ueber das Fundament des philosophischen Wissens nebst einigen Erläuterungen über die Theorie des Vorstellungsvermögens* (Jena: Johann Michael Mauke, 1791), p. 73.

readers had apparently missed the intent of his *Versuch einer neuen Theorie des menschlichen Vorstellungsvermögens,* published in 1789 and again in 1795, Reinhold emphasized, in his essay on the relationship between that work and Kant's First *Critique,* his "purpose of setting out the premisses of the critical philosophy."[14] Reinhold's name for the basic part of his reconstruction was *Elementarphilosophie.* Only through the latter could philosophy become what Kant had programmatically proclaimed it to be: the complete scientific system of pure reason. Others soon came to agree with Reinhold. Fichte's pertinent reflections, out of which grew his famous review of *Aenesidemus*[15] and then his *Grundlage der gesammten Wissenschaftslehre,* bore the telling title *Eigne Meditationen über Elementar-Philosophie.*[16] And Schelling, who, while still a student at Tübingen, had intensively concerned himself with Reinhold's works,[17] agreed in a letter to Hegel that "Kant has provided the conclusions; the premisses are still lacking."[18] Schelling's paraphrase here of Reinhold is of interest because it shows agreement with Reinhold's assessment of Kant's work and, consequently, with the former's program but not with the extant implementation of this program. The result was that, as de Vleeschauwer rightly notes, "The systematic search for the unique principle, from which transcendentalism in its entirety would be seen to flow, constitutes the true motivating force of philosophy in this feverish *fin de siecle.*"[19] As Reinhold predicted in 1791, his program would be widely accepted in twenty years.[20]

Kant, old, frail, and physically distant from the centers of these efforts, notably Jena and Göttingen, remained silent in their regard for a decade. Finally, in 1799, he published his two-page "Declaration" against

14. Karl Leonhard Reinhold, "Ueber das Verhältniss der Theorie des Vorstellungsvermögens, zur Kritik der reinen Vernunft," in *Beyträge zur Berichtigung bisheriger Missverständnisse der Philosophen,* 1.259.

15. Johann Gottlieb Fichte, "Ohne Druckort: *Aenesidemus oder über die Fundamente der von dem Hrn. Prof. Reinhold in Jena gelieferten Elementar-Philosophie. Nebst einer Vertheidigung des Skepticismus gegen die Anmassungen der Vernunftkritik.* 1792. 445 S. 8," in *Allgemeine Literatur-Zeitung* (Jena: Expedition, 1794), Numbers 47–49. Reprinted in J. G. Fichte, *Gesamtausgabe der Bayrischen Akademie der Wissenschaften,* 26 vols., ed. Reinhard Lauth and Hans Gliwitzki (Stuttgart-Bad Cannstatt: Friedrich Frommann Verlag Günther Holzboog, 1965), 1.2. 41–67.

16. Fichte, *Gesamtausgabe der Bayrischen Akademie der Wissenschaften,* 2.3.8.

17. Martin Bondeli, *Das Anfangsproblem bei Karl Leonhard Reinhold: Eine systematische und entwicklungsgeschichtliche Untersuchung zur Philosophie Reinholds in der Zeit von 1789 bis 1803* (Frankfurt am Main: Vittorio Klostermann, 1995), p. 264n14.

18. Friedrich Wilhelm Joseph Schelling, letter to Hegel, dated Eve of the Feast of Three Kings, 1795, in Georg Wilhelm Friedrich Hegel, *Sämtliche Werke,* 30 vols., ed. Johannes Hoffmeister (Hamburg: Verlag Felix Meiner, 1952), 27.14.

19. Herman-J. de Vleeschauwer, *The Development of Kantian Thought* (London: Thomas Nelson and Sons, 1962), pp. 166–67.

20. Reinhold, *Ueber das Fundament des philosophischen Wissens,* pp. 137–38.

Fichte, expelling the latter not only from the ranks of critical philosophers but, given his conception of the development of reason, from philosophy altogether.[21] This became very clear the following year in a one-page Preface Kant provided for Jachmann's *Prüfung der Kantischen Religionsphilosophie*. In this, his last philosophical publication, Kant characterized attempts to develop transcendentalism from a highest principle as "pseudophilosophy," which he also called "mysticism." The latter term was used to denote not, as in earlier years, a dogmatic metaphysics such as Plato's but rather "the exact opposite of all philosophy."[22]

This became the basis of the first of the myths I mentioned. When German idealism came to be repudiated, many of these repudiations marched to the battle cry with which Otto Liebmann in 1865 closed each chapter of his *Kant und die Epigonen:* "Hence it is necessary to return to Kant!"[23] This neo-Kantian return to Kant was shaped both by the rapid advance of the empirical sciences and by the equation, drawn by Hegel and accepted by his opponents, of absolute idealism with metaphysics in its final form. The Kant returned to was thus an antimetaphysical analyst or theorist of scientific knowledge generally or, more specifically, of Newtonian mechanics. From this perspective—and it is important to recall how many of the major historians of the pertinent period shared this perspective—Reinhold's *Elementarphilosophie* was the psychologistic beginning of a fall into metaphysical mysticism, while the rest of Reinhold's work was too alien to merit discussion. The underlying animus showed up in various ways. Thus, when R. Schmidt reissued Reinhold's *Briefe*, he noted that he did so solely "for the sake of Immanuel Kant and the study of his philosophy."[24] Lest the meaning of this remark be missed by his reader, he added: "This reissue thus occurs only indirectly in honor of Reinhold. No Reinhold renaissance is to be conjured up thereby."[25] Even E. Cassirer, who admitted that the neo-Kantian picture of this body of

21. Immanuel Kant, "Erklärung in Beziehung auf Fichtes Wissenschaftslehre," in *Werke*, 11 vols., ed. Ernst Cassirer (Berlin: Bruno Cassirer, 1922), 8.515–16. For an excellent tracing of Kant's gradual appropriation of the notion of criticism to his own work exclusively, see Kurt Röttgers, *Kritik und Praxis: Zur Geschichte des Kritikbegriffs von Kant bis Marx* (Berlin: Walter de Gruyter, 1975), esp. pp. 61–62. In regard to Kant's gradual identification of propaedeutic and system, see de Vleeschauwer, *Development of Kantian Thought*, chap. 4.

22. Immanuel Kant, "Vorrede zu Jachmanns Prüfung der Kantischen Religionsphilosophie," in *Werke*, 8.229–31.

23. Otto Liebmann, *Kant und die Epigonen: eine kritische Abhandlung* (Berlin: Reuther and Reichard, 1912).

24. Raymund Schmidt, "Vorwort des Herausgebers," in Karl Leonhard Reinhold, *Briefe über die Kantische Philosophie*, ed. Dr. Raymund Schmidt (Leipzig: Verlag von Philipp Reclam jun., [1923]), p. 3.

25. Ibid., p. 5.

work was in need of revision,[26] managed very little in the way of such revision. Buttressed by such extraneous factors as Mill's influential and independently arrived at equation of metaphysics and mysticism[27] and the perceived effectiveness of Russell and Moore in combating British Hegelianism, this view became widespread in the English-speaking world.

Reinhold's philosophical development involved a number of phases which, given the metaphilosophic preoccupation of the time with "system," meant a number of system changes. From defending Kant's philosophy, he moved to the articulation, in several systematic forms, of his own *Elementarphilosophie*. He then adopted a modified form of Fichte's *Wissenschaftslehre*, only to move to a position between the latter and the views of Jacobi. He then articulated a "rational realism" that built on the "logical realism" of Bardili,[28] and proceeded on that basis to studies in the philosophy of language. These contributed both to his relinquishing Bardili's doctrines and to the formulation of another system all his own. The latter—Reinhold's last—reminds me, at least, of medieval thought, though it is clearly the product of what Reinhold had learned both from his own work in German idealism and from English philosophers as well.

While Reinhold's changes within the general ambit of German idealism were praised as philosophically important,[29] the situation changed dramatically when Reinhold, who first conceptualized the movement from Kant through the *Elementarphilosophie* to Fichte's absolute subjectivism to the identity systems of Schelling and Hegel as a necessary development, jumped out of this line of development altogether in the direction of realism. Fichte, Schelling, and Hegel—probably for the only time in their respective careers—made a common front against him. Fichte spoke of "this miserable wretch"[30] who had "never had a spark of transcendental spirit."[31] Schelling who, as he himself noted, had a "personal

---

26. Ernst Cassirer, *Das Erkenntnisproblem in der Philosophie und Wissenschaft der neueren Zeit* (Berlin: Bruno Cassirer, 1922), p. 34.

27. John Stuart Mill, *A System of Logic, Ratiocinative and Inductive, Being a Connected View of the Principles of Evidence and the Methods of Scientific Investigation*, 2 vols. (London: J. W. Parker, 1843), Vol. 1, Book I, chapter 4.

28. C. G. Bardili, *Grundriß der Ersten Logik, gereiniget von den Irrthümern bisheriger Logiken überhaupt, der Kantischen insbesondere; Keine Kritik sondern eine Medicina mentis, brauchbar hauptsächlich für Deutschlands Kritische Philosophie* (Stuttgart: Franz Christian Löflund, 1800 [de facto: 1799]).

29. Johann Gottlieb Fichte, letter to Reinhold, dated March 21, 1797, in Fichte, *Gesamtausgabe der Bayrischen Akademie der Wissenschaften*, 3.3.56–57.

30. Johann Gottlieb Fichte, letter to Schelling, dated June 9, 1800, in J. G. Fichte, *Briefwechsel*, 2 vols., ed. Hans Schulz (Hildesheim: Georg Olms Verlagsbuchhandlung, 1967), 2.236.

31. Johann Gottlieb Fichte, letter to G. E. Mehmel, dated November 4–11, 1800, in Fichte, *Briefwechsel*, 2.278.

and, I could almost say, physical antipathy" to Reinhold,[32] characterized him as this "wind blown reed,"[33] and as a "simpleton."[34] Rather than substantively concerning himself with the quality of reasons prompting Reinhold's changes—the latter's "Accounting for My Changes of System,"[35] published in 1803, was analyzed by neither Fichte nor Schelling nor Hegel—Schelling made fun of these changes[36] and took them as signs of a "philosophical imbecility."[37] Hegel, in his *Differenzschrift*, followed the example of his friend, though without name-calling. This work, insofar as it is concerned specifically with Reinhold's thought, is not such as to enhance Hegel's status as a philosophical critic.

Taken literally, Hegel's main claim, that Reinhold seemed not to have recognized a difference between Schelling and Fichte,[38] is "simply and without any qualification substantively false."[39] Hegel based his claim primarily on the first issue of Reinhold's *Beyträge zur leichtern Uebersicht* . . . , in which Schelling was discussed relatively little, and not on either the second issue of this journal, where Schelling was analyzed very extensively, or Reinhold's lengthy review of Schelling's *System des transcendentalen Idealismus* in the prior year—both familiar to Hegel. Hence R. Lauth goes even further and accuses Hegel of having "demonstrably said knowingly what is untrue."[40] But even in terms of Reinhold's relatively brief account of Schelling in the initial issue of *Beyträge zur leichtern Uebersicht* . . . , this claim by Hegel and such others as the claim, that Reinhold confused a part of Schelling's philosophy with the latter's whole system,

---

32. Friedrich Wilhelm Joseph Schelling, letter to Fichte, dated May 24, 1801, in Fichte, *Briefwechsel*, 2.320.

33. Friedrich Wilhelm Joseph Schelling, letter to Fichte, dated May 14, 1800, in Fichte, *Briefwechsel*, 2.224.

34. Friedrich Wilhelm Joseph Schelling, "Ueber das absolute Identitäts-System und sein Verhältniss zu dem neuesten (Reinholdischen) Dualismus. Ein Gespräch zwischen dem Verfasser und einem Freund," in *Kritisches Journal der Philosophie*, ed. F. W. J. Schelling and G.W.F. Hegel (Hildesheim: Georg Olms Verlagsbuchhandlung, 1967), vol. 1, issue 1, p. 88.

35. Karl Leonhard Reinhold, "Rechenschaft über mein Systemwechseln," in *Beyträge zur leichtern Uebersicht des Zustandes der Philosophie beym Anfange des 19. Jahrhunderts* (Hamburg: Friedrich Perthes, 1803), issue 5, pp. 23–46.

36. Friedrich Wilhelm Joseph Schelling, "Ein Brief von Zettel an Squenz," in *Kritisches Journal der Philosophie*, pp. 122–30.

37. Friedrich Wilhelm Joseph Schelling, "Vorerinnerung," in *Darstellung meines Systems der Philosophie 1801*, in *Schellings Werke*, 6 vols., ed. Manfred Schröter (Munich: C. H. Beck'sche Verlagsbuchhandlung, 1958), 3.7.

38. Hegel, *Differenz des Fichte'schen und Schelling'schen Systems der Philosophie*, p. 94.

39. Helmut Girndt, "Hegel und Reinhold," in *Philosophie aus einem Prinzip Karl Leonhard Reinhold*, ed. Reinhard Lauth (Bonn: Bouvier Verlag Herbert Grundmann, 1974), p. 222.

40. Reinhard Lauth, "Reinholds Vorwurf des Subjektivismus gegen die Wissenschaftslehre," in *Philosophie aus einem Prinzip Karl Leonhard Reinhold*, ed. Lauth, p. 292.

must be taken as "complete fabrications."[41] Indeed, these claims were directly contradicted shortly thereafter by Schelling himself.[42] If, on the other hand, one takes Hegel to have been speaking loosely and really to have meant that Reinhold did not rightly construe the differences between Fichte and Schelling as an opposition of principle, then the proper addressee of this criticism should have been Schelling, who at this juncture was denying any such opposition.[43]

Of course, Hegel's *Differenzschrift* also made plenty of legitimate criticisms, whose subsequent role would make fascinating philosophical reading. Some of his criticisms hit their mark. Thus the critique of Bardili's (and Reinhold's) "logical realism"[44] undoubtedly contributed to Reinhold's relinquishing, in the next several years, the ultimate principle involved—Bardili's "untenable concept of thought"—and consequently most of the system built thereon.[45] Other criticisms, such as Hegel's claim that the principle of "popular philosophy"—"the absolute nonidentity of finite and infinite"—was simply spurious, continued to receive Reinhold's considered rejection on the basis of their resting on a nest of linguistic confusions.[46] (Ironically, Hegel's implicit presupposition here, shared by Fichte and Schelling, that the mediation of life and philosophy occurs in philosophy, was denied by Reinhold throughout his career except during his Bardili phase, which was the phase being attacked by Hegel.) Likewise, Hegel's charge that Reinhold viewed truth as given, the absolute as something true in and for itself, rather than as produced by reason,[47] was accepted by the latter, though he found no failing in this.[48] In regard to other charges, the situation was more complex. Thus Hegel's complaint about Reinhold's grounding the beginning of philosophy's quest for the *Urwahre* in a "problematic and hypothetical" truth[49] contained various strands and thus consequences. In the

41. Helmut Girndt, "Hegel und Reinhold," p. 219.
42. See the lengthy discussion in Reinhard Lauth, "Reinholds Vorwurf des Subjektivismus gegen die Wissenschaftslehre," in *Philosophie aus einem Prinzip Karl Leonhard Reinhold*, ed. Lauth, esp. pp. 278–79.
43. Ibid., pp. 222–23.
44. Hegel, *Differenz des Fichte'schen und Schelling'schen Systems der Philosophie*, pp. 105–10.
45. See the autobiographical remarks in Karl Leonhard Reinhold, *Die alte Frage: Was ist die Wahrheit? bey den erneuerten Streitigkeiten über die göttliche Offenbarung und die menschliche Vernunft, in nähere Erwägung gezogen* (Altona: Johann Friedrich Hammerich, 1820), pp. 162–63.
46. E.g., in Reinhold, *Die alte Frage*, pp. 15–16, 46–47, 74.
47. Hegel, *Differenz des Fichte'schen und Schelling'schen Systems der Philosophie*, p. 103.
48. Not coincidentally does he preface the book just cited with a citation from Dugald Steward's *Philosophical Essays:* "Knowledge no wise constitutes these truths, which are its objects. The previous Existence of the Truths is manifestly implied in the very Supposition of their being Objects of the Knowledge."
49. Hegel, *Differenz des Fichte'schen und Schelling'schen Systems der Philosophie*, p. 103.

final issue of his *Beyträge zur leichtern Uebersicht* . . . , Reinhold would, as a result, modify his view of the truth with which philosophy must begin to include its being something familiar and foundational to common sense, yet initially indistinct conceptually and clouded by semblance.[50] And, in his final works, he would relinquish philosophy's hypothetical beginning. Hegel, on the other hand, would come to recognize the problematic character of the beginning of philosophy, indeed to give Reinhold credit in this regard in the First Book of the greater *Logic*.[51] And he would accept Reinhold's related idea of a philosophical introduction to the system of philosophy in the *Phenomenology of Spirit*. More generally, Hegel would later also come to echo a number of Reinhold's earlier criticisms of Schelling. In short, there was a mutual though rarely acknowledged give-and-take.[52]

Instead of investigating Hegel's charges or tracing the give-and-take just mentioned, the great Hegelian historians of philosophy in the nineteenth century contented themselves with the overall caricature of Reinhold's work found in the *Differenzschrift*—Hegel's only sustained treatment of Reinhold—and with Schelling's seemingly endless derision. This produced the second myth I mentioned.

In terms of this myth, Reinhold received credit for popularizing Kant who, after all, was viewed as "the foundation and point of departure of recent German philosophy."[53] He was also credited with drawing attention to the foundational shortcomings of the latter's work and thereby, as well as by means of his own attempts to remedy these shortcomings, serving as a transition to Fichte's *Doctrine of Science*. As I indicated earlier, no attempt was made to assess the reasons for Reinhold's subsequent substantive changes of mind. Instead, he was subjected to character aspersions. Thus his former student W. T. Krug already pointed in this direction, in spite of the admiration also evident:

As concerns Reinhold's philosophy, it is probably no exaggeration to say that no philosopher of significance combined so great a love for the truth and so great an effort in its investigation with so much submission [*Hingabe*] to others and,

50. Karl Leonhard Reinhold. "Neue Auflösung der alten Aufgabe der Philosophie," in *Beyträge zur leichtern Uebersicht des Zustandes der Philosophie beym Anfange des 19. Jahrhunderts* (Hamburg: Friedrich Perthes, 1803), issue 6, pp. 14ff. This is a variant of a view Reinhold had already come to embrace in 1792. See Marcelo Stamm, "Das Programm des methodologischen Monismus: Subjekttheoretische und methodologische Aspekte der Elementarphilosophie K. L. Reinholds," in "Ansätze der Philosophie um 1800," ed. Rüdiger Bubner, Konrad Cramer, and Reiner Wiehl, *Neue Hefte für Philosophie* 35 (1995): 21.
51. Georg Wilhelm Friedrich Hegel, *Wissenschaft der Logik*, 2 vols., ed. Georg Lasson (Leipzig: Verlag von Felix Meiner, 1951), 1.55.
52. For an excellent account of the pertinent points, see Bondeli, *Das Anfangsproblem bei Karl Leonhard Reinhold*, pp. 30–33, 353–64, 376–414.
53. Hegel, *Wissenschaft der Logik*, 1.44n.

precisely for this reason, so little autonomy in philosophizing as precisely this man. The reason for this probably lay partly in his early monastic education and partly in Reinhold's spiritual nature insofar as the latter was more feminine or receptive than manly or creative.[54]

This view then continued. Rosenkranz found "a residue of Catholicism, which is used to subordination in spiritual matters,"[55] while Fischer pointed to "a sort of feminine leaning on."[56] Apart from the contributions mentioned, Reinhold was thus viewed as too changeable and too little autonomous to be taken seriously as a philosopher.[57] His final investigations into language were taken as confirming this view. Hence Rosenkranz's overall assessment was dismissive. Reinhold was a pop philosopher both in the sense that his best work consisted of popularization and in the further sense that his frame of mind overly resembled that of the public. Since the latter was "inclined to derive differences of philosophy from an excessive neglect of language which thinks for us, Reinhold finally sank that low as well, though always with decorum."[58]

This Hegelian view of Reinhold—and of the period of the emergence of German idealism—has exercised immense influence on subsequent writing in the history of philosophy. It runs from Erdmann and Michelet through Rosenkranz and Fischer on into the neo-Hegelian revival, which grew out of neo-Kantianism, of Kroner and others.

The upshot of each of these myths and of their combination is that Reinhold is truly "a forgotten philosopher," as I indicated by my earlier reference to Copleston's *A History of Philosophy*. A further result is that many of Reinhold's major reviews, articles, and books have never even

---

54. Wilhelm Traugott Krug, *Allgemeines Handwörterbuch der philosophischen Wissenschaften, nebst ihrer Literatur und Geschichte*, 5 vols. (Leipzig: F. A. Brockhaus, 1833), 3.491.

55. Karl Rosenkranz, *Geschichte der Kant'schen Philosophie*, in Immanuel Kant, *Sämmtliche Werke*, 14 vols., ed. Karl Rosenkranz and Friedrich Wilhelm Schubert (Leipzig: Leopold Voss, 1840), 12.389.

56. Kuno Fischer, *Geschichte der neuern Philosophie*, 10 vols. (Heidelberg: Carl Winter's Universitätsbuchhandlung, 1890), 5.120.

57. It is worth noting that the person who probably knew Reinhold and his works best finally judged in this regard as follows:

> Jens Baggesen not only entirely takes back his judgment about Professor Reinhold's character as philosopher (insofar as the latter appeared to him inconstant, slavish and without character), but declares that, after having studied this character more precisely in all of its expressions, including its latest manifestation, he takes the latter to be the solely true, genuine, God-pleasing philosophical character, the most unconstrained and unegotistical character he knows.

See Jens Baggesen, letter to Reinhold, dated November 20, 1801, in *Aus Jens Baggesen's Briefwechsel mit Karl Leonhard Reinhold und Friedrich Heinrich Jacobi*, 2 vols., ed. K. Baggesen and A. Baggesen (Leipzig: F. A. Brockhaus, 1831), 2.355–56.

58. Rosenkranz, *Geschichte der Kant'schen Philosophie*, pp. 387–400.

received any scrutiny at all.⁵⁹ Instead, Reinhold's name has become a cultural icon for eclecticism, as in Samuel Beckett's *First Love:* "Yes, there are moments, particularly in the afternoon, when I go all syncretist, a la Reinhold. What equilibrium."⁶⁰ M. Zahn aptly notes in regard to recent efforts at Reinhold scholarship what I have urged thus far:

> It becomes visible here as well, how unavoidable it is to investigate anew the classical epoch of German philosophy in its entire complexity and thereby, in particular, to assess critically the interpretive models used hitherto which do not do justice to the richness of the pertinent disputes and in part tendentiously foreshorten or disfigure them out of self-interest.⁶¹

I thus wish to acknowledge my appreciation to the editors of this volume. For it seems to me that, once the forgetting I have traced is undone, Reinhold can be recognized as, at least, worth close study in regard to the emergence of German idealism.

As the encomia I cited earlier make clear, Reinhold was a very smart man. As also already suggested, he worked very hard. He published more than a hundred books and articles and nearly twice that number of reviews and notes.⁶² And the publisher of his correspondence expects the extant letters, many of which are of philosophical interest, to fill six large volumes of which only the first is in print thus far.⁶³ This large body of work is, in good part, the product of Reinhold's resolve—expressed in the title of this paper—to keep up with his age. Because of this resolve, he not only wrote a lot like many of his philosophic colleagues but, unlike some of them, also read assiduously.⁶⁴ "He digested the philosophical literature of his time almost exhaustively" and was thus able to follow current developments "with greater precision than his famous philosophical contemporaries."⁶⁵ Many of Reinhold's major works, notably the two volumes of his *Beyträge zur Berichtigung bisheriger Missverständnisse der Philosophen* (1790, 1794) and the six issues of his *Beyträge zur leichtern Uebersicht des Zustandes der Philosophie beym Anfange des 19. Jahrhunderts* (1801–1803), contain lengthy and detailed analyses of Kant,

---

59. Alexander von Schönborn, *Karl Leonhard Reinhold: Eine annotierte Bibliographie* (Stuttgart-Bad Cannstatt: Friedrich Frommann Verlag Günther Holzboog, 1991), pp. 35–38, 45–49.
60. Samuel Beckett, *First Love* (London: Calder and Boyars, 1973), p. 27.
61. Manfred Zahn, "Einleitung," in *Philosophie aus einem Prinzip Karl Leonhard Reinhold*, ed. Lauth, p. 6.
62. von Schönborn, *Karl Leonhard Reinhold: Eine annotierte Bibliographie*.
63. Lauth, Heller, and Hiller, eds., *Karl Leonhard Reinhold Korrespondenzausgabe*.
64. Reinhold, *Leben und litterarisches Wirken*, p. 120.
65. "Vorwort," in *Karl Leonhard Reinhold Korrespondenzausgabe*, ed. Lauth, Heller, and Hiller, p. xi.

Fichte, Schelling, and Bardili. He wrote several major reviews each on works by Kant, Fichte, and Schelling. He reviewed, or wrote books about, the works of lesser luminaries who are nevertheless important to understanding the disputes of the time: F. L. Bouterwek, J. A. Eberhard, J. F. Flatt, J. F. Fries, J. F. Herbart, J. G. v. Herder, K. H. Heydenreich, L. H. Jakob, J.G.C. Kiesewetter, W. T. Krug, J. K. Lavater, K.C.E. Schmid and G. E. Schulze. And he sought to draw attention to foreign philosophical writings such as J. Harris's *Hermes: or, A philosophical inquiry concerning language and universal grammar*.[66]

Given his distinctive willingness to learn, Reinhold everywhere sought dialogue and candid discussion with his contemporaries. He thus became—frequently mediating, clarifying, ordering and delimiting—a central figure for the discussion of his time. It is largely due to him that this discussion attained a certain homogeneity in terms of posing problems and of level.[67]

It is thus not surprising that, in his excellent recent book *Das Anfangsproblem bei Karl Leonhard Reinhold*, M. Bondeli persuasively characterizes Reinhold as not only "the initiator" but also the "indefatigable reformer and profound critic" of the post-Kantian philosophical systems.[68]

It is thus particularly unfortunate that Reinhold is so little known. His "forgottenness" has exacted heavy costs. Apart from a handful of exceptions, his works have not been republished. They are thus hard to obtain; several are no longer to be found even in German libraries. Translations into English are practically nonexistent. The major portion of one of his important works[69] and one of his popular works[70] are the only items available in English. In terms of secondary literature, those readers able to read German have the distinct advantage of several good books,[71]

---

66. James Harris, *Hermes: or, A philosophical inquiry concerning language and universal grammar* (London: Printed by H. Woodfall for J. Nourse and P. Valiant, 1751). This work went through many editions throughout the rest of the century. Its second, improved edition (1765) is reprinted in Hildesheim: Georg Olms, 1976.
67. Zahn, "Einleitung," p. 3.
68. Bondeli, *Das Anfangsproblem bei Karl Leonhard Reinhold*, p. 13.
69. K. L. Reinhold, *The Foundation of Philosophical Knowledge*, in *Between Kant and Hegel: Texts in the Development of Post-Kantian Idealism*, ed. and trans. George di Giovanni and H. S. Harris (Albany: State University of New York Press, 1985), pp. 52–106.
70. Sabine Roehr, *A Primer on German Enlightenment: With a Translation of Karl Leonhard Reinhold's "The Fundamental Concepts and Principles of Ethics"* (Columbia: University of Missouri Press, 1995).
71. For an account of Reinhold's doings and writings prior to his discovery of Kant, I would recommend Werner Sauer's "Josephinische Aufklärung und Kantischer Vernunftglauben," in his *Österreichische Philosophie zwischen Aufklärung und Restauration: Beiträge zur Geschichte des Frühkantianismus in der Donaumonarchie* (Amsterdam: Rodopi, 1982), chap. 3, pp. 57–106. For Reinhold's Kantian and *Elementarphilosophie* phases, I would recommend Alfred Klemmt's *Karl Leonhard Reinholds Elementarphilosophie*. Given Klemmt's animus against German idealism, which affects his construal of Reinhold, I would also recommend

those able to read Italian have at least one.⁷² In English, sadly, the longest meaty treatment is one chapter in F. Beiser's *The Fate of Reason*.⁷³ But as I noted earlier, many of Reinhold's writings have never been scrutinized in print by anyone, in any language.

The consequence and further costs of this scarcity of material are not only our skewed understanding of the emergence of German idealism but Reinhold's virtual absence from current philosophical discussion. D. Henrich mentions a distinction crucial for a theory of self-consciousness first drawn by Reinhold, which Henrich had, earlier in his career, attributed to Fichte.⁷⁴ G. Prauss approvingly cites Reinhold's criticisms of Kant's account of will⁷⁵ and thus forces a defender of Kant's account like H. Allison to discuss these criticisms.⁷⁶ The rest seems an oppressive silence.

In undertaking the preceding necessary ground-clearing—in effect, a plea to look at Reinhold's philosophical output—I have, unfortunately, used up a significant portion of the space allotted to this paper. As Zahn and Bondeli have suggested, and as I very briefly illustrated in regard to Hegel's *Differenzschrift*, the give-and-take between Fichte, Hegel, Reinhold, and Schelling was a significant part of the development of each philosopher's final views. Each developed several "systems"; each did so in significant part due to the criticisms of the others. Charting and making sense of this give-and-take insofar as Reinhold is involved, in regard to the particular issue and specific time frame indicated in his title, takes Bondeli some 445 pages. I shall therefore use my remaining

---

for these phases Wilhelm Teichner's *Rekonstruktion oder Reproduktion des Grundes: Die Begründung der Philosophie als Wissenschaft durch Kant und Reinhold* (Bonn: Bouvier Verlag Herbert Grundmann, 1976). For brief treatments of the phases discussed thus far and more elaborate studies of Reinhold's Fichte period, with some helpful discussions of Jacobi, Schelling, and Hegel in relation to Reinhold as well, see Reinhard Lauth, ed., *Philosophie aus einem Prinzip Karl Leonhard Reinhold*. (One caution in regard to this volume: The Fichtean perspective of its contributors is better at detecting what Reinhold is not yet than what Fichte is no longer.) Finally, the best account of Reinhold, covering all the phases mentioned thus far and Reinhold's very difficult Bardili phase, is the very recent Martin Bondeli, *Das Anfangsproblem bei Karl Leonhard Reinhold*. Within the restrictions indicated by its title, this work contains more helpful information and good, detailed analysis than any other secondary source on Reinhold. It covers much of the latter's role in the emergence of German idealism and does so fairly and in depth.

72. Angelo Pupi, *La formazione della filosofia di K. L. Reinhold 1784–1794* (Milan: Società Editrice Vita e Pensiero, 1966).

73. Frederick C. Beiser, *The Fate of Reason: German Philosophy from Kant to Fichte* (Cambridge: Harvard University Press, 1987), pp. 226–65.

74. Dieter Henrich, "Die Anfänge der Theorie des Subjekts (1789)," in *Zwischenbetrachtungen: Im Prozess der Aufklärung*, ed. Axel Honneth (Frankfurt am Main: Suhrkamp Verlag, 1989), p. 150n18.

75. Gerold Prauss, *Kant über Freiheit als Autonomie* (Frankfurt am Main: Vittorio Klostermann, 1983), pp. 84–91.

76. Henry E. Allison, *Kant's Theory of Freedom* (New York: Cambridge University Press, 1990), pp. 133–36.

space to indicate roughly Reinhold's development, referring the reader, for the actual disputes and the pertinent arguments offered, to the works I recommended above. Given the claims about Reinhold's eclecticism and inconstancy, tracing that development strikes me as valuable.

In his "Accounting for My Changes of System," Reinhold remarked:

> But a presentiment of the in itself absolute, of the first simpliciter, of the originally true in the true—through which philosophizing from the beginning only mattered to me as a getting to the bottom [*des Ergründens*]—has, for that reason, never left me in the entire course of my life thus far.[77]

Nine years later, in the Preface of his *Synonymik* addressed to Jacobi, Reinhold declared the latter to have had a longer and more beneficial influence on his efforts than anyone else.[78] I would like to use these two remarks as clues to his development. Doing so requires turning to his youth.

Reinhold was born—in 1757 in Vienna—into a devout family and, at age fifteen, enrolled in a Jesuit seminary. When the Society of Jesus was suppressed less than a year later, he switched within a couple of months to the seminary of the Barnabite monks. An extant letter, written by Reinhold on the news of this suppression,[79] bears out the truth of his later remark that "through the manner in which he was raised, religion ... was made not just the main but in a sense the sole concern of his early life."[80] After his priestly ordination, Reinhold worked as a teacher of philosophy, master of novices, and parish priest.[81] Apparently, he performed these tasks very well. The testimony of a Barnabite, Don Martinus, dated July 1783, praised Reinhold not only as a teacher but as someone who "*in omnis suis muneribus*" exhibited scientific cultivation and a religious disposition.[82] But at the time of this testimonial, Reinhold was already as well a member of the elite Masonic lodge To True Harmony[83] and of the *Illuminati* (with the code name "Decius"). As speaker

---

77. Reinhold, "Rechenschaft über mein Systemwechseln," p. 36.
78. Karl Leonhard Reinhold, *Grundlegung einer Synonymik für den allgemeinen Sprachgebrauch in den philosophischen Wissenschaften* (Kiel: August Schmidt, 1812), p. xxx.
79. Karl Leonhard Reinhold, letter to his father, dated September 13, 1773, in *Karl Leonhard Reinhold Korrespondenzausgabe*, ed. Lauth, Heller, and Hiller, pp. 1–8.
80. Karl Leonhard Reinhold, *Versuch einer neuen Theorie des menschlichen Vorstellungsvermögens* (Prague and Jena: C. Widtmann and J. M. Mauke, 1789), p. 52.
81. Reinhard Lauth, "Nouvelles recherches sur Reinhold et l'Aufklärung," *Archives de philosophie* 42, no. 4 (1979): 594.
82. Cited in Robert Keil, ed., "Wiener Freunde 1784–1808. Beitraege zur Jugendgeschichte der Deutsch-Oesterreichischen Literatur," in *Beitraege zur Geschichte der deutschen Literatur und des geistigen Lebens in Oesterreich*, ed. Jakob Minor, August Sauer, and Richard Maria Werner (Vienna: Verlag Carl Konegen, 1883), issue 2, p. 4.
83. The emperor did not allow promulgation of the papal ban on Catholics becoming members in the lands under the Habsburg crown.

of his lodge and as a very active reviewer at the Viennese *Realzeitung*, he was a fiery advocate of the reforms characterized by the rubric "Josephinism."[84] In short, he was in the midst of a complex crisis. Since this crisis made an indelible impression such that its gradual resolution provided central themes for the rest of Reinhold's life, I shall sketch some of its important aspects.

The first and arguably main aspect was religious and had both personal and social aspects. The study of philosophy made it impossible for Reinhold "to believe blindly, as before."[85] His Catholic supernaturalism gave way to materialistic atheism, from which he extricated himself through Leibniz's philosophical theism only to lapse into Humean skepticism.[86] Institutionally, he was master of novices in an order of monks while inveighing, as advocate of Josephinism, against celibacy, monks, and the "monkish spirit" present in much of Catholicism. Moreover, he saw that he was not alone in this situation. During his most formative years, the changes in Austria from baroque Catholicism, engendered by both the neo-Jansenist reform movement[87] and the imperial initiatives to foster the Enlightenment as a means of strengthening Austria in the wake of the Seven Years War,[88] were both very rapid and far-reaching. An increasingly poignant polarization between traditional supernaturalism and scoffing disbelief in the name of reason—evidenced by the radical French Enlightenment—was consequently felt by many.[89]

---

84. For details on these reforms and their advocacy by Reinhold, see Zwi Batscha, "Einleitung," in Karl Leonhard Reinhold, *Schriften zur Religionskritik und Aufklärung, 1782–1784* (Bremen: Jacobi-Verlag, 1977).

85. Reinhold, *Versuch einer neuen Theorie des menschlichen Vorstellungsvermögens*, p. 53.

86. Letter from Reinhold to Friedrich Nicolai, dated October 12, 1789, in Lauth, "Nouvelles recherches sur Reinhold et l'Aufklärung," p. 611.

87. Peter Hersche, *Der Spätjansenismus in Österreich* (Vienna: Verlag der Österreichischen Akademie der Wissenschaften, 1977).

88. Ernst Wangermann, "Reform Catholicism and Political Radicalism in the Austrian Enlightenment," in *The Enlightenment in National Context*, ed. Roy Porter and Mikulás Teich (Cambridge: Cambridge University Press, 1981), pp. 127–40.

89. The poet Aloys Blumauer, Reinhold's childhood friend and fellow member of the same Masonic lodge and its *Illuminati* core, put the point in his poem "*Glaubensbekenntnis eines nach Wahrheit Ringenden*" (Creed of One Struggling for the Truth):

Sieh' diesen schweren Kampf, den mein Gewissen
Mit dem Verstande kämpft, mitleidig an,
Und lehre mich ein Mittel, wie mein Wissen
Mit meinem Glauben sich vereinen kann.—
Und hast du denn von dieser meiner Bitte
Dein gütig Ohr auf immer weggewandt,
So nimm—ich fleh's, o Herr! zu deiner Güte—
Nimm mir den Glauben oder den Verstand.

See Edith Rosenstrauch-Königsberg, *Freimauerei im josephinischen Wien. Aloys Blumauers Weg vom Jesuiten zum Jakobiner* (Vienna: Wilhelm Braumüller, 1975), p. 46. For Reinhold's ex-

In this existential tug of war between reason and faith, Reinhold found no help in philosophy as he knew it. As he clearly recognized, the latter, "while proffering more than one scheme to accommodate either his head or his heart, had not a single scheme to offer which might be capable of satisfying the serious demands of both at once."[90]

Where Reinhold did find support—psychological, financial, and ideational—was among his Masonic brethren. *To True Harmony*, under the leadership of Ignaz von Born—Mozart's Sarastro in the *Magic Flute*—had quickly become "a center for literary and scientific ambitions which was to serve as substitute for an academy of sciences lacking in Vienna."[91] It must have been a profound eye-opener for the rather unworldly young monk to find himself closely observing such cosmopolitan practice of enlightenment as individuals like Born, Haydn and Sonnenfels were able to display. The modeling performed by these and the other brethren provided psychological support, and the lodge underwrote Reinhold's expenses when he suddenly in the fall of 1784—whether because of his untenable social situation[92] or for additional political[93] or even amatory[94] reasons is unclear—fled Vienna to Leipzig and then to Weimar. But the chief support he received was ideational. To clarify the latter requires saying something about the *Illuminatenbund*.[95]

This secret society, founded in 1776 by the later Kant adversary Adam Weishaupt, was the radical wing of German Masonry.[96] It not only developed out of the Enlightenment but was, as well, a response to conservative reactions to enlightened absolutism as represented by the Rosicru-

---

pression of the same sentiments in prose, see the citation in Hans Gliwitzky, "Carl Leonhard Reinhold's erster Standpunktwechsel," in *Philosophie aus einem Prinzip: Karl Leonhard Reinhold*, ed. Lauth, p. 33.

90. Reinhold, *Versuch einer neuen Theorie des menschlichen Vorstellungsvermögens*, p. 53.
91. Sauer, *Osterreichische Philosophie zwischen Aufklärung und Restauration*, p. 47.
92. Reinhold, *Leben und litterarisches Wirken*, pp. 19–21.
93. Lauth, "Nouvelles recherches sur Reinhold et l'Aufklärung," pp. 612–13.
94. Gliwitzky, "Carl Leonhard Reinhold's erster Standpunktwechsel," p. 19.
95. Those working in the history of philosophy during this period have not done much with the institutional and ideational relevance of Masonry to philosophy. That this connection is worth exploring is clear from Reinhard Koselleck, *Kritik und Krise. Ein Beitrag zur Pathogenese der bürgerlichen Welt* (Freiburg and Munich: Verlag Karl Alber, 1959).
96. Some of the convictions and many of the activities of this society and of its members are still shrouded in mystery. After its suppression in Bavaria in 1785 and the selectively edited publication of some of its documents, it became fashionable to view the society as having advocated the violent overthrow of governments generally and, later, of having played an important role in fomenting the French Revolution. Conservative reactions to that event still take this view. Thus Reinhard Lauth assigns to Reinhold "un certain rôle d' initiateur" of this revolution (see "Nouvelles recherches sur Reinhold et l'Aufklärung," p. 621). Most current research, as found in the other pertinent works I cite, denies the violent intentions in general. Reinhold's political views were always moderately liberal.

cians, among whose members was that even greater Kantian nemesis, Prussian minister of state J. C. von Wöllner.[97] This responsive feature is worth mentioning because it made necessary a reflective differentiation between genuine and spurious enlightenment.[98] While many of the ideas articulated by Weishaupt and the *Illuminati* were standard Masonic fare—for example, inveighing against what separates persons, fundamentally their religions, states, and estates—a distinctive contribution seems to have been a philosophy of history.[99] The latter viewed history as a phased movement, based on the development of human needs, toward the perfection of the human race. The pertinent phases exhibited a kind of dialectical relationship in that oppression, for example, needed to push to the limit in order to arouse a need to react against it. In the last of the major phases of this historical development, a society's best, most enlightened members had to join together in secret societies aiming at keeping whatever attainments in freedom and enlightenment had been produced by princely self-interest, while working toward the day when all political domination would become superfluous and reason would be "humanity's sole book of law." As R. van Dülmen notes in this context, when Weishaupt spoke of "enlightenment," he meant "a moral and political quality." "Enlightenment meant for him not knowledge of abstract, speculative and theoretical ideas and problems but rather something that improves the 'heart.'"[100] The morality in question was that of Jesus and his initial followers before being ecclesiastically corrupted.[101] And since this enlightenment was not merely an individual attainment but the common good of humanity, the view of history under discussion entailed fostering interest in current affairs and, especially, the education of the young.[102]

97. See Michael W. Fischer, *Die Aufklärung und ihr Gegenteil. Die Rolle der Geheimbünde in Wissenschaft und Politik* (Berlin: Dunker und Humblot, 1982).
98. Thus Reinhold will attack Lavater and the Rosicrucians for their irrational *Schwärmerei* in his *Herzenserleichterung zweyer Menschenfreunde, in vertraulichen Briefen über Johann Caspar Lavarers Glaubensbekentnis* (Frankfurt and Leipzig: Weidmann Verlag, 1785). Distinguishing between genuine and spurious enlightenment will prove to be a major feature of his essay "Gedanken über Aufklärung" (reprinted in Karl Leonhard Reinhold, *Schriften zur Religionskritik und Aufklärung, 1782–1784*, ed. Batscha, pp.352–396) and of his book *Verhandlungen über die Grundbegriffe und Grundsätze der Moralität aus dem Gesichtspunkte des gemeinen und gesunden Verstandes, zum Behuf der Beurtheilung der sittlichen, rechtlichen, politischen und religiösen Angelegenheiten* (Lübeck and Leipzig: Friedrich Bohn, 1798) (translated in Sabine Roehr, *A Primer on German Enlightenment*).
99. Koselleck, *Kritik und Krise*, p. 108.
100. Richard van Dülmen, *Der Geheimbund der Illuminaten. Darstellung, Analyse, Dokumentation* (Stuttgart-Bad Cannstatt: Friedrich Frommann Verlag Günther Holzboog, 1975), pp. 108–9. The citations are from p. 109.
101. Ibid., p. 110.
102. Rosenstrauch-Königsberg, *Freimauerei im josephinischen Wien*, pp. 56–57.

Given the crisis produced both in his own situation and observable all around him, Reinhold was deeply influenced by what, in terms of institutions, conduct, and ideas, pointed in the direction of resolving his crisis. His commitment to true, that is, moral enlightenment and to Masonry proved lifelong.[103] Reinhold would, with a brief aberration during his Bardili phase, view morality as the underpinning to both true philosophy and true religion, rather than being dependent on either.[104] He would also seek to further popular enlightenment by addressing current issues[105] in writings and lectures specifically differentiated from his philosophical work.[106] In both types of efforts, his works exhibited, as Fichte was to note astutely, "a practical warmth," the hope of "improving human beings through philosophy."[107] Reinhold also worked hard, and very successfully, at his teaching,[108] claiming that "My goal was and is to awaken, to exercise and to animate the cognitive abilities and the moral feeling of my hearers, not to teach them the pure truth—which I do not possess—through some infallible system."[109] His acute awareness of rapid historical change made him appreciate the Illuminatist claim that a philosophy of history is crucial, that, as he noted in his *Ueber die kabirischen Mysterien*, understanding history contributes most to self-understanding.[110] Much of his subsequent work in philosophy would involve substantive reconstructions in the history of philosophy to make

---

103. [A. H. Baggesen,] "Reinholds Todtenfeier, den 5. August 1823. Ein maurerisches Denkmal," in *Zeitschrift für Freimaurerei* (Altenburg: Literatur-Comptoir, 1824), issue 1, pp. 95–122. I thus cannot agree with Lauth's claim that Reinhold's development as *Aufklärer*, especially in regard to religious matters, ceased with his encounter in 1792 with Fichte's *Versuch einer Critik aller Offenbarung*. See Lauth, "Nouvelles recherches sur Reinhold et l'Aufklärung," pp. 625–26. To see this, one needs only to browse through Roehr, *A Primer on German Enlightenment*, or through Reinhold's last published work.
104. [Karl Leonhard Reinhold,] *Herzenserleichterung zweyer Menschenfreunde*, p. 13. [Karl Leonhard Reinhold,] "Schreiben des Pfarrers zu *** an den H. des T. M. Ueber eine Recension von Herders Ideen zur Philosophie der Geschichte der Menschheit," in *Der Teutsche Merkur*, 66 vols. (Weimar: Carl Rudolf Hofmann, 1785), 1.164.
105. Examples are the Spinozism debate, the Catholicism debate, the atheism debate, German reactions to the French Revolution, and duelling on university campuses.
106. Reinhold, "Vorrede," in *Beyträge zur Berichtigung*, p. iv.
107. Letter to Reinhold, dated April 22, 1799, in Fichte, *Gesamtausgabe der Bayrischen Akademie*, III (Letters) 3.327.
108. In his last Jena semester, Reinhold's three lecture courses had an enrollment of 600 students out of a total university enrollment of around 860. Additional students were in the Privatissima Reinhold held evenings to discuss philosophical issues. In Kiel, the crowding in his classes was even greater. See Reinhold, *Leben und litterarisches Wirken*, pp. 63–71; and Kurt Röttgers, *Kritik und Praxis*, p. 800; *Geschichte der Christian-Albrechts-Universität Kiel* (Neumunster: Karl Wachholz Verlag, 1969), 5.1.34–35.
109. Letter to Fichte, dated January 7, 1795, in Fichte, *Gesamtausgabe der Bayrischen Akademie*, III (Letters), 2.247.
110. [Karl Leonhard Reinhold,] "Ueber die kabirischen Mysterien. von Br. R**," in *Journal für Freimaurer* (Vienna: Christian Friedrich Wappler, 1785), year 2, issue 1, p. 5.

sense of the emergence of a given position.[111] Finally, though by no means least, Reinhold saw the mediation of philosophy and life or, since religious faith is taken as an outgrowth of a moral life, the mediation of philosophy and faith, as having to occur in one's life. For Reinhold, the apotheosis of the human condition is not the philosopher, as Fichte and Hegel were to claim, nor yet the aesthetic genius, proclaimed by Schiller and differently by Schelling, but rather the ordinary moral agent seeking to approximate a holy will.

Given these themes, it is now possible to sketch very briefly some of Reinhold's intellectual and more properly philosophical developments. As Sauer shows well, the theme of many of Reinhold's earliest Viennese reviews was "the relation between irrational superstition and true belief, between disbelieving illusory reason and true reason."[112] Moreover, these reviews also exhibited increasingly Protestant sympathies. Hence Reinhold formally converted to Lutheranism within a month of his arrival in Weimar. His first publication there, in Wieland's *Der Teutsche Merkur,* was an enthusiastic review of Herder's *Ideen zur Philosophie der Geschichte der Menschheit*—a work he then also defended later against an anonymous review by Kant[113]—followed by his *Gedanken über Aufklärung* and then by a large number of other writings until August 1786, when the first two of his *Letters Concerning the Kantian Philosophy* appeared in this same journal.

The content of this group of largely historical writings consists of the themes I have been discussing, with Protestantism the one major addition. In regard to the latter, Reinhold viewed it as historically a major step toward the Enlightenment, though distinguishing between its principle, the free use of reason in religious matters, and its incomplete historical realization.[114] Now what is important about this principle is that it provided Reinhold with a partial solution to his initial difficulty of finding a synthesis between knowledge and faith that would not degenerate into either supernaturalist superstition or scoffing disbelief. As Sauer notes, the Protestant principle, as itself a synthesis of faith and reason, worked against the first of these dangers, excesses of faith, but

111. Karl Leonhard Reinhold, "Über den Begrif der Geschichte der Philosophie. Eine akademische Vorlesung," in *Beyträge zur Geschichte der Philosophie,* ed. Georg Gustav Fülleborn (Züllichau and Freystadt: Frommannische Buchhandlung, 1791), issue 1, pp. 5–35.
112. Sauer, *Osterreichische Philosophie zwischen Aufklärung und Restauration,* p. 59.
113. [Karl Leonhard Reinhold,] "Schreiben des Pfarrers zu *** an den H. des T. M. . . . ," pp. 148–74.
114. See, e.g., Karl Leonhard Reinhold, *Ehrenrettung der Lutherischen Reformation gegen zwey Kapitel in des K. K. Hofraths Herrn I. M. Schmids Geschichte der Teutschen nebst einigen Bemerkungen über die gegenwärtige katholische Reformation im Oesterreichschen* (Jena: Christian Heinrich Cuno's Erben, 1789 [de facto: 1788]).

not against excesses of reason. The latter, the radical enlightenment of disbelief, called for distinctions within reason rather than faith. For reason, Jacobi had recently proclaimed in initiating the pantheism or Spinozism debate, could if consistent have no other consequence than such radical enlightenment. But no such analysis of reason, much less one able to accommodate a grounding of religion in morality, was available thus far to Reinhold, in spite of his pertinent programmatic remarks.

Reinhold's original concern was enlightenment in regard to the Enlightenment. This concern has come to entail a further task. What is now required is enlightenment concerning reason. Put in Kant's language, in which the concepts "enlightenment" and "critique" coincide, what is required is a critique of reason.[115]

That, of course, is what Reinhold found in Kant. Hence his first letter to the latter was permeated by a deep gratitude. Reinhold there indicated that the study of the *Critique of Pure Reason* cured him of disbelief and thereby showed him that Kant had provided the synthesis he so long had sought to bridge "the unhappy alternatives of superstition and disbelief." His joy over his cure, coupled with the wish to contribute to "the spreading of a medication still so little appreciated," thus prompted the writing of the *Letters Concerning the Kantian Philosophy*.[116] The latter thus celebrate that "gospel of pure reason," which "leads on the path of reason from morality to religion and illuminates the darkness of the historical religion while avoiding the coldness of its philosophical counterpart."[117] As Reinhold put it in the enlarged book version, Kant's work resolved his doubts "in a manner fully satisfying head and heart."[118]

Reinhold realized that an attempt to lead unprepared readers into the depths of Kant's philosophy was more likely to have them "recoil in fright than to prove inviting." Hence, to spread that "medication still so little appreciated," he decided to "lift out the most striking results" of the *Critique of Pure Reason* and to present these in connection with "the needs of our time."[119] And, in a note at the start of the Fourth Letter in the original version, he reminded his readers that he wished to present only some of the most important results of the *Critique* "but by no means

---

115. Sauer, *Osterreichische Philosophie zwischen Aufklärung und Restauration*, p. 76.
116. Letter to Kant, dated October 12, 1787, in *Karl Leonhard Reinhold Korrespondenzausgabe*, pp. 272–73.
117. Karl Leonhard Reinhold, Third Letter, in "Briefe über die Kantische Philosophie," in *Der Teutsche Merkur*, 66 vols. (Weimar: Carl Rudolf Hofmann, 1787), 1.38–39.
118. Karl Leonhard Reinhold, *Briefe über die Kantische Philosophie*, 2 vols. (Leipzig: Georg Joachim Göschen, 1790), 1.106–7.
119. Letter to Christian Gottlob von Voigt, dated the beginning of November, 1786, in *Karl Leonhard Reinhold Korrespondenzausgabe*, ed. Lauth, Heller, and Hiller, p. 153.

the inner grounds of these," in regard to which he asked his readers to withhold their judgment until that examination would occur "to which he wishes to invite and for which he wishes to prepare."[120]

The *Briefe* might thus be summarized as an interpretation of the crisis of the time in regard to its Kantian/Illuminatist resolution—the latter, of course, without attribution. The First Letter depicts the current crisis of both reason and religion. Reinhold portrays a decrease in enlightenment by pointing to the increasing indifference by Protestants to their distinctive principle, as evident in the Catholicism debate raging already for some years; to the general indifference to reason as manifest in regard to its highest manifestation, metaphysics, in the writings of the *Popularphilosophen;* and to the pantheism debate between Jacobi and Mendelson, made even more virulent by Wizenmann's defense of Jacobi. The portrayal of this crisis takes the interesting form of incorporating Kant's notion of the antinomy of reason into the Illuminatist account of history. Sauer summarizes Reinhold in this regard:

Enlightenment is the realization of reason in history. Since the initially always dogmatic-naive stance of reason leads unavoidably to antinomies, an antinomic situation must arise in the process of Enlightenment. And just as, in the narrower domain of theoretical thought, these antinomies provide the occasion of surmounting the dogmatic-naive view in favor of the critical one, so too the Enlightenment will, with increasing insight into the peculiarity of its crisis, base itself on the critical concept of reason, thereby resolving its crisis and removing legitimation from the tendencies running counter to the Enlightenment.[121]

For the crisis engenders the new need of asking what reason is genuinely capable of or, as the title of this initial letter puts it, "The Need of a Critique of Reason." Only by meeting this need could the spiritual crisis be resolved and the enlightened unification of the contending parties be brought about.

The second of the original *Briefe* then illustratively provides the Kantian answer to the question of what reason is truly capable in regard to the problem of God's existence, a key aspect of the debate between naturalistic metaphysics and fiducial supernaturalism in the pantheism debate. The Third and Fourth Letters then again assimilate Kant and Illuminatism. The critique of reason shows that the rational belief based on practical reason is, on the level of reflective reason, the reconstitution of the unity of rational morality and religion which, prereflectively on the part of religion, was the original content of Christ's message before its ecclesi-

120. Karl Leonhard Reinhold, Fourth Letter, in "Briefe über die Kantische Philosophie," in *Der Teutsche Merkur,* 1.117.
121. Sauer, *Osterreichische Philosophie zwischen Aufklärung und Restauratio,* p. 83.

astic perversion.¹²² Reinhold is thus quite literal when he hails the second Immanuel's "gospel of pure reason." The Fifth and Sixth Letters then take up another aspect of the crisis sketched in the First Letter, the immortality of the soul, and deal with it analogously to the treatment of the existence of God in the Second Letter. Finally, the last two letters trace the development of "the psychological idea" and hence of conceptions concerning the differentiation between the body and the soul. In particular reference to Greek philosophy of mind, Reinhold makes novel use of Kant's distinctions in the First *Critique* to show how the pertinent positions arose out of conflating understanding with inner sense, on the one hand, and of outer sense with the sense organs, on the other.¹²³ It is worth noting that in these last letters, as well as in the earlier ones, Reinhold draws attention to the particular importance of Kant's doctrine of pure sensibility. He thus from the beginning grasps that this doctrine and that of the reality of the concept of freedom form, as Kant will himself note much later, the "twin pivots" on which the critical philosophy turns.¹²⁴

The *Briefe* had three immediate consequences. They made Kant—and Reinhold—famous; they garnered for Reinhold the position of extraordinary professor at the University of Jena; and they forced Reinhold to undertake both what he had promised in this work and what his new professorial duties required of him: an examination of the "inner grounds" for the Kantian "results" he had so eloquently portrayed.

Kant was not wholly unknown before the *Briefe*. There were some pockets of academic interest in his work, Jena chief among these.¹²⁵ And Jena's *Allgemeine Literatur-Zeitung*, under its editor C. G. Schütz, had already begun proselytizing on Kant's behalf.¹²⁶ Nevertheless, Kant himself spoke of "the silence with which [the learned public] for a long time honored my *Critique*."¹²⁷ That silence was permanently broken by the *Briefe*. As the preacher D. Jenisch informed Kant, they created "the most impressive sensation," so that "all philosophical minds in Germany seem

122. Ibid., p. 87.
123. I would refer readers not having ready access to the initial set of eight "Letters ..." to my bibliography, cited earlier, for information concerning which of these correspond, and with what modifications, to those in the later, enlarged book versions.
124. Immanuel Kant, *Welches sind die wirklichen Fortschritte, die die Metaphysik seit Leibnizens und Wolffs Zeiten in Deutschland gemacht hat?*, in *Werke in sechs Bänden*, vols., ed. Wilhelm Weischedel (Wiesbaden: Insel-Verlag, 1960), 3.652.
125. Norbert Hinske, Erhard Lange, and Horst Schröpfer, eds., *Der Aufbruch in den Kantianismus: Der Frühkantianismus an der Universität Jena von 1785–1800 und seine Vorgeschichte* (Stuttgart-Bad Cannstatt: Friedrich Frommann Verlag Günther Holzboog, 1995).
126. Ibid., chap. 2.
127. Immanuel Kant, *Prolegomena to Any Future Metaphysics That Will Be Able to Come Forward as Science* (Indianapolis, Ind.: Hackett, 1985), p. 119.

to have awakened from their indifference against all speculative philosophy to the most lively interest in you."[128] Nor was this awakening limited to philosophers. "The entire literary public in Germany was made to take an interest."[129] It was not just philosophers, but jurists, doctors, landowners, scientists, and poets who henceforth journeyed to Jena to hear Reinhold expound Kant. And, as already mentioned, Reinhold strove hard, in his teaching and subsequent publishing, to deserve that trust.

As Reinhold turned to the examination of the "inner grounds" for the "results" he had published, his enthusiasm became increasingly muted. And he was clearly taken aback, in terms of his desire to end sectarianism, by the fact that the "medication," which had effected his cure, continued to be "still so little appreciated" by Wolffians, Lockeans, and skeptics alike. In the large output of the next five years, the phase of his *Elementarphilosophie*, he sought to supply what Kant both did not and could not provide. Primarily, this concerned the formal aspects of the Kantian philosophy. Let me mention three pertinent aspects. Key concepts were insufficiently clarified by Kant; the structure of the critique made Kant's claims vis-à-vis the prior rationalists and empiricists appear as question-begging; and Kant either did not or even could not do justice to his own program.

Kant, according to Reinhold, did not sufficiently clarify key notions, thereby opening the door to diverse construals by friend and foe alike. Thus the notion of representation, a necessary component of Kant's explication of knowledge, was merely characterized in terms of its extension but not its content, thus allowing the bringing in of conceptual notes, including various notions of the subject of representation, that do not belong.[130] Representation is a basic fact of consciousness and the concept of consciousness remains in Kant indeterminate as well.[131]

Though Reinhold was convinced that the First *Critique* in fact showed both empiricism and rationalism to be mistaken, the form of its exposition did not allow proper recognition of this achievement. For the ground or foundation on which this work rests is experience.[132] Now if, as Kant puts it, experience is possible only "through a representation of

---

128. Daniel Jenisch, letter to Kant, dated May 14, 1787, cited in Sauer, *Osterreichische Philosophie zwischen Aufklärung und Restauration*, p. 87.

129. Reinhold, *Leben und litterarisches Wirken*, p. 43.

130. Reinhold, *Versuch einer neuen Theorie des menschlichen Vorstellungsvermögens*, pp. 62ff. As a result, Kant himself is at times misled—in his characterization, for example, of space and time as representations, which they are not. See Reinhold, "Ueber das Verhältniss der Theorie des Vorstellungsvermögens, zur Kritik der reinen Vernunft," p. 302.

131. Reinhold, "Ueber das Verhältniss der Theorie des Vorstellungsvermögens, zur Kritik der reinen Vernunft," p. 305.

132. Ibid., p. 278.

necessary connection of perceptions,"[133] then not only can experience not be explained, in Kant's terms, without circularity,[134] but anyone not already committed to the presence of "necessary connection" in perception will be free to deny the entire edifice built on this foundation, including specifically the existence of synthetic a priori judgments.[135] Hence Kant's claims needed a new and different manner of justification.

Finally and most importantly, Kant's program was, in a formal regard, not yet implemented. Kant had insisted that "rational knowledge is *cognitio ex principiis*"[136] and that, if this knowledge is to be possible as philosophical science, it must exhibit systematic unity.[137] This unity of principle, Reinhold added, requires that philosophy find its proper foundation in a single principle.[138] Such a first principle is not to be found in Kant. Kant, of course, speaks of principles in various places in his *Critique of Pure Reason*. Thus, he tells us that "The principle of apperception is the highest principle in the whole sphere of human knowledge."[139] But he does not state this principle in propositional form, and he does not indicate its precise relationships to the "supreme principle"[140] of sensibility and to that of understanding, nor to the "highest principle"[141] of analytic and of synthetic judgments. Taking the last of these, the highest principle of synthetic judgments, as the highest principle of the *Critique of Pure Reason*, Reinhold pointed out that this principle cannot be demonstrated without circularity in that work,[142] a point seemingly granted by Kant himself.[143] The demonstration must occur in a discipline systematically prior to criticism as propaedeutic to metaphysics—Kant's specific concern. For this prior discipline, Kant provided the "materials,"

---

133. Immanuel Kant, *Critique of Pure Reason*, trans. Norman Kemp Smith (New York: St. Martin's Press, 1961), B219, p. 209.

134. Reinhold, "Ueber das Verhältniss der Theorie des Vorstellungsvermögens, zur Kritik der reinen Vernunft," p. 281. See note 143 below.

135. Ibid., pp. 286-87.

136. Kant, *Critique of Pure Reason*, A836/B 864, p. 655.

137. Ibid., A 832/B60, p. 653.

138. Karl Leonhard Reinhold,"Ueber das Bedürfniss die Möglichkeit und die Eigenschaften eines allgemeingeltenden ersten Grundsatzes der Philosophie," in *Beyträge zur Berichtigung bisheriger Missverständnisse der Philosophen*, 1.94.

139. Kant, *Critique of Pure Reason*, B135, p. 154.

140. Ibid., B136, p. 155.

141. Ibid., A150/B189, p. 189; A154/B193, p. 191.

142. Reinhold, *Ueber das Fundament des philosophischen Wissens*, p. 69.

143. Kant writes in regard to the causal principle, which is a specification of the highest principle of synthetic judgments, as follows: "But though it needs proof, it should be entitled a *principle*, not a *theorem*, because it has the peculiar character that it makes possible the very experience which is its own ground of proof, and that in this experience it must always itself be presupposed." See *Critique of Pure Reason*, A737/B765, p. 592.

but not the "theory."[144] The prior, "elementary" discipline—hence *Elementarphilosophie*—must, moreover, be "the science of the principles of all of philosophy, of theoretical and practical, formal and material philosophy, not just of metaphysics."[145] This elementary science must, of course, have its own first principle, which will thus be the first principle of philosophy. The latter principle, which Reinhold terms the "principle of consciousness," is

> a proposition completely determined through itself. It is indeed the only possible such proposition. All others can only proffer concepts determinable through yet other propositions. Thus their conceptual notes must in the end be referred back to the ones originally determined in the principle of consciousness.[146]

The basic proposition, in one of its various formulations by Reinhold, is: "In consciousness, the representation is distinguished by the subject from the subject and the object and related to both."[147]

Establishing its basic proposition is only part of the task of the *Elementarphilosophie*. Another obvious part is specifying the form of derivation that holds between the basic proposition and those of subsidiary philosophical disciplines, as well as those philosophical knowledge claims that do not have the status of principles. Here Reinhold worked initially with linear models, both in the sense of formal deduction and in weaker senses. I say "initially," because increasingly elements of the circular model of derivation—hitherto claimed in the literature as first introduced by Fichte—were made use of by Reinhold.

As is only now becoming fully apparent through the research connected with the Jena Programm directed by D. Henrich, Reinhold's conception of the *Elementarphilosophie* underwent a major crisis in 1792, primarily as the result of objections raised by his students C. I. Dietz and J. B. Erhard.[148] Reinhold came to recognize that, on whatever model of derivation, the propositions needing to be derived required appeal to more facts than just the fact of consciousness articulated as first principle. The restructuring resulting from this insight, only programmati-

---

144. Reinhold, "Ueber das Verhältniss der Theorie des Vorstellungsvermögens, zur Kritik der reinen Vernunft," pp. 273–74.
145. Ibid., p. 278.
146. Karl Leonhard Reinhold, "Ueber die Möglichkeit der Philosophie als strenge Wissenschaft," in *Beyträge zur Berichtigung bisheriger Missverständnisse der Philosophen*, 1.354.
147. Karl Leonhard Reinhold, "Neue Darstellung der Hauptmomente der Elementarphilosophie," in *Beyträge zur Berichtigung bisheriger Missverständnisse der Philosophen*, 1.167.
148. See in particular the final chapter of Dieter Henrich, *Konstellationen. Probleme und Debatten am Ursprung der idealistischen Philosophie* (Stuttgart: Cotta Verlag, 1991).

cally sketched in print,[149] required the system of philosophy to become bidimensional. The analytic ascent to the highest principle was no longer preliminary to the system but its integral first half.[150] The starting point for this ascent via abstraction and reflection was a plurality of basic empirical facts, located in inner sense and already articulated in fundamental convictions of common sense.[151] The status of self-consciousness changed from being derivable from consciousness to being that datum of inner sense from which the derivations of the second part of the system were to originate. Reinhold thus "took inner experience, insofar as it depends on the subject of pure self-consciousness and consists of the facts of this self-consciousness, to be the foundation of the elementary philosophy."[152]

What was initially less obvious to Reinhold in this concern with the systematic features of the reformulation of "the foundation and point of departure of recent German philosophy" was its entailment of revisions in most of Kant's major claims. The claim that all of philosophy stood under a single highest principle entailed the integration of practical reason into the theoretical. This in turn meant that the concepts of "object" and "thing-in-itself" acquired a differing meaning and structure and that Kant's dualisms between a priori and a posteriori knowledge, between analytic and synthetic judgments, and between constitutive and regulative principles had to be given up. All of these changes came to play crucial roles in the emergence of German idealism. Additional points of pertinent interest concerned a shift, in regard to philosophical knowledge, from a basis in judgment to one in inference, a broadening of the meaning of "practical" from its frequent equivalence with "moral" in Kant, and an overcoming of the semantic atomicity and immobility of the Kantian categories. Reinhold's contributions in all of these respects, together with their impact on Fichte, Hegel, and Schelling, can now be found very competently discussed in M. Bondeli's book.

Partly as a result of his increasing interest, due to the changing structure of the *Elementarphilosophie,* in the data of inner sense as articulated

---

149. Karl Leonhard Reinhold, "Ueber den Unterschied zwischen dem gesunden Verstande und der philosophierenden Vernunft in Rücksicht auf die Fundamente des durch beyde möglichen Wissens," in *Beyträge zur Berichtigung bisheriger Missverständnisse der Philosophen,* 2 vols. (Jena: Johann Michael Mauke, 1794), 2.1–72. Karl Leonhard Reinhold, "Ueber den gegenwärtigen Zustand der Metaphysik und der transcendentalen Philosophie überhaupt. Neue um die Hälfte vermehrte Ausgabe meiner Beantwortung der Berlin. Preisfrage über die Fortschritte der Metaphysik seit Leibnitz und Wolf," in *Auswahl vermischter Schriften,* 2 vols. (Jena: Johann Michael Mauke, 1797), 2.248–79, esp. pp. 276–79.

150. Bondeli, *Das Anfangsproblem bei Karl Leonhard Reinhold,* pp. 22–23, 128–32, 150–53, 239–43.

151. Stamm, "Das Programm des methodologischen Monismus," p. 21.

152. Reinhold, "Ueber den gegenwärtigen Zustand der Metaphysik und der transcendentalen Philosophie überhaupt," p. 276.

in common sense; partly due to his perennial interest in conscience as one of these; and presumably partly due to a need to return to the evidences of his life experience in the face of the difficulties encountered in framing a viable system, Reinhold began to concern himself intensively, early in 1792, with the difference between the artificial use of reason in philosophy and its natural use, which he called "healthy common sense" (*der gemeine und gesunde Verstand*). "Health" was defined as that state "which is commensurate with the basic natural capabilities and with the ultimate purpose of their use."[153] It is not only physical and psychological but moral "insofar as it depends on the free, general and firm resolve to act rightly."[154] It is especially moral health that interested Reinhold, and he carefully attempted "to present moral truths independently of all theoretical scientific presuppositions."[155]

This careful focus on the moral dimension of ordinary life deserves mention for two reasons. It became the basis of some substantive disagreements with Kant. And it not only reappropriated Reinhold's Viennese commitments but pointed to aspects of Reinhold's further development.

Reinhold came to construe the difference between theoretical and practical rules of reason as consisting simply in the latter's application to the satisfaction or nonsatisfaction of a demand by desire. Hence a concept of morality that does not include sensibility becomes unthinkable. Furthermore, Reinhold differed sharply in his conception of willing. Will was not a causality of reason, nor yet a disposition to act in terms of represented laws; will was rather the person's capability, distinct from both reason and sensibility, to determine herself to the satisfaction or nonsatisfaction of a demand by desire. Kant's own view of will entailed, according to Reinhold, the impossibilities of making sense of immoral actions as actions for which persons are accountable and of distinguishing moral merit from sheer luck.[156]

Whatever the appropriate systematical form of philosophy as theory, it as a whole has its foundation in a morally good life, according to Reinhold. Theory as a seeking of the truth for its own sake has its ground in moral commitment. "Pure truth can consequently only be sought and

153. Ibid., pp. 19–20.
154. Ibid., p. 20. See also the essay written three years earlier, "Ueber den Unterschied zwischen dem gesunden Verstande und der philosophierenden Vernunft in Rücksicht auf die Fundamente des durch beyde möglichen Wissens."
155. Karl Leonhard Reinhold, letter to Jens Baggesen, dated February 21, 1797, in *Aus Jens Baggesen's Briefwechsel mit Karl Leonhard Reinhold und Friedrich Heinrich Jacobi*, ed. Baggesen and Baggesen, p. 167.
156. Karl Leonhard Reinhold, "4. Ueber das vollständige Fundament der Moral," in *Beyträge zur Berichtigung bisheriger Missverständnisse der Philosophen*, 2.221–26.

found through a morally good will."[157] This morally good will, as completely morally good or holy, is what human life ought ultimately to be about. Not surprisingly, moral will would continue to be, as in Kant, the foundation of the convictions constitutive of purely (nonecclesiastically) religious faith.[158] This view of the moral foundation of religion and philosophy—which Reinhold would, in his final system, develop into a mutuality of *fides quaerens intellectum and intellectus quaerens fidem*[159]—became central in his further development.

The year 1797 represented the next milestone in this development. In this year, Reinhold embraced Fichte's *Wissenschaftslehre*. He would also begin reflecting on Kant's just-published *Metaphysics of Morals*, reflections that will prove important in his move, two years later, away from Fichte and towards Jacobi and Bardili.

Reinhold motivated his acknowledgment of the superiority of the *Wissenschaftslehre* with self-criticisms reminiscent of those he had leveled against Kant. The *Elementarphilosophie* had taken the connections and differences between the transcendental and the empirical as just given, not principled, and thus rested on both a pure and—here like Kant—an empirical foundation. Put differently, the problem of the "thing-in-itself" had not been adequately resolved.[160] And practical philosophy remained a sort of ancillary edifice alongside the theoretical.[161]

That Reinhold understood Fichte's positions very well—Hegel's contrary insinuations in the *Differenzschrift* not withstanding—cannot be doubted. One only needs to read his lengthy review of all of Fichte's theoretical writings in the following year.[162] That his adherence to these views was not slavish becomes clear when one compares this review with Reinhold's own exposition of the "newest philosophy" in his 1799 *Ueber die Paradoxien der neuesten Philosophie*. In the review, Reinhold had shown that Fichte's system both started and concluded with an act of freedom both absolute and moral. But in the *Paradoxien*, Reinhold sharply distinguished between the absolute freedom with which philosophy begins and the moral freedom which it presupposes and cannot incorporate within itself. The reason he offered is that, while absolute freedom re-

---

157. Karl Leonhard Reinhold, "Ueber den Einfluss der Moralität des Philosophen auf den Inhalt seiner Philosophie," in *Auswahl vermischter Schriften*, 1.35.
158. Karl Leonhard Reinhold, "5. Ueber das Fundament der moralischen Religion," in *Beyträge zur Berichtigung bisheriger Missverständnisse der Philosophen*, 2.295–368.
159. Reinhold, *Die alte Frage: Was ist die Wahrheit?*, pp. 98–138.
160. Karl Leonhard Reinhold, "Vorbericht," in *Auswahl vermischter Schriften*, 2.vii–xi.
161. Reinhold, "Ueber den gegenwärtigen Zustand der Metaphysik und der transcendentalen Philosophie überhaupt," p. 324.
162. Karl Leonhard Reinhold, in *Allgemeine Literatur-Zeitung*, 1798, numbers 5–9, from January 5 through January 8.

quires, as Fichte acknowledges, abstraction from all that is real, moral freedom precludes such absolute abstraction because requiring reflection on the real situation upon which one ought to act. A further consequence of this distinction is that the *Wissenschaftslehre* loses its circular structure in favor of absolute freedom's endless self-determination.[163]

Philosophy and the domain of moral freedom, with the moral-religious convictions implied by its proper exercise, mutually correct and augment each other. The how, where, and when of the respective augmentation is not the business of the philosopher but of the healthy, that is, morally judging person. Without naming Fichte, Reinhold here warned against confusing the philosopher with the human being, consequently the theory of the practical with the practical, and thereby contaminating both.[164]

Reinhold thus found a way of accommodating both Fichte and Jacobi by separating philosophy from life and its religious convictions. Though Fichte was pleased by this—at the time of the publication of these ideas, he himself saw no way of going beyond the moral order to the life of God, and Reinhold's separation allowed him to defend Fichte against the charge of atheism, which had just brought about the latter's release by the University of Jena—Reinhold quickly saw its inadequacy. For he recognized that a faith that goes beyond the absolute objectivity of the moral world order cannot be compatible with a "knowledge for which absolute subjectivity is first and last and which is thus only compatible with a faith for which, insofar as it is faith, absolute objectivity must be first and last."[165] Moreover, Kant's explication of his doctrine of the moral postulates in Part 2 of the *Metaphysics of Morals* as not involving true beliefs but only an analogy, an acting "as if" moral finite reason were God, convinced Reinhold[166] that the doctrine of practical reason was not, after all, the suitable explication of his "presentiment of the in itself absolute, of the first simpliciter, of the originally true in the true." Given that he viewed the philosophy of identity being developed by Schelling and then Hegel, with its "confusion" of nature with God, as a necessary further development of transcendental philosophy as it had thus far de-

---

163. Karl Leonhard Reinhold, *Ueber die Paradoxien der neuesten Philosophie* (Hamburg: Friedrich Perthes, 1799), pp. 68–69, 75.
164. Ibid., pp. 98–99. For more detail on this set of aspects in the philosophical dialogue between Fichte and Reinhold, see my "Fichte und Reinhold über die Begrenzung der Philosophie" (paper presented at 200 Jahre Wissenschaftslehre—die Philosophie Johann Gottlieb Fichte, Internationaler Fichte Kongress, Jena, September 1994). This paper has now appeared in *Fichte-Studien*, 9.241–255.
165. Reinhold, "Rechenschaft über mein Systemwechseln," pp. 40–41.
166. Karl Leonhard Reinhold, *Anleitung zur Kenntniß und Beurtheilung der Philosophie in ihren sämmtlichen Lehrgebäuden* (Vienna: J. V. Degen, 1805), pp. 125–30, 141–47.

veloped from Kant through his own work to Fichte, Reinhold turned away from this entire idealist development.[167] He turned to Bardili's logical realism and, after recognizing the untenability of the latter's conception of thought as calculation (on the model of Leibniz), to the development of his own final system as presented in *Die alte Frage: Was ist die Wahrheit?* ...

Since these last two phases of Reinhold's development take us beyond the focus of this volume, let me close with a parting comment by Reinhold on the development of German idealism that points in the direction of his own last efforts:

Perhaps in no time and among no other people since Plato and Aristotle among the Greeks has there been so much serious and zealous philosophizing about the proper character of philosophy as among the Germans from the appearance of Kant's critique of reason to the present. In regard to these discussions about the possibility of philosophy as a science, which have distinguished this period in the history of philosophy, it is an undeniable though hardly noted fact—which, however, is very much worth noting—that the relation of thinking to speaking and the character of linguistic usage in philosophizing in no way came under scrutiny and to formulation.[168]

167. Reinhold, "Rechenschaft über mein Systemwechseln," pp. 42–44. See also the following essay in this same issue of the *Beyträge zur leichteren Uebersicht*: "Ueber die Verwechselung und die Vereinigung der Natur und Gott. Ein Gespräch durch Schelling's *Bruno* veranlaßt."

168. Reinhold, *Grundlegung einer Synonymik*, p. 8. See also Karl Leonhard Reinhold, *Das menschliche Erkenntnißvermögen, aus dem Gesichtspunkte des durch die Wortsprache vermittelten Zusammenhangs zwischen der Sinnlichkeit und dem Denkvermögen* (Kiel: im Verlage der academischen Buchhandlung, 1816), pp. 2–3.

3 The Role of Skepticism in the Emergence of German Idealism
MICHAEL BAUR

1. *Introduction*

According to Immanuel Kant's well-known account of his own intellectual development, it was the skeptic David Hume who roused him from his dogmatic slumber.[1] According to some popular accounts of post-Kantian philosophy, it was the soporific speculation of the idealists that quickly returned German philosophy to the Procrustean bed of unverifiable metaphysics, where it dogmatically slept for half of the nineteenth century. This popular picture of post-Kantian German philosophy receives some apparent support from the relevant evidence. After all, Kant had allegedly demonstrated the illegitimacy of all metaphysical speculation that transcends the bounds of experience, and the writings of the German idealists—filled as they are with references to what is putatively "absolute" and "unconditioned"—seem to violate Kant's strictures.

In place of this popular conception, I seek to sketch out a rather different picture of German idealism. The development of post-Kantian German idealism is best described, not as a turning away from skepticism, but rather as a *radicalization* of it. The radicalization of skepticism from Kant through Fichte to Hegel, however, does not lead away from systematic philosophy. The movement of thought from Kant to Hegel coincides with the gradual realization that skeptical thought is not external to systematic philosophy, but is in fact internal to, or even identical with, it.[2] This thesis concerning the progressive "radicalization" or "inter-

---

1. Immanuel Kant, *Prolegomena to Any Future Metaphysics*, trans. Paul Carus, rev. James W. Ellington (Indianapolis, Ind.: Hackett, 1977), p. 5.
2. Thus I believe that Michael Forster is correct to say that the German idealists were "distinguished by a shared recognition of the importance of skepticism and by a determined effort to answer it on behalf of their systems"; see Michael Forster, *Hegel and Skepticism* (Cambridge, MA: Harvard University Press, 1989), p. 99. Nevertheless, I would contend that it is somewhat misleading to say, as Forster does, that the German idealists sought

nalization" of skepticism in German idealism receives some prima facie support from the relevant writings of Kant, Fichte, and Hegel.

In his *Critique of Pure Reason*, in the section on "The Antinomy of Pure Reason," Kant explains that the skeptical method, or the method of provoking "a conflict of assertions," is "essential" for the development of a genuinely scientific transcendental philosophy.[3] The skeptical method, however, cannot resolve the conflict of assertions that it reveals. At best, the skeptical method is "a means to awakening [reason] from its sweet dogmatic dreams, and of inducing it to enter upon a more careful examination of its own position" (*CPR*, A757/B785). Echoing Kant, Fichte also acknowledges the indispensability of the skeptical method in the development of systematic philosophy: "It is undeniable that philosophizing reason owes all the human progress which it has made so far to the observations of skepticism concerning the insecurity of every resting place yet obtained by reason."[4] But Fichte goes beyond Kant to suggest that the skeptical method is not merely a means to an external end, but that skepticism's own immanent *telos* is nothing other than systematic philosophy: "Nothing is more to be desired," writes Fichte, "than that skepticism might crown its [own] labors and drive inquiring reason on to the attainment of its lofty goal," namely, the transformation of philosophy into a science.[5] Going beyond both Kant and Fichte, Hegel suggests that skepticism and scientific philosophy (properly understood) amount to the same thing. In his 1802 essay on the "Relationship of Skepticism to Philosophy," Hegel claims that "skepticism itself is in its

---

to provide an "answer *to*" or a "defense *against*" skepticism (p. 117; emphasis added). This is misleading because (as I seek to show) the strategy of the German idealists was not merely to offer an externally related *alternative* to skepticism; instead, their strategy was to show that the dangers of skepticism could be avoided only if self-conscious skepticism and systematic philosophy were shown to be in some sense identical.

3. Immanuel Kant, *Critique of Pure Reason*, trans. Norman Kemp Smith (London: Macmillan, 1989), p. 395 (A423–24/B451–52). All subsequent references to Kant's *Critique of Pure Reason* will be made parenthetically in the text, using the acronym CPR and the page numbers of the A and B editions.

4. Johann Gottlieb Fichte, "Review of *Aenesidemus*," in *Fichte: Early Philosophical Writings*, trans. Daniel Breazeale (Ithaca, N.Y.: Cornell University Press, 1988), p. 59.

5. Ibid. Following Fichte, Schelling also observes that transcendental philosophy necessarily begins with "general doubt as to the reality of the objective." For Schelling, this general doubt must be a kind of "absolute scepticism—not the half-scepticism which merely contends against the common prejudices of mankind, while never looking to fundamentals, but rather that thoroughgoing scepticism which is directed, not against individual prejudices, but against the basic preconception, whose rejection leads automatically to the collapse of everything else." See F.W.J. Schelling, *System of Transcendental Idealism*, trans. Peter Heath (Charlottesville: University Press of Virginia, 1978), pp. 7–8. Unlike Fichte and Hegel, Schelling allows his skepticism to be quickly overtaken by his nonskeptical, speculative impulses. As a result, the philosophy of Schelling will not figure prominently in my analysis of "the role of skepticism in the emergence of German idealism."

inmost heart at one with every true philosophy."⁶ And in his *Phenomenology of Spirit* of 1807, Hegel argues that the doubting, despairing pathway toward scientific philosophy, a pathway that is itself already scientific, must be nothing other than the pathway of "self-fulfilling skepticism" (*dieser sich vollbringende Skeptizismus*).⁷

As I shall try to show, the development of German idealism can be understood as the gradual unfolding of the basic claim that skeptical thought, when properly radicalized and raised to the level of self-consciousness, amounts to systematic, scientific philosophy. If this thesis is correct, then German idealism can be understood as a reenactment of Socrates' fundamental insight: ignorance that has become self-conscious of itself *as* ignorance is not simply a blind, empty state of not-knowing, but is in fact a form of wisdom.⁸

2. *Kant, Skeptics, and Supporters*

Kant understands skepticism, or the skeptical method, as essentially external to genuine, systematic philosophy. More specifically, Kant sees skepticism as a midway stage in reason's ascent to self-knowledge. The first stage of reason, reason in its infancy, is the dogmatic stage; the second stage, the skeptical stage, subjects reason to doubt and thus induces reason to begin asking about its own powers and limits; the third stage, the criticism of reason (exemplified by Kant's own philosophy), undertakes "to subject to examination, not the facts of reason, but reason itself, in the whole extent of its powers, and as regards its aptitude for pure *apriori* modes of knowledge" (*CPR*, A761/B789). According to Kant, the stage of skepticism is only "a [temporary] resting place for human reason. . . . But it is no dwelling place for permanent settlement" (*CPR*, A761/B789). At most, the skeptical method "*prepares the way* [to systematic philosophy] by arousing reason to circumspection," but it "cannot of itself yield any *satisfying* answer to the questions of reason" (*CPR*, A769/B797). In order to satisfy the questions of reason and thus overcome the threat of skepticism, one must move to a third position that is external to and beyond both dogmatism and skepticism. That third position is constituted by adequate self-knowledge, provided by "transcendental philosophy."

6. G.W.F. Hegel, "Relationship of Skepticism to Philosophy, Exposition of Its Different Modifications and Comparison to the Latest Form with the Ancient One," trans. H. S. Harris, in *Between Kant and Hegel*, ed. George di Giovanni and H. S. Harris (Albany: State University of New York Press, 1985), pp. 322–23.
7. *Hegel's Phenomenology of Spirit*, trans. A. V. Miller (Oxford: Oxford University Press, 1977) p. 50.
8. See Plato, *Apology* 21c–e.

Early in his *Critique of Pure Reason,* Kant tells us: "I entitle *transcendental* all knowledge which is occupied not so much with objects as with our way of knowing objects [*unsere Erkenntnisart von Gegenständen*] insofar as this way of knowing is to be possible *apriori*" (*CPR*, A11–12).[9] Transcendental philosophy thus entails a kind of "return to the subject," or "call to self-knowledge" (*CPR*, Axi). Through transcendental philosophy, one attains knowledge of one's own knowing insofar as such knowing is possible a priori. That which is a priori in our knowing is "indispensable for the possibility of experience itself" (*CPR*, B5), and thus what is a priori in our knowing is itself a condition of the possibility of our having experience at all. Accordingly, the aim of transcendental philosophy is to effect a "return to the subject" in order to grasp our way of knowing insofar as this is not conditioned by, but is rather a condition of, experience.

With his return to the subject and his articulation of the a priori conditions of our knowledge of objects within experience, Kant claims to have set philosophy in general and metaphysics in particular onto the sure path of a science. Since all that is a priori in our knowledge has its own systematic unity (*CPR*, Axiii; A67/B92; A474/B502; A845/B873), and since it is just such unity that raises a mere aggregate of knowledge to the rank of science (*CPR*, A832/B860), it follows that transcendental philosophy can be assured of its unity and completeness and thus can claim the status of a "science." In virtue of its scientificity, Kant argues, transcendental philosophy can also show the way by which metaphysics can become scientific. The metaphysics that is scientifically grounded through transcendental philosophy would be immune to any further revision or elaboration, save in the manner by which it might be expressed or taught (*CPR*, Axx; Bxxiv; Bxxxviii). Metaphysics, once it has been placed upon the sure path of science, will no longer have to retrace its steps, or attempt any new lines of approach (*CPR*, Bvii); the sure path of science, "once it has been trodden, can never be overgrown, and permits of no wandering" (*CPR*, A850/B878).

With his transcendental philosophy, Kant thought that he had cleared the path by which genuine philosophy could leave skeptical doubts behind once and for all. However, critics began planting new seeds of doubt upon Kant's "sure path of science" almost as soon as the path had been cleared. From the point of view of the later German idealists, Kant's "sure path of science" remained vulnerable to such doubts, precisely because Kant regarded the activity of skeptical questioning as something essentially *other* than the activity of systematic philosophizing. Kant's strategy of exclusion ultimately doomed his project to failure, because any system

---

9. Here I have modified Kemp Smith's translation slightly.

of philosophy that tries to leave skeptical questioning behind as something external to itself automatically renders itself partial and less than comprehensive through that very act of exclusion. In turn, a system of philosophy that is not comprehensive cannot be fully systematic, and thus cannot adequately stand up to the attacks of skepticism. In order to address skepticism adequately, systematic philosophy must learn to see the doubting, questioning activity of the skeptic as nothing other than the not-yet-self-conscious activity of systematic philosophy itself.[10]

This basic failing, as seen by the German idealists, can be expressed in slightly different terms. Kant erroneously regarded skepticism as a temporary stage that could eventually be left behind, to be replaced by true self-knowledge. Accordingly, Kant believed that the content of genuine self-knowledge must be derived from some principle or source that is essentially *other* than skeptical doubting. As a result, genuine self-knowledge for Kant must present itself as external to skeptical doubt, as an alternative to such doubt. However, the essence of *radical* skepticism is to question the validity of *any* claim that presents itself as an alternative to doubt. Thus any putative claim to self-knowledge that appears as external to skeptical doubt will be vulnerable to further attack.[11] If one is to address the challenge of *radical* skepticism, then self-knowledge must be regarded not as external to skepticism, but as the same as skeptical questioning, only raised to the level of self-consciousness. In order to prevent a perpetual oscillation between epistemic claims and skeptical attacks, one must learn to see how skepticism and systematic philosophy are actually identical, in spite of their immediate opposition.

For the post-Kantian idealists, then, there is an essential identity-in-difference between skeptical questioning and systematic philosophy. However, this identity-in-difference remained hidden from Kant and his immediate critics.[12] As a result, the early skeptical concerns about the Kantian system at first appeared to spring from sources entirely *external*

---

10. Similarly, Socrates realized that the threat of skepticism is not to be met by leaving skepticism behind and seeking refuge in some principle or source that is allegedly available to us in a realm beyond, and immune from, such skeptical questioning. An answer to skepticism can be achieved only by entering into dialogue with the skeptic and by demonstrating how a certain kind of knowledge is implicit in the skeptic's own questioning. In short, one can philosophize in a manner that is immune to skeptical questioning only by radicalizing the skeptic's own questioning and showing how that questioning is not ultimately different from systematic philosophy.

11. Hegel alludes to this problem when he addresses the question of *how* genuine philosophy is to make its appearance in the midst of skeptical concerns: "But Science, just because it comes on the scene, is itself an appearance: in coming on the scene it is not yet Science in its developed and unfolded truth.... *One* bare assurance is worth just as much as another." See *Hegel's Phenomenology of Spirit*, pp. 48–49.

12. Among the early critics, it seems that only Maimon had an implicit sense of the necessary identity-in-difference of skepticism and systematic philosophy.

to the Kantian system, rather than from the *internal* failings of the Kantian system itself. In order to address the skepticism adequately, Kant would have to make his philosophy more systematic by making it more skeptical. That task, however, was left to the later German idealists.

The early skeptical attacks upon Kant took on many forms, but the most powerful and important early criticisms centered around the basic conviction that Kant had failed to respond adequately to the skeptical challenge of Hume. Kant's alleged failure to meet the Humean challenge can be expressed in three fundamental claims: (1) Kant's notion of the thing-in-itself is riddled with inconsistencies; (2) Kant's metaphysical deduction is only inductively valid and thus lacks the necessity and completeness that are proper to science; and (3) Kant's transcendental deduction is essentially circular and thus question-begging.[13]

Perhaps the most famous critique of Kant's notion of the thing-in-itself was articulated by F. H. Jacobi. Jacobi's critique focuses on the notion of "transcendental objects," or objects beyond consciousness that allegedly cause representations within consciousness. In the "Appendix" to a book appropriately entitled *David Hume,* Jacobi argues that Kant's appeal to transcendental objects is a necessary feature of the Kantian system, but also inconsistent with the system. For Jacobi, the notion of a transcendental object is necessary to the Kantian system, since Kant starts by assuming that human sensibility is purely passive. As a necessary correlate to this assumption, Kant must posit the existence of some external object or objects that act upon sensibility and with respect to which human sensibility is passive. Within the same system, however, Kant also argued that human knowledge cannot transcend the bounds of possible experience; thus we cannot have knowledge of anything that lies beyond experience. Accordingly, we cannot have any knowledge about the alleged existence or activity of those transcendental objects with respect to which sensibility is said to be passive. Thus the notion of a transcendental object (or thing-in-itself) is both mandated and outlawed by the Kantian system: "I need the assumption of things-in-themselves to enter the Kantian system; but with this assumption it is not possible for me to remain inside it."[14]

Skeptics like Platner, Schulze, and Maimon articulated similar arguments against Kant's notion of the thing-in-itself. In his *Philosophische*

---

13. The self that provides the basis for self-knowledge in Kant is not the self that is simply the activity of radical, self-conscious questioning (as in Socrates); rather, it is the ready-made self that finds itself endowed with categories, full-blown from the head of Aristotle.

14. See F. H. Jacobi, "Beylage," to *David Hume über den Glauben, oder Idealismus und Realismus, ein Gespräch,* in *Werke,* 6 vols., ed. F. H. Jacobi and F. Köppen (Leipzig: Fleischer, 1812), 2.304. See also Jacobi's *Werke,* 6 vols. (Leipzig: Fleischer, 1815), 3.304.

Aphorismen, Platner argues that even Kant's denial that we can have knowledge of the thing-in-itself is insufficiently skeptical. If we really could have no knowledge of the thing-in-itself, Platner argues, then we would not even know whether the thing-in-itself is unknowable. For Platner, then, genuine skepticism requires that we remain open to the possibility that the thing-in-itself might actually be knowable to us as something existing in space and time.[15] Schulze argues that any belief in a transcendental object beyond consciousness is inconsistent with Kant's own restriction of human knowledge to the objects of possible experience, regardless of whether the transcendental object is conceived as a thing-in-itself, a noumenon, or a transcendental idea.[16] Maimon's critique of Kant's thing-in-itself is perhaps the most penetrating of all. According to Maimon, if Kant were true to his own skepticism regarding the thing-in-itself, then there would be no purpose in postulating the existence of the thing-in-itself; for if the thing-in-itself were genuinely unknowable, then it would be empty of all explanatory content. The notion of the thing-in-itself is not only inconsistent with the Kantian system as a whole, it is superfluous.[17]

The second skeptical charge against Kant alleges that the metaphysical deduction, or Kant's derivation of the categories of the understanding from the forms of judgment, has only empirical or inductive validity. Gottlob August Tittel, for example, argues that Kant's derivation and organization of the categories is merely "rhapsodic."[18] According to Tittel, Kant arrived at his table of categories by observing and abstracting from the kinds of judgments that we actually make about objects within our experience. Since the categories are inductively derived, there can be no guarantee that the table of categories is complete. And because Kant has not shown that the table of categories is comprehensive, he cannot justifiably claim that his critical philosophy has really achieved the status of a science.[19] In short, the doubts that Hume had articulated concerning induction in general can apply equally to Kant's derivation of the categories: the same lack of necessity and universality that Hume had

15. See E. Platner, *Philosophische Aphorismen* (Leipzig: Sigwart, 1784), pp. viii ff.
16. G. E. Schulze, *Aenesidemus oder über die Fundamente der von dem Herrn Professor Reinhold in Jena gelieferten Elementarphilosophie,* ed. A. Liebert (Berlin: Reuther und Reichhard, 1912), pp. 116–30.
17. S. Maimon, *Gesammelte Werke,* 7 vols., ed. V. Verra (Hildesheim: Olms, 1965), 2.372; 4.415; 5.404–6, 412–13.
18. Gottlob August Tittel, *Kantische Denkformen oder Kategorien* (Frankfurt: Gebhardt, 1787), pp. 44, 94.
19. Similar criticisms of Kant are expressed by Garve and Weishaupt. See Garve, "Kritik der reinen Vernunft," *Allgemeine deutsche Bibliothek,* supp. to 37–52 (1783), 842 ff.; and Weishaupt, *Gründe und Gewissheit des menschlichen Erkennens: Zur Prüfung der kantischen Critic der reinen Vernunft* (Nurenberg: Gratenau, 1788), pp. 48–49.

demonstrated with regard to our knowledge of objects also affects Kant's derivation of the categories. Of course, Kant would argue that the categories are not merely derived from experience, but constitute the a priori conditions of experience itself. But the objection cannot be so easily dismissed; for even if the categories themselves do not have their source in experience, the fact remains that Kant's own "hitting upon" these particular categories (and no others) has taken place within experience, and thus (in the absence of any further justification) Kant's derivation of the categories is vulnerable to doubt.

The third skeptical charge against the Kantian system alleges that the transcendental deduction is viciously circular and thus question-begging. The purpose of Kant's transcendental deduction is to demonstrate how the categories of the understanding can relate a priori to the objects of our possible experience; Kant's demonstration of the validity of the categories consists in showing that the objects of possible experience would not be constituted *as* objects if it were not for the a priori categories of the understanding. This demonstration, however, entails a fundamental circularity. In effect, Kant tried to demonstrate the validity of the categories by referring them to our regular and orderly experience; but conversely, he tried to demonstrate the orderliness and regularity of experience by referring experience back to the categories. If asked how we can know that the objects of our experience really do exhibit the necessary and universal structures that we attribute to them, Kant would have to appeal to the a priori structures that we bring to experience. But then, if asked how we can know whether these a priori structures actually do underlie our experience, Kant would have to appeal to experience itself. Thus a vicious circularity infects the transcendental deduction. Because of this circularity, the transcendental deduction can only be question-begging in the face of Humean doubt. As Platner argues: Kant has only shown that, *if* we have regular and orderly experience, then such experience will necessarily conform to the a priori structures of our knowing. Of course, it is the necessity of such regularity and orderliness that skeptics like Hume question in the first place.[20]

These three skeptical criticisms aimed at Kant are interrelated, since the fundamental failings in Kant that make him vulnerable to such criticisms are themselves interrelated. For example, Kant finds it necessary

---

20. Platner, *Philosophische Aphorismen*, § 699. Reinhold also acknowledges that Kant's very notion of experience implies that there is a necessary and lawlike connection among perceptions. As a result, any antiskeptical argument that *begins* with Kant's notion of experience will be circular. See Karl Leonhard Reinhold, "Über das Verhältnis der Theorie des Vorstellungsvermögens zur Kritik der reinen Vernunft," in *Beyträge zur Berichtigung bisheriger Mißverständnisse der Philosophen* (Jena: Johann Michael Mauke, 1790), 1.281.

to appeal to a reality outside of consciousness as that in relation to which sensibility is passive, since Kant simply assumed that there is an absolute dichotomy between receptivity and spontaneity. Once he accepted this dichotomy as given, Kant was forced to appeal to something outside of the spontaneous activity of the knowing self (the thing-in-itself) as the ground of the self's receptivity. Kant's acceptance of the dichotomy between receptivity and spontaneity also explains the inductive or rhapsodic character of his derivation of the categories in the metaphysical deduction. Because Kant simply accepts the dichotomy of sensibility and understanding as given, he is forced to regard sensibility and understanding as two different faculties that are simply found alongside one another. Because these two faculties remain only contingently related, Kant is unable to find anything other than a contingent unity among the various acts of judgment (i.e., the acts within which the heterogeneous contributions of sensibility and understanding are combined). Since the unity of the table of judgments is empirically based, Kant's derivation of the categories from the table of judgments can have only inductive validity.

Finally, the question-begging nature of Kant's transcendental deduction is related to the problems outlined above. The purpose of the transcendental deduction was to demonstrate how the categories of the understanding can relate a priori to the objects of possible experience. Unfortunately, Kant cannot demonstrate this in a non-question-begging way, since he starts by presupposing the heterogeneity of sensibility and understanding. Because Kant takes sensibility and understanding to be heterogeneous as matter of fact, he cannot demonstrate noncircularly how the categories of the understanding relate a priori to what is given a posteriori through the intuitions of sensibility. Kant's acceptance of the dichotomy between sensibility and understanding *as given* makes it impossible for him to demonstrate that there exists anything but an a posteriori, contingent relation between the two. Once again, Maimon seems to offer the most penetrating analysis of the problem. Maimon notes that the transcendental deduction becomes necessary within the Kantian system because Kant presupposes a dualism between sensibility and understanding; if receptivity and spontaneity in human knowing were not assumed to be heterogeneous in the first place, then there would be no need to demonstrate how the concepts of the understanding could relate a priori to the objects given within experience. On the other hand, the Kantian dualism between sensibility and understanding also prevents the transcendental deduction from being anything but circular and question-begging. Taken together, this means: the assumption that makes the transcendental deduction necessary for Kant (i.e., the assumption of the fundamental heterogeneity of receptivity and spontaneity) also makes the transcendental deduction impossible. In short, there is a fundamental tension in Kant's understanding of the aims and limits of his own transcendental project.[21]

In the wake of these and other skeptical attacks, Karl Leonhard Reinhold came to the defense of the Kantian system. Through the publication of his "Letters Concerning the Kantian Philosophy" (1786–1787), Reinhold had already earned public recognition, as well as the approval of Kant himself. While still a committed Kantian, Reinhold gradually came to believe that the Kantian system could not claim the status of a science, and thus could not successfully withstand the attacks of skepticism, unless it were reformed and revised. Reinhold does not question the truth of the propositions that make up the Kantian system; he does, however, argue that Kant had not properly demonstrated the scientific character of his own system. Kant had presupposed the validity of several claims and distinctions that constitute his system, but he did not show how these various claims and distinctions could be derived formally and rigorously from a single, self-evident first principle. Reinhold's proposal for systematic reform takes its inspiration from Kant himself. Kant had argued that the scientific character of philosophy is guaranteed by its systematic unity and completeness (*CPR*, A832/B860). In order to demonstrate the unity and completeness of the Kantian system, Reinhold argues, one must not simply accept Kant's various claims and distinctions as given; rather, one must show how these claims and distinctions can be derived from a single, self-evident, first principle. For Reinhold, the requisite derivation is only implicit in the Kantian system,[22] and must be made explicit.

The single, self-evident first principle that provides the basis for Reinhold's reformulation of the Kantian system is called the "principle of consciousness" (*Satz des Bewußtseins*). For Reinhold, the most general concept within consciousness and the concept that is presupposed by all other possible contents of consciousness, is the concept of "representation" (*Vorstellung*). The principle of consciousness declares: "In consciousness the subject distinguishes the representation from the subject and the object and relates [the representation] to both [subject and object]."[23] According to Reinhold, all conscious states exhibit the same basic structure, the structure of representation, or *Vorstellung*; thus all consciousness involves not only a subject and an object, but also a distinguishing

21. See S. Maimon, *Werke*, 2.62–65, 182–83, 362–64.
22. E.g., Kant suggests that sensibility and understanding might have a single "common root" (*CPR*, A15/B29).
23. Reinhold, "Neue Darstellung der Hauptmomente der Elementarphilosophie," in *Beyträge zur Berichtigung bisheriger Missverständnisse der Philosophen*, 1.167.

and relating that holds between subject, object, and representation. In all representation, the subject of consciousness makes a distinction between itself and its representation and between its representation and the object of which it is a representation. Furthermore, within consciousness, the subject relates the representation to itself and relates the representation to the object of which it is the representation. With this, Reinhold is not making any claims about the "independent" existence of the object of representation. He is only claiming that the activity of conscious representing necessarily implies a set of *relations* and *differences* among the representation, the subject (which does the representing), and the object (of which the representation is a representation). It is quite possible that the "object" is not "independent" at all, but entirely contingent upon consciousness itself.

For Reinhold, the skeptic may very well be able to doubt whether there is anything at all outside of consciousness; however, even the most radical skeptic cannot deny the principle of consciousness itself. The principle of consciousness is immediately self-evident to anyone who is conscious at all: "*Consciousness* forces everyone to agree that to every representation there pertains a representing subject and a represented object, *both* of which must be *distinguished* from the *representation* to which they pertain."[24] According to Reinhold, one can begin with nothing more than the principle of consciousness itself and derive from it all the specific content of the Kantian system, including, for example: the regularity and orderliness of experience, the dichotomy between sensibility and understanding, the two forms of intuition, the twelve categories, and even the unknowability (or nonrepresentability) of the thing-in-itself.[25] Reinhold offers just such a derivation in his *Elementarphilosophie*.[26]

We need not examine the details of Reinhold's derivation in order to appreciate the significance of his role in the emergence of German idealism. Reinhold's groundbreaking claim is that one can derive all the specific content of Kant's system, even the *apparent* externality of the thing-in-itself, from entirely within the *immanence* of consciousness itself. In making this claim, Reinhold is effectively arguing that objective consciousness (our consciousness of objects) is to be understood as a modification of self-consciousness. This, of course, is a step toward idealism that Kant himself refused to take; but it is equally a moment in the radi-

---

24. Reinhold, *Versuch einer neuen Theorie des menschlichen Vorstellungsvermögens* (Prague and Jena: Widtmann und Mauke, 1789), p. 200.
25. For Reinhold's derivation of the unknowability of the thing-in-itself, see, e.g., Reinhold, *Beyträge*, 1.185, and *Versuch*, p. 299.
26. For a helpful and illuminating account, see Daniel Breazeale, "Between Kant and Fichte: Karl Leonhard Reinhold's 'Elementary Philosophy,'" *Review of Metaphysics* 35 (1982): 785–821.

calization of skepticism. In making this claim, Reinhold is saying that the genuinely scientific philosopher need not and should not begin by presupposing the existence of anything whatsoever outside of consciousness, or—correlatively—by presupposing the dichotomy between sensibility and understanding. A genuinely scientific demonstration of transcendental philosophy should begin by exercising extreme skepticism regarding both the dichotomy between sensibility and understanding *within* consciousness and the alleged existence of anything *beyond* consciousness. Precisely because Kant did not begin with sufficient skepticism about these kinds of claims, his presentation of transcendental philosophy remained vulnerable to skeptical challenge.[27]

Reinhold's thought aims to be purely descriptive, accepting only what is accessible within consciousness itself. For Reinhold, what is accessible within consciousness is the concept of representation. The "object" with respect to which the representation is said to be a representation does not necessarily refer to anything outside of consciousness itself. Similarly, the "subject" that relates itself to and distinguishes itself from the representation is not the Kantian subject that appears on the scene already outfitted with the forms of intuition and categories of the understanding, full-blown from the head of Aristotle. Instead, the "self" that constitutes the originary source for self-knowledge in Reinhold's reformulation of transcendental philosophy is a highly purified self. The self, for Reinhold, must start out as nothing more than the self that has representations, relating itself to and distinguishing itself from both the representation and the object to which the representation refers. All further claims and distinctions are supposed to be derived rigorously from what is immediately self-evident in the structure of representation itself.

Reinhold was certainly more sensitive to the challenge of skepticism than Kant was; yet from the point of view of later German idealism, Reinhold himself was still not sufficiently skeptical. For Fichte and Hegel, the problem with Reinhold was that he sought to address the challenge of skepticism by radicalizing skepticism only up to a point. In other words, Reinhold sought to radicalize skepticism only until he hit upon a concept or first principle that would itself be immune to skeptical doubt. This concept or first principle was then supposed to provide an unshakable foundation for deriving the specific content of a scientific, transcendental philosophy. In short, Reinhold radicalized skepticism beyond Kant, but then he sought to overcome skepticism by appealing to a foun-

27. In seeking to derive all the content of the Kantian system (including the thing-in-itself) from within the immanence of consciousness, Reinhold effectively replaced the Kantian dichotomy between what is "inside" and what is "outside" the knower with his own dichotomy between what is "conscious" and what is "unconscious" in knowing.

dation that is itself essentially *different* from the activity of skeptical doubting itself. Thus he did not radicalize skepticism as far as he could have. For Fichte and Hegel, the problem of skepticism can be addressed adequately only if skepticism is fully radicalized and (what amounts to the same thing) if the "foundation" that provides the "way out" of skepticism is in some sense identical to the activity of skeptical questioning itself.

The first crucial step in the radicalization of skepticism after Reinhold was taken by Gottlob Ernst Schulze, in a work entitled *Aenesidemus oder über die Fundamente der von dem Herrn Prof. Reinhold in Jena gelieferten Elementar-Philosophie* (1792).[28] This work presents itself as a dialogue between Hermias, a proponent of transcendental philosophy, and Aenesidemus, a Humean skeptic.[29] Using Aenesidemus as his mouthpiece, Schulze points to a number of weaknesses in Reinhold's attempt to demonstrate the scientific character of transcendental philosophy. Two major aspects of Schulze's attack are of particular importance here.

First of all, Schulze argues that the concept of representation as it is articulated by Reinhold cannot possibly be the first and highest concept of consciousness. Schulze bases this criticism on Reinhold's own "principle of consciousness." Reinhold, we will recall, held that all consciousness involves a dual relationship between subject and representation: the subject distinguishes itself from its representation while at the same time relating this representation to itself as subject. Without this dual relationship of distinguishing and relating, the subject would not be a conscious subject. Schulze, however, observes that if all consciousness involves a conscious distinguishing and relating between subject and representation, and if this activity of distinguishing and relating occurs within consciousness itself (as Reinhold says it does), then the subject that distinguishes itself from and relates itself to the representation must itself be known through some further kind of representation. That is, the subject's own awareness of itself (which is necessary for distinguishing itself *from* and relating itself *to* a representation) must take place through some kind of representation; but if the subject that does the distinguishing and relating is aware of itself through some kind of representation, then we need yet another subject to distinguish itself from and relate itself to that representation of the first subject, and so ad infi-

28. Gottlob Ernst Schulze, *Aenesidemus oder über die Fundamente der von dem Herrn Prof. Reinhold in Jena gelieferten Elementar-Philosophie*, ed. A. Liebert (Berlin: Reuther und Reichhard, 1911). Reprinted in *Aeteas Kantiana* (Brussels: Culture et Civilisation, 1969).
29. For a brief account of this work and its influence on subsequent thought, see Daniel Breazeale, "Fichte's *Aenesidemus* Review and the Transformation of German Idealism," *Review of Metaphysics* 34 (1981): 545–68.

nitum. On Reinhold's own terms, then, the concept of representation cannot serve as the highest and most general concept for establishing a systematic and unified philosophy of consciousness: *either* we find ourselves stuck with an infinite regress (which is contrary to the very idea of a systematic, unified transcendental philosophy), *or else* there would have to be something "behind" or "beyond" the concept of representation that would provide the true foundation for a rigorous, scientific demonstration of transcendental philosophy. Since Reinhold has not identified the requisite condition "behind" or "beyond" the concept of representation, his system cannot claim to be truly scientific.[30]

The second, more general aspect of Schulze's skeptical attack on transcendental philosophy emerges from the first. Schulze suggests that the same basic problem that affects Reinhold's attempted demonstration of the scientific character of transcendental philosophy will also affect any other attempted demonstration as well. This is because any concept or first principle, so long as it has any determinate explanatory content at all (including content based on the internal structure of representation), must be the result of some act of abstraction from (internal or external) experience. Such abstraction, by definition, must leave at least something out of account. As a result, one can never know for sure whether a principle that is thus derived actually has universal, or merely inductive, validity. It is always possible that there is something beyond the scope of the principle itself that relativizes the principle's validity. Any attempt to capture what is beyond the scope of the principle will require yet another principle, which, in turn, may have only relative validity, and so on ad infinitum. In order to avoid this infinite regress, one might suggest that we appeal to some concept or first principle that is not the product of any act of abstraction. This strategy, however, is plausible only in theory. For in fact, any concept or principle that has any intelligible, determinate content at all will have to be the product of some act of abstraction. Where there is no abstraction at all, there is no intelligible conceptual content, and thus no explanatory potential.

For Schulze, Reinhold failed to demonstrate that the concept of representation as expressed in the principle of consciousness is universally valid, that is, valid for every possible state of consciousness. At most, Reinhold demonstrated only that the structure of representation is valid for some forms of consciousness, but not necessarily all.[31] Thus the skep-

30. See sections 2–5, *Aenesidemus*. For another account of the problem of this infinite regress, see Frederick Neuhouser, *Fichte's Theory of Subjectivity* (Cambridge: Cambridge University Press, 1990), p. 71.
31. Schulze, *Aenesidemus*, pp. 53–55, 65.

tic remains free to doubt the universal validity of the structure of representation as it is articulated by Reinhold. According to Schulze, Reinhold's project fails not because of any personal lack or individual oversight, but rather because the project of scientific philosophy is itself doomed from the start. For Schulze, no intelligible, determinate principle (i.e., no principle that is derived from an act of abstraction) can ever provide an adequate starting point for a scientifically grounded philosophy, for the alleged universality of such a principle can always be questioned. Conversely, no contentless, indeterminate principle (if such a term makes sense at all) can ground a scientific philosophy, for such a principle is devoid of all explanatory content. In short, one can purchase determinate content (and thus explanatory power) only at the expense of universality, and universality only at the expense of content (and thus explanatory power). With this critical observation, Schulze injects radical skepticism into the very heart of transcendental philosophy, rending apart what Kant and Reinhold had tried to unite, namely, the synthetic (that which introduces determinate content) and the a priori (that which is necessary and universal).[32]

3. Fichte

Schulze's skeptical criticism of Reinhold had a dramatic effect upon Fichte, as Fichte himself acknowledged in a letter to J. F. Flatt:

> *Aenesidemus*, which I consider to be one of the most remarkable products of our decade, has convinced me of something which I admittedly already suspected: that even after the labors of Kant and Reinhold, philosophy is still not a science. Aenesidemus has shaken my system to its very foundations.[33]

Schulze had convinced Fichte that Reinhold's reformulation of the Kantian system had failed; nevertheless, Fichte was still not convinced that scientific philosophy itself was impossible. In fact, Schulze's attack upon Reinhold helped inspire Fichte to attempt the scientific demonstration that had eluded both Kant and Reinhold. Fichte attempts to establish philosophy as a science, not by seeking refuge in some concept or principle that is allegedly immune to skeptical doubt, but by accepting the radical doubt in all of its severity and by articulating what is implicit in the activity of doubting.

32. Some have questioned whether Schulze misunderstood Reinhold and Kant by regarding the transcendental argumentation as an empirical generalization.
33. Letter to J. F. Flatt, November or December 1793. From *Fichte: Early Philosophical Writings*, trans. and ed. Daniel Breazeale (Ithaca, NY, and London: Cornell University Press, 1988), p. 366.

For Fichte, Reinhold displayed the right kind of skeptical strategy when he sought to bracket all belief in the existence of an external world and then derive the specific content of transcendental philosophy from within the immanence of consciousness itself. Reinhold, however, was insufficiently skeptical insofar as he did not turn his doubt upon all possible facts that can be found even *within* consciousness. Thus Schulze was able to show that no first principle based on any given fact whatsoever (regardless of whether that fact is alleged to be internal or external to consciousness) can provide an adequate starting point for a scientific, systematic philosophy. Fichte accepts Schulze's demonstration up to this point; however, he does not accept Schulze's claim that the project of scientific philosophy is necessarily doomed to failure. Fichte seeks to avoid Schulze's conclusion by rejecting a basic assumption, an assumption that *both* Reinhold and Schulze shared. Both of these thinkers wrongly assumed that *if* transcendental philosophy is to be scientifically grounded in a first principle, *then* the first principle must be based on a fact, such as the fact articulated in the principle of consciousness (describing the basic structure of representation).[34] Against both Reinhold and Schulze, Fichte argues that the starting point of philosophy need not be based on any given fact at all.

If Fichte does not begin with at least some given fact, then how can he begin at all? Fichte's starting point is not any fixed fact or claim, but simply the activity of being radically skeptical. To be radically skeptical is to be aware that all given content (including the content contained in Reinhold's principle of consciousness) is subject to doubt. To be radically skeptical is to be aware that no given content is necessarily determinative for the self's thinking, that no given content necessarily imposes itself on the self and causes the self to accept it as binding. Thus to be radically skeptical is to be aware that the self's thinking is not determined by any external necessity. To refer to any kind of external necessity or causality upon the self would be to assume the existence or efficacy of something that is outside of the self; but such an assumption has already been ruled out by the radicalization of skepticism. Finally, to be aware that the self's thinking is not determined by any external necessity is to be aware that the self is radically undetermined and *free* as a thinking self.

In order to remain true to this radical skepticism, one must be careful not to conceive of the radically skeptical, radically free, thinking self in terms of any particular content or idea that might be subject to doubt. Thus Fichte understands the self as nothing other than the activity of

---

34. See Fichte, "Review of *Aenesidemus*," in *Fichte: Early Philosophical Writings*, pp. 60–61.

being aware of oneself as radically doubting and radically free, undetermined by any given content. The skeptical self cannot consistently define itself by reference to anything *other* than such activity, for that would involve the nonskeptical claim that the self can have knowledge of some determinate state or condition that is allegedly external to its own thinking. The self is simply the activity of thinking of itself as radically free and undetermined by anything external to itself.

From this it follows that the self's awareness (or thinking) of itself as radically skeptical and free must be a *nonrepresentational* kind of awareness. After all, any determinate representation would involve at least some content that is given to the self. Since all such given contents are subject to doubt, the skeptical self may not understand itself by reference to any such given content. The self's awareness is entirely nonrepresentational. The term "awareness" is potentially misleading here. The awareness that constitutes the self's being does not depend on any given content or fact (*Tatsache*) whatsoever, but is simply an activity (*Tathandlung*), namely, the activity of being aware, in a nonrepresentational way, of oneself as free and undetermined by any given content. Of course, there is a circularity here. What is the self? It is the nonrepresentational activity of self-awareness. What is the content of this awareness? Nothing other than the nonrepresentational activity itself. If the act of awareness and the content of the awareness did not fully coincide, then the self would implicitly be claiming to have knowledge of something that is *external* to its own self or (what amounts to the same thing) external to its own self-awareness. But such a claim would contradict the policy of radicalized skepticism. As a fully self-referential activity, this self-awareness is something that one must *do* for oneself.

The nonrepresentational self-awareness that constitutes the self's being is described by the first principle of Fichte's *Grundlage der gesamten Wissenschaftslehre:* the pure *Ich = Ich*.[35] Fichte also discusses this nonrepresentational self-awareness as the activity of self-positing, or pure "being *for* self." The "content" of the first principle of the *Grundlage* is not really any content at all, but is simply the activity of self-positing, or being *for* self in a nonrepresentational way. In this activity, the act of self-awareness and the "content" of the act fully coincide; all that the self is, is simply its own selfhood as the act of being for self: "*To posit oneself* and *to be* are, as applied to the self, perfectly identical. Thus the proposition, 'I am, because I have posited myself' can also be stated as: '*I am absolutely* [*schlechthin*]*, because I am.*' "[36]

---

35. J. G. Fichte, *The Science of Knowledge*, trans. Peter Heath and John Lachs (Cambridge: Cambridge University Press, 1982), p. 96.
36. Ibid., p. 99.

In describing the radically skeptical, self-positing self, Fichte uses terms such as *absolut, unbedingt,* and *schlechthin;* however, this terminology can be misleading. To say that the self "absolutely" or "unconditionally" posits itself is not an attempt to infinitize or absolutize the self, but rather an attempt to express the radicalness of the self's skepticism. To say that the self "absolutely" or "unconditionally" posits itself is to say that the self is so self-consciously skeptical that it may not explain itself or (what amounts to the same thing) explain its awareness of itself by appealing to any thing that is other than itself. Any attempt to explain the self by appealing to something that is *other* than the self (i.e., some external state of affairs) would run counter to the self's radical skepticism. To say that the skeptical self posits itself unconditionally (*unbedingt*) is to say that it cannot explain itself by reference to any thing (*Ding*) that is allegedly other than itself.

Just as the skeptical self cannot explain itself by reference to any external thing or state of affairs, so too it cannot think of itself as any kind of substance or thing that differs from the bare activity of being skeptical. To refer to any substrate or substance as the basis of the self would be to refer to some form of being or existence that can allegedly be known to exist as it is in itself, apart from the activity of the self's thinking. Thus any reference to some underlying substance or substrate would contradict the activity of skepticism that the self *is*. As Fichte writes, the radically free, skeptical self "is an act, and absolutely [*absolut*] nothing more; we should not even call it an *active* something [*ein Thätiges*]."[37] In short, the radically skeptical self is simply the "pure activity" of nonrepresentational, nonsubstantialist self-awareness.

Thus far, Fichte's radicalization of skepticism has yielded a highly purified and abstract notion of the self. But if the radically skeptical self cannot consistently base any of its claims on any given content or representation, then how can the analysis proceed any further? It would seem that such an abstract and empty notion of the self can provide no explanatory content at all. For Fichte, genuine explanatory content begins to emerge as soon as the self begins to understand what is implied by its own radically skeptical activity. The radically skeptical self knows that no given representation or content necessarily imposes itself on the self. However, one "thing" that does "impose" itself on the self is the "fact" that the self must have *come-to-be* aware of itself as thus radically skeptical and undetermined by any given content. The self's coming-to-be the radically skeptical self that it is must "happen" to the self, apart from any deliberate or self-conscious choosing by the self. The radically skeptical

37. Ibid., p. 21.

self can never freely or self-consciously choose to become the self that it has become; after all, "prior" to this coming-to-be, the self is "not yet" a self-consciously skeptical or free self at all. The radically skeptical self necessarily emerges *out of* a "prior" state of *not* being the radically skeptical self that it is. Since the self-positing self was not *always* the self that it is, the self-positing self cannot be the totality of all that is, for coming-to-be necessarily implies some form of otherness. Insofar as the self-positing self is not the totality of everything that is, there must be something "other" to the self, or a not-self *(Nicht-Ich)*. This not-self is the subject matter of the second principle of Fichte's *Grundlage der gesamten Wissenschaftslehre*.[38]

The necessity of the not-self can also be explained by reference to the skeptical self's ability to ask questions. All question-asking implies some sense of otherness. As long as any question is not yet answered, there is something that persists as an *other* to the self's awareness of itself as a self (an awareness that is the same as the self's being). Insofar as there is some otherness to the self, the self is not the totality of all that is, and there must be a not-self. One might challenge this conclusion by arguing that the sense of otherness implied by question-asking does not necessarily pertain to a *real* otherness, but might refer only to an *illusory* otherness (in which case the self just might be the totality of all that is). This argumentation, however, only confirms the necessity of the not-self. If the otherness implied by the self's question-asking referred only to an illusory otherness, then the self's being (its awareness of itself) would already be the totality of all that is. But if that were the case, then the self would already know that much, for it would already know everything about everything by virtue of being aware of its own self. Yet if that were the case, then the self could not even *begin* to wonder whether the sense of otherness were real or illusory. It would already know. Indeed, the self could not even begin to wonder about anything at all. In short, even the *appearance* of a *possible* otherness is necessarily a *real* otherness for a self whose being consists in the bare activity of self-awareness.[39]

---

38. In his *Foundations of Transcendental Philosophy*, Fichte explains more fully how this "prior" state of not being fully self-conscious corresponds to the sphere of the not-self. See *Fichte: Foundations of Transcendental Philosophy Wissenschaftslehre (novo methodo)*, trans. Daniel Breazeale (Ithaca, N.Y.: Cornell University Press, 1992), pp. 121–33.

39. The necessity of the not-self can be explained still differently. A careful analysis of self-positing will reveal that the self could not be *for* itself, if there were no not-self *out of which* the self reflected upon or returned to itself. In other words, if there were no not-self, then the self would be an unchecked activity extending out to infinity without reflecting back on itself; but in that case, the self would not be *for* itself, and thus the self would not be a self at all. While the necessity of the not-self can be expressed in a variety of ways, it seems that Fichte found it pedagogically helpful to explain it by reference to the self's own "prior" state of inactivity, or *not*-being the fully self-positing self that it is.

The radically skeptical, self-conscious self must acknowledge the existence of a not-self. Thus Fichte's radicalization of skepticism does not lead to a complete solipsism or nihilism or emptiness. The negating power of skepticism, when radicalized and made self-conscious, acknowledges and preserves its own indebtedness to the otherness out of which it has arisen (the sphere of the not-self). Thus the power of negation that characterizes Fichte's radicalized skepticism is not an abstract, annihilating form of negation, but is rather a form of negation that preserves some relation to otherness: it is a *determinate negation*.[40] While Fichte radicalizes skepticism, he nevertheless avoids wholesale solipsism; and he does so without limiting his skepticism or relying ultimately on the validity of some content as given. Instead, solipsism is avoided insofar as the skeptical self becomes self-conscious and acknowledges its own relatedness-to-otherness (without which it would not be the question-asking, skeptical self that it is).

In order to be a fully self-conscious, skeptical self, the Fichtean self must acknowledge its own relatedness to a not-self. This necessary relatedness of the self to the not-self constitutes the primordial unity of *spontaneity* (corresponding to the purely self-positing self) and *receptivity* (corresponding to the sphere of the not-self) in the Fichtean system. Unlike Kant, Fichte does not have to speculate about the possible unity of these two "stems" of human knowledge (*CPR*, A15/B29); according to Fichte, the self's own activity of self-conscious skepticism *shows* the necessary unity of the two. Similarly, Fichte does not find it necessary to posit a thing-in-itself as the external ground of the subject's receptivity. For Fichte, the self's pure spontaneity, as self-conscious, necessarily implies the existence of a not-self, and therefore implies receptivity within the self's own being. Without the problematic postulate of the thing-in-itself, Fichte can develop a system of knowledge that avoids the various difficulties that plagued the Kantian system.

The Fichtean self, as presented thus far, is an intrinsically contradictory self. On the one hand, the self's radicalized skepticism implied that the self may not consistently explain or account for itself by reference to anything allegedly other than, or external, to itself. The self's being is

---

40. While the terminology of "determinate negation" comes from Hegel, it was Fichte who first showed how such determinate negation actually takes place. Hegel's contrast between "abstract negation" and "determinate negation" adequately describes how Fichte's self-conscious skepticism is different from abstract, empty skepticism. Hegel writes: "The scepticism that ends up with the bare abstraction of nothingness or emptiness cannot get any further from there, but must wait to see whether something new comes along.... But when, on the other hand, the result is conceived as it is in truth, namely, as a *determinate* negation, a new form has thereby immediately arisen." See *Hegel's Phenomenology of Spirit*, p. 51.

fully exhausted by its awareness, and its awareness is simply the nonrepresentational awareness of itself as radically free and not determined by any given content. Thus the self is simply the pure act of self-awareness, where the act of self-awareness and the content of the act of self-awareness fully coincide. On the other hand, the skeptical self also had to acknowledge that it has come to be. In order for the self to have come to be, there must be an other *for* the self, or a not-self (corresponding to the self's prior state of not being the fully self-positing self that it is). However, if there is an other *for* the self, an other that somehow coexists alongside the self's awareness of itself, then the self cannot be the pure and simple act of being for self, where the act and the content of the act fully coincide. Thus the Fichtean self is self-contradictory.

If this contradiction were left to stand in its immediacy, then consciousness would be impossible. This is because the activity of pure self-positing (pure self-consciousness) is *by definition* incompatible with any relation to otherness (empirical consciousness). Pure consciousness of self seems both to require and to exclude all consciousness of otherness. It thus becomes necessary to overcome this contradiction, while still preserving the two sides that are necessary for conscious selfhood (pure self-positing and relation-to-other). As Fichte writes, it is necessary to eradicate this fundamental contradiction, yet "without doing away with the identity of consciousness."[41] Indeed, the *Grundlage der gesamten Wissenschaftslehre* can be understood as an extended series of attempts to eradicate this basic contradiction. Throughout the *Grundlage*, the self-conscious, self-contradictory self seeks to resolve its internal contradiction, as we philosophical observers look on.

Every attempt in the *Grundlage* to eradicate the basic contradiction within consciousness ultimately fails. However, the result is not merely negative, since the enactment and failure of the series of attempts demonstrates two things. First of all, it shows that the resolution of the contradiction is not be conceived as an accomplished *fact* that the self actually experiences, but only as a *process*, a perpetual *task*. Secondly, the failure of the various attempts to eliminate the contradiction does not amount to a dead end, but in fact yields a set of thought categories, namely, the categories by which the contradictory self seeks to explain itself. The thought categories are not self-consciously "chosen" by the self-contradictory, skeptical self, but emerge "behind its back" as a *necessary* part of the strategy by which the self seeks to eliminate the contradiction that it is. As a result, the skeptical self at first does not recognize the thought categories as the products of its own freedom. With philo-

---

41. Fichte, *Science of Knowledge*, p. 107.

sophical hindsight, we observers realize that the emerging thought categories constitute the hidden conditions of the possibility of the self's own ability to think at all. Our ability to observe the emergence of the categories and to grasp them together in their necessary unity constitutes a fully rigorous transcendental deduction. For example, in its attempt to account for itself as a unified self, the skeptical self *must* think of the category of "limit," for the unified coexistence of self and not-self *requires* that the two sides mutually limit one another.[42] In turn, the self's ability to think of the category of limit depends on the category of "quantity,"[43] and so forth. When the end of the series coincides with the beginning (and thus when the entire system forms a circle), the transcendental deduction is complete and we have a fully consistent, self-accounting system of knowledge. In this way, Fichte shows how all the self's thought categories emerge *necessarily* from the its own internal struggle as the radically *free*, skeptical self that it is. Thus, unlike Kant, Fichte does not need to borrow the categories as ready-made from Aristotle or any other external source. Similarly, Fichte shows how the very concept of "representation" (*Vorstellung*) originally emerges from the self's own self-related activity.[44] Thus unlike Reinhold, Fichte does not have to *begin* by presupposing the concept of representation as given.

Fichte's *Grundlage* recounts the "history of the human mind."[45] In recollecting this "history," we philosophical observers comprehend how the self's own self-related activity generates a series of thought categories in terms of which the self *must* think in order to be the radically skeptical, *free* self that it is. The contradictory unity of self and not-self constitutes the fundamental synthetic a priori from which all other synthetic a priori contents are systematically and rigorously derived. We can now see how skeptical questioning, properly understood and raised to the level of self-consciousness, does not amount to an empty state of not-knowing or to the annihilation of all determinate content, but rather to a system of knowledge that generates content of its own. Fichte's transcendental deduction of the categories does not depend on any contingently derived content, but simply on the self's own attempts to explain itself as both self-conscious and conscious of otherness. The specific content of systematic philosophy is derived, yet without compromising or restricting the skepticism that gave rise to the need for systematic philosophy in the first place. The content of transcendental philosophy emerges out of the very activity of radicalized, skeptical questioning becoming self-con-

42. Ibid., pp. 105–19.   43. Ibid., pp. 128–30.
44. See Fichte's "Deduction of Presentation [*Vorstellung*]," in *Science of Knowledge*, pp. 203–18.
45. Fichte, *Science of Knowledge*, pp. 198–99.

scious.[46] Precisely because the activity of skeptical questioning produces its own content, the content that is thus derived has more than inductive validity, and is immune to skeptical doubt. Indeed, the content thus derived is shown to be the *necessary* condition of self-conscious, skeptical doubting. Skepticism is thus answered by being radicalized and made self-conscious. Finally, Fichte's demonstration addresses Schulze's skeptical claim that one can secure determinate content for philosophy only at the expense of universality, or universality only at the expense of determinate content. Schulze's observation clearly applies to content that is derived from a source that is external to the skeptical self; however, it does not apply to the Fichtean strategy of recollecting the thought categories that *necessarily* emerge from the self's attempts to account for its own radicalized skepticism.

4. Hegel

Fichte's *Grundlage* tells the story of a radically skeptical, self-contradictory self whose attempts to grapple with its self-contradiction generate the content of a fully critical, systematic philosophy. In many ways, Hegel's *Phenomenology* is similar to Fichte's *Grundlage*. Like the *Grundlage*, Hegel's *Phenomenology* presents a series of attempts whereby consciousness seeks to account for itself as both purely self-positing and yet related to some form of otherness. As consciousness attempts to account for itself in its relation to the other, we philosophical observers look on and "recollect" the emergence of the thought categories as they are generated "behind the back" of consciousness itself. The entirety of the series of thought categories thus derived grounds the Hegelian system of knowledge.

While there are significant similarities between Fichte and Hegel, there are also substantial differences. For example, Hegel asserts, contra Fichte, that the self's various attempts to eradicate the self-contradiction at the heart of its being do not all end in failure, and the desire for theoretical self-consistency or wholeness need not play itself out as a perpetual striving. On the face of it, the Hegelian assertion of the possibility of consistency and closure seems to undermine the claim that Hegel's

---

46. In a similar vein, Fichte argues, in his *Grundlage des Naturrechts nach Principien der Wissenschaftslehre*, that all the determinate content of practical philosophy, including a theory of rights, emerges from the activity of radicalized skepticism becoming self-conscious. He argues, for example, that the not-self which exists for the self must be another free self whose relation to the first self is mediated by property relations, and so forth. See J. G. Fichte, *Grundlage des Naturrechts nach Principien der Wissenschaftslehre*, in *J. G. Fichte Gesamtausgabe*, ed. Reinhard Lauth and Hans Jacob (Stuttgart-Bad Cannstatt: Friedrich Frommann Verlag, 1966), 1.3–4.

systematic philosophy can be understood as the radicalization of skepticism beyond Fichte. This claim can begin to make sense, however, if we situate Fichte's radicalized skepticism within the context of Hegel's *Phenomenology*.

Roughly speaking, the skeptical, self-contradictory self that sets up the main problem to be resolved in Fichte's *Grundlage* finds its logical parallel in the "skepticism" section of Hegel's *Phenomenology*. In the "skepticism" section, the self realizes that no given content is necessarily determinative for it: "the wholly unessential and non-independent character of [the] other becomes explicit *for consciousness.*"[47] Skeptical thinking "annihilates the being of the world in all its manifold determinateness, and the negativity of free self-consciousness comes to know itself."[48] Unlike earlier forms of consciousness, which experience the vanishing of objective content as something that just "happens," skepticism knows that it is itself responsible; it knows that it "*makes* this 'other' which claims to be real, vanish."[49] Through its awareness of its power to negate, skeptical consciousness "procures for its own self the certainty of its freedom."[50] Skeptical consciousness thus experiences itself as fully self-positing, unable to explain itself in relation to anything other than itself, for its "self-certainty does not issue from something alien."[51] However, instead of being purely self-identical and related only to itself (which is what a purely self-positing self *would* be), the radically skeptical self experiences some form of otherness outside of it. This is shown by the fact that the skeptical self still has unanswered questions and is confused; that is, the skeptical self does not already know everything that is to be known. Since there exists some form of otherness for it, the skeptical self cannot be purely self-related and self-identical. By virtue of this otherness, the self is rendered "contingent, single, and separate."[52] Accordingly, the skeptical self finds itself oscillating between "the one extreme of self-identical self-consciousness" and "the other extreme of the contingent consciousness" that is related to and conditioned by an other, a not-self.[53]

In skepticism, Hegel writes, "consciousness truly experiences itself as internally contradictory."[54] If skeptical consciousness were only the contradictory unity of self-identity and relation-to-otherness, and nothing more than that, then it would not be aware of itself *as* contradictory; it would be a *blind* oscillation between pure self-identity and relation-to-otherness. Skepticism, however, is explicitly conscious of its contradic-

47. *Hegel's Phenomenology of Spirit*, p. 123.
48. Ibid., p. 123.
49. Ibid., p. 124.
50. Ibid.
51. Ibid.
52. Ibid., p. 125.
53. Ibid.
54. Ibid., p. 126.

tory state; thus it is "*one* consciousness which contains within itself these two modes."⁵⁵ Nevertheless, skeptical consciousness cannot yet explain the strange unity that it is. The next shape of consciousness, the Unhappy Consciousness, explicitly addresses the problem of reconciling the two contradictory modes of skeptical consciousness: that is, the pure, unchangeable self-positing, self-identical self (which can be called the transcendental self), and the contingent, changeable self that finds itself related to some otherness (which can be called the empirical self). The task of reconciliation is undertaken by the Unhappy Consciousness in the religious language of the reconciliation between God (the purely self-identical unchangeable consciousness) and the human pilgrim (the contingent, changeable, dependent consciousness).

The Unhappy Consciousness, Hegel writes, is really *both* the unchangeable and the changeable consciousness at once. However, the possible unity of the two sides, as they are immediately given, remains an unsolved problem, and so the question of their reconciliation is approached from the point of view of the contingent, changeable consciousness. The changeable consciousness at first takes the two sides to be, not the same, but *opposites* in need of being brought together; furthermore, it views itself as inessential and the unchangeable as essential.⁵⁶ Now the problem of articulating the unity of the unchangeable (purely self-related, transcendental) self and the changeable (other-related, empirical) self is logically equivalent to the fundamental problem that animates Fichte's *Grundlage*. For Hegel, Fichte was quite right to set up the basic problem as the problem of articulating the unity of transcendental selfhood (purely self-positing, self-identical selfhood) and empirical selfhood (selfhood that has an other for it). However, Fichte was not sufficiently skeptical about his own approach to the problem. Fichte correctly identified the terms to be reconciled; however, he uncritically assumed that his identification of the terms to be reconciled already included an adequate understanding of the *meaning* of those terms (i.e., the meaning of the transcendental self and the empirical self). For Hegel, the meaning of the terms is not transparent at the outset of the analysis, but emerges only gradually as a *result* of the analysis itself. And just as the *meaning* of the terms becomes clear through the analysis, so too does the *possibility* of their fundamental *unity*. By accepting the *meaning* of the terms as given at the beginning of his analysis, Fichte effectively prevented himself from seeing how the two terms could actually be reconciled. The grounds of this logical problem can be gleaned from Hegel's section on the Unhappy Consciousness.

55. Ibid.   56. Ibid., pp. 126–27.

At the beginning of the section on the Unhappy Consciousness, the changeable consciousness takes the two sides in need of reconciliation to be *opposites,* and regards itself as inessential and the unchangeable as essential.[57] With this starting point (which corresponds to Fichte's starting point in the *Grundlage*), the unity of the changeable and the unchangeable becomes possible only to the extent that the changeable sheds the relatedness-to-otherness that makes it the contingent, particular self that is. After all, as long as there is any particularity or otherness attached to the changeable, empirical self, it must be *different* from the purely self-positing, unchangeable self with which it seeks to be united. Unfortunately, the changeable, empirical self's loss of particularity or relation-to-otherness would also entail its loss of consciousness. For without some relation-to-otherness, the self would be an unchecked activity extending out to infinity without reflecting back on itself; and if that were the case, then the self would not be a conscious self at all. Given the basic terms of the analysis, then, the changeable self can never (consciously) *experience* its reconciliation with the unchangeable, transcendental self.

In accordance with the foregoing problem, the changeable self conceives of its reconciliation with the unchangeable as something "beyond" its present, conscious state. Within the context of the Unhappy Consciousness, this is the religious "beyond" of the afterlife; within the context of Fichte's philosophy, this is the practical "beyond" of the self's unfulfilled, perpetual striving. Furthermore, the changeable self must conceive of its reconciliation with the unchangeable as something that *happens to it* by virtue of an agency *outside* of itself. After all, the reconciliation cannot result from the self's own conscious, deliberate activity. For as long as the self remains conscious at all, there must be an other for it, in which case it must be *different* from the purely self-positing, unchangeable self with which it seeks to be united. The changeable self's own consciousness thus prevents, rather than facilitates, its unity with the unchangeable self.[58] The reconciliation can be effected only by an external agency. Within the context of the Unhappy Consciousness, the external agency is the religious minister, who effects the unity of changeable and unchangeable by stripping the religious pilgrim of all the particularity that makes the pilgrim a particular, conscious self (something that the pilgrim cannot do to himself).[59] Within the context of Fichte's

57. Ibid.
58. An analogy may be helpful here: just as the changeable, empirical self cannot *consciously* relinquish the particularity and other-relatedness that make it conscious, so too a person cannot *consciously* cause himself to go to sleep.
59. See *Hegel's Phenomenology of Spirit,* pp. 136–37.

philosophy, the external agency is the Ephorate, which stands above the people and oversees the harmony of the general will and particular wills (since no particular will *within* the populace can ever conceive of the general will while still remaining a conscious, particular will).[60]

What emerges from Hegel's analysis of the Unhappy Consciousness is an implicit criticism of Fichte's insufficiently skeptical starting point. Fichte began by assuming that the terms to be reconciled (self-positing selfhood and empirically conditioned selfhood) were essentially different. Thus within the Fichtean system, the changeable, empirical self is able to conceive of its unity with the unchangeable, transcendental self only as something "beyond" and only as something that *happens to* it by virtue of some agency outside of itself. That is, the changeable self can conceive of its unity with the unchangeable only if it imagines itself from a point of view *outside* of itself and conceives of itself as being stripped of its particular consciousness.[61] As Hegel points out, however, this position is contradictory. The empirical self, qua empirical self, cannot even begin to imagine itself as being stripped of all particularity while still remaining an empirical self.[62] Furthermore, the imaginary position of viewing oneself from a point of view outside of oneself is suspiciously similar to the uncritical claim of the realist that Fichte had already criticized (i.e., the claim that one can know the object as it is "in itself," as if from a point of view outside of all contingent subjectivity). In short, Fichte's insufficiently skeptical starting point forced him in the end to make untenable claims about how one must understand the unity of transcendental selfhood and empirical selfhood.

If the Fichtean approach fails because of its insufficient skepticism, then the Hegelian solution is to radicalize the skepticism. Accordingly, Hegel questions Fichte's presumption that the meaning of the terms as given (the pure, self-related, transcendental self and the contingent, other-related, empirical self) must be determinative for the entire course of the analysis. In their givenness, the two terms certainly do appear to be *opposites;* however, one should be open to their possible identity. Thus at the beginning of the section on the Unhappy Consciousness, Hegel warns that it would be wrong to assume that the reconciliation of the changeable and the unchangeable must be the movement of one side alone. It is possible that the terms to be reconciled are *not* essen-

---

60. Fichte, *Grundlage des Naturrechts nach Principien der Wissenschaftslehre,* in *J. G. Fichte — Gesamtausgabe,* 1.3.440ff.
61. *Hegel's Phenomenology of Spirit,* p. 137.
62. As Hegel puts it, the changeable consciousness is implicitly contradictory because it "disclaims all power pertaining to its own independent existence, ascribing it all to a gift from above, but which in this very disclaimer, holds on to its own particular existence" (*Hegel's Phenomenology,* p. 137).

tially different, and that the story of the pilgrimage of the believer is equally the story of God's own coming-to-be.[63] Fichte was not open to this possibility, since he began his analysis by thinking of the act of self-positing as an immediate act that is radically discontinuous with all objectivity. Thus Fichte famously insisted that one could enter into his system only by making an immediate and radical break with all dependence on otherness.[64] The immediacy of Fichte's starting point compelled him to think of transcendental and empirical selfhood as essentially different, and thus incapable of being reconciled *for* the contingent, empirical self. By contrast, Hegel implicitly questions whether the pure, self-positing, transcendental self must be what it *appears* to be at first, and thus whether it is really discontinuous with all otherness.

Hegel's *Phenomenology* does not begin with an immediate act of self-positing that requires a break with all otherness. For Hegel, it is sufficient to begin with a minimalist sense of self-positing. For Hegel, self-positing is not an activity that is radically other than all given objectivity, but is rather an activity that manifests itself only *in* the objective appearances themselves. The sense of self-positing with which Hegel begins is simply the (limited) ability of ordinary consciousness to exist "beyond" what is immediately given to it ("beyond" the appearance) and to question its own relation to what is thus given. Already included in this very ability to question is a basic sense of being-for-self, or self-relation, "beyond" the given. Unlike Fichte's notion of self-positing, the meaning of self-positing as it appears in the various stages of the *Phenomenology* is intrinsically related to and conditioned by the appearances as given. As the movement of the *Phenomenology* unfolds, the meaning of this activity of self-positing will be enriched, and we philosophical observers will realize that "pure" self-positing is both pure and not pure at once. It will reveal itself as the perpetual ability of the self to be "beyond" any given appearance, while always simultaneously interpreting itself *out of* some particular appearance. Unlike Fichte, Hegel holds that self-positing is not essentially different from all relation-to-otherness, but actually depends on the determinacy of the other in order to be the pure self-positing that it is. The act of pure self-positing is intrinsically dependent on the movement of objectivity; or stated more precisely, the activity of pure self-positing is *identical* to the movement of objectivity-becoming-conscious.

With this insight, we return (appropriately) to our starting point, the slumber-disrupting skepticism of Hume. From the Hegelian point of

63. Ibid., p. 128.
64. See, e.g., Fichte's "First Introduction to the Science of Knowledge," in the *Science of Knowledge,* where he argues that the starting points of realism and idealism are absolutely incompatible.

view, one might say that the skeptic Hume was correct to show that the knowing self can never find itself as an independent, stable entity within experience. What one calls the "self" is not a self-sufficient, self-transparent being at all, but is simply the product or effect of the movements of objectivity. However, Hegel would also say that Hume was wrong to conclude that selfhood is fully explicable as the effect of objectivity and nothing else. For if the self's being were exhausted by its being-affected by the movement of objectivity (e.g., through custom and habituation), then the self could never become conscious of this alleged fact about its own self. That is, if the self were merely the plaything of objective occurrences, then this very fact about it would remain just beyond its own awareness. The self would never catch *itself* in the act of being affected, but could only speak of a *past* self being affected. For Hegel, then, the Humean skeptic is right to assert the fundamental *identity* of subjectivity and objectivity. But beyond Hume, fully self-conscious skepticism also implies a *difference:* subjectivity is not just objectivity as given, but is objectivity in the act of becoming conscious of itself.

PART III
ABSTRACT REALISM AND THE PRIMACY OF THE PRACTICAL: ESSAYS ON FICHTE

PART III

4   Fichte's Abstract Realism
DANIEL BREAZEALE

Few features of Fichte's early *Wissenschaftslehre* have proven a greater stumbling block to his admirers or a greater object of derision for his detractors than his notorious doctrine of the *Anstoß* or "check" that is somehow supposed to limit what is presumed to be an "absolutely posited, infinite I." There have been two traditional strategies for eliminating what seems to be the egregious contradiction between Fichte's alleged claim concerning the absolute character of the self and his apparent admission of the need for some external "check" upon the activity of the same: One popular option is to explain the "check" in question as nothing more than a roundabout way in which the I surreptitiously "affects" itself (so that it can then proceed to posit an external world as a sphere for its own practical endeavors—a sort of moral gymnasium in which it can then work out).[1] The other strategy, which perhaps goes back to Hegel and has been recently revived by Dieter Henrich, is simply to eliminate altogether the doctrine of the *Anstoß*, to dismiss it as a "dogmatic" relic, incompatible with what is taken to be the "speculative spirit" of Fichte's philosophy.[2] In the remarks that follow I will explore a third option, one that emphasizes *both* the irreducibility of the *Anstoß* to the activity of the I *and* the absolutely essential role of this doctrine within the overall account of subjectivity proposed in the Jena *Wissenschaftslehre*. I will then try to show how an accurate understanding of this last point exposes the wholly misguided nature of some of the more persistent misunderstandings of Fichte's thought and prepares the way for a just appreciation of what I would describe, somewhat tendentiously to be sure, as "Fichte's abstract realism."

    1. See, e.g., Emile Bréhier, *The History of Philosophy*, vol. 6: *The Nineteenth Century: Period of Systems, 1800–1850*, trans. Wade Baskin (Chicago: University of Chicago Press, 1968 [orig. French ed. 1932]), p. 118.
    2. See, e.g., Dieter Henrich, *Fichtes ursprüngliche Einsicht* (Frankfurt: Klostermann, 1967), p. 41.

1. The Doctrine of the Anstoß in the 1794–1795 Wissenschaftslehre

A glance at Grimm's *Deutsches Wörterbuch* reveals that the term *"Anstoß"* was employed in the late eighteenth century with quite a number of overlapping and often figurative meanings, two of which are particularly relevant to Fichte's usage. On the one hand, an *Anstoß* is an "obstacle" or "hindrance" *(Hindernis* or *Hemmung);* on the other, it is an "impetus" or "stimulus" *(Anlass* or *Anregung).* In the rational mechanics of the period the term *Anstoß* designates the "original impulse" that sets a physical system in motion.[3]

Keeping in mind this dual meaning, let us turn to the *Grundlage der gesamten Wissenschaftslehre*, and see how the term *Anstoß* is actually employed in this work.[4] We first encounter this term near the end of the second "theoretical" part of the text, just after it has been concluded that the I can posit itself only as a finite I, and, in turn, can posit itself in this way only by simultaneously opposing itself to something radically other: the limited Not-I. Such mediate positing of the I and the Not-I, moreover, is shown to be possible only by virtue of the presence within consciousness of a particular *Bestimmtsein* or determinacy, for it is only this that permits the intellect to posit any boundary between itself and its other. If, therefore, representational consciousness is to be possible at all, then it must contain, in addition to a self-active or "subjective" element, a passive or "objective" one—that is, a moment of sheer determinacy or givenness, which Fichte describes simply as *"etwas überhaupt."*[5]

Enter the *Anstoß*, which makes its initial appearance simply as the most abstract way of designating the aforementioned "realistic" or "ob-

---

3. See Pierre-Philippe Druet, "'L'Anstoss' fichtéen: Essai d'élucidation d'une métaphore," *Revue philosophique de Louvain* 70 (1972): 384–92.

4. Of course, there are passages in Fichte's writings where the term *Anstoß* is employed in a thoroughly unproblematic and nontechnical manner. Here, however, we will be concerned only with those usages that cast possible light upon Fichte's theory of the I. (According to Druet's study, the term occurs a total of thirty-two times in the I. H. Fichte edition of Fichte's writings, and most of these occurrences are indeed to be found in the *Grundlage*.) Note that Fichte's writings are here cited according to the Critical Edition edited by Reinhard Lauth and Hans Gliwitzky, *J. G Fichte—Gesamtausgabe der Bayerischen Akademie der Wissenschaften* (Stuttgart-Bad Cannstatt: Frommannn, 1964–), abbreviated as *GA* and cited by series, volume, and page number. For the convenience of readers without access to GA, reference is also provided, wherever possible, to the edition of Fichte's writings edited by his son, I. H. Fichte, *Johann Gottlieb Fichtes sämmtliche Werke* (Berlin: Viet, 1845–1846), abbreviated as SW and cited by volume and page number. All English translations are my own.

5. "Something or other must be present, something within which the active I traces a boundary delimiting what is subjective and consigns what remains to what is objective" (GA, 1.2.351–52 [SW, 1.206]).

jective" moment of consciousness: the original presence to consciousness of *etwas überhaupt*. Note, however, that in order to explain objective consciousness, it is not necessary to presuppose the *actual presence* of any particular object. Instead, writes Fichte,

> All that is needed, if I may so express myself, is the presence of an *Anstoß* for the I. That is to say, the subjective element [*das subjektive*] must, for some reason that simply lies outside of the activity of the I, be unable to extend any further.... Such an *Anstoß* would not limit the I as active, but would give it the task of limiting itself. All limitation, however, occurs through opposition, and thus, simply in order to be able to satisfy this task, the I would have to oppose something objective to the subjective element that is to be limited and would then have to unite both synthetically, in the manner just indicated. And thus the entire representation could be derived in this way. This manner of explanation is, as is immediately obvious, realistic, yet it is based upon a much more abstract form of realism than any of the other, previously discussed varieties of realism. What it assumes is not a Not-I that is present outside of the I, and not even a determination that is present within the I, but rather, the mere task, on the part of the I itself, of undertaking a determination within itself—that is, *the mere determinability* of the I.[6]

This single passage nicely summarizes Fichte's case for the *necessity* of such an *Anstoß* for the very *possibility* of any theoretical consciousness (i.e., any objective cognition) at the same time that it points to the dual role of the *Anstoß* as both "obstacle" and "stimulus" to the activity of the I.

First of all, it is clear that, whatever else it might be, the Fichtean *Anstoß*, to the extent that it signifies "*eine Unmöglichkeit des weitern Ausdehnens*" or "an impossibility of further extension", is indeed an *obstacle* or *hindrance* to what is described here only as "the activity of the I."

Second, though the *Anstoß* is admittedly a check upon the I, it does not follow from this that it is necessarily an *external* obstacle to the same. Instead, all we can say about this abstract remnant of objectivity is that it *functions* within the *Grundlage* as the ultimate real ground upon which all subsequent positing of the Not-I (and indeed, all subsequent positing of the I itself) is based.

Nor is the *Anstoß* to be identified with any particular determination of the knowing I itself (the I qua intellect); that is, it is not to be understood as a *Vorstellung* or "representation." This is the meaning of Fichte's obscure assertion that the *Anstoß* does not limit the intellect so much as it "gives it the task of limiting itself." As such, it presupposes and indeed "incites" the I's own capacity for spontaneous self-determination— which is what is meant here by the phrase "the determinability of the I." Once set in motion by the *Anstoß*, the cognitive powers of the I ultimately

---

6. GA, 1.2.354–55 (SW, 1.210–212).

do succeed, of course, in generating actual determinations of the intellect, that is, "representations." There is, however, another sense in which the *Anstoß* itself *can* be described as a "determination" (and indeed an "original determination") of the I—not of the knowing I, or "intellect," but of the practically striving I.

A third point concerning the relationship of the *Anstoß* to theoretical consciousness must, however, immediately be added to the preceding two: namely, that nothing can be either an obstacle or a stimulus to the activity of the I unless it is posited as such *by the I itself;* and nothing can exist *for* the I except what is posited *in* the I. In other words, whatever else it may be, the *Anstoß* is not some sort of independently existing *Ding an sich.* Instead, the *Anstoß* must, in some sense yet to be explained, *be an original aspect of the I itself.* Even though the *Anstoß* is not, as such, freely posited by the I, it still must, according to Fichte, somehow "occur as a result of the I's own self-positing," since otherwise it would not exist "for the I" at all. More specifically, if the I did not constantly strive to "extend itself," then it simply could not be "checked" or *angestoßen* in the relevant, Fichtean sense: its activity could not be "reflected back into itself," nor would it have any occasion to determine itself any further qua intellect. (Note that in order to understand this "infinite striving" we will eventually be forced to turn from the "theoretical" to the "practical" portion of the *Grundlage.*) In this sense, therefore—though only in this sense—the *Anstoß* does depend upon the I and can even be said to be "grounded in the absolute I itself."[7] As Fichte himself puts it:

The *Anstoß* (which is not posited by the positing I) occurs to the I insofar as it is active, and is thus an *Anstoß* only insofar as the I is active. Its possibility is conditioned by the activity of the I: no activity of the I, no *Anstoß*. And vice versa: the I's activity of determining itself would, in turn, be conditioned by the *Anstoß:* no *Anstoß*, no self-determination. Moreover, no self-determination, nothing objective, etc.[8]

Finally, even as the *Anstoß* represents a sort of "limit" or "check" upon the activity of the I, as well as a stimulus to the further activity of the same, it is equally clear that the I, even understood purely as an intellect or cognizing subject, must also *transcend* and *proceed beyond* this "limit"— since otherwise it would be unable to posit the latter as a limit *for itself,* and hence unable to *posit itself as limited.* Not only, therefore, must the *Anstoß* resist the activity of the I,[9] but the I must also possess another sort of (purely intellectual) activity, thanks to which it is able to posit for itself

---

7. GA, 1.2.405 (SW, 1.272).   8. GA, 1.2.356 (SW, 1.212).
9. On "resistance" (*Widerstand*) as a synonym for *Anstoß*, see GA, 1.2.358 (SW, 1.214).

its own limitation. The very concept of a subject conscious of its own finitude (in contrast, e.g., with the concept of a finite object) thus implies that one and the same subject must be simultaneously limited (with respect to the sheer occurrence of the *Anstoß*) and unlimited (with respect to the positing thereof).

If the theoretical portion of the *Grundlage* succeeds in demonstrating the *necessity* of the *Anstoß* for the possibility of any consciousness whatsoever, much still remains to be said concerning precisely *how* such a determinate "check" or "impulse" presents itself to the I and concerning the sort of *evidence* that can be cited in support of the claim that such an *Anstoß* actually *does* occur. And this in turn requires a careful investigation of the various "activities" of the I—which is precisely the task of Part 3 of the *Grundlage*, in which Fichte erects his entire "pragmatic history of the human mind" upon an account of the "striving I" and of the various "drives" of the same.[10]

Without pretending to summarize this complex account, let me simply recall the remarkable manner in which Fichte's analysis of the practical powers of the I transforms what is at first taken to be a wholly "external contradiction" between the activities of the I and of the Not-I into a purely "internal" contradiction between the various "infinite" and "finite" activities of the I itself. In the course of this analysis, we observe how the two theoretical (or "ideal") activities of the self discussed in Part 2—namely, the infinite (self-reverting or "simply self-positing") activity of the I and its finite ("objective" or "representing") activity—presuppose an equally fundamental "practical" (or "real") activity, described by Fichte somewhat obscurely as an indeterminate striving to "fill out infinity," to overcome all external and internal hindrances, and to make itself totally independent of the same. It is this latter, practical activity of the I that is originally "checked" by the occurrence of the *Anstoß*, and without which the latter could not subsequently be posited by the intellect and thus—thanks to the power of the productive imagination—transformed into a determinate "representation." In the famous formula, "no striving, no object."[11]

It has previously been established that *all* positing, whether of the I itself or of the Not-I must presuppose and start with the positing of something that is both "purely subjective" (since otherwise we would once again run aground on the reef of dogmatic realism, which is never able to fill the gap it itself posits between mental representations and independently existing things-in-themselves) and, at the same time, is not

---

10. See GA, 1.2.361–62 (SW, 1.218). 11. GA, 1.2.397 (SW, 1.262).

produced by the activity of the I (since, according to Fichte's own admission, the I cannot "simply posit" its own limitations). Neither object-consciousness nor self-consciousness is possible unless, in Fichte's words, "there emerges within the I itself a disparity and thus something alien [*etwas fremdartiges*]."[12]

Previously, that is, in the account of theoretical consciousness presented in Part 2 of the *Grundlage*, this foreign "something" was designated only by the abstract term *"Anstoß"*; but now, in the context of an examination of the "practical" elements of consciousness, it receives a new, more familiar name, a name that calls explicit attention not merely to the *formal function* of the *Anstoß* with respect to various activities and features of the active, conscious self, but to its *actual content*, and hence to its essential contribution to *what* we actually experience.[13] This new name is *Gefühl* or "feeling," which is simply another way of designating that "original" or "highest fact of consciousness,"[14] which must be present if any experience whatsoever—and hence any self at all—is to be possible.

Feelings satisfy the two requirements mentioned above: they are subjective states of the I (all feelings are, at least originally, *"Selbstgefühle"*),[15] and they possess a determinacy that is not freely determined by the activity of the I. Feelings can therefore perform both of the functions previously attributed to the *Anstoß:* First of all, feelings serve to *constrain* or to *check* the free, outwardly striving, practical activity of the same. From the purely practical standpoint, this sense of *"Nichtkönnen"* or "inability" is a primary ingredient, if not in every, then certainly in most, types of feeling, and feeling is, in the first instance, a feeling of limitation and constraint—and indeed of one's *own* limited state or constitution (*Beschaffenheit*).[16] Secondly, these same feelings serve to *stimulate* or to *set in motion* the objective, cognitive activity of the I. According to Fichte's account, these feelings provide the "original impetus"[17] for those reiterated acts of positing described abstractly in the "Deduction of Representation" with which Part 2 of the *Grundlage* concludes. It is by virtue of these acts of positing and repositing these "original facts of consciousness" that the intellect succeeds in constituting for itself "a system of

---

12. *"Es tut in ihm sich ein Ungleichheit, und darum etwas fremdartiges hervor"* (GA, 1.2.400 [SW, 1.265]).

13. See GA, 1.2.416 (SW, 1.285–86).   14. GA, 1.2.390 (SW, 1.253).

15. "Feeling is entirely *subjective*. For an *explanation* of feeling, which is an act of theorizing, we certainly require *something that limits*. This, however, is not required for a *deduction* of feeling insofar as it is supposed to be present within the I" (GA, 1.2.419 [SW, 1.289]). "The I never feels an object, but only itself. . . . Yet the I cannot produce any feeling within itself" (GA, 1.2.433 [SW, 1.306]). See too GA, 1.2.427–29 (SW, 1.298–301).

16. See GA, 1.2.426 (SW, 1.297).   17. See GA, 1.2.411 (SW, 1.279).

representations accompanied by a feeling of necessity," at the same time that it posits itself as a finite, embodied agent within this same world.

(In reply to the charge, first raised by Dieter Henrich and reiterated by Manfred Frank, that Fichte, even though he was the first to successfully challenge the dyadic, reflective model of self-consciousness, failed to remain true to this insight and again and again fell back into the discredited position that separates the subject and object of consciousness, the act of self-positing from the I's consciousness of this act, and is therefore guilty of reifying the I as a quasi-substantial "ego," one might reply that it is not *Fichte* who is guilty of this dualism and reification so much as it is *the conscious I itself*! For what the Jena *Wissenschaftslehre* demonstrates is that a free subject cannot posit itself as such except as materially *embodied* and spatiotemporally situated—and, in this sense, "reified." And, of course, no sooner does it do this than it inevitably *distinguishes itself* as a freely self-positing subject from this bodily "ego.")[18]

2. Anstoß *and* Aufforderung *in the Later Jena* Wissenschaftslehre

Before turning to a brief consideration of some of the more important implications of the doctrine of the *Anstoß*—or, if you prefer, of this clear recognition of the underivability of finitude—for Fichte's overall account of subjectivity, as well as for his philosophy as a whole, some mention—however cursory—must be made of a significant ambiguity in the use of the term *Anstoß* in the 1794–1795 *Grundlage* and of the problematic relationship of the same to the later, revised version of the Jena *Wissenschaftslehre*. In the *Grundlage* the doctrine of the *Anstoß* is presented at the highest possible level of abstraction. All that we can say about the actual *content* of the *Anstoß* is that it is supposed to be identified with "feeling." But what *sorts* of feelings are actually suited for "checking" and "stimulating" the activity of the I in the manner required by Fichte's account?

The most obvious answer to this question is sense impressions, that is, feelings or sensations such as "sweet," "hot," or "blue." And, indeed, Fichte himself cites precisely such examples, both in the *Grundlage* and in his 1795 elaboration of the "distinctive character of the *Wissenschaftslehre* with respect to the theoretical power,"[19] and he repeats this in his discussions of "feeling" qua "original limitation" of the I in the *Wissen-*

---

18. See Manfred Frank, *Die Unhintergehbarkeit von Individualität* (Frankfurt: Suhrkamp, 1986), p. 34.
19. See, e.g., *Grundriß*, GA, 1.3.155 (SW, 1.13), where the *Anstoß* is identified with "sensible impressions" (*Eindrücke*) affecting the I. See too 1.2.437–46 (SW, 1.311–12).

schaftslehre nova methodo and in the *Versuch einer neuen Darstellung* (where, incidentally, the term *Anstoß* does not occur at all, though the account of the role of "original feeling" in the self-constitution of the I is explicitly reaffirmed, along with the clear recognition that such an "original limitation" of the I can never be "derived" from anything higher).[20]

Nevertheless, in Fichte's writings and lectures after 1795 it becomes increasingly apparent that, in addition to and alongside sensible *qualia*, there are present to the I immediate feelings of a radically different sort, feelings even better suited to the role assigned to the *Anstoß* in the *Grundlage*. The "feelings" in question are those associated with one's immediate sense of "being summoned" or "solicited" (Fichte's word is *aufgefordert*) to limit one's own freedom in recognition of and out of respect for the freedom of others. As in the case of such later philosophers as Hegel

---

20. See the discussion of the "original limitation of the I" in § 6 of the "Zweite Einleitung" to the *Versuch*, where we are reminded that,

> just as certainly as I posit myself at all, I posit myself as limited, and this occurs as a consequence of my intuition of my own act of self-positing. I am finite in virtue of this intuition.
>
> Since this limitation of mine conditions my positing of myself, it constitutes an original limitation.—One might still demand some further explanation of this; and thus one might try to account for my limitation as the object of reflection by referring to my necessary limitation as the reflecting subject—an explanation that would imply that the reason I am finite for myself is because I can think only of what is finite. Or, conversely, one might try to account for the limitation of the reflecting subject by referring to the limitation of the object of reflection—an explanation that would imply that the reason I think only of what is finite is because I myself am finite. But neither of these explanations would explain anything at all; for I am originally neither the reflecting subject nor the object of reflection, and neither of these is determined by the other. Instead, I am *both of these in their unity with each other*; though I am admittedly unable to think of this unity, because whenever I think, I must distinguish the object of reflection from the reflecting subject.
>
> By virtue of its intuition and of its concept, every limitation is a *completely determinate* limitation; no limitation is, as it were, a limitation "as such" or "in general."
>
> As we can see, the necessity *of some limitation of the I* has been derived from the very possibility of the I. The *specific determinacy* of this limitation is, however, not something that can be derived in this way; because, as we can also see, such determinacy is itself what provides the condition for the very possibility of all I-hood. Consequently, we have arrived at the point at which all deduction comes to an end. The determinacy in question appears to be something absolutely contingent and furnishes us with the *merely empirical* element in our cognition. It is because of this determinacy, for example, that I am, of all possible rational beings, a *human being*, and that, of all human beings, I am this *specific* person, etc.
>
> The determinate character of my limitation manifests itself as a limitation of my practical power (this is the point where philosophy is driven from the theoretical to the practical realm). This determinate limitation is immediately perceived as a *feeling*: sweet, red, cold, etc. (GA, 1.4.242–43 [SW, 1.489–90])

For further elaboration of this point, see, above all, the discussion, in § 8 of the *Wissenschaftslehre novo methodo*, of the "system of feeling."

and Sartre, Fichte treats intersubjectivity not primarily as an epistemological issue concerning "our knowledge of other minds," but rather as an immediate and essential modification of self-consciousness itself. Though there are perhaps traces and anticipations of this account of intersubjectivity in some of Fichte's earlier writings, it is, I would maintain, first made explicit in 1796, in Part 1 of Fichte's *Grundlage des Naturrechts*, which commences with a justly famous demonstration that the very possibility of self-consciousness depends upon one's consciousness of oneself as an individual person, which in turn depends upon one's free recognition of other free individuals—a recognition accomplished and signaled by the aforementioned voluntary self-limitation of one's own freedom out of respect for the freedom of others.

This new appreciation on Fichte's part of the role of mutual recognition in the constitution of consciousness had significant repercussions for the new presentation of the basic principles of the *Wissenschaftslehre* that he began expounding in his lectures on *Wissenschaftslehre nova methodo* and elsewhere. In this new presentation, as in the *Grundlage des Naturrechts*, it is clear that not only must the I contain within itself those "original limitations" that we have described above as sensible feelings, but it must also contain within itself an immediate awareness—a "feeling," if you will—of the freedom of other finite, rational beings. And all of this is possible only insofar as the I is immediately conscious of an *Aufforderung*, that is, of a "summons" to limit its own freedom out of recognition of the freedom of the other.

Clearly, there is an intimate connection between this doctrine of the *Aufforderung* and the previously discussed doctrine of the *Anstoß*, a connection emphasized by Fichte himself in § 3 of the *Naturrecht*, where he explicitly identifies the *Aufforderung* as a kind of *Anstoß*.[21] Thus one could

---

21. In the preceding section of the *Grundlage des Naturrechts*, self-consciousness has been shown to be possible only if the conscious subject is able to perceive its own free self-activity. But how is such a synthesis of objectivity and self-activity possible as an object of consciousness? Fichte's answer is as follows:

Both are completely united when we think of a *subject's being determined to determine itself*, a summons [*Aufforderung*] to the subject to decide to act efficaciously.

Insofar as what is required is an object, it must be given to sensation, and indeed to *outer* sensation.... But this object is not comprehended otherwise, and cannot be comprehended otherwise, than as a mere summons of the subject to act [*eine bloße Aufforderung des Subjeks zum Handeln*]. As certainly, therefore, as the subject comprehends this object, then it just as certainly has a concept of its own freedom and self-activity—and indeed, as a concept given to it from outside. It receives the concept of its free efficacy, not as something that *exists* in the present moment, for that would be a true contradiction, but as something that *ought to* exist in some future moment.

(The question was: how is the subject able to discover itself as an object? In order to discover *itself*, it must discover itself only as self-active, otherwise it does not discover

say that, at least by the year 1796,[22] Fichte recognized not one, but two sorts of *Anstoß:* first, that original "system of feeling," thanks to which the I posits for itself an external, phenomenal world and posits itself as an internally and externally limited agent therein; and second, an immediately felt, but nonsensible "summons" to exercise one's own freedom and to do so in a manner that respects and recognizes the freedom of others, thereby affirming one's place in the supersensible or noumenal realm—again, not as an "absolute I," but as a limited (in this case, to be sure, a "freely limited") individual.[23] Such a scheme is, in my view at least, present in both the unpublished lectures on *Wissenschaftslehre novo*

---

itself; . . . In order to discover itself as the *object* (of its own reflection) the subject cannot discover itself as *determining* itself to self-activity (how the matter may be, in itself, viewed from the transcendental standpoint, is not the question here, but only, how it must appear to the subject which is to be investigated); instead, it must discover itself as determined to self-activity by an external *Anstoß*, though one which must nevertheless leave him his full freedom for self-determination, since otherwise the first point would be lost and the subject would not discover itself as an I.

In order to make the last point clearer I will take for granted some things to which we will return in the future. The subject cannot discover itself to be required actually to act, even in a general sense, for then it would not be free, nor would it be an I. Should it decide to act, it can even less discover itself to be required to act in this or that determinate way, for then, once again, it would not be free, nor would it be an I. How then and in what sense is it determined to efficacy, in order to discover itself as an object? Only insofar as it discovers itself to be something that *could* act efficaciously here, something that is summoned [*aufgefordert*] to act efficaciously, but which can just as well not act.) (GA, 1.3.342–43 [SW, 3.33–34])

22. Some distinguished readers of Fichte, including Reinhard Lauth, Alexis Philonenko, and Thomas Hohler, find the doctrine of intersubjectivity, and hence the interpretation of the *Anstoß* as *Aufforderung*, to be at least implicit in the "Deduction of Representation" in Part 2 of the *Grundlage*. See Lauth, "Das Problem der Interpersonalität bei Fichte," in *Transzendentale Entwicklungslinien von Descartes bis zu Marx und Dostojewski* (Hamburg: Meiner, 1989), pp. 180–95, esp. pp. 184–87; Philonenko, *La liberté humaine dans la philosophie de Fichte* (Paris: Vrin, 1966), p. 328; and Hohler, *Imagination and Reflection: Intersubjectivity. Fichte's "Grundlage" of 1794* (The Hague: Martinus Nijoff, 1982), pp. 68ff.

I must confess, however, that, despite Fichte's remark, *"kein Du kein Ich; kein Ich, kein Du"* (GA, 1.2.337 [SW, 1.189]), I remain unconvinced on this point, and would contend that, while nothing in the *Grundlage* is inconsistent with such an interpretation of the *Anstoß*, this is nevertheless not what Fichte had specifically in mind in the 1794–1795 presentation, though it is certainly present in the version of 1796–1799. For an interpretation that supports my own, see Claudio Cesa's essay in *Difettività e fondmento*, ed. A. Masullo (Naples, 1984), pp. 39–60.

23. One of the most brilliant of the new generation of Fichte scholars, Alain Perrinjaquet, has recently argued for recognizing the necessary presence of a *third* type of *Anstoß* in the overall system of the Jena *Wissenschaftslehre:* viz., the necessary "checking" of the "pure will" by the "natural drive" described in the *System der Sittenlehre*—without which there could no distinctively "moral will." See Perrinjaquet, "Le fondement de la philosophie pratique des années 1796–1800: *Grundlage der gesammten Wissenschaftslehre* ou *Wissenschaftslehre nova methodo?*," *Les Cahiers de Philosophie* [numèro hors sèrie, *La bicentenaire de la doctrine de la science de Fichte (1794–1994)*, (Lille, 1995): 149–67].

methhodo and in the published *System der Sittenlehre*, even if the word *Anstoß* hardly appears in either of these texts.[24]

This substantial enrichment of the earlier and more abstract doctrine of the *Anstoß* surely raises a number of important questions—concerning, for example, the precise relationship between the various sorts of *Anstoß*,[25] or concerning the relationship between the phenomenal and the noumenal realms or between "belief" and "knowledge"—not to mention a serious metaquestion concerning the possibility of satisfactorily answering such questions within the framework of the Jena *Wissenschaftslehre*. Such questions, however, must all be postponed. The only point I wish to make on this occasion is that the doctrine of the *Aufforderung* by no means mitigates but merely reinforces the most important result of our examination of the doctrine of the *Anstoß* as presented in the *Grundlage:* that is, the necessary finitude of all subjectivity and the unavoidable element of alien contingency—"facticity," if you will—at the heart of the Fichtean self.

3. On Human Finitude: Anstoß *as Affront*

In addition to the two senses that have already been discussed, the word *Anstoß* has another common, and vaguely biblical, meaning, a meaning that is also not without relevance to Fichte's technical usage of the term. More than a mere obstacle or hindrance, an *Anstoß*, understood in this third sense, is an *affront* to one's pride or intelligence, an *offense* against one's self-importance and sense of dignity, and hence a source of *umbrage* or *chagrin*. This is the sense reflected in Luther's choice of the German phrase *Stein des Anstoßens* to render the familiar

---

24. To be sure, the term *Anstoß* is almost completely absent from this revised presentation (occurring only once in the "Halle transcript" of the lectures on *Wissenschaftslehre nova methodo* and twice in the "Krause transcript" of the same). Instead, Fichte talks simply about *Gefühl* and *Aufforderung*.

The few occurrence of the term *Anstoß* that do occur in the *Wissenschaftslehre nova methodo*, however, simply confirm the interpretation of *Anstoß* as signifying the *Gebundenheit* or "constrained condition" of the I's real and ideal activities. See 4.2.68 and Fichte, *Wissenschaftslehre nova methodo*, ed. Erich Fuchs (Hamburg: Meiner, 1982), pp. 73 and 126.

25. It is perhaps worth calling attention, even if only in passing, to a recently published and little-known note from the winter of 1794–1795 or 1795–1796 that seems to have a direct—if problematic—bearing on the relation between the various senses of *Anstoß*:

> Even the philosopher explains this production [of representation by the productive imagination] by referring to an *Anstoß*. As we have seen, my *activity* is *limited*. This original limitation is a limitation that occurs through a duty. Every other limitation is, in turn, only a *sensible* presentation [*Darstellung*], by means of the imagination, of this original limitation. (GA, 2.4.360)

description (in 1 Peter 2.8) of Christian faith as "a stone of stumbling and a rock of offense" for the unbeliever[26]—indeed, as something of a *scandal*.

The *Anstoß* of the Jena *Wissenschaftslehre* is one in this sense as well, not for the philosopher, of course, but for the proudly self-positing I, which insists upon its own essential independence from all that it itself has not freely determined and hence finds itself chagrined and humiliated by having to recognize the unavoidable element of sheer contingency and limitation present not simply within the world, but within the I itself. For a subject that identifies its own dignity with its assertion of its self-sufficiency and freedom, such a discovery is not a welcome one. It is an affront to that very self-conception.

Its reputation to the contrary notwithstanding, Fichte's Jena *Wissenschaftslehre* is in fact a merciless and uncompromising exposé of the vanity of the "absolutely self-positing I" and an attempt to demonstrate—starting from the presumptive perspective of just such an autonomous and self-sufficient subject—the utter untenability of such a claim. Allow me to elaborate: It should be evident from what has already been said that the I can be an I only if it is limited, and moreover, only if it is limited *for itself*. An I that cannot posit (i.e., reflect upon) itself is not an I at all. The I, however, can reflect upon itself only insofar as it reflects upon itself as a finite, determinate self; and it can reflect upon itself as a determinate self only insofar as it relates itself to and indeed finds itself to be a part of a world of material objects related to one another in space and time, as well as an individual "citizen" in a republic of other free agents, whose very freedom makes certain claims upon its own freedom. At the same time that the I posits itself as finite and determinate, however, it inevitably (at least according to Fichte) finds itself dissatisfied with this very determinacy and finitude, since the latter conflicts with its immediate practical awareness of—indeed insistence upon—its own lack of any essential determinacy. In other words, the Fichtean self does not merely "register" or "recognize" the presence within its own immediate consciousness of limitation and hindrance; instead, it takes the *Anstoß* personally, as it were; it is *offended* or *affronted* thereby. This conflict between our immediate awareness of our own limitations and our equally immediate awareness of our own freedom presents itself within ordinary consciousness primarily as a vague sense of "longing" to overcome the very limits in question, coupled with or supplemented by a categorical awareness, first, of one's obligation to "determine the Not-I" by transforming it from whatever it actually "is" into what it "ought to be," and, second,

---

26. See too, e.g., Romans 12.13, 1 Corinthians 8.9.

of the need to construct a just political order in which individual freedom can be preserved.

Whereas it is certainly correct to characterize the early *Wissenschaftslehre* as a "philosophy of striving," it is vital to recall that only a finite, limited I can strive in the manner described within this system. Indeed, that is precisely the main thesis of the *Grundlage:* only a finite I can be an I at all. Thus, if it is true, as the first principle of the *Grundlage* asserts, that "*das Ich setzt sich selbst schlechthin*"—"the I simply posits itself" (or "the I posits itself absolutely")—then it must also be true that the I simply posits itself *as limited*. This, however, is not to say that the limits in question are posited (in the sense of being produced) by the I itself. On the contrary, the one thing that freedom, according to Fichte, cannot do is posit its own limitations. The limits in question have to be *discovered* not *created* by the freely self-positing subject. And if it is to posit *itself* as limited, then it must recognize these limits as *its own*. But these limits themselves must be, for their part, just as "ungrounded" and "ungroundable" as is the original freedom of the I; and hence the positing of the former must be just as "absolute" as that of the latter. Both I and Not-I, or rather, both the freedom and the determinacy of the finite I must be *schlechthin gesetzt*.[27] To put the same point somewhat paradoxically, though the I must "absolutely posit" itself, it is absolutely not absolute.

Far, then, from being wholly self-determined, the Fichtean I necessarily possesses a determinacy wholly beyond its own control, and only on this condition does it possess either freedom or consciousness. This original determinacy closely resembles what some later philosophers have described as the necessary "facticity" of the I. As in these later philosophies, so too in the Jena *Wissenschaftslehre:* the inescapable facticity or original determinacy of the self is not merely an obstacle to its free projects and hence an affront to its proud pretensions of self-sufficiency—though it *is* both of these things. At the same time, this facticity is also a necessary and essential condition for the possibility of both the theoretical and the practical activities of the I, without which there could be neither an I nor a Not-I.

But it is only through transcendental analysis of ordinary experience that we can grasp this point. Within everyday experience itself, the finite I tends to identify itself wholly—or at least wholeheartedly—only with one side of its own divided nature, namely, with its capacity for free self-determination, and hence to treat everything else as "Not-I." Not that there is anything wrong with such a practical, everyday self-under-

---

27. Indeed, this point is made exlicitly by Fichte himself; see GA, 1.2.292–94 (SW, 1.255–57).

standing: on the contrary, this is precisely the image of ourselves and of our responsibilities that, according to Fichte, we are morally obliged to affirm. Philosophy neither can nor should do anything to undermine this practical self-conception: it can only "explain" it.

Returning to our examination of Fichte's account of subjectivity, we can now appreciate how thoroughly the traditional caricature of the "absolutely free and self-contained" Fichtean self misrepresents and distorts the actual theory of selfhood that emerges from the *Wissenschaftslehre*, according to which consciousness always possesses an essential *openness* to the world. The task of somehow eliminating the gap between the conscious self and the objective world is simply not a task that can arise within the context of the *Wissenschaftslehre*, which considers the synthetic link between self and world, *Tathandlung* and *Anstoß*, to be a fundamental condition for the very possibility of any consciousness whatsoever. Far from being either a solipsistic fantasy or a narcissistic nightmare, the Fichtean self is a subject that is always and inevitably *engaged* in a realm that it, to be sure, helps constitute in its full "objectivity," but that always escapes and eludes its control. This is the import of Fichte's clear recognition that if the I is to encounter anything foreign at all, then it must encounter it *within itself*, since "if any difference is ever to enter into the I, difference must already be originally present within the I itself."[28] And this is why the doctrine of the *Anstoß*, far from being some sort of dogmatic residue of dualism or vestige of the "reflective model of consciousness,"[29] is, in fact, absolutely central, not just to the *Grundlage*, but—under the names "feeling" and "solicitation"—to the entire Jena *Wissenschaftslehre*.

In the systematic context of the *Grundlage*, neither *Tathandlung* nor *Anstoß* can be reduced to the other, and thus neither can be "accounted for" in the transcendental sense of being "derived" from something higher. On the other hand, the *necessity* of each can be derived from the positing of the other. If I am to be free, then I must be a finite part of the natural world; if there is to be a world for me, then I must be free: hence Fichte's frequent reference to what he calls the "original duality"

---

28. GA, 1.2.405 (SW, 1.272). See too GA, 1.2.408–9 (SW, 1.276). Thus, when Fichte claims that his philosophy goes beyond Kant's in its recognition that experience is not merely (as in the case of Kant) *conditioned,* but also *determined* by consciousness, it must be remembered that the consciousness in question is itself characterized by an *original determinacy* of its own. (See "Zweite Einleitung," GA, 1.4.229 [SW, 1.477].) A similar caveat applies to the interpretation of Fichte's easily misunderstood claim, in "Annalen des philosophischen Tons" and elsewhere, concerning the original identity between the realms of the a priori and the a posteriori (GA, 1.4.304–310 [SW, 2.471–79]).

29. See Henrich, *Fichtes ursprüngliche Einsicht*, p. 41.

of the self.³⁰ Struggle as we may—and must—this original conflict within the self can never be eliminated, for the simple reason that this conflict is the condition for the very possibility of the self.³¹

In an early letter to Niethammer, Fichte expressed his belief that "pure philosophy is acquainted with only a *single* I, and this one I ought not to contradict itself."³² Unfortunately—or rather, fortunately!—however, it always does. And, as Fichte came to see with greater and greater clarity, the I always *must* contradict itself, however much it may—and indeed *must*—struggle endlessly to overcome its own self-contradiction. In the end, the unity of the self is a necessary, infinite Idea of reason— nothing less, but also nothing more.³³ The real self is always the divided self, the self that simultaneously affirms its own radical autonomy and remains open to and constrained by a realm beyond its own devising— a realm both of material things and of other rational individuals. The I, however, is by no means determined by this necessary relationship to its other, but, as a freely self-determining practical agent, constantly reasserts and realizes its (always relative and partial) independence thereof—which is precisely what it means to be a "finite self."³⁴

4. *Fichte's Abstract Realism*

Insofar as Fichte's account of consciousness and experience recognizes and ultimately presupposes the sheer facticity of the *Anstoß*, then

---

30. It is thus appropriate that the *Grundlage* should conclude with a reaffirmation of this same original duality, viz., with an eloquent description of "the duality of striving and reflection" and of their reciprocal interdependence (1.2.423 [SW, 1.294]; see too 1.2.432 [SW, 1.304-305]).

31. Note that, since this conflict depends upon something more than the productive activity of the I (inasmuch as it presupposes the equally "groundless" presence within the I of the *Anstoß*), it is misleading of Henrichs and others to attribute to Fichte a "production theory" of the I.

The claim that the Fichtean I "produces itself" has also been challenged, albeit from a somewhat different direction, by Reinhard Hiltscher, in his essay "Stellt Fichtes Theorie von 'Ich' in der WL von 1794/95 eine Produktionstheorie des 'Ich' dar?," *Fichte-Studien* 5 (1993): 107-16. Against the "production theory of the I," Hiltscher too notes that even though "reason provides an a priori foundation for the *possibility* of the *Anstoß*, it nevertheless no longer grounds the *fact* thereof" (p. 115).

32. Letter to F. I. Niethammer, December 6, 1793.

33. See 1.2.403-4 (SW, 1.269-70).

34. For interpretations of Fichte that emphasize the essential *finitude* of the Fichtean self, see, in addition to Philonenko's seminal *La liberté humaine:* Luigi Pareyson, "La deduzione del finito nella prima dottrina della scienza di Fichte," *Filosofia* 1 (1950): 13-40; Thomas P. Hohler, "Fichte and the Problem of Finitude," *Southwestern Journal of Philosophy* 7 (1976): 15-33; and Frederick Neuhouser, *Fichte's Theory of Subjectivity* (Cambridge: Cambridge University Press, 1990).

he is certainly correct in asserting, in the passage we have already cited, that "this manner of explanation is, as is immediately obvious, realistic, yet it is based upon a much more abstract form of realism than any of the other, previously discussed varieties of realism."[35] Consequently, Fichtean idealism must always be balanced by Fichtean realism, the core of which is the doctrine of *practical feeling* reaffirmed in the following passage from § 5 of the *Grundlage*:

> The *Wissenschaftslehre* is thus *realistic*. It shows that the consciousness of finite natures simply cannot be explained unless one assumes the presence of a force that is independent of them and completely opposed to them, upon which they themselves depend for their empirical existence. However, it asserts no more than this: that there is such an opposed force, which is not cognized but only felt by the finite creature in question.[36]

(This is the same doctrine of feeling that is somewhat awkwardly and misleadingly signaled, in a footnote to the Preface of the first edition of *Ueber den Begriff der Wissenschaftslehre*, by the assertion that "things are *represented* as *appearances*, whereas they are *felt as things in themselves*; ... no representations at all would be possible without feeling; but ... things in themselves can be recognized only *subjectively*, i.e., insofar as they affect our feeling [*insofern sie auf unser Gefühl wirken*].")[37]

This, then, is the essence of Fichtean "realism": the recognition that the I cannot "simply posit" its own limitations, but must instead "discover" them; and the original locus of such a discovery is that determinate "system of feeling" that is simply "there." It is equally true, of course, that in order for the I to "discover" such immediate feelings at all, it must explicitly "posit them" for itself, thereby transforming them from practical limitations of its own striving into theoretically knowable components of an objective, material world—in a process elaborately described in the various "deductions of representation" that feature so prominently in Fichte's early presentations of his system. In other words, Fichtean realism must constantly be balanced by Fichtean idealism, the cardinal principle of which is the insistence that all being is being for a subject, and hence, that all *Sein* is *Gesetztsein*.

The most sophisticated form of pure idealism recognized in the *Grundlage* is what Fichte calls "quantitative idealism" and explicitly describes as "even more abstract" than all of the preceding forms of idealism.[38] The principle of such "abstract idealism" is this: *"The I is finite, simply because it is finite."*[39] That is, such idealism maintains that the neces-

---

35. GA, 1.2.355 (SW, 1.210).
37. GA, 1.2.109 (SW, 1.29).
39. GA, 1.2.333 (SW, 1.184).

36. GA, 1.2.411 (SW, 1.280).
38. See GA, 1.2.333 (SW, 1.184).

sary finitude of the I is simply a consequence of its own absolute positing. But even this most sophisticated form of pure idealism must be rejected in favor of a still more sophisticated position, one that recognizes the incoherence of the claim that the original limits of the I can be understood as products of free positing. Instead, this still more sophisticated position correctly insists upon the "*real presence of a limitation of the I*, without any contribution on the part of the I as such, either through absolute activity, as the qualitative idealist maintains, or by virtue of a law inherent in its nature, as is held by the quantitative idealist."[40] Fichte's name for this position, which he considers superior to any form of pure idealism, is "critical, quantitative realism." What the quantitative realist asserts is not the independent existence of a realm of external things-in-themselves, but rather "the reality, independent of the I, of a mere *determination* [*Bestimmung*]. There is a determination present in the I, the ground of which is not to be posited in the I: for him, this is a fact, and he is cut off from inquiring into the ground of this determination *as such*. That is to say, for him it is purely and simply present and without any ground or reason."[41] A more familiar name for such "critical quantitative idealism" is "critical idealism." The major difference, according to Fichte, between this "critical idealism" or "quantitative realism" and the foregoing "quantitative idealism"—as well as the main reason for the superiority of the former—is that the former, unlike the latter, does not attempt to ground the reality of the I's original determinacy in anything higher; more specifically, it does not attempt to ground it in the absolute self-positing of the self. It simply recognizes such determinacy for what it is—a contingent and inexplicable fact about the I itself.[42]

Nevertheless, even quantitative realism is not the last word in philosophy, since, like all forms of realism, it cannot explain positing as such, and thus it cannot explain the transition from determinacy to consciousness, from, in Fichte's language, the real to the ideal series, the finite to the infinite. What is called for, then, is a synthesis of quantitative idealism—which can explain the "transition" in question—and quantitative realism—which correctly recognizes the contingency of sheer facticity. This highest standpoint, the standpoint of the *Wissenschaftslehre* itself, is therefore described by Fichte as "critical quantitative idealism," or, more perspicuously, as "real-idealism" or "ideal-realism."[43] Such a position frankly acknowledges its own inability to adduce any higher "ground" for the original limitation of the I. Like quantitative realism, it views these limits as contingently given and hence as merely discovered. But,

40. GA, 1.2.334 (SW, 1.185).
42. GA, 1.2.336 (SW, 1.186–87).
41. GA, 1.2.334–35 (SW, 1.186).
43. GA, 1.2.412 (SW, 1.281).

like quantitative idealism, it also recognizes that a limit is a limit for the I only when it has, in turn, been posited as such. The real-idealism of the *Wissenschaftslehre* thus confirms what Fichte calls "the law of the mediacy of positing," according to which the I cannot posit itself as a subject without also positing an object, and cannot posit an object without positing itself as the subject for which this object exists, thereby demonstrating, in Fichte's own words, "no ideality, no reality, and vice versa."[44]

We now return, finally, to the doctrine of the *Anstoß* and the implications of the same for Fichte's distinctive philosophical position: For all of its reliance upon the immediacy of mere "feeling," Fichte's doctrine must never be confused either with a philosophy of direct feeling (such as Jacobi's) or with any sort of "commonsense" or "direct" realism (such as, perhaps, Reid's). We are no more conscious of our immediate "feelings" than we are of the immediate unity of subject and object that is expressed in the *Tathandlung* with which we began our analysis and that is implicitly present in every act of free self-determination as well as in every moment of mere object consciousness. Both of these absolute poles of Fichte's transcendental explanation of subjectivity and of experience become objects of thetic consciousness only within philosophical reflection, where they are of course abstracted from the full, rich context of lived experience. On the other hand, though transcendental analysis may perhaps succeed in convincing someone that an *Anstoß* or "original fact of the mind" of the sort described in the early *Wissenschaftslehre* is essential for the possibility of ordinary consciousness, no mere philosophy is able to demonstrate the *actual occurrence* of such an *Anstoß;* just as Fichte's own systematic presentation of philosophy is equally unable to prove the reality of that freedom with which it begins. From the standpoint of transcendental philosophy, both freedom and the occurrence of the *Anstoß* are simply presuppositions taken over from everyday life— within which alone their reality can be exhibited. Hence, according to Fichte, the only proper response to anyone who would contest the reality of the *Anstoß* is not to urge him to read more philosophy, but rather to refer him to the testimony of his own inner experience, within which alone the reality of the *Anstoß*—and hence of anything else—can be, not proven (*erweisen*), but displayed or shown (*dartun*).[45] Philosophy can prove *that* such an *Anstoß* must occur *if* consciousness is to be possible; but it cannot prove that it *does* occur.[46] (This is not exactly like Dr. John-

---

44. See GA, 1.2.332–333 (SW, 1.183).
45. See GA, 1.2.390, 400, and 408 (SW, 1.252, 265, and 275).
46. "The infinitely extending activity of the I is, at some point or another, supposed to be checked and driven back into itself. *That* this occurs as a fact is something that simply

son's kicking a stone to refute Berkeley, but there is this similarity: namely, the recognition that our experience of "objectivity" is always a consequence of our own goal-oriented activity.)

Like the self it describes, the Jena *Wissenschaftslehre* is a system that remains forever open to the "infinite richness of experience."[47] For this is a philosophy that acknowledges the presence, within the I itself, of a realm of irreducible otherness, absolute contingency, and ultimate incomprehensibility. To be sure, Fichte believed that we can explain a great deal about the world and ourselves through a combination of empirical research and transcendental analysis. But the question "Why does the world have the particular experiential properties that it does?"—that is, "Why does the I, and hence the world, possess the original determinacy or constitution that it does?"—is a question that has no answer, and certainly no philosophical one. Only a complete neglect of the doctrine of the *Anstoß* and an ignorance of the implications of the same can explain how a philosopher as astute as Josiah Royce could have criticized the *Wissenschaftslehre* for its failure to answer such questions as "Why do I create a world that has a belt of asteroids between the orbits of Mars and Jupiter?"[48] However appropriate such a question might be when directed toward the speculative idealism of a Schelling or a Hegel, it has no force at all against Fichte's more modest and purely transcendental project—according to which not just Angelus Selesius's rose, but every *Anstoß* whatsoever *ist ohne Warum*.

This is the point of Fichte's repeated insistence that, though philosophy can indeed derive the necessity of the *Anstoß* for the possibility of consciousness, it is utterly unable to derive or to demonstrate either the *actuality* or the *specific content* of the same. Instead, the *Wissenschaftslehre* seeks to reconcile us to what Fichte described as "the incomprehensible boundaries within which we simply find ourselves to be confined," a reconciliation obtained by demonstrating that it is only *within* such boundaries that we can possess either theoretical consciousness or practical freedom.[49] As for the boundaries themselves—facticity and freedom—

---

cannot be derived from the I, as we have often mentioned. However, it certainly can be shown that it must occur *if* any actual consciousness is to be possible" (GA, 1.2.408 [SW, 1.275]).

47. One of the few readers to appreciate and to call attention to this aspect of the *Wissenschaftslehre* is Jean Hyppolite, who praises Fichte's philosophy precisely for its ability to answer the question "How is encounter possible?" without resorting to any sort of transcendent leap beyond the limits of consciousness. See "L'idée fichtéene de la doctrine de la science et le projet Husserlien," in *Figures de la pensée philosophique* (Paris: Presses Universitaires de France, 1971), 1.177.

48. *The Spirit of Modern Philosophy* (Boston: Houghton, Mifflin, 1892), p. 167.

49. GA, 1.5.353 (SW, 5.184).

whether we follow Fichte in employing abstract, figurative names like *"Anstoß"* and *"Tathandlung,"* or prefer metonymies such as "the starry heavens above" and "the moral law within," in either case the search for a ground, and hence all philosophical explanation, comes at an end at just these two extremes. Understood in this manner, philosophy can be construed as using all of the analytical and dialectical tools at its disposal merely to confirm and to reestablish the sense of "wonder" with which it so naively began.

By now it should long since have become clear that Fichte remains a dualist, albeit of a peculiar sort. The dualism of the *Wissenschaftslehre* is not that of the I and the Not-I, but is instead a dualism of the finite and infinite aspects or activities of one and the same I. And just as the *Wissenschaftslehre* is ultimately dualistic, so is the self it describes: the Fichtean self remains a profoundly divided self; and, for Fichte, difference is not merely the opposite of identity, it is the condition for its possibility. The undifferentiated unity of consciousness—the congruence of the I with its own practical self-conception—can never be more than an infinite goal. Just as Fichte explicitly recognized the reciprocal relationship between identity and difference, he also viewed the quest for unity—and hence the fact of contradiction—as the moving force not only of systematic philosophy, but, more importantly, of both theoretical self-consciousness and practical self-activity. For this reason the "real-idealism" of the Jena *Wissenschaftslehre* could also be described as a *dialectical dualism*.[50]

This indeed is one of the main reasons why Fichte's conception of the self has proven so difficult to grasp and to categorize. For self-consciousness is portrayed in this philosophy as a dynamic, unstable, and unending synthetic *process,* each moment of which refers us to every other moment. Thus, though we must (for essentially practical reasons) begin our systematic philosophizing with the assertion of the sheer freedom of the I, this freedom is no sooner posited unconditionally (*schlechthin gesetzt*) than it is discovered to be conditioned by something else—until ultimately it is revealed to be conditioned by the presence of a particular *Bestimmtsein*, an involuntary *Anstoß*, that would appear to be the very opposite of freedom. Fichte's point is that it is precisely within the dynamic field produced by the tension between these "opposites" that all life and consciousness, all acting and knowing—in short, everything that per-

---

50. On the profoundly "dialectical" character of the Jena *Wissenschaftslehre*, as well as the ineradicable dualism implicit in Fichte's conception of the finite I, see, above all, Reinhard Lauth, "Der Ursprung der Dialektik in Fichtes Philosophie," in *Transzendentale Entwicklungslinien*, pp. 209–26.

tains to what he sometimes called the *"der Kreislauf der Funktionen des Ich"*[51]—become possible.

51. See 1.2.423 (SW, 1.294). Note the similarities between Fichte's description of this "circle of the functions of the I" and Sartre's account, in Part 2 of *L'être et le néant*, of "the circle of selfhood" (*le circuit de l'ipséité*). Hegel, too, especially in the Introduction to the *Phänomenologie des Geistes*, calls attention to the deeply "circular" character of the relationship between the object of consciousness and the conscious, self-examining subject. Significantly, however, Fichte's account is closer to Sartre's than to Hegel's, inasmuch as neither Fichte nor Sartre hold out the possibility of ever escaping from this "circle"—of moving, with Hegel, from the dyadic and riven "standpoint of consciousness" to the supposedly higher and more unified "standpoint of spirit."

5 Fichte's Appeal Today: The Hidden Primacy of the Practical
KARL AMERIKS

Today's resurgence of interest in Fichte's philosophy is for the most part tied closely to Fichte's claim to develop and improve upon *Kant's* work. The current interest in Kant's philosophy, in turn, is often tied to its focus on the *self,* and, more specifically, to its focus on the self's *activity.* And this focus, in turn, is often expressed—in a natural but too narrow way—in terms of the famous doctrine of the "primacy of the *practical.*"

The popular appeal of Fichte's philosophy can be understood easily enough in terms of its being the first important radicalization of this doctrine. But although the impact of the doctrine of the primacy of the practical should in no way be minimized, one should also never forget that this doctrine, for both Kant and Fichte, is embedded in more general considerations, and especially in an underlying philosophical conception of the self. On a number of other occasions I have critically examined Fichte's radicalization of Kant's theory of the self's activity of *apperception,* for it is precisely Fichte's revision of the Kantian conception of this basic power that has formed the point of departure for much of the most interesting recent work on Fichte—for example, studies by Dieter Henrich, Frederick Neuhouser, and Manfred Frank.[1] This work often

---

[1]. See esp. D. Henrich, *Fichtes ursprüngliche Einsicht* (Frankfurt: Klostermann, 1967), *Identität und Objektivität* (Heidelberg: Carl Winter, 1976), and "The Identity of the Subject in the Transcendental Deduction," in *Reading Kant,* ed. E. Schaper and W. Vossenkuhl (Oxford: Blackwell, 1989), pp. 250–80; Frederick Neuhouser, *Fichte's Theory of Subjectivity* (Cambridge: Cambridge University Press, 1990); Manfred Frank, *Selbstbewusstsein und Selbsterkenntnis* (Stuttgart: Reclam, 1991), and *Selbstbewusstseinstheorien von Fichte bis Sartre* (Frankfurt: Suhrkamp, 1991). Cf. also Robert Pippin, *Hegel's Idealism: The Satisfactions of Self-Consciousness* (Cambridge: Cambridge University Press, 1989), and, for a powerful Kantian and non-Fichtean theory of radical self-activity, Gerold Prauss, *Die Welt und wir* 2 vols. (Stuttgart: Metzler, 1990, 1993). See my discussion of Henrich in "Kant and Guyer on Apperception," *Archiv für Geschichte der Philosophie* 65 (1983): 174–86, and "Kant and the Self: A Retrospective," in *Figuring the Self,* ed. D. Klemm and G. Zöller (Albany: State University of New York Press, 1997), pp. 55–72; of Neuhouser in "Kant and the Self"; of Frank

proceeds by closely connecting two of Fichte's most basic concerns: the notion of the self and the notion of activity. My contention here, however, will be that there is one crucial point that this work often does not make clear enough, namely, that although in Fichte the general phenomenon of self-activity *reflects* interest in the practical, it is still not quite the same thing as that interest. This is because, in its most general meaning, the self's activity, and even the fundamental activity of apperception, is not itself strictly practical in Fichte's favored sense of the term. Thus, whereas before I have stressed problems in recent Fichtean interpretations of *theoretical* self-activity, and, in particular, of apperception, on this occasion I will be taking a critical perspective on the recent Fichtean treatment—or, more exactly, lack of treatment—of the fundamental role of *practical* self-activity, and, in particular, of morality.

Fichte's concern with the practical has two main dimensions: the dimension of *actual* sociohistorical *praxis*, and the dimension of the doctrine of practical *reason* as the primary form of reason and as fundamentally *moral* in that role. With respect to the first dimension, it is sufficient here simply to note the general form of Fichte's career, his lifetime sympathy for the French Revolution, and his engagement in the institutional renovation of German academic and political life.[2] Fichte's activism was extremely important, but my focus here will rather concern the second (and of course not unrelated) dimension of his primarily practical orientation, namely, the very foundations of his philosophy. That philosophy gives practical reason an absolute primacy in a multitude of ways—and in all these ways it is important to remember that Fichte, like Kant, usu-

---

in "The Ineliminable Subject: From Kant to Frank," in *The Modern Subject: Conceptions of the Self in Classical German Philosophy*, ed. K. Ameriks and D. Sturma (Albany: State University of New York Press, 1995); of Pippin in "Hegel and Idealism," *Monist* 74 (1991): 386–402; and of Prauss in "Contemporary German Epistemology," *Inquiry* 25 (1982): 125–38. The broadest presentation of my interpretation of the Fichtean era is in "Kant, Fichte, and Short Arguments to Idealism," *Archiv für Geschichte der Philosophie* 72 (1990): 63–85.

2. Among Fichte's earliest tracts were passionate and influential defenses of the French Revolution ("A Discourse on the Reclamation of the Freedom of Thought from the Princes of Europe, Who Have Hitherto Suppressed It," 1793; "Contribution toward Rectifying the Public's Judgment of the French Revolution," 1793–1794); his first academic appointment, in Jena, inspired the revolutionary cultural movement of German romanticism; his first academic treatise (*Attempt at a Critique of All Revelation*, 1792) was an anticipation of Kant's liberal views on church and religion, and led eventually to the famous "Atheismusstreit" (1798–1799), or political dispute over teaching atheism; and he anticipated Kant again by publishing a detailed critical political and ethical system (*Foundations of Natural Right* [the "Naturrecht"], 1796; *System of Ethical Theory* [the "Sittenlehre"], 1798), one that in important ways also led beyond Kant by developing cornerstones of later Hegelian and socialist doctrines. For brief overviews, see Allen Wood, "Fichte's Philosophical Revolution," *Philosophical Topics* 19 (1991): 1–28; and D. Breazeale, "Fichte and Schelling: The Jena Period," in *The Routledge History of Philosophy*, vol. 6: *The Age of German Idealism*, ed. R. Solomon and K. Higgins (London: Routledge, 1993), pp. 138–60.

ally used the term "practical" in its pure sense, as equivalent to "moral," and that he understood "morality" in turn as defined by freedom and autonomy. More specifically, "the practical" involves both the executive power to determine oneself absolutely, in absolute freedom, as an uncaused cause, and also the legislative capacity to do so with an orientation to the thought of Kantian *duty*, the thought that the self determines itself from laws of its own essence, its own rationality. In this context, the doctrine of the primacy of the practical therefore has to do primarily with a preeminence of deontological moral reason. This preeminence, however, can be and was taken in different ways by Kant and by Fichte.

For Kant, the preeminence of pure practical reason was a matter of its (1) *significance* and of its (2) *detail*, but not of its (3) *method*. Kant spoke of our awareness of duty as revealing a fundamental "fact of reason," namely, the fact that we recognize the call of pure practical reason to follow the moral law, the categorical imperative. This law is (1) the most significant object of our attention, for it has the highest and broadest value. It alone also provides (2) the detail for determining our own ultimate reality, as well as even the ultimate shape that we should believe nature and history takes. Nonetheless, (3) methodologically, practical reason has a secondary status for Kant, and it is appropriately treated only in the Second *Critique*, since the crucial ensurance that we really *can* have the absolute freedom needed to be able to heed the call of morality presupposes the First *Critique*'s metaphysics of transcendental idealism.[3] For Kant, this metaphysics is crucial because *only* it can show that the spatiotemporal laws that govern the ordinary appearances of our life need not constrain our inner or noumenal reality, and so, rather than having to give up morality in the face of a law-governed nature, we can and should accept morality as the guide to a nonspatiotemporal realm that exists and is more fundamental than nature. Thus Kant argues: "If we grant that morality necessarily presupposes freedom in the strictest sense . . . and if at the same time we grant that speculative reason has proved that such freedom does not allow of being thought, then . . . morality would have to yield to the mechanism of nature."[4]

---

3. This interpretation is disputed by some scholars, e.g., Richard Velkley, in *Freedom and the End of Reason* (Chicago: University of Chicago Press, 1989), and Onora O'Neill, in *Constructions of Reason* (Cambridge: Cambridge University Press, 1989). While I have the greatest respect for their work, and agree that their perspective sheds significant light on Kant's texts, I believe that it leads to difficulties if taken too far, e.g., as implying that the principles of Kant's Analogies of Experience, or even his logic, rest on practical reason.

4. Kant, *Critique of Pure Reason*, trans. N. K. Smith (London: Macmillan, 1929), Bxxix. The A/B pagination is the standard reference to the first/second edition of Kant's *Critique of Pure Reason*.

Fichte could not accept Kant's metaphysics because he believed that Kant's first critics (especially Jacobi) had already shown the doctrine of transcendental idealism to be inconsistent.[5] Here we need not go into the details of this disagreement. The main point is that it left Fichte with the thought that Kant's philosophy, as it stood, was no more capable than any other metaphysics or theoretical philosophy of saving (what he took to be) our commonsense belief in absolute freedom and the claim of the moral law upon us. The only options for him were either to renounce morality as a "phantom," or to question the methodological preeminence of theoretical philosophy. Fichte himself could never imagine questioning morality, and he was keen on downgrading theoretical philosophy for a number of reasons. Influenced again by Kant's first critics (especially his teacher, G. Schulze), he thought that in addition to the specific complications of transcendental idealism, there was the problem that it could be shown that no sheerly theoretical philosophy could be reconciled with the basic commonsense belief in an external world, a world beyond our mere representations.[6] For Fichte, the solution was not to become a skeptic but rather to accept the call of practical reason without any prior consideration of its theoretical possibility. If one accepts morality as absolute, one already has made a commitment to freedom; one can then claim that it is this commitment in turn that leads one to posit the world beyond representations that theoretical philosophy could not in any case deliver. Thus, practical reason has methodological primacy; it gives us not only the details for answering the questions we take to be most significant (e.g., What is our "determination, destiny, vocation"?); it also gives the first truths of philosophy in general. Theoretical philosophy has its first condition in practical philosophy, rather than vice versa, as with Kant. Fichte was very explicit about his procedure: "observe the logical sequence of the ideas here presented. Our contention is not: I ought since I can [i.e., since I have a prior, theoretical proof that there really can be a power of transcendental freedom]; it is rather: I can since I ought. That I ought and what I ought to do comes first and is most immediately evident."[7] The primacy of practi-

5. See, e.g., the "Second Introduction to the Science of Knowledge," in *Fichte: Science of Knowledge (Wissenschaftslehre), with the First and Second Introductions,* trans. and ed. P. Heath and J. Lachs (Cambridge: Cambridge University Press, 1982). J. G. Fichtes, *Johann Gottlieb Fichtes sämmtliche Werke,* 8 vols., ed. I. H. Fichte (Berlin: Veit, 1845–1846), 1.481; hereafter cited as *SW*.
6. See Fichte's 1794 "Review of Aenesidemus," in *Fichte: Early Philosophical Writings,* ed. D. Breazeale (Ithaca, N.Y.: Cornell University Press, 1988), pp. 59–77.
7. Fichte, "On the Foundation of Our Belief in a Divine Government of the Universe," trans. Paul Edwards, in *Nineteenth Century Philosophy,* ed. Patrick Gardiner (New York: Free Press, 1969), p. 23.

cal reason thus becomes a primacy in not merely one or two respects, but a primacy in all the basic respects noted earlier.

In his *Vocation of Man* (1800), Fichte gave the classical statement of this strategy by dividing the work into three sections: Doubt, Knowledge, and Faith (*Glaube*). "Doubt" is his term for the blind alleys of modern pre-Kantian theoretical philosophy, the familiar conundrums that arise from Cartesian dualism, that is, the confrontation of a deterministic nature and an inner sphere of mere appearances. "Knowledge" is here Fichte's ironic term for his understanding of Kant's strategy, that is, his attempt to get to objects by building an empirical realism upon a transcendental idealism, an attempt that supposedly leads only to contradictions and "empty knowing" (i.e., mere rules for connecting representations, not for determining the ultimate nature of what is outside or within us). "Faith," then, is the term used to describe what is left when we abandon all theoretical approaches and take as our foundation only belief, specifically, belief in the moral law and what it requires. All this fits Fichte's explicit claim that we are to take the "ought" of morality to ground our belief in the "can," that is, the possibility of absolute freedom, rather than vice versa (as would happen if one started with Kantian transcendental idealism).

Fichte is very careful about his procedure here. He notes (at the beginning of Book 3) that one might try to get to a foundation, a disclosure of our absolute nature, by focusing on the fact that some of our ideas seem to be archetypes rather than images, that is, seem to function as guides to our activity rather than our mere receptivity. Fichte observes the strong *temptation* to think that this impression of ourselves as agents rather than spectators affords proof enough of our freedom and the reality of its intended objects. But he resolutely refuses to accept evidence of such a broadly "practical" nature as his foundation. Rather, he insists that it is only with specifically moral intentions that one cannot avoid thinking of oneself as free. For any nonmoral practical intention, just as with any sheerly theoretical intention (e.g., an alleged perception of an external object), Fichte says we could always take it to be the case that things are not at all as we suppose them to be.[8] It is supposedly only with moral thoughts that (unless one is a scoundrel not worth dealing with) one can no longer take seriously the possibility of illusion—which is not to deny that it is theoretically possible.

---

8. "Do I then indeed *feel* that real power of free action? By no means.... I cannot *will* to act, for according to that [nonmoral] system, I cannot *know* whether I can really act." From selections from Fichte's *The Vocation of Man*, in *Nineteenth Century Philosophy*, ed. Patrick Gardiner and trans. W. Smith (New York: Free Press, 1969), pp. 29, 30.

The true foundation of all of Fichte's thought lies in this moralistic strategy, a strategy that sees the limits in all arguments from any general, nonmoral notion—be it a merely passive speculative notion or the notion of activity itself. Instead of reviewing the virtues and details of this remarkable system, I will be concentrating on bringing out its most basic structure, and some of its most basic, still unappreciated, difficulties. In particular, I will be stressing one major flaw from a Kantian perspective. Against Fichte, one can hold, as Kant did, that even if one regards practical reason as preeminent in some very important respects, it is not at all clear that theoretical philosophy is bankrupt or totally secondary. That is, since it need not be seen (even in Kant) as limited to the representationalist theories that Fichte always begins with and then lampoons, it should have at least as much claim to our attention as Fichte's approach. The most important point that Kant reminds us of here is that even if theoretical philosophy were to appear to entail a metaphysics that blocks our moral-practical presumptions, our first course should be to reconsider these presumptions and their alleged preconditions and consequences rather than to jump immediately to insisting on a radical primacy of the practical. Kant also held that in the end the only solution here is to try to save these practical presumptions through a transcendental idealist metaphysics; but there are other alternatives available to us besides this orthodox Kantian strategy or Fichte's radical option. For example, one can reconsider compatibilism, or deny that our theoretical knowledge any longer makes determinism a strong doctrine.[9] Hence, we can have good reason to wait before building everything on a "practical" ground—especially if, as with Fichte, that practical ground makes very strong and controversial claims, and if the prospects for theoretical philosophy are not as dim or limited as they are at first assumed to be.

Because of these difficulties with a direct and radical advocacy of the primacy of the practical, it is understandable that Fichte's fans today have been tempted by another strategy. This strategy would try to found an idealist philosophy on a phenomenon that is not as contentious as an absolute primacy of practical reason nor as restricted as a typical "objectivist" theoretical philosophy. The special phenomenon that has thus become the focus of many Fichteans once again is the bare activity of apperception. It has the marvelous quality of appearing to be fundamental in many passages of both Kant and Fichte's work, and of seeming to undergo a positive and radical transformation under Fichte's care, a transformation that would seem to allow an alternative and less conten-

---

9. See my "Kant and Hegel on Freedom: Two New Interpretations," *Inquiry* 35 (1992): 219–32.

tious way of making sense of Fichte's work as a genuine improvement on Kant, and as an improvement that still has something to do with the feature of activity.

Encouragement for finding a foundation for a philosophy of freedom in the phenomenon of apperception can be found not only in current interpreters but also in Fichte himself, and even in texts from Kant that Fichte relied on and that current Kant interpreters also take in a broadly Fichtean manner, that is, as providing a foundation for philosophy that finds freedom in the most general activity of the mind, apperception. Elsewhere I have challenged various versions of this reading of Kant, and in another place I have also criticized the most sophisticated presentation of Fichte's work along this line, namely, Frederick Neuhouser's very impressive attempt to defend ways in which Fichte appears to present a *non*practical demonstration of the absoluteness of our subjectivity.[10] Rather than repeat those criticisms, here I will be offering some further documentation for my general contention that Fichte is to be read as committed to a radical doctrine of the primacy of the practical, and then I will apply this evidence to indicate limitations in some other important recent Fichte interpretations.

There is a historical complication that may seem to affect the force of what I have argued so far. Like many interpreters, Neuhouser makes a distinction between works of the early and the later Fichte, so my appeal to what I take to be the clear and decisive text of the *Vocation of Man* of 1800 may seem irrelevant to the issue of whether there is a strong "nonmoralistic" strand in Fichte's best-known systematic work, his *pre*-1800 writings. The issue is further muddied by the fact that undoubtedly in Fichte's *very* early reflections in the 1790s (e.g., in the "Eignen Meditationen über Elementarphilosophie" of 1793–1794)[11] there are considerations that fairly clearly (though in an undeveloped way) appear to go from the *non*moral feature of apperception to the claim that subjectivity is an absolutely spontaneous ground of philosophy.

On my view, the natural way to understand these matters is, first, to concede that for at least a short period Fichte (like Kant as well) had an initial fascination with the idea of a nonpractical ground (and in particular a "neutral" ground underlying and unifying both practical and theoretical reason), and then, second, to stress that nonetheless Fichte's own commentary on the first official but rushed version of his system, namely, his famous two "Introductions" to the new presentation of his *Wissenschaftslehre* (1797), show clearly enough his underlying commit-

10. See note 1 above.
11. See the analysis by Jürgen Stolzenberg, in *Fichtes Begriff der intellektuellen Anschauung* (Stuttgart: Klett-Cotta, 1986), chap. 1.

ment to the primacy of the practical. Moreover, this commitment is very clearly reiterated in the *Sittenlehre* of 1798, and thus already earlier than the *Vocation of Man*, and in a work that cannot be regarded as "merely popular." My main point is that if Fichte had thought his expressions of commitment to this primacy were a modification of his system (and not just of some unpublished very early views), he could have made this clear enough in his own immediate published interpretation of his system.

Here is how the issue is approached in the so-called First Introduction to the *Wissenschaftslehre*. Fichte begins (Sec. 1) by noting as basic in our experience the distinction between representations that seem free and those that seem necessary (*SW,* 1.423). He then (Sec. 2) defines philosophy as the explanation of the ground of this distinction, or, as he puts it, as a search for the "ground of experience" (*SW,* 1.425). Fichte goes on (Sec. 3) to distinguish the fundamental options in philosophy in terms of identifying this ground either "dogmatically" with a transcendent thing-in-itself (which he strangely *presumes could not operate* freely), or "idealistically" with an "I" (which he strangely *presumes must* operate freely). Since the "thing-in-itself" is here *defined* by Fichte as a mere figment of imagination (and thus it really is not understood in the manner of the *Critique of Pure Reason*—where its cognitive status has rather to be established, since Kant does not begin by defining things-in-themselves as totally beyond us), the only profitable procedure is (Sec. 4) to explore the "I." This I is what Fichte says comes into view whenever we focus on what is thinking, irrespective of the content of what is thought. Fichte claims two immediate advantages for this I: it (unlike the "thing-in-itself") is at least something that comes into view; and it is something that we believe "each person can freely create in himself" (*SW, 1.428,* 429). This is not to say that our reflecting literally generates the "existence" of the self; rather, it is said to be responsible simply for "determining" the self, for making it what it is on a particular occasion (*SW,* 1.427). Fichte adds that this is still not to give an "explanation" of how the I is a "ground" of experience (*SW,* 1.428). He also goes on (Sec. 5) to concede that idealism has not yet refuted dogmatism, and thus he has already reached the conclusion that also structures the later *Vocation of Man*, the conclusion that "from the speculative point of view" alone dogmatism will appear to be as valid as idealism. Fichte stresses that while it may be true that we *believe* our reflection on the self is a manifestation of a "free activity" (since it has "free range," it can find this thinking self, whatever the content that happens to be thought), this very belief in "freedom" (and the initial activity of the I that is the precondition and focus of the belief) may nonetheless be rooted in a hidden unfree ground (*SW,* 1.430).

It is at this point that Fichte claims that one's standpoint on the conflict between idealism and dogmatism is solely a reflection of one's "interest" (*SW,* 1.433). "Interest," of course, is Kant's term for the orientations of reason, and here Fichte is surely playing on Kant's view that it is practical, that is, moral, concerns that determine a highest and inescapable interest for us. In the final two sections of this Introduction Fichte reviews (Sec. 6) the inability of dogmatism to provide an explanatory ground of experience (for we can know nothing of how a thing defined as beyond experience can act on experience; and, supposedly, within experience we "understand only mechanical action" [*SW,* 1.438]), and he now introduces (Sec. 7) a way in which idealism can offer an explanation after all. This explanation also comes from Kantian ideas,[12] and in particular from the idea that the mind can be conceived as legislative, as determining in a lawlike manner. However, its manner of determination is not spelled out explicitly here; Fichte simply invokes the notion that the I, precisely since it is being *contrasted* with a "thing," should be considered as an "activity." Given his reference to "interest," it seems that Fichte surely has in mind activity that is rooted in moral contexts, but he complicates matters by merely referring back to earlier works in which he had called upon his readers "to think a certain concept freely," that is, to think of their very thinking, abstracting from whatever their object of thought is (*SW,* 1.445). Obviously what Fichte needs to do is to spell out that *this* reference to "free" thinking is not, like his discussion at the beginning of the Introduction, something that can be neutralized simply because "from a speculative point of view" the counterassertion of an underlying necessity is still possible. Hence, the only sense in which the last part of the Introduction can make sense as an *advance* in argument is if the reference to "free" thinking is meant to be understood as *backed up* by a connection with a "nonspeculative" perspective, that is, a practical view of ourselves as moral legislators that is to be given primacy because of a general principle that where the nonpractical does not refute the practical, the implications of the practical are overriding.

It is precisely this move that is spelled out in more detail in the "Second Introduction," published some months later in August and November 1797. After a review of the now familiar options of idealism and dogmatism (Sec. 1), Fichte states (Sec. 2) clearly that the idealist position rests "on the highest law of reason, that of autonomy (*practical* legislation), to which *all* other rational laws are subject" (my emphasis), and it cannot be put forth on "objective" grounds (*SW,* 1.456). Matters become complicated again because Fichte goes on (Secs. 3–5) to charac-

---

12. See esp. Kant, *Critique of Pure Reason,* B430–31.

terize idealism also in terms of the idea that the possibility of self-consciousness ("reverting" into itself; "*in sich zurück gehen*"), of existing "for oneself," is the "condition" of "all other acts of consciousness" (*SW*, 1.462). (This sounds like a radical idea, but it could also be taken as the fairly innocuous claim that consciousness cannot be structured such that it immediately makes self-consciousness *impossible*.) Here he also characterizes this self-consciousness as a kind of activity, indeed a "free" activity (*SW*, 1.460), and so it still might look like there is a nonpractical argument, an argument from mere thinking, to absolute freedom and the ultimate ground of experience. But once again Fichte makes clear enough that this appearance is but a phase in his real line of argument. He insists that as soon as we want to "explain" the "possibility" of this activity, as soon as we need to "confirm" and "vindicate" that it is a matter of genuine freedom, we can do so "*solely* by exhibition of the moral law" (*SW*, 1.466; my emphasis): "The consciousness of this law, which is itself doubtless an immediate consciousness derived from no other, forms the basis for the intuition of self-activity and freedom ... only through this medium of a moral law do I behold *myself*" (*SW*, 1.466).

Fichte borrows Schelling's positive use of the term "intellectual intuition" to designate this "immediate consciousness" at the base of his system, but he contrasts his procedure here explicitly with some nonmoral Schellingian accounts that would try to base an idealistic philosophy on theoretical representations such as space and time rather than on concepts of right and virtue (*SW*, 1.467–68). Fichte even defends his use of the term "intellectual intuition" as Kantian, for he claims that Kant rejects intellectual intuition only if it is understood in terms of theoretical access to a *transcendent* thing-in-itself. As long as we rather understand this intuition merely in terms of consciousness of the "categorical imperative," Fichte claims it is clearly something that must be accepted and not rejected by Kant (*SW*, 1.472).

Much of the rest of the lengthy Second Introduction includes digressions about the structure of apperception that, read in isolation, can again easily generate the mistaken impression that a theoretical phenomenon is the basis of Fichte's philosophy. Fortunately, he continues to insert reminders of his real strategy, for example, by saying that it is not "consciousness of individuality," but rather the "concept of the pure self" (*SW*, 1.476, 505) that is fundamental. And each time this reminder is made, the reader has to recall that the purity of this self is tied to its "free activity"—and that Fichte has by now made clear enough that "solely" moral grounds allow us to "explain" and "confirm" that there is genuine freedom here, and not a mere appearance.

These points also fit the great systematic ethical works of this period: the *Foundations of Natural Right* (1796) and the *System of Ethical Theory* (1798)—in other words, the main works flanking the "Introductions" that give Fichte's own immediate and most direct reflections about the ultimate basis of his published *Wissenschaftslehre*. (For the sake of simplicity I bracket discussion of the unpublished lectures on the *Wissenschaftslehre* "nova methodo" of 1796–1797 and 1798–1799.) Fichte's position is not so easy to see in the argument of the *Naturrecht* simply because, like most philosophers in the area, he employs a basically relative and political notion of freedom that is not directly related to the question of one's absolute metaphysical freedom. Moreover, the focus on rights here involves a notion of the practical that is not restricted by moral considerations. Even if people are not assumed to be interested in moral ends as such, or even to be the ultimate source of any of their ends, one can still compare how much legal "freedom" various systems of rights provide them. Nonetheless, when Fichte says that the "innermost root of the I is practical" (*SW,* 3.6), he has sworn off any sheerly theoretical ground for his philosophy, even if he has not yet worked out his full view about what the primacy of the practical must consist in.

All this is clearer in the *Sittenlehre*, where there is not only a familiar stress on "rational nature" in general as ultimate (*SW,* 4.14), and a reminder of the primacy of practical reason (*SW,* 4.53–54, 165), but also an explicit insistence on understanding the practical in terms of the moral "ought" (*SW,* 4.61, 169–70). Once more, the bottom line is that the "primacy of practical reason" means that "the ultimate foundation of all my knowledge is my duty. This is the intelligible 'in itself'" (*SW,* 4.169). Here again Fichte is invoking Kant while going beyond him in the controversial methodological way indicated earlier; he is making moral knowledge the ground of *all* knowledge, and not something that relies on any prior theoretical conditions (as it does with Kant).

Other commentators have also stressed Fichte's moral orientation here; recently Alain Perrinjaquet has argued along this line in an especially persuasive manner.[13] Nonetheless, at certain points even Perrin-

13. Alain Perrinjaquet, "Some Remarks Concerning the Circularity of Philosophy and the Evidence of Its First Principle in the Jena *Wissenschaftslehre*," in *Fichte: Historical Contexts/ Contemporary Controversies*, ed. Daniel Breazeale and Thomas Rockmore (Atlantic Highlands, N.J.: Humanities Press, 1994), pp. 71–95. See esp. pp. 80ff.: "Awareness of the certainty of the first principle of philosophy depends upon a moral attitude." Perrinjaquet (p. 82) also cites the *Sittenlehre:* "Certainty is possible for me only insofar as I am a moral being, for the criterion of all theoretical truth is not itself, in turn, theoretical . . . but is, instead, a practical criterion, based upon duty" (*SW,* 4.169–70). In addition, Perrinjaquet ("Circularity," p. 83n68 and n69; see note 7 above) refers to work of Fichte's "*Atheismusstreit*": "On the Foundations of Our Belief in a Divine Government of the Universe" (1798) and "Appeal to the Public" (1799).

jaquet's remarks reveal some entrapment in the ambiguities of the Fichtean position. Perrinjaquet notes that Fichte distinguishes between a "real" and a "pure" sense of "intellectual intuition." The "real" sense comes with the moral awareness of ordinary consciousness, and the "pure" sense comes with the consciousness of the philosopher who reflects upon the moral law and its conditions:

> Consciousness of freedom thus appears on two levels. In the *series of the I* it appears as *real* intellectual intuition (consciousness of the moral law, self-determination). In the *series of the philosopher* it appears as pure intellectual intuition. The latter is possible only thanks to the reality of the former: The philosopher would not be able to exert his freedom of reflection and abstraction were he not already free as a human being and had he not at least an indistinct consciousness of this freedom. He would not be able to obey the "postulate of philosophy," "think of yourself."[14]

The proper point of these considerations is to remind us that for Fichte freedom does not have its existence and confirmation originally at a reflective, theoretical level. However, in this passage there is also the dangerous suggestion (found also in Fichte's own texts) that somehow a philosopher's thinking (i.e., his responding to the injunction "think of yourself") *must* itself also be a manifestation of freedom. The difficulty here comes from the fact that although in a way one could not "truly" obey the injunction to "think of oneself,"[15] in the sense in which it is intended, if one were not free (since injunctions could be understood as meant only for free beings), still one could, given Fichte's own arguments, *to all appearances* "obey" such an injunction without being absolutely free. That is, if the logical possibility that the dogmatic determinist-realist accepts is in fact true—and nothing has been demonstrated by Fichte to exclude that possibility—then what might happen is that people could reflect on themselves and their moral consciousnesses and naturally characterize themselves as free even when no real freedom

---

14. Perrinjaquet, "Circularity," p. 84.

15. Of course, this injunction to "think of oneself" also plays a fundamental role in Fichte's famous argument that there is a kind of self-awareness that is immediate and nonobjective. Cf. *SW*, 1.526–27: "a consciousness of the wall is possible only in so far as you are conscious of your thinking.... But if it is claimed that in this self-consciousness I am an object to myself, then ... it [the subject] becomes an object, and requires a new subject, and so on ad infinitum." See my "Kant and the Self: A Retrospective," for a discussion of the implications of this argument for the theory of apperception. Cf. also Manfred Frank, "Intellektuale Anschauung," in *Die Aktualität der Frühromantik*, ed. E. Behler and J. Hörisch (Paderborn: Schöningh, 1987), pp. 96–126. It is striking that Fichte uses the same basic term, "intellectual intuition," to stand sometimes for this immediate but theoretical mode of self-consciousness, and sometimes rather to stand explicitly for moral consciousness. This ambiguity reflects the fundamental ambiguity of his system, although I believe Fichte follows a clear tendency over time to treat the practical usage as primary in a more explicit way.

need have taken place, in either the "ordinary" or reflective series of events. Of course, *if* the original consciousness is free, then the direct reflection on it will be by one and the same being, and *on this given condition*, that being will have to be free; but this fact can hardly be used to *show* that reflection as such, or the mere act of "thinking of oneself," demonstrates freedom.

Matters are made even more complicated by the fact that when Fichte appeals to the idea that there is no speculative refutation of the dogmatist, and that one's philosophy rests on one's "interest," he almost seems to be saying that this very fact is a proof or indication of freedom. That is, in Perrinjaquet's words, "the dogmatist cannot possibly be *constrained* to adopt the starting point of the [Fichtean] transcendental idealist . . . because the principle of transcendental philosophy cannot be enforced from outside, since it requires an act of freedom—that is, attention to one's freedom."[16] There is a confusion here that involves an ambiguity in the notion of "constraint." The bad Fichtean suggestion is that if there were a theoretical argument proving one is free, then somehow this itself would wipe out that freedom, for one would be "constrained" to accept the conclusion. This is a confused thought, because if there really were such an argument proving the existence of freedom, it need not follow that the *normative* constraint of "having to accept" the conclusion of the argument involves any kind of *real* constraint that would amount to a "having to act," rather than a free acting, in the original context that the argument is about.

A further confusion that arises here concerns the suggestion that since "attention to freedom," and "thinking of oneself" are not necessary actions, in the sense that they do not happen "by themselves," in the ordinary prereflective course of experience, then they must be free actions. But the most that follows is that they are contingent actions, actions that one must take an extra step to carry out. When they are carried out, these actions may reflect and repeat a freedom that we already have; but, on the other hand, they also may not. From the fact that we are really involved in an act of thinking, one ought not, precisely on Fichte's own grounds, conclude that one must be absolutely free in such a context. Action (being involved in something that has an effect) need not be free action (being an uncaused cause of that effect).

I belabor these points only because they still seem to be passed over in the very best work on Fichte—and not only by Perrinjaquet and Neuhouser, for example, but also sometimes by Daniel Breazeale, who has

---

16. Perrinjaquet, "Circularity," pp. 79–80.

done the most recently to make Fichte's work available in English and to become a significant part of the current philosophical scene.[17]

Breazeale has stressed that Fichte is a "practical foundationalist," a philosopher whose system ultimately rests (as I have argued) on an appeal to strong moral considerations. And yet Breazeale is tempted by Fichte's suggestions of an "original positing of self-consciousness" wherein the theoretical and the practical are equiprimordial. One striking way he has of summarizing this view is in terms of the clever adage "no consciousness without conscience."[18] This adage points to a whole line of Fichtean argument that is deeply ambiguous. The line proceeds by reflecting on the conditions of consciousness, and in particular on the conditions of consciousness in the "full sense" that involves genuine self-consciousness, and then by arguing that, for this, morality and thus freedom is required. This kind of argument can appear to be in keeping with the general strategy of the "primacy of the practical" because it is affirming that we cannot make sense of our own selves without ultimate recourse to a practical, that is, moral, perspective. In another sense, however, this very strategy goes against the basic Fichtean notion of the primacy of the practical, for it would entail that "neutral" considerations about consciousness alone would be what would entail claims about the existence of morality and freedom. Thus, the procedure would become the direct opposite of Kant's: theory would be the *ratio cognoscendi* of the purely practical, and the purely practical would become the *ratio essendi* of theory (for Kant, the moral law is rather the *ratio cognoscendi* of the fact of absolute freedom; and this freedom is the *ratio essendi* of moral law).[19] But such a procedure is not only un-Kantian, it is intrinsically unpromising and unrepresentative of Fichte's own clearest views. How, after all, can one maintain that "consciousness without conscience" is *impossible*? Such a consciousness is precisely what the skeptic or "dogmatic realist" actually maintains; and the actual cannot be impossible.

Fichte does want to show (as Breazeale notes) that morality and freedom are the "explanatory base" of all consciousness, but this is to be done by showing that the practical perspective is *sufficient* to explain all consciousness, not that it is immediately *necessary*. Fichte sees dogmatism

---

17. I leave to another occasion an explanation of how my interpretation relates to that of another leading Fichtean: Allen Wood. See my "The Practical Foundation of Philosophy in Kant, Fichte, and After," in *The Reception of Kant's Critical Philosophy: Fichte, Schelling and Hegel*, ed. Sally Sedgwick (Cambridge: Cambridge University Press, forthcoming).
18. Daniel Breazeale, "Why Fichte Now?," *Journal of Philosophy* 88 (1991): 526. Cf. Perrinjaquet, "Circularity," p. 87: "self-consciousness would be inexplicable without the demand made by the moral law."
19. Kant, *Critique of Practical Reason*, 4n (original pagination).

also as offering a possible alternative; it just turns out to be an account that is supposedly quite weak and insufficient. It is true that Fichte argues that one would not "perceive the world" if one were not a "practical being."[20] But this still is not an argument that being practical, that is, being free, is necessary for consciousness or theory as such. Fichte's view is rather simply that "theory" alone never *proves* a *world;* from a strictly theoretical perspective one could, in a phenomenalist fashion, still hold that one has a mere series of representations without a really distinct world. And Fichte does hold that if one is a true practical being, then one will have to believe that one is dealing with a distinct world, a distinct realm in relation to which one can have genuine obligations. But this again is at most to say that the practical perspective, and it alone, is sufficient for what our ordinary consciousness is supposedly committed to; it is not to argue that someone with a traditional narrow construal of that consciousness has to accept the practical perspective as a necessary condition for its existence.

In sum, the exact meaning of Fichte's doctrine of the primacy of the practical has yet to be appreciated by even his most careful admirers. The proper critical response to its radicality and its limitations can develop only once this meaning has been brought into the open.[21]

20. Breazeale, "Why Fichte Now?," p. 526, quoting from *J. G. Fichte: Gesamtausgabe der Bayerischen Akademie der Wissenschaften*, ed. R. Lauth, H. Jacobs, and H. Gliwitzky (Stuttgart-Bad Cannstatt: Frommann, 1964–), 1.4, 332.

21. Portions of this essay were presented at The Catholic University of America and DePaul University. I am indebted to audiences there, and also to discussions of Fichte with scholars at the Universities of Iowa, Notre Dame, Berlin, and Tübingen. Special thanks go to Michael Baur and Daniel Dahlstrom.

PART IV

THE AESTHETIC TURN: ESSAYS ON SCHILLER, HÖLDERLIN, AND THE ROMANTICS

6   Schiller, Hegel, and the Aesthetics of German Idealism

JOHN MCCUMBER

If we are to believe Hegel, the relation between Schiller's aesthetics and those of German idealism is quite simple: the one *is* the other:

> It is *Schiller* (1759–1805) who must be given great credit for breaking through the Kantian subjectivity and abstraction of thinking and for venturing on an attempt to get beyond this by intellectually grasping unity and reconciliation as the truth and by actualizing them in artistic production. For Schiller in his aesthetic writings has not merely taken good note of art and its interest, without any regard for its relation to philosophy proper, but he has also compared his interest in the beauty of art with philosophical principles, and only by starting from them and with their aid did he penetrate into the deeper nature and concept of the beautiful.... This *unity* of universal and particular, which Schiller grasped scientifically as the principle and essence of art and which he laboured unremittingly to call into actual life by art and aesthetic education, has now, as the *Idea itself*, been made the principle of knowledge and existence, and the Idea has become recognized as that which alone is true and actual. Thereby philosophy has attained, with Schelling, its absolute standpoint.[1]

If Schiller went beyond Kant in grasping truth as reconciliation (*Versöhnung*), and if this is philosophically equivalent to the "Idea" itself that constitutes the "absolute standpoint," then he has not left much for later philosophers to do except apply his ideas. But one suspects that these compliments would not have been returned. In 1805, the year of his death, Schiller had written to Wilhelm von Humboldt:

> Speculative philosophy, if it ever claimed me, has scared me away through its hollow formulas; I find in this barren field [*kahlen Gefild*] no living source and no nourishment for myself.[2]

---

    1. G. F. W. Hegel, *Aesthetics*, 2 vols., with consecutive pagination, trans. T. M. Knox (Oxford: Oxford University Press, 1975), pp. 61–63.
    2. Friedrich Schiller, *Schillers Werke* Nationausgabe, 43 vols., ed. Axel Gellhaus (Weimar: Hermann Böhlauys Nachfolger, 1984), 23.208.

True, Schiller goes on to say that the "deep basic ideas" of idealistic philosophy remain an "eternal treasure," and that one must congratulate oneself for living in the time of its efflorescence. And it is also true that this was written before Hegel had published a thing. But it rings prescient of later views of Hegelian philosophy as a "bloodless play of concepts," a criticism that was first advanced within philosophy by Schelling (who was certainly publishing in 1805), and thence became canonical.[3] So we may doubt that Schiller would have retracted it.

How, then, is Schiller to be integrated into the history of German idealism? The above quotes seem to leave us with two stories. According to Schiller's own testimony, after his famous "two decades with Kant" ("One to understand you, one to free myself from you"),[4] he reacted against German idealism, even abandoned it. This has independent support, for certainly Schiller's later philosophical efforts were entirely restricted to ethical and aesthetic concerns; and such concerns, though they can be "idealistic" in a variety of ways, cannot immediately be equated with idealism itself, which is fundamentally concerned with metaphysics.[5] In regard to metaphysics, however, Schiller seems clearly to remain outside the development of German idealism after Kant—for, as Emil Wilm has written, he never associated himself with the single most important gesture in the rebirth of metaphysics in German idealism: with the "expulsion or assimilation" of the thing-in-itself.[6]

But there is the other story. For Hegel's view of Schiller has support of its own. For one thing, it has a certain initial plausibility. For to the extent that Schiller "freed himself" from Kant without leaving philosophy entirely behind, he was by definition a post-Kantian. He was also an important pre-Hegelian, at least if we accept the testimony, just adduced, of Hegel himself, who for all his intellectual faults was in a position to recognize clearly just who should count as an important pre-Hegelian. In general, moreover, it is dangerous, when dealing with the German idealists, to assume that any domain of philosophy—be it aesthetics, metaphysics, epistemology, social philosophy, or philosophy of religion—can be separated off from the rest. It is entirely possible that what in Schiller took the form of purely aesthetic and ethical thinking influ-

---

3. Schelling's critique of Hegel is ably stated and explored in Alan White, *Absolute Knowledge* (Athens: Ohio University Press, 1983).

4. This phrase can be found in Arthur Kutscher, ed., *Schillers Werke: Erster Teil*, 6 vols. (Berlin: Bong & Co., n. d.), 1.395.

5. As Emil Wilm also points out, in his *The Philosophy of Schiller in Its Historical Relations* (Boston: John W. Luce, 1912), p. 159.

6. Ibid., pp. 159ff.

enced the philosophies of his successors among the German idealists much more broadly.[7]

So the question can still be asked: Is Schiller relevant, through his aesthetic thought, to the subsequent development of German idealism itself? Even, perhaps, to its metaphysical component? And if he is, what is the middle term connecting his aesthetics and ethics with the metaphysics of German idealism?

1. Schiller's Entry into the History of German Idealism

Schiller's main criticism of Kant concerned his moral "rigorism." The idea that a moral act is one performed in utter indifference to one's own inclinations (*Neigungen*—the Kantian word for desires, appetites, ambitions, and indeed every conceivable sort of motive except "respect for the moral law")[8] was something that Schiller seems to have found not only unrealistic, but repugnant. His reaction to it is summed up in a piece of doggerel that he wrote in 1796:

> Gladly I serve my friends
> But do it, unfortunately, because I am inclined to;
> And it often rankles me
> That I am so immoral.[9]

From this point of view, the key to improving upon Kant lies in somehow finding positive ethical significance for at least some inclinations. Hence it is unsurprising that what Schiller found admirable in Kant, that is, in the Kant from which he did not wish to free himself, was the Third *Critique*, not the morally rigorous Second. For the problem with inclinations, for Kant, is that they arise from the senses, and hence originate not in the "autonomy" of reason but in the "heteronomy" of our corporeal existence among other bodies. It was in the *Critique of Judgment* that Kant articulated the idea of an aesthetic relation of sense to intellect that would be one not of domination or indifference, but of free play and mutual accord.[10] "Improving upon Kant," then, means taking the aes-

---

7. Such a suspect separation of aesthetics from philosophy is used by George Armstrong Kelly to argue that Schiller's influence on Hegel was negligible; see his *Hegel's Retreat from Eleusis* (Princeton, N.J.: Princeton University Press, 1978), pp. 58–59.

8. See Kant, *Grundlegung der Metaphysik der Sitten*, Akademie-Ausgabe, 29 vols. (Berlin: Reimer, 1902), 5.71–89.

9. The poem from which this is taken—*Die Philosophen*—can be found in *Schillers Werke*, 10 vols., ed. Arthur Kutscher (Berlin: Nong and Co., n.d.), 1.138.

10. For an account of this, see my *Poetic Interaction* (Chicago: University of Chicago Press, 1989), pp. 259–69.

thetic relation of sense to intellect articulated in the Third *Critique* and modifying it into an ethical relation of reason to inclination.

This is the approach that is worked out in detail (and with un-Kantian historical sensitivity) in the book Hegel liked so much, the *Letters on Aesthetic Education*.[11] There, the harmony of mind and body, of sense and intellect, is advanced not only as an aesthetic but as a moral and even as a political ideal.[12] It is an ideal that finds an obviously central place in Hegel's own philosophy, throughout which the harmonizing of oppositions is nothing short of rampant.

On this account, Schiller's ethical critique of Kantian ethics is the middle term that integrates him into the development of German idealism: through that critique, Schiller led to developments in the aesthetics, ethics, and politics of German idealism—if not to developments in its metaphysics.

This account, however, places Schiller, if not outside the standard story of German idealism, at least on its sidelines. For that development is usually presented as leading from Kant through Fichte and Schelling to Hegel. Schiller's divergence from that story occurs with Fichte, for whom (at least in Hegel's own view) the dominance of reason over sense, of the moral will over a recalcitrant reality, was the key to achieving what Kant never did: a unified account of the faculties of the human mind.[13]

Schiller and Fichte, in other words, departed from Kant in two different directions while hoping to arrive at the same place. Fichte sought to achieve a unified theory of the human mind by developing the Second *Critique*'s version of the dominance of reason over inclination (as well as over other realities): he made practical reason primary. Schiller departed via the Third *Critique*, not to enhance the dominance of reason over reality, but to replace that domination by harmony. The Fichtean version of the dominance of practical reason, questioned by Schelling, was (as I have noted) rejected by Hegel as early as *Glauben und Wissen* and the *Differenzschrift*. Their attempts to achieve a unified theory of the human mind thus presumably followed Schiller in departing from the Third *Critique*.

The domination of reason over the senses was justified for Fichte, according to these early texts of Hegel, through Fichte's strict and fixed separation of the rational from the irrational: what is rational must be

---

11. Cf. Hegel, *Aesthetics*, pp. 61–63.
12. Cf. on this Philip J. Kain, *Schiller Hegel Marx* (Kingston, Quebec, Canada: McGill-Queen's University Press, 1982), pp. 13–33.
13. For an account of Hegel's criticism, in *Glauben und Wissen* and the *Differenzschrift*, of Fichte's instatement of the dominance of reason, see my *The Company of Words: Hegel, Language, and Systematic Philosophy* (Evanston, Ill.: Northwestern University Press, 1989), pp. 15–18.

wholly rational, and what is not rational must be *wholly* irrational. It follows that, if reason and sense are opposed, just because reason is rational sense must be wholly irrational. It cannot be accommodated to or "reasoned with," then, but must be dominated: it is mere material for realizing moral ideals. This is the view that the young Hegel wanted to fight, in a fight for which, according to the old Hegel quoted above, Schiller provided ammunition.

Hence the basic thrust of the *Letters on Aesthetic Education*. In it, the central problem of the age is identified as the problem of finding a way to articulate and justify the harmonious union of sense and intellect. And this is to be accomplished through an account of aesthetic experience that shows it to be at once sensory and intellectual, with neither side dominating. Construed in this way, Schiller's attempt to harmonize reason with sense cannot remain wholly aesthetic or wholly ethical and political. For it depends on finding some sort of rationality to the sensory world—and in particular to that which gives us access to that world, our body. And the human body is not only the very source of our inclinations, but a material object. Matter itself, in other words, must be shown—at least in the case of the human body—to be somehow rational.

2. Schiller: History, Mind, and Matter

Schiller's attempt to improve upon Kant has yet another burden, for we do not "improve upon" what we think is wholly mistaken; we simply throw it out (as the logical positivists famously attempted to throw out "metaphysics"). Hence, Schiller must show how Kant's opposition of mind and matter, sense and intellect, reason and inclination, is in some limited way justified. Schiller's account of this is both holistic and historically sensitive: it sees human nature as something that has developed over time, in conjunction with the overall development of the human race itself. Kant's "oppositional" account of the mind is faithful not to the eternal nature of the human mind itself, but merely to one stage—the most recent stage—of that history.

As Schiller presents it, what has happened is this: The Greeks were creatures of sense, enraptured by the natural world and the play of appetites and sensations it affords; but they had no awareness of higher moral concepts. This is because such concepts are abstract, and the Greeks, as creatures of sense, were unused to abstract thought: mankind had not yet developed the concepts necessary to carry it out.[14]

14. Friedrich Schiller, *On the Aesthetic Education of Man in a Series of Letters*, English text with facing German, ed. and trans. Elizabeth M. Wilkinson and L. A. Willoughby (Oxford: Clarendon Press, 1967), Letter 6, pp. 32ff.

The subsequent history of Western thought (or, as Schiller calls it, "of the human race") is the gradual development and articulation of such abstract and universal concepts as right, good, just, humanity, and so on. But in developing these concepts, humanity has turned against their origins, that is, against the sensory world itself. Eager to explore the higher regions of pure reason, we have left the rich diversity of sensory experience behind, with the result that our sensibility has atrophied and our minds are directed against what remains of it—trying, futilely, to dominate it. This historical development is why German idealism, as it existed at the time of Schiller's letter to von Humboldt, could be both a *"kahlen Gefild"* and an "eternal jewel." For though the development of abstract thought was an enriching one, it has left us divided against ourselves and unhappy in ways that the Greeks, those happily unified children, were not. This process, with its Kantian outcome, was not a mistake: we hardly wish to go back to the Greek world, with its culture of uncontrolled sexuality, slavery, and infanticide. We want to retain the eternal moral truths that we have come, slowly and with much effort, to recognize. But we also cannot remain, for long, in the frustration and futility of attempts to satisfy Kantian or Fichtean rigorism.

It is art, then, that can save us, that can show us how to restore Greek self-unity without sacrificing modern morality. For a work of art is at once a rational and a sensory being. It is neither a mere abstract concept nor a haphazard play of material forces, but a set of sensory materials intelligently arranged for a purpose. Each detail can be argumentatively justified by appreciating its contribution to the achievement of that purpose, so a work of art is not a mere clump of matter but something rationally structured. The purpose in question is, for its part, the conveyance of a moral lesson—as in *Wallenstein,* in which a noble attempt to unify Germany is defeated by the very means used to achieve it.[15] Thus, for Schiller, in contemplating a work of art, as Ernst Cassirer has put it, we enter the world of ideas—but without leaving the sensory world behind.[16]

Nowhere in this argument does Schiller reject such Kantian concepts as duty or the categorical imperative (nor did Hegel).[17] Nor does he reject the Kantian view of them as universal and necessary (nor did Hegel).[18] Rather, and this is important, he sees their relation to the sensory world differently than Kant did. They are not to be followed in opposition or

---

15. Cf. Hegel, *Aesthetics,* p. 1229.
16. Ernst Cassirer, "Die Methodik des Idealismus in Schillers philosophischen Schriften," in his *Idee und Gestalt,* 2d ed. (Berlin: Verlag Bruno Cassirer, 1929), p. 81–111, esp. p. 106.
17. G.F.W. Hegel, *Philosophy of Right,* trans. T. M. Knox (Oxford: Oxford University Press, 1967), ¶¶ 105–14.
18. On this, see Cassirer, "Die Methodik," p. 91.

indifference to desires and inclinations, but out of them. The specific inclination that incites us to follow moral prescriptions is pleasure in beauty; for this is a "free" pleasure, and freedom, for Schiller, as for Kant, is the ground of morality. "Inclination to duty" is thus, as Emil Wilm has written, "the heart of Schiller's ethics, and the gist of his criticism of Kantian rigorism."[19]

So viewed, aesthetic experience presents the solution to a moral problem. We moderns are pulled in two ways: our response to the senses is our *Stofftrieb* or "drive to matter," and our response to reason is our *Formtrieb*, or "drive to form." Each of these drives wants to take us over, and make of us either ancient Greeks or Kantians, respectively. In a truly moral person, that is, a person who is inclined to do what is right, the two drives are balanced, and only art can teach us how to achieve this balance. Hence the importance for Schiller not merely of aesthetic *experience*, but of aesthetic *education*. Schiller goes so far, indeed, as to draw a political implication: the balanced experience that is afforded by works of art now belongs, according to the last page of the *Letters*, to a "few privileged circles." But the book closes with the expressed hope that as a result of aesthetic education, those circles will expand to constitute entire societies in the future "aesthetic state."[20] If for Fichte, as Cassirer has also written, ethics swallowed up aesthetics[21]—and, I would add, critique as well—then for Schiller aesthetics has swallowed up both ethics and critique. The moral life coincides with the beautiful life.

Schiller's effort to improve upon Kant thus begins with aesthetics, but leads explicitly to ethics and politics. It does so by way of a reinstatement of rationality to certain kinds of matter: for both the matter of the artwork and of the body that perceives it must be rationally structured if aesthetic experience is to do for us what Schiller claims it can do. But his basic insight into the need to reconcile oppositions may extend even farther than that. For, Schiller suggests, the ways in which we experience art are ways in which we experience nature itself. *On the Naïve and Sentimental in Literature* opens with the following words:

There are moments in our lives when we extend a kind of love and tender respect toward nature in plants, minerals, animals, landscapes. . . . We do this, not because it makes us feel good and not even because it satisfies our intellect or taste (in both cases the reverse can often occur)[,] but merely *because it is nature*.[22]

---

19. Wilm, *Philosophy of Schiller*, p. 127.
20. Schiller, *On the Aesthetic Education of Man*, Letter 27, p. 216.
21. Cassirer, "Die Methodik," pp. 96, 98f.
22. Schiller, *On the Naïve and Sentimental in Literature*, in *Friedrich Schiller: Essays*, trans. Walter Hinderer and Daniel O. Dahlstrom (New York: Continuum, 1993), p. 179.

Independently of our appreciation of it, nature is worthy of respect because it is in its own way what I will call "pre-moral": it prefigures morality to us. Schiller suggests this more specifically in the *Letters on Aesthetic Education:*

> Nature in her physical creation points the way we have to take in the moral. Not until the strife of elemental forces in the lower organisms has been assuaged does she turn to the nobler creation of physical man.[23]

The natural world is thus not merely—as I had it earlier—a play of elemental forces. It is, much more subtly, their balancing out. And this leads to a number of further suggestions that Schiller never develops explicitly. For if the existence of natural beings in and through the balancing of opposed elemental forces prefigures morality; and if morality is the creation of reason; then must not that balancing prefigure reason as well? Does not the orbit of a planet, which balances the pull of gravity with centrifugal force, prefigure (for example) the reconciliation of the intellect with sense that is the crucial task of reason in the present age? The balancing of elemental forces so as to constitute natural objects would then present not merely a "pre-moral" aspect of the material world, but a "prerational" one as well: it prefigures not only morality but reason.

On such a view, it would be not merely art objects and our own bodies that are more than mere matter but natural bodies of any kind (and especially, of course, living organisms). Schiller's basic insight would then have spread, if not all the way to metaphysics, at least to that little-understood but important subdiscipline of German idealism, "philosophy of nature." And it may spread even farther: for it trades upon a new definition of "rationality" itself. On this new definition, reason is no longer what it was for the canonical philosophers of "modernity" (including many today): the making of clear conceptual and empirical distinctions. It must also include the harmonizing of what is distinguished, so that the oppositions that result from such distinctions are balanced.

3. Metaphysics Reborn

That these views, which Schiller does not himself explicitly develop, strongly prefigure the dialectics of Hegel's entire philosophical project is too obvious to need comment.[24] Hegel's aesthetics, for their part, will remain on basically Schillerian terrain. Its point will be to show how works of art achieve the "reconciliation" of sense and intellect, by giving

---

23. Schiller, *On the Aesthetic Education of Man,* Letter 7, p. 45.
24. Cf. on this Michael Hoffheimer, "The Influence of Schiller's Philosophy of Nature on Hegel's Philosophical Development," *Journal of the History of Ideas* 46 (1985): 231–44.

epiphanic sensory expression to a guiding conceptual truth.[25] But something will have changed, and this change will have to do with the rebirth of metaphysics out of critique. Seeing how Hegel's reception of Schiller functioned to aid this rebirth will, I think, tell us something about what kind of metaphysics was reborn.

For Wilm, the rebirth of metaphysics in Hegel was neither aided nor facilitated by Schiller, but instead includes a major misunderstanding of him:

> Hegel's error consists in interpreting as a metaphysical theory of reality Schiller's notion of the unity of the spiritual and the natural, the universal and particular, which was intended by Schiller to be merely an ethical precept or ideal.[26]

The passages quoted above from Schiller and Hegel suggest that Wilm's suspicions may be overstated. It seems, on the one hand, that Schiller's views on the "unity of the spiritual and the natural" did comport certain "metaphysical" views about what I will call the "prerationality" of matter. And Hegel, in my opening quote from him, does clearly distinguish Schiller's aesthetic interest and motivation from the philosophical concerns that he also attributes to Schiller.

But there is no denying that Hegel has rather massively falsified Schiller: for he makes the philosophical, indeed metaphysical, implications of Schiller's doctrines much more central than Schiller himself ever did. What can still be asked, however, is whether the falsification was a mere witless blunder or not. Perhaps it was motivated by important, but unstated, philosophical insights that govern Hegel's account of Schiller and indeed make Schiller productive in Hegel's scheme of things. What could be responsible, in other words, for such an obvious misreading? How deep a misreading is it? In what sense is Schiller's aesthetics really so unmetaphysical?

The view that matter prefigures rationality, I have suggested, leads to insights into the philosophy of nature: it concerns how we can experience the material world. It does not lead to metaphysics, which is a theory not of how we experience the world but of what beyond us makes possible the world of our experience.

In this regard, the key issue in German idealism was the rejection of the Kantian thing-in-itself. Things-in-themselves play a metaphysical role for Kant in that one of their functions is to make possible the world of appearances. This move beyond my experience itself to conditions of it that are asserted to exist outside me is, as "metaphysical," basically

---

25. For an account of aesthetic reconciliation in Hegel, see my *Poetic Interaction*, pp. 63–86.
26. Wilm, *Philosophy of Schiller*, p. 168.

illegitimate within Kant's own philosophical framework. It is necessary, he sometimes argues, because any appearance must be an appearance of something else—which itself, therefore, can never appear.[27] Hegel and other German idealists rejected both this argument, itself notably skimpy, and the idea behind it: that of things-in-themselves. Schiller, as I mentioned, never associated himself with this rejection; indeed, as Cassirer points out,[28] Schiller's adherence to the doctrine of things-in-themselves was essential for his turn to art. For Schiller, as for Kant, our purest concepts are in no way images of things: they are what they are not because of the objects outside us that they refer to, but because of the nature of our own minds. This is a motive for turning to art. For art, like all our experience but more clearly than most of it, is not reality "in itself" but mere appearance, *Schein*. Turning to works of art avoids the temptation to take our concepts as referring to objects-in-themselves, then; we remain purely on the level of *Schein*.

Because our concepts do not refer to objects, the question of whether they accurately mirror the nature of things outside us recedes: a concept tends to be judged not by how it captures some nonconceptual reality, but in terms of how well it coheres with other concepts and with the laws of reason itself. In particular, since groups of concepts cohere together to constitute entire "idioms" of thinking, it is important to investigate the coherence of such idioms with one another. Hence the importance, which I have already noted, of history to Schiller: Greek and modern thought constitute two such idioms, and his aim is to see how they might fit together. When they do, it is because they cohere with the only things immutable for Schiller: the eternal laws of reason.[29] Those laws of reason, then—*as* laws of reason—demand their sensory realization or embodiment: that is the overall "law" of our nature that requires us to turn, at last, to art.

Appearances *(Schein)* are thus, for Schiller as for Kant, our only access to matter. Because they are, in art, susceptible to conceptual structuring and articulation, they are rational—or rationalizable. Art is the place where this happens; it is, as Cassirer puts it, "*Schein* on the way to *Wesen*": appearance on the way to essence.[30]

Philosophy, suggests Schiller (in *Anmuth und Würde*), cannot understand anything that poetry has not already felt.[31] So understood, philosophy would be the rational articulation of *Schein* on the way to *Wesen:* of the coherence of our basic concepts, not with reality outside us, but with

---

27. Cf. Kant, *Critique of Pure Reason*, Akademie-Ausgabe, A249/B306.
28. See on this Cassirer, "Die Methodik," p. 91.
29. Ibid., p. 92.   30. Ibid., p. 93.
31. Schiller, *Anmuth und Würde*, in *Schillers Werke*, ed. Kutscher, 4.255.

each other and with the laws of reason. But this sounds like good Hegelianism; indeed, it reads like an advertisement for Hegel's Logic. For what does that Logic do but show the mutual coherence of the various concepts it develops? And since Hegel says that his Logic is to stand in the place of what was previously metaphysics,[32] it seems that Schiller is indeed quite close to the latter. But what has happened, now, to the great "rejection" of the thing-in-itself, which supposedly separated Hegel from Schiller and explained why Hegel, but not Schiller, was a metaphysician?

The rejection of the Kantian thing-in-itself, which to us seems so momentous, is treated by Hegel in a notably offhand way: indeed, almost as a mere semantic adjustment.[33] It is as if, in Hegel's view, when we have described something in our experience, it is actually *empty* to go on and say, "and this thing that I have discussed is merely an appearance." Hence, his arguments *against* the metaphysical role of the thing-in-itself are as brief as Kant's argument *for* it.

Though I think this is part of what Hegel intends by "rejecting" the doctrine of the thing-in-itself, there is, of course, more to it. For one thing, Hegel has to argue that Kant's antinomies cannot be resolved by distinguishing between appearances and things-in-themselves, which in the First *Critique* was the great motivator for that very distinction. Hegel does this by claiming that the generation of antinomies is not due to ignoring that distinction but is part of the job of every concept.[34] Hegel must also argue against the various ethical uses Kant made of the idea of things-in-themselves—and in particular against the "noumenal" status of the idea of freedom.

But further discussion of these issues is, thankfully, unnecessary. The main point here is that Hegel does not really reject the Kantian concept of the "in-itself" any more than he rejects the Kantian categorical imperative; rather, and once again, he rethinks its relation to experience. Instead of locating things-in-themselves in some nonempirical realm we can never reach, he gives them an empirical embodiment. "All things," he writes, "are in the first instance *an sich*, in themselves."[35] What he has in mind is the characteristics a thing has that are, indeed, unexperienceable—but only because they are still latent within the thing, have not yet been brought out by its development. A child, for Hegel, is "in-itself" a mature human being; an acorn is "in-itself" an oak; and each stage of the

32. G.F.W. Hegel, *Science of Logic*, trans. A. V. Miller (New York: Humanities Press, 1976), p. 27 ("Preface to the First Edition").
33. See my *The Company of Words*, pp. 126ff., and G.F.W. Hegel, *Hegel's Logic*, trans. William Wallace (Oxford: Clarendon Press, 1975), ¶¶ 124 Suppl., 140 Suppl.; also see Hegel, *Phenomenology of Spirit*, trans. A. V. Miller (Oxford: Oxford University Press, 1979), p. 12, and more generally, pp. 31ff.
34. Hegel, *Science of Logic*, p. 191.   35. Hegel, *Hegel's Logic*, ¶ 124 Suppl.

Phenomenology is "in-itself" the next. So understood, Hegel's "rejection of the in-itself" is much in the spirit of Aristotle's rejection of the Platonic χωρισμός, the separation of Forms from sensibles and the instatement of Forms in another world that we cannot sense. Just as Aristotle argued that Forms exist, but here in the empirical world (as species), so Hegel argues concerning things-in-themselves. The Hegelian in-itself is not an indeterminable something beyond experience, but an indeterminacy that is found as such within experience, and which is called so because it goes on to determine, or actualize, itself in further experiences.

Thus, for Hegel, "*Schein* on the way to *Wesen*" is not the appearance of something else but reality itself, on the way to (conceptual) determinacy. Reality just is what we experience; locating it beyond our experience, so that metaphysics is a nonempirical discipline, is a defect in Kant's empiricism. From this point of view, a theory of human experience will be a theory of reality.

So for Schiller's theory of aesthetic experience: from Hegel's perspective, it is already and inescapably metaphysical, a theory of reality itself. In Hegel's view, if Schiller had cared to carry out the philosophical program he himself envisaged, that of articulating what poetry feels in the form of mutually coherent concepts, he would have been doing a type of metaphysics, though his ongoing faith in the Kantian version of things-in-themselves would have led him to deny it.

The metaphysics in question would have been an updated version of what Kant calls *metaphysica specialis:* the theory of one specific domain of ultimate reality (such as God or the rational soul). But this does not capture Hegel's version of what metaphysics is: for when Hegel says that his Logic stands in the place of previous metaphysics, he does not restrict the claim to any special branch of metaphysics; he is talking, rather, of *metaphysica generalis,* the general theory of ultimate reality as such. To accommodate Schiller's views on aesthetic experience to this conception of metaphysics would require broadening their content beyond the domain of aesthetics, ethics, and politics.

We have seen Schiller suggesting just such a broadening when he talks about nature as the balancing of elemental forces, and hence as premoral—as well as, I suggested, prerational. That we can experience nature itself, as well as the human world, aesthetically suggests that Schiller's views on aesthetic experience can be broadened into an overall account of human experience in general. And "metaphysics," for Hegel, can mean nothing more than that.

Hegel's misrepresentation of Schiller as offering a "metaphysical" theory is thus grounded, first, in Hegel's own rejection of Kantian things-in-themselves. This leaves nothing for metaphysics to be about except basic features of experience. It is grounded, secondly, in the suggestion Schiller makes that we can experience nature itself in a way akin to the aesthetic, for it exhibits the balancing of forces. But Hegel's "reawakening" of metaphysics in fact takes him beyond Schiller in another way, one that also shows the depth of his debt to Schiller.

For Schiller does, in a sense, reject the Kantian thing-in-itself: he rejects the nonsensory existence of those things-in-themselves which, though never given in experience, are rationally justifiable, things as thought through the reason alone. For Kant, these were ideas of reason, such as freedom. For Schiller, as we have seen, such ideas are to be aesthetically presented: they are not to be left in some abstract realm, even that of reason itself, but must be accessible to art. Only then can they participate in the harmonious unity of the faculties, instead of dominating (or, as Kant would call it, "regulating") our behavior in this world from a position outside it. For Schiller, in other words, ideas of reason are to become embodied in a work of art.

It is this conception of "embodiment" that I think shows Hegel's ultimate debt to Schiller, even as he moves beyond him into a reborn metaphysics. For Schiller, what embodies moral ideas is, we have seen, a work of art. Because the ideas are moral, Schiller is an ethicist; because the embodiment is artistic, he is an aesthetician. For Hegel, and much more broadly than for Schiller, language itself is such an embodiment, is a sensory realization of the intelligible:

> We know about our thoughts and have determinate, real thoughts only when we give them the form of *objectivity*, of *being distinguished from our interiority*—only, then, when we give them the form of *externality*—of such an externality, to be sure, as bears the imprint of the highest interiority. The only such interior externality is the *articulated tone,* the word.[36]

Language in general—and as actually sounding, as a "tone"—is thus one form of the intellect's embodiment. It is, in fact, the most perfect for Hegel, because a mere word (unlike a bodily part or an artifact) has very little matter to be reckoned with: it is merely a "tone," a movement of the air, something sensible but evanescent and controllable. The job of philosophy, as a work of thought, is to take words (not "concepts," which as divorced from the words that convey them would be wholly interior, indeterminate, and unreal) and show how they cohere with one another and with the laws of reason.

This means that philosophy has a much wider task than any Schiller would have envisioned for it in his own thought. For it means that aes-

---

36. Ibid., ¶ 462 Suppl. For further discussion of this issue, see my *The Company of Words,* pp. 215–49, 303–31.

thetics will form just one part of philosophy, which must also deal with words from the natural and social sciences, jurisprudence, and especially, of course, religion. If for Schiller philosophy "can understand nothing that poetry has not already felt," for Hegel it can think nothing that language has not already spoken out or articulated. The most basic things thus spoken, the fundamental words that Hegel treats in his Logic, constitute the subject of metaphysics for him.

It is, to be sure, a peculiar form of "metaphysics" that has been reborn with Hegel: if I am right, it is a metaphysics that treats not of what we would normally call "reality," but of words. If pushed, Hegel would have had to justify calling this "metaphysics" in a more traditional sense with a Wittgensteinianism: "The limits of my language mean the limits of my world."[37] Hegelian metaphysics, as I see it, is thus a sort of linguistic analysis, different from Wittgenstein's and other more recent kinds in being systematic (words should cohere with one another and with reason) and dialectical (i.e., not uncritical of the words it inherits, which it undertakes to transform in regulated ways so as to bring out their coherence and rationality, or to achieve such when it is missing). If Hegel has been led to this by his concern, shared with and learned from Schiller, for the harmonious embodiment of reason, he has also gone beyond him. For as von Humboldt pointed out at the time, "it is to be lamented in the highest degree... that Schiller, in his reasoning about the development of the human race, does not even a single time mention language."[38]

37. Ludwig Wittgenstein, *Tractatus Logico-Philosophicus*, trans. D. F. Pears and B. F. McGuinness (London: Routledge & Kegan Paul, 1961), # 5.6, p. 115.
38. See Wolfgang Düsing, *Friedrich Schiller. Über die ästhetischen Erziehung des Menschen in einer Reihe von Briefen: Text. Materialen. Kommentar* (Munich: C. Hanseon, 1981), p. 184.

7   The Epochal Threshold and the Classical Ideal: Hölderlin contra Hegel
KARSTEN HARRIES

I

When invited to speak in a series entitled "From Transcendental Philosophy to Metaphysics: The Emergence of German Idealism" on "Hölderlin and the Hellenistic Ideal," my first reaction was a certain bewilderment: to be sure, German idealism emerged in an epoch in which the classical ideal was present in a way that most of us, products of a very different education, can scarcely imagine. But what does this *Tyranny of Greece over Germany*[1] have to do with the emergence of German idealism? Is the latter not much more essentially a product of enlightened efforts to transform divine spirit into human reason, religion into philosophy? More specifically, in the case of Hegel, Schelling, and Hölderlin, the product of an attempt to use the critical philosophy of Kant, as mediated by Fichte, to effect such a transformation, in reaction to, but at the same time still very much in the spirit of, the pietistic theology that dominated the Tübingen seminary, with its chiliastic expectation of an age of everlasting peace, *The Golden Age*—the title of a book by Friedrich Christoph Oetinger?[2] Nietzsche's observation in the *Antichrist* came to mind:

Among Germans I am immediately understood when I say that philosophy has been corrupted by theologians' blood. The Protestant parson is the grandfather of German philosophy. Protestantism itself its *peccatum originale*. Definition of Protestantism: the partial paralysis of Christianity—and of reason. One need only say "Tübingen Seminary" to understand what German philosophy is at bottom, an insidious theology. The Swabians are the best liars in Germany: they lie innocently.[3]

---

1. E. M. Butler, *The Tyranny of Greece over Germany* (Boston: Beacon Press, 1958).
2. See Jochen Schmidt, *Hölderlins geschichtsphilosophische Hymnen: "Friedensfeier"—"Der Einzige"—"Patmos"* (Darmstadt: Wissenschaftliche Buchgesellschaft, 1990), p. 89.
3. Friedrich Nietzsche, *The Antichrist*, 10, in *The Portable Nietzsche*, ed. and trans. Walter Kaufmann (New York: Viking Press, 1959), p. 10.

This much at least must be granted: any thorough investigation into the prehistory of transcendental idealism has to include some consideration of the *Tübinger Stift*, where Hegel and Hölderlin, both born in 1770, and the precocious Schelling, born in 1775, became friends and shared religious concerns, including their unhappiness with Protestant orthodoxy and chiliastic expectations; an enthusiasm for the French Revolution, which for a short time seemed to promise a secular version of the golden age; an interest in Plato, Spinoza, Rousseau, Kant, and Fichte; a love of antiquity and poetry; an interest in myth—and a distaste for the ministry for which they were ostensibly preparing themselves. Philosophers like Dieter Henrich,[4] Otto Pöggeler,[5] Christoph Jamme,[6] and Takako Shikaya[7] have demonstrated the importance of Hölderlin's contribution to the development of German idealism. But despite that contribution, Hölderlin himself left no doubt about his allegiance to poetry: in a letter to his friend Neuffer he thus called philosophy "a hospital" in which a shipwrecked poet can honorably seek refuge.[8] Heidegger seems to me right when he insists that if Hölderlin continues to present philosophy today with an important challenge, it is not the philosopher, but the poet who presents the challenge,[9] and where inseparable from that challenge is the challenge poetry presents to philosophy.

When considering Hölderlin's influence, we should not forget that, while today his place among the world's great poets is assured, for a hundred years he remained pretty much unknown. There were, to be sure, exceptions, such as Gustav Schwab, Clemens von Brentano, and Bettina and Achim von Arnim, but when the fifteen-year-old Nietzsche proclaimed Hölderlin his *Lieblingsdichter*, his favorite poet, he also remarked that the majority of his compatriots had not heard of him.[10] And if Hölderlin was of only marginal significance for the development of nineteenth-century poetry, no one in the nineteenth century would

---

4. Dieter Henrich, "Hölderlin über Urteil und Sein," *Hölderlin-Jahrbuch* 14 (1965–1966): 73–96.
5. See esp. Otto Pöggeler, *Hegels Idee einer Phänomenologie des Geistes*, 2d ed. (Freiburg: Alber, 1993).
6. Christoph Jamme, *"Ein ungelehrtes Buch." Die philosophische Gemeinschaft zwischen Hölderlin und Hegel in Frankfurt 1797–1800*. Hegel-Studien, No. 23 (Bonn: Bouvier, 1983).
7. Takako Shikaya, "Hölderlin, Dichter jenseits des Idealismus," in *Idealismus mit Folgen. Die Epochenschwelle um 1800 in Kunst und Geisteswissenschaften, Festschrift zum 65. Geburtstag von Otto Pöggeler*, ed. Hans-Jürgen Gawoll and Christoph Jamme (Munich: Fink, 1994), pp. 263–72.
8. Letter to Christian Ludwig Neuffer, November 12, 1798, in *Hölderlin, Sämtliche Werke und Briefe*, 2 vols., ed. Günter Mieth (Munich: Hanser, 1973), 2.728.
9. Martin Heidegger, *Hölderlins Hymnen "Germanien" und "Der Rhein,"* in *Gesamtausgabe*, 79 vols. (Frankfurt: Klostermann, 1980), 39.6.
10. See *Dichter über Hölderlin*, ed. Jochen Schmidt (Frankfurt: Insel, 1969), p. 109.

have thought of him as having made a significant contribution to the emergence of German idealism, certainly not Hegel, who could be said to have outgrown Hölderlin shortly after 1800. Soon Hegel was to "criticize the art of his day as 'dreaming' and Hölderlin's Empedocles, a kind of self-portrait, as a 'beautiful soul,' fleeing life."[11] Hegel's description of the beautiful soul in his *Phenomenology of the Spirit*,[12] as a consciousness concerned to save its purity of heart, condemned to unhappiness by its refusal to realize itself in the world, may be read as also a description of Hölderlin. As the spirit's progress in the *Phenomenology* has to leave the beautiful soul behind, has to leave art behind, so Hegel's progress leaves Hölderlin behind. The mature Hegel buried Hölderlin in silence.

The decision to include a lecture on Hölderlin in this series would, I suspect, not have been made except for Heidegger's understanding of Hölderlin: precisely "because he is our greatest *poet*," Heidegger insists, he is also "one of our greatest, that is, most futural *thinkers*,"[13] a thinker whose work is said to present all of us, but especially the German people, with a profound challenge, where part of that challenge, as Heidegger understands it, is the continuing challenge presented by Greece. Heidegger's high estimation of Hölderlin—where his focus is, as it should be, on the late hymns—was of course not original with him. Crucial, as he acknowledges, was Norbert von Hellingrath's Hölderlin edition, especially its fourth volume, which, appearing in 1914, for the first time made these hymns available. For his Hölderlin understanding, Heidegger, then, like so many of his contemporaries, for example, Rilke, is indebted to the circle around Stefan George, to which von Hellingrath belonged. Heidegger himself has been quite explicit about this debt.

When Heidegger celebrates Hölderlin not just as a great poet, but also as a great thinker, he places his own thinking in self-conscious opposition to the metaphysical thinking of the mature Hegel, who, in the spirit of considerations presented already in Plato's *Republic*, was unable to take poetry seriously as a rival claimant to truth. This is not to call into question the importance of the countless discussions in which Hölderlin and Hegel engaged, first in Tübingen (Hölderlin and Hegel became friends in 1790; the following year Schelling joined the circle), later, from January 1797 to 1800, in Frankfurt. After all, it was Hölderlin to whom Hegel dedicated his best-known poem, "Eleusis," written in August 1796, a poem that looks forward to rejoining the friend, whom

11. Shikaya, "Hölderlin, Dichter jenseits des Idealismus," p. 264. See Herma Nohl, ed., *Hegels theologische Jugendschriften* (Tübingen: Mohr, 1907), p. 285f.
12. Georg Wilhelm Friedrich Hegel, *Phänomenologie des Geistes*, ed. Johannes Hofmeister (Hamburg: Meiner, 1952), p. 463.
13. Heidegger, *Hölderlins Hymnen "Germanien" und "Der Rhein,"* p. 6.

Hegel here calls *Geliebter*.[14] But soon their thoughts and paths began to diverge, and we can say that only *because* Hegel—and something similar can be said of Schelling—was able to leave Hölderlin behind, could German idealism develop as it did.

Heidegger, of course, insists that the confrontation with Hölderlin still awaits us and claims that to understand his own thought, one has to understand it as serving and therefore as standing in an essential relationship to Hölderlin's poetry.[15] Socrates' teaching in the *Republic* is here reversed: the primacy of the poet over the philosopher is explicitly acknowledged. To speak on Hölderlin and the Greeks with reference to the evolution of Heidegger's thought is thus an easy task: such a talk might well point out that Heidegger's turn to Hölderlin is bound up with his call for a step beyond the entire tradition of metaphysics, a tradition that is said to culminate in the work of Hegel, where that step is also understood as a step beyond modernity. If Heidegger is right, that tradition had to end in nihilism and just because of this we need to confront Hölderlin. Be this as it may, this much is clear: Heidegger's Hölderlin reception does not lead one to expect from this poet a decisive contribution to the turn from transcendental philosophy to a new metaphysics, but quite the opposite: an invitation to leave metaphysics behind, as the once "timely" philosophers Schelling and Hegel left Hölderlin, this now "timely," then "untimely," poet, behind.

2

Those who want to argue in favor of Hölderlin's importance to the genesis of German idealism can cite a great deal in support of their thesis. A particularly weighty piece of evidence is the tantalizing fragment that has been published as "Das älteste Systemprogramm des deutschen Idealismus," the "Earliest System-Programme of German Idealism,"[16] dating presumably from late 1796 or early 1797 (in January 1797 Hegel joined his friend in Frankfurt and the two engaged in particularly intense philosophical discussions). The author, speaking in the first person, begins with the idea of "myself" as a "free absolute being"; in Fichtean fashion, he turns next to the world, which is said to appear together

14. Georg Wilhelm Friedrich Hegel, *Werke* 1, *Theorie Werkausgabe, Frühe Schriften* (Frankfurt: Suhrkamp, 1971), p. 230.
15. Martin Heidegger, "The *Spiegel* Interview," in *Martin Heidegger and National Socialism: Questions and Answers*, ed. Günther Neske and Emil Kettering, trans. Lisa Harries (New York: Paragon House, 1990), p. 62.
16. Hegel, *Werke*, 1.234–236.

with this I, demanding a physics guided by ideas born from the question: "How does the world have to be for a moral being?"—a demand that may be thought to foreshadow Hegel's later philosophy of nature; the fragment next addresses the political sphere, where it calls for the abolition of the state as a mechanism incompatible with genuine freedom; it culminates in an appeal to the idea of beauty, taken "in its highest Platonic sense," as the Idea that joins truth and goodness: the highest act of reason is here said to be an aesthetic act. "Our philosophers, who cling to the letter, lack an aesthetic sense. The philosophy of the spirit is an aesthetic philosophy." With this turn to the aesthetic, poetry "gains a higher dignity. Poetry will become in the end what she was in the beginning—the *teacher of humanity;* for then there will be no philosophy, no history any longer. The art of poetry alone will survive all the other sciences and arts"[17]—the dependence on Schiller's *Letters on the Aesthetic Education of Man*, where beauty is conceived to be the mediation of sense and spirit, is evident,[18] and it is worth noting that it was in this connection that Schiller used for the first time the word *aufheben* to mean both "to abolish *and* to preserve"; here Hegel found this key term of his dialectic:[19] in Schiller's *Letters*, then, German idealism has an obvious root. In the "Systemprogramm," not only the masses, but the philosopher, too, is said to be in need of a *sinnliche Religion*, a sensible—or should it be sensuous?—religion, where the paradigmatic example of such a religion, not named in the programme, but surely present, is provided by the Greeks. "Monotheism of reason and heart, polytheism of imagination and art, this is what we need."[20] The fragment proceeds to call for "a new mythology, but this mythology must stand in the service of the ideas, must be a mythology of reason. Before we make the ideas aesthetic, i.e. mythological, they hold no interest for the people; and, the other way around, before mythology is reasonable, the philosopher has to be ashamed of it."[21] "A higher spirit, sent by heaven, has to found this new religion among us; it will be humanity's last, greatest work."[22] This higher spirit presumably will not be a pure philosopher, but a philosophizing poet such as Hölderlin thought himself. Sensing the presence of the divine in the world, such a poet would have to find the strength to once again name the gods.

17. Ibid., 1.235.
18. See Friedrich Schiller, *On the Aesthetic Education of Man*, ed. and trans. with an introduction, commentary, and glossary of terms by Elizabeth M. Wilkinson and L. A. Willoughby (Oxford: Clarendon Press, 1967), pp. 304–5.
19. Ibid., pp. 304–5.
20. Hegel, *Werke*, 1.235–36.
21. Ibid.,1.236.
22. Ibid., 1.236.

The fragment thus looks forward to a synthesis of the monotheism of spirit and reason and the polytheism of the imagination, that is to say, to a synthesis of an enlightened Christianity and paganism. Such remarks make it tempting to claim the entire text, with its extravagant praise for poetry, for Hölderlin,[23] despite all that suggests, as Otto Pöggeler has once again shown, that Hegel is indeed its author, as the handwriting argues,[24] although Schelling's authorship has also been claimed.[25] But the very fact that a case has been made for each of the three friends shows how close they were in their thinking at that time, and how close they were too to Schiller. That Hölderlin, if not the author of the programme, yet had a profound influence at least on its aesthetic second part, which seems to strike a rather different note than the first with its emphasis on freedom, seems difficult to deny. He certainly was thinking along these lines, as is shown by his letter to Schiller of September 4, 1795:

> I seek to develop for myself the idea of an infinite progress of philosophy, I want to show, that the persistent demand which must be made of every system, the unification of subject and object in an absolute—I, or whatever one wants to call it, can indeed be achieved aesthetically, in intellectual intuition, but theoretically only through an infinite approximation, like the approximation of the square to the circle, and that to realize such a system of thought, an infinity is just as necessary, as it is for a system of acting.[26]

Theory's claim to lay hold of reality in a system is as vain as the attempt to square the circle.

This letter was written after Hölderlin's departure from Jena, to which he had been drawn to be nearer to his heroes Schiller and Fichte, also hoping for some appointment in philosophy, but which he soon left, penniless, disappointed in his quest to find a suitable position, and suspicious of the airy flights of metaphysical speculation. Despite his dense and rather opaque contributions to philosophy and aesthetics, despite his hopes to get an appointment in philosophy, Hölderlin was hardly a philosopher. For that he had, from the very beginning, too deep a suspi-

---

23. As suggested by Wilhelm Böhm (1926), and refuted by Ludwig Strauß. For a brief summary of the controversy, see the editorial comment in Hegel, *Werke*, 1.628.

24. Otto Pöggeler, "Hegel, Verfasser des ältesten Systemprogramms," in *Hegel-Tage Urbino, 1965*, ed. Hans-Georg Gadamer (Bonn, 1969), pp. 17–32. See also Pöggeler, "Philosophie im Schatten Hölderlins," in *Der Idealismus und seine Gegenwart*, ed. U. Guzzoni, B. Lang, and L. Siep (Hamburg, 1976), pp. 361–77. For the relationship between Hegel and Hölderlin, see also Christoph Jamme, *"Ein ungelehrtes Buch,"* pp. 354ff.

25. Franz Rosenzweig, who published the fragment in 1917, recognized Hegel's handwriting of ca. 1796, but argued that the content suggested that its real author was the precocious Schelling. See editorial comment, *Werke*, vol. 1, 628.

26. Hölderlin, *Sämtliche Werke und Briefe*, 2.667.

cion of reason, too high an opinion of the poetic imagination. That such an elevation of aesthetic intuition above theory, with its attendant suggestion of an elevation of poetry above philosophy, is profoundly incompatible with the philosophy of the mature Hegel requires no comment. Clear also is the danger such enthusiastic praise of aesthetic intuition poses to philosophical reflection.

3

The programme's reference to polytheism returns me to the second part of my charge: within the context of "the emergence of German idealism" I am supposed to address the topic "Hölderlin and the Hellenistic Ideal." The "Earliest System-Programme of German Idealism" does indeed invite us to think of German idealism as the product of an attempt to arrive at a synthesis of a rationalized Christianity and pagan polytheism, to envision a recovery of the latter on the basis of the former, an impossible attempt perhaps, as is suggested by William Desmond when he claims that Hölderlin is shattered "in the tension between Greek paganism and Christianity in the tremendous effort to wed together in a perhaps impossible marriage the figures of Christ and Dionysus."[27]

The felt need for such a synthesis, which rules out any simple repetition of what the ancients achieved, presupposes a then widely shared experience of the age as what Hölderlin in the hymn "Brot und Wein" calls *die dürftige Zeit*, "the destitute age," an experience bound up with a conviction that Christianity, with its one-sided emphasis on inwardness and spirit, was somehow responsible for the poverty of the modern age—just this idea lay behind Schiller's argument for the moral and political significance of an aesthetic education—bound up also with idealizations of ancient Greece as the unsurpassed exemplar of beauty and full humanity. Winckelmann had interpreted the multifaceted geography of Greece, which discouraged authoritarian rule, and its mild climate as favorable to a free humanity dwelling in beauty, and both Goethe and Schiller wrote poems that exemplify the kind of literary fare on which the young Hölderlin was raised and which provided him with a framework in which to place what he experienced. Consider, for example, Schiller's "Die Götter Griechenlands" (1788, 1793), which nostalgically looks back to a beautiful, loving world, joyfully presided over by the gods, which the poem significantly calls

---

27. William Desmond, *Art and the Absolute: A Study of Hegel's Aesthetics* (Albany: State University of New York Press, 1986), p. 109.

Schöne Wesen aus dem Fabelland!

Beautiful beings from the realm of fable![28]

Schiller contrasts an image of nature, when Helios guided his golden chariot across the sky, when oreads filled the heights, when a dryad lived in every tree, when streams sprang from the urns of naiads, and when death did not threaten as a gruesome, scythe-rattling skeleton, but life ended gently with a kiss, with the soulless world of today. His lament is characteristic of the romantic classicism inaugurated by Winckelmann.

Schiller also names the power that destroyed this world, whose only trace is preserved in the *Feenland der Lieder*, the fairy land of songs.

Einen zu bereichern unter allen,
Mußte diese Götterwelt vergehn.

To enrich *one* among all,
This world of gods had to perish.

The Christian God who suffers no other gods besides himself is here blamed for *Die entgötterte Natur*, for nature denied divinity.

Hölderlin addresses this same theme in one of his late hymns, "Der Einzige," which also begins with an invocation of a Greece full with the presence of the gods, but only to call for Christ:

Viel hab' ich Schönes gesehn,
Und gesungen Gottes Bild,
Hab' ich, das lebet unter
Den Menschen, aber dennoch
Ihr alten Götter und all
Ihr tapfern Söhne der Götter
Noch Einen such ich, den
Ich liebe unter euch,
Wo ihr den letzten eures Geschlechts,
Des Haußes Kleinod mir
Dem fremden Gaste verberget. (Erste Fassung)

[I] Have looked upon much that is lovely
And sung the image of God
As here among human kind
It lives, and yet, and yet,
You ancient gods and all
You valiant sons of the gods,
One other I look for whom
Within your ranks I love,
Where hidden from the alien guest, from me,

28. Where a translator is not given, the translation is my own.

You keep the last of your kind,
The treasured gem of the house.[29]

The Greek world is visible. Christ, however, remains hidden. And yet this hidden Christ, said to be of one race with the gods and the sons of the gods, although unique precisely as the last, the god to end all gods, is the object of the poet's special love.

> Mein Meister und Herr!
> O du, mein Lehrer
> Was bist du ferne
> Geblieben? und da
> Ich fragte unter den Alten,
> Die Helden und
> Die Götter, warum bliebest
> Du aus? Und jetzt ist voll
> Von Trauern meine Seele
> Als eifertet, ihr Himmlischen, selbst
> Daß, dien' ich einem, mir
> Das andere fehlet. (Erste Fassung)

> My Master and Lord!
> O you, my teacher!
> Why did you keep
> Away? And when
> I asked among the ancients,
> The heroes and
> The gods, then why were you
> Not there? And now my soul
> Is full of sadness as though
> You Heavenly yourselves excitedly cried
> That if I serve one I
> must lack the other.[30]

Hölderlin speaks of his love for the invisible Christ, but at the same time he considers this love a fault that needs to be remedied:

> Es hänget aber an Einem
> Die Liebe. Diesesmal
> Ist nemlich vom eigenen Herzen
> Zu sehr gegangen der Gesang,
> Gut machen will ich den Fehl
> Wenn ich noch andere singe (Erste Fassung)

> To One alone, however,
> Love clings. For this time too much
> From my own heart the song

---

29. The English translation of "Der Einzige" is by Michael Hamburger; see his *Poems and Fragments* (London: Routledge and Kegan Paul, 1961), pp. 446–61.
30. Hamburger, trans., *Poems and Fragments*, p. 449.

> Has come; if other songs follow
> I'll make amends for the fault

Hölderlin speaks of the guilt incurred by such love:

> Ich weiß es aber, eigene Schuld
> Ists! Denn zu sehr,
> O Christus! häng' ich an dir,
> Wiewohl Herakles Bruder.
> Und kühn bekenn' ich, du
> Bist Bruder auch des Eviers, der
> An die Wagen spannte
> Die Tyger ... (Erste Fassung)
>
> And yet, I know, it is my
> Own fault! For too greatly,
> O Christ, I'm attached to you,
> Although Heracles' brother.
> And boldly I confess,
> You are the brother also of Evius
> Who to his chariot harnessed
> The tigers ...

Daringly the poet proclaims Christ the brother of Heracles and Dionysus, but one of the sons of the highest, but one manifestation of the divine. A polytheistic pantheism is announced, reminiscent of the call of the "Systemprogramm" for a synthesis of a "monotheism of reason and heart" and a "polytheism of imagination and art."[31] Yet the poem also insists on a decisive difference between Christ, on the one hand, and Heracles and Dionysus, on the other:

> Es hindert aber eine Schaam
> Mich dir zu vergleichen
> Die weltlichen Männer ... (Erste Fassung)
>
> And yet a shame forbids me
> To associate with you
> The worldly men ...

Hölderlin's spiritual development makes him ashamed to compare the otherworldly Christ to the worldly gods of Greece. But that very shame is called into question by the poet's profession of guilt, which suggests that Hölderlin feels that he should not thus feel ashamed, that he needs to outgrow such shame.

This charge of personal guilt is underscored by one of Hölderlin's epigrams:

---

31. See Schmidt, *Hölderlins geschichtsphilosophische Hymnen,* pp. 109–15.

Wurzel alles Übels
Einig zu sein ist göttlich und gut; woher die Sucht denn
Unter den Menschen, daß nur *einer* und *eines* nur sei?

Root of All Evil
To be at one is divine and good; whence then the rage
Among human beings, that *only one* and *one thing* should be?

It is tempting to answer Hölderlin's question with the epigram's own word: Isn't it precisely because "To be at one is divine and good" that we seek to raise one thing, person, or god above all others and thus to gather what is fragmented into a whole?[32] And yet the epigram calls the desire to thus single out one as the only one a *Sucht*, a disease, which the title terms the root of all evil. Evil here is said to have its origin in the idolatrous idealization of some particular person or being so that it becomes the only one and tolerates no equals. Such idealization freezes the heart, prevents it from remaining open to contrary claims.

But the fragment gestures not only backward, to the pluralism of the Greek gods in which the invisible Godhead is thought to manifest itself, but also forward to a unity no longer based on any particular, to the universal as the only adequate realization of the divine spirit. From this vantage point Christ and the Greek gods are recognized as brothers; at the same time it allows for a recognition of the epochal significance of Christ's death:[33] Christ mediates the divine in a way that left no room for other divine mediators, indeed left no room finally even for himself as a visible presence. His death thus issues in the age of the dead, the absent God. As Hölderlin writes in a later version of the elegy "Brot und Wein":

In Ephesus ein Aergerniß aber ist Tempel und Bild.[34]

But in Ephesus temple and image are a scandal.

The reference is to Paul's visit to Ephesus, which caused people to say that "gods made with hands are not gods" and to depose "the great goddess Artemis . . . from her significance."[35] Precisely the death of Christ allows him to be reborn in the spirit in each individual, a thought familiar also to Schelling and Hegel: the plastic principle of the Greeks had to yield to the Christian pneumatic principle. As Jochen Schmidt suggests in his discussion of the hymn,

---

32. See also Karsten Harries, "The Root of All Evil: Lessons of an Epigram," *International Journal of Philosophical Studies* 1, no. 1 (1993): 1–20.
33. Schmidt, *Hölderlins geschichtsphilosophische Hymnen*, p. 106.
34. See ibid., p. 135.   35. Acts 19.26, 27.

But Christ is here the appearance of the epochal revolution. On one hand he embodies the form-bound, humanly mediating principle of the Greek pantheon. He is therefore called he who took on "human form." On the other hand he represents a pneumatic principle. The consolation through the Holy Spirit, at his farewell, points to this.[36]

4

But unlike Hegel, Hölderlin finds it difficult to accept the loss of the Greek plastic principle, even if it is preserved in memory and song. The late hymn "Der Einzige" thus communicates a tragic tension between the poet's love of Greece, which he says he loves more than his *Vaterland*, and his love of Christ. The poem's conclusion, which likens the poet to Christ, opens up the possibility that a new epoch might be beginning, in which not the disembodied spirit, but its incarnation in the living word, not the philosopher, but the poet, assumes the essential task of mediating between the Highest and the people.

> Denn wie der Meister
> Gewandelt auf Erden
> Ein gefangener Aar,
>
> Und viele, die
> Ihn sahen, fürchteten sich,
> Dieweil sein Äußerstes that
> Der Vater und sein Bestes unter
> den Menschen wirkete wirklich,
> Und sehr betrübt war auch
> Der Sohn so lange, bis er
> Gen Himmel fuhr in den Lüften,
> Dem gleich ist gefangen die Seele der Helden.
> Die Dichter müssen auch
> Die geistigen weltlich seyn (Erste Fassung)

> For as the Master
> Once moved on earth,
> A captive eagle,
>
> And many who,
> Looked on him were afraid,
> While the Father did
> His utmost, effectively bringing
> The best to bear upon men,
> And sorely troubled in mind
> The Son was also until
> To Heaven he rose in the winds,

---

36. Schmidt, *Hölderlins geschichtsphilosophische Hymnen*, p. 135.

So too, the souls of the heroes are captive.
The poets, and those no less who
Are spiritual, must be worldly.

The poet-hero is likened to the suffering Christ and thus also to Heracles and Dionysus: he, too, a son of the highest, receives from him high thoughts and a great soul. Like the philosopher in the *Republic*, so the poet, although spiritual, has to descend into the world, even if such worldliness is experienced as a kind of imprisonment. This conclusion should be read together with the first stanza, which also had called the poet fettered and imprisoned, although that stanza spoke not of a worldly but of a heavenly imprisonment. What imprisons the poet in the beginning of the poem is his love of ancient Greece, this transfigured world:

> Denn wie in himmlische
> Gefangenschaft verkaufft,
> Dort bin ich, wo Apollo gieng,
> In Königsgestalt,
> Und zu unschuldigen Jünglingen sich
> Herablies Zeus, und Söhn' in heiliger Art
> Und Töchter zeugte
> Der Hohe unter den Menschen. (Erste Fassung)

> For as though into heavenly
> Captivity sold,
> I am where Apollo walked
> In the guise of a king,
> And Zeus condescended
> To innocent youths, and sons in a holy fashion
> Begot, and daughters,
> The exalted amid mankind.

This backward-looking reference, not to a worldly imprisonment, but to a heavenly one, does not oppose world and heaven. The heavenly ones, the Greek gods, are at the same time worldly. As perfect mediations of sense and spirit, they are paradigms of beauty. In them the opposition of heaven and world was healed, a formulation that suggests Hegel's understanding of the classical as the adequate realization of the spiritual in the sensuous, even as it suggests the Incarnation—in *Patmos* Hölderlin thus refers to Christ as he, *An dem am meisten die Schönheit hing,* to whom beauty clung most. But in "Der Einzige" it is the Greek gods who forcibly fetter the poet to blessed shores, far removed from the world of his contemporaries, and make him a stranger in this modern world. Hegel might have commented that precisely because he did not find the strength to break these fetters, Hölderlin was condemned to remain a *schöne Seele*.

Two loves then struggle in Hölderlin. A love of beauty and the synthesis that it implies and a love of Christ. Can there be a higher synthesis, a synthesis of these two loves? Hegel might have replied, as we may be tempted to reply: Grow up! The art religion of the Greeks is dead and lies behind us. An awareness of the death and therefore the irreality of the Greek world, also of the irreality of the beautiful, so evident in Kant's *Critique of Judgment,* is part of neoclassicism and distinguishes it from other classicisms or, perhaps better, renaissances, which sought to repeat and if possible surpass the achievements of the ancients. But the late eighteenth century experienced the ancient world as a world that had perished, a world in ruins, not only in the obvious sense that its art and architecture had survived only in fragments, but also in the sense that the spiritual world that once supported it had disintegrated. Nature and time have triumphed over the ideal. The conclusion of Winckelmann's *Geschichte der Kunst des Altertums* has symptomatic significance:

Although in looking at this decline I felt almost like a person who in writing the history of his own fatherland had to touch on its destruction, which he himself had experienced, I yet could not stop following the fates of these works as far as my eye would reach. Just as a loved girl, standing by the side of the ocean, looks with tears in her eyes after her departing lover, without any hope of ever seeing him again, believing to see his face in the distant sail, we have, as it were, only the shadowgraph of the object of our desire, which for this reason awakens an all the stronger longing for what has been lost. . . .[37]

Such melancholy, which also colors many of Hölderlin's poems, invites us to extend Hegel's characterization of the *schöne Seele* to all of neoclassicism, which thus appears as but one manifestation of romanticism. To do so is to presuppose that the melancholy of neoclassicism is misplaced, that the death of the Greek world must be affirmed, even admitting the unsurpassed splendor of Greek art: it is a presupposition of the spirit's progress, of humanity's coming of age. This is how Hegel would have us understand the death of classical art; he here follows Herder, who for that reason considered the aesthetic ideal of the Greeks suitable for the innocence of youth.[38] Of the adult a different kind of seriousness is demanded. But Hölderlin, even as he recognizes the strength of such considerations, a strength reinforced by the eschatological understanding of history that was part of his, as of Hegel's and Schelling's, pietistic inheritance, finds it difficult to relegate the Greek gods to a world that had to perish and lies irrecoverably behind us. He himself claims to have lived in the presence of the gods. What Schiller relegates to a wonderful,

---

37. Johann Joachim Winckelmann, *Geschichte der Kunst des Altertums* (Darmstadt: Wissenschaftliche Buchgesellschaft, 1982), p. 393.
38. See Desmond, *Art and the Absolute,* p. 108.

but forever lost, past, whose trace lives only in the *Fabelland der Lieder*, in the fabulous realm of songs, Hölderlin experienced as reality, opening himself to the charge that he confused, as children or adolescents are wont to do, reality with an aesthetic construction. How differently did Hölderlin and Hegel respond to the Alps: what the poet experienced as the divinely built castle of the gods, the philosopher saw as a mute wasteland that soon left him bored.[39] Hölderlin could not follow Hegel when the latter transformed the Holy Spirit into the at-one-and-the-same-time human and divine world spirit and understood nature as spirit alienated from itself, present first of all as an obstacle on the spirit's path, as initially obscure, mute matter to be subdued and comprehended, until in the end no longer experienced as a mute given, let alone as a gift coming from without, but as itself the product of spirit, *aufgehoben* in the spirit— an understanding in which, severed from its in Hegel still theological foundation, that is, severed from his absolute, we can recognize the understanding of nature that guides our modern science and technology. Logic here triumphs over reality. *Aufhebung* in its more spiritual, Hegelian sense, triumphs over *Aufhebung* in its original aesthetic, Schillerian sense. Hölderlin cannot follow Hegel in his devaluating *Aufhebung* of the particular, both of the sensuous and the individual, of life, in the name of the "absolute spirit," whose throne's "reality, truth, and certainty" the end of the *Phenomenology* identifies with its "recollection and Golgatha," with "comprehended history."[40] But if Hölderlin cannot follow Hegel, he also is unable to return to Schiller; he is too aware of the tensions that stand in the way of such an aesthetic synthesis. His, then, is a more profoundly tragic understanding of history than that of Hegel, for whom every tragedy ends in a *Versöhnung*, a reconciliation, where the death of Socrates, this tragedy of the Greek spirit, provides the paradigm: communal *Sittlichkeit* and individual subjectivity here collide, but this collision prepares for a higher morality that joins individual and community; for the sake of that synthesis the "beautiful religion" of the Greeks had to perish.[41] The difference between Hegel's and Hölderlin's understanding of tragedy is evident in their different understanding of Sophocles'

---

39. Already the young Hegel dismissed thus the natural sublime, as is made clear by an entry in his *Tagebuch der Reise in die Berner Oberalpen:*
Reason finds in the thought of the permanence of these mountains or in the kind of sublimity that one ascribes to them nothing that imposes it, that compels it to respond with wonder and admiration. Seeing the eternally dead masses gave me nothing but the monotonous and, stretched out, boring idea: *this is the way it is* [*es ist so*]. (*Werke*, 1.618)
40. Hegel, *Phänomenologie*, p. 564.
41. Hegel, "Das Verderben der griechischen Sittlichkeit," in *Vorlesungen über die Philosophie der Weltgeschichte, Sämtliche Werke*, ed. Georg Lasson, vol. 8 (Leipzig: Meiner, 1919–20), pp. 638–47.

Antigone. For Hegel, Antigone and Creon must perish because the colliding moralities they represent are one-sided and must perish. Thus justice, thus the progress of morality demands it. According to Hölderlin, what collides in the tragedy is the infinite and the finite: the individual who, in the spirit of God, acts as if *against* God, and thus knows the spirit of God *gesetzlos*, "without a law," and the individual, who accepting fate, honors God as something that has been posited, "*das Ehren Gottes, als eines gesetzten.*"[42] Not different laws collide here, but law and the lawless, the inevitable singularization or definition of God, and the abysmal essence of God.[43] That collision permits no *Aufhebung*, no reconciliation. Tragic representation thus depends for Hölderlin on the fact that

> the immediate God is completely *one* with the human being (for the God of an apostle is mediated, is highest understanding in the highest spirit), so that *infinite* enthusiam grasps itself *infinitely*, in oppositions, in consciousness that cancels and preserves [*aufhebt*] consciousness, grasps itself departing in holiness, and God is present in the guise of death.[44]

Hölderlin's late hymns present history as a tragedy in this sense, balancing the eschatological understanding of history common to both pietism and Hegel with a Sophoclean openness to the abyss. To show this in some detail I would like to spend the last part of this lecture on the hymn "Patmos."

5

The first stanza is both a request, answered by the rest of the poem, and a statement that anticipates much of what is to follow, but expressing it in so concentrated a fashion as to demand a further, explanatory movement. The stanza is made up of four sentences, with each successive sentence longer than the one that preceded it. The first, simply but enigmatically, states God's relationship to man:

Nah ist
Und schwer zu fassen der Gott (1.1–2)

Near is
And difficult to grasp, the God[45]

---

42. Hölderlin, "Anmerkungen zum Oedipus," in *Sämtliche Werke*, ed. Paul Stapf (Berlin and Darmstadt: Tempel, 1960), p. 1064.
43. Cf. Reiner Schürmann, "A Brutal Awakening to the Tragic Condition of Being: On Heidegger's *Beiträge zur Philosophie*," in *Martin Heidegger: Politics, Art, and Technology*, ed. Karsten Harries and Christoph Jamme (New York: Holmes and Meier, 1994), pp. 89–105.
44. Hölderlin, "Anmerkungen zum Oedipus," p. 1064.
45. The English translation of "Patmos" is by Hamburger; see his *Poems and Fragments*, pp. 462–87. The numbers refer to stanzas and lines.

The nearness of God is the nearness of a threatening abyss. The second sentence, related to the first by sound and rhythm, links danger to salvation:

> Wo aber Gefahr ist, wächst
> Das Rettende auch (1.3–4)
>
> But where danger threatens
> That which saves from it also grows

The human being is in danger because, although close to God, he finds it difficult to grasp him. The abyss, of course, cannot be grasped and so it is not surprising that later versions show that Hölderlin was not quite satisfied with this beginning. One such version thus has:

> Voll Gût' ist; keiner aber fasset
> Allein Gott.
>
> Most kind is; but no one by himself
> Can grasp God.

God is now said to be "most kind," and instead of saying that it is difficult to grasp God, Hölderlin now insists that this is impossible for the solitary individual. Knowledge of God must be communal. We sense here a change that has taken place in Hölderlin's thinking. To mark this change one should compare "Patmos" to the earlier backward-looking poem "Da ich ein Knabe war. . . ." Hölderlin there spoke of having been raised in the arms of the gods, who are said to have been far closer to him than his fellow human beings:

> Doch kannt' ich Euch besser
> Als ich je die Menschen gekannt
> Ich verstand die Stille des Äthers,
> Der Menschen Worte verstand ich nie.
>
> Yet I knew you better
> Than ever I have known men,
> I understood the silence of the Aether
> But human words I've never understood.[46]

Before he learns to name, not God, but the gods, Helios, Endymion, Luna, he already knew them, listening to the voices of nature, to sun and moon, to the quiet of the ether, to flowers and whispering trees. He knows that our ordinary ways of speaking, *das Geschrei der Menschen*, drown out these voices. The young poet thus sensed the presence of the

---

46. The English translation of "Da ich ein Knabe war . . ." is by Hamburger; see his *Poems and Fragments*, pp. 80–81.

holy in particular shapes. Dwelling in the presence of the gods gave him the strength to name them. But this privilege was bought at a price, and later he was to accuse himself of having sinned against his fellow human beings: since as a poet he neither loved nor served them in human fashion, they did not show themselves to him as human. The very first lines of "Patmos," at least in their revised form, reject this opposition between poetry and community.

The next four lines speak of beings who live securely in the face of danger.

> Im Finstern wohnen
> Die Adler und furchtlos gehen
> Die Söhne der Alpen über den Abgrund weg
> Auf leichtgebaueten Brücken (1.5–8)
>
> In gloomy places dwell
> The eagles, and fearless over
> The chasm walk the sons of the Alps
> On bridges lightly built.

We have already encountered the eagle as a metaphor for both Christ and the poet. But the eagle is also the attribute of John. The wing's of the spirit allow us to dwell in the dark without fear and to pass over the abyss of time. The stanza's last sentence is a request, based on a further description of the present situation:

> Drum, da gehäuft sind rings
> Die Gipfel der Zeit,
> Und die Liebsten
> Nah wohnen, ermattend auf
> Getrenntesten Bergen (1.9–13)
>
> Therefore, since round about
> Are heaped the summits of Time
> And the most loved live near, growing faint
> On mountains most separate,

Time is now seen as a mountain range. Its peaks, as the following stanzas make clear, are the high points of history, especially the age of the Greeks and the time of Christ. And yet their proximity to us is coupled with a lack of reality. The loved ones dwell near, but cannot be reached. Destructive time separates the poet not only from the Greeks and their gods, from Christ and his disciples, but also from those whom he once knew and was separated from by death. *Die Liebsten* thus includes also Susette Gontard, his Diotima.

We can now be somewhat more specific about the community the poet has in mind. Those he loves, while near, yet languish on most distant mountains. Every lover knows that memory is a very inadequate bridge across the abyss of time. Such inadequacy leads to the request with which the stanza closes:

> So gieb unschuldig Wasser,
> O Fittige gib uns, treuesten Sinns
> Hinüberzugehn und wiederzukehren. (1.14–16)

> Give us innocent water,
> O pinions give us, with minds most faithful
> To cross over and to return.

The request may seem surprising. One might have expected a request that God show himself in such a way that he can be grasped; instead the request is for wings that allow us to fly across the abyss of time. Yet the two requests are not unrelated: for God has shown himself to us in Christ. But this, too, now belongs to the past: just another peak of time, with its power, too, waning. We no longer live in the presence of the divine. The request thus becomes a request to join those who once saw him.

Important is the line:

> To cross over and to return.

Especially for Hölderlin, whose "beautiful soul" found it easy to seek refuge in an idealized past, yet had difficulty finding its place in the contemporary world, the request again to return is a request that the desired community not be bought at the cost of his world.[47]

The next two stanzas pose fewer problems. Less dense than the first, they are made up of just two sentences. The first suggests that the request has been granted: a Genius, a poetic spirit, abducts him and leads him far way from home. The next twenty-six lines form one extended sentence, describing a movement across space and time, away from the forests and brooks of his youth, across Greece, to the eastern edge of the Aegean, to Asia. As later revisions suggest, nature presented itself to the young poet in human form:

> Es kleideten sich
> Im Zwielicht, Menschen ähnlich, da ich gieng
> Der schattige Wald
> Und die sehnsüchtigen Bäche
> Der Heimat

> There clothed themselves,
> Like men, in the twilight, as I went,
> The shadowy wood

---

47. See, e.g., the last stanza of "Dichterberuf."

And the yearning streams of
My homeland.

Hegel points out that, when we experience nature as if dressed in human form, we dwell near the Greek gods. But this time the journey carries the poet beyond Greece, to its eastern edge, to Patmos, this island, where, according to legend, the apostle John, who, following tradition, was identified with the evangelist, author of the pneumatic gospel, wrote down the Apocalypse, for pietists like Friedrich Christoph Oetinger and Johann Albrecht Bengel the very model of an inspired text.[48] In the fifth stanza this turn to Patmos is tied to calamities:

> Und wenn vom Schiffbruch oder klagend
> Um die Heimath oder
> Den abgeschiedenen Freund
> Ihr nahet einer
> Der Fremden, hört sie es gern, . . .

> And when, after shipwreck or lamenting for
> His homeland or else for
> The friend departed from him,
> A stranger draws near
> To her, she is glad to hear it, . . .

Shipwreck and loss of home and friend refer here not just to the apostle but also to the homeless poet, struggling with the loss of his Diotima and his loneliness.

The sixth stanza brings a change. The poem becomes denser, the rhythm more complicated. Especially toward the end of the stanza sentences become very brief. More than to any other part of the poem, Hölderlin kept returning to this stanza. Thus in a later version the first four lines become three stanzas.

Striking are parallels between poet and disciple. Not only has John, too, lost home and the one he loved, but he appears here as the paradigm of a poet who saw the face of, not just a god, but the God who presented himself as the only one. John wrote as someone who not only saw, but had been loved and called by, God. And yet this God had died on the cross and no new gods have appeared to take his place. The problem facing Hölderlin is this: What is the place of the poet, given the death of God? How are we to hold on to God, given abysmal time. Later versions dwell on this point:

> Begreiffen müssen
> Diß wir zuvor. Wie Morgenluft sind nemlich die Nahmen

---

48. Schmidt, *Hölderlins geschichtsphilosophische Hymnen*, pp. 190–97.

Seit Christus. Werden Träume. Fallen wie Irrtum
Auf das Herz und tödtend, wenn nicht einer

   Erwäget, was sie sind und begreift.

This first we
Must understand. For like morning air are the names
Since Christ. Become dreams. Fall on the heart
Like error, and killing, if one does not

   Consider what they are and understand.

The death of God tempts the poet to make himself into a false priest, as Hölderlin describes himself in the last fragmentary stanza of "Wie wenn am Feiertage . . . ," significantly repressed by Heidegger.[49] The poet who, without being called, usurps the place of the prophet can only mislead, for his words have no substance. Yet even the words of former prophets have become hollow. Orthodoxy thus threatens to imprison the spirit in now meaningless but established ways of speaking. To guard against this, we need to weigh and comprehend them.

Metaphors of lightning, thunder, and rainbow keep echoing through this poem. In this stanza Christ is thus called "der *Gewittertragende*," a phrase that suggest the opening of "Wie wenn am Feiertage . . . ," central to Hölderlin's determination of the place of the poet:

Doch uns gebührt es, unter Gottes Gewittern,
Ihr Dichter! mit entblößtem Haupte zu stehen,
Des Vaters Stral, ihn selbst, mit eigner Hand
Zu fassen und dem Volke ins Lied
Gehüllt die himmlische Gabe zu reichen.

Yet, fellow poets, us it behoves to stand
Bare-headed beneath God's thunderstorms,
To grasp the Father's ray, no less, with our own two hands
And, wrapping in song the heavenly gift,
To offer it to the people.[50]

The poet appears here as mediator between God and the people. The divine, as so often with Hölderlin, expresses itself as terrifying and potentially destructive. The poet must expose himself to God's lightning. And yet there is hubris in this idea that the poet should grasp "the Father's ray, no less," with his own two hands. John was free of such hubris. God showed himself to him in definite shape so that he could be grasped

---

49. Martin Heidegger, "Wie wenn am Feiertage . . . ," in *Erläuterungen zu Hölderlins Dichtung, Gesamtausgabe* (Frankfurt: Klostermann, 1981), 4.49–77; see esp. p. 51.

50. The English translation of "Wie wenn am Feiertage . . ." is by Hamburger; see his *Poems and Fragments*, pp. 372–73.

without danger. But the divine becomes destructive whenever a human being reaches for it, without waiting for a divine mediator, when the poet usurps the place of such a mediator. The fragmented, terrifying last stanza of "Wie wenn am Feiertage . . ." makes this point:

Und sag ich gleich,

Ich sei genaht, die Himmlischen zu schauen
Sie selbst warfen mich tief unter die Lebenden
Den falschen Priester ins Dunkel, daß ich
Das warnende Lied, den Gelehrigen singe.
Dort

And although I say

That I approached to see the Heavenly,
They themselves cast me down, deep down
Below the living, into the dark cast down
The false priest that I am, to sing,
For those who have ears to hear, the warning song.
There[51]

The imaginary journey that carries the poet to Patmos fails to carry him into the presence of God, only to the island that once offered refuge to the Seer, who in "blessed youth" walked with "the son of the highest"—the parallels between the poet and John are unmistakable—only to experience the death of God; thus it carries him to the edge of the night in which we still dwell. Like John, we have to learn to let go of "blessed youth" and learn to accept the death of God. Yet like the disciples we find it difficult to let go of the light of day, which for Hölderlin means also to let go of the Greek world and its plastic principle, and also of his beloved Diotima:

aber sie liebten unter der Sonne
Das Leben und lassen wollten sie nicht
Vom Angesichte des Herrn
Und der Heimat. Eingetrieben war,
Wie Feuer im Eisen, das, und ihnen gieng
Zur Seite der Schatte des Lieben. (7.5–9)

but under the sun they loved
This life and were loath to part from
The visible face of the Lord
And their homeland. Driven in,
Like fire into iron, was this, and beside them
The loved one's shadow walked.

---

51. Hamburger, *Poems and Fragments*, pp. 376–77.

Later versions add *Wie eine Seuche,* "like a disease." And memories of life "under the sun" can indeed prevent us from taking our place in this world of night that is our destiny. It is not up to us to name God or the gods. They themselves must claim us. We can only wait for the gift of a new day, wait for the god who is to come. Impatient attempts to reveal the divine must fail in one of two ways: either the words of the would-be prophet will become empty and hollow, or the unmediated God, still so near as to be one with the self, will break the shell of words and render the poet mute. In this night authentic poetry, in its attempt to name the transcendent, will again and again approach silence.

To say that the gods have fled is not to say that there is no mediation at all:

> Und es grünen
> Tief an den Bergen auch lebendige Bilder (8.14–15)

> And low down at
> The foot of the mountains, too, will living images thrive

And again:

> der Vater aber liebt
> Der über allen waltet,
> Am meisten, daß gepfleget werde
> Der veste Buchstab, und bestehendes gut
> Gedeutet (15.10–15)

> but what the Father
> Who reigns over all loves most
> Is that the solid letter
> Be given scrupulous care, and the existing
> Be well interpreted.

Nature and what has been established in the words of seers who, like John, lived in the light of day, are the mediations left to us.[52] And yet what sacred texts speak of becomes more and more dreamlike and nature does not speak clearly enough to found on such speech a common way of life. With the death of God all genuine community is threatened, for community presupposes a common language that joins individuals in a larger order. Such a language issued from Christ; but with the death of God this language appears to have lost both founder and foundation.

52. As we read in a later version of "Der Einzige":

Mit Stimmen erscheinet Gott als
Natur von aussen. Mittelbar
In heiligen Schriften.

The old order falls apart. Individuals, and especially those most committed to the divine, find themselves alone with the abyss.

> Doch furchtbar ist, wie da und dort
> Unendlich hin zerstreut das Lebende Gott. (9.1-2)

> Yet dreadful it is how here and there
> Unendingly God disperses whatever lives.

The ninth stanza is grammatically the most confusing in the poem. Much remains unsaid that is yet necessary to even grammatically complete what appears. Communicating uncertainty and loss, they lead to the desperate question that is the tenth stanza. What is the meaning of the process in which we find ourselves caught up?

Three times the word *wenn* introduces a description that points to what makes this process so questionable:

> Wenn aber stirbt alsdenn
> An dem am meisten
> Die Schönheit hieng, daß an der Gestalt
> Ein Wunder war und die Himmlischen gedeutet
> Auf ihn (10.1-5)

> But when thereupon he dies
> To whom beauty most adhered, so that
> A miracle was wrought in his person and
> The Heavenly had pointed at him

Hölderlin speaks of the beauty of the incarnated God. With his death all beauty becomes questionable. That includes the beauty of the Greek gods, includes also the beauty of Hölderlin's Diotima.

> ... und wenn, ein Räthsel füreinander
> Sie sich nicht fassen können
> Einander, die zusammenlebten
> Im Gedächtniß, und nicht den Sand nur oder
> Die Weiden es hinwegnimmt und die Tempel
> Ergreifft (10.5-10)

> And when, an enigma to one another
> For ever, they cannot understand
> One another who lived together
> Conjoined by remembrance, and not only
> The sand or the willows it takes away,
> And seizes the temples

Time appears here as a force that takes away not only sand and willows, but even the temples in which the gods and God were once present. Time forces us to acknowledge that ultimately we are alone; even those whom we loved, with whom we lived together, while still so near, yet become strange and alien, a riddle we are unable to solve.

> ... wenn die Ehre
> Des Halbgotts und der Seinen
> Verweht und selber sein Angesicht
> Der Höchste wendet
> Darob, daß nirgends ein
> Unsterbliches mehr am Himmel zu sehn ist
> Oder auf grüner Erde, was ist diß? (10.10–15)

> when even
> The demigod's honour and that of his friends
> Is blown away by the wind, and the Highest
> Himself averts his face
> Because nowhere now
> An immortal is to be seen in the skies or
> On our green earth, what is this?

Christ himself is forgotten and God has turned away from a world subject to the seemingly meaningless rule of time.

The *was ist diß?* with which the stanza closes is the cesura, the interruption that breaks into the poetic progress and marks off what has preceded from what follows. Very gently, parable-like, the eleventh stanza attempts an answer. Recalling two New Testament parables (Mark 4.3–9; Math. 3.12), the poet suggests that God is like the sower who separates the wheat from the chaff, and is rich enough not to care if some gets lost:

> Und nicht ein Übel ists, wenn einiges
> Verloren gehet und von der Rede
> Verhallet der lebendige Laut,
> Denn göttliches Werk auch gleicht dem unsern
> Nicht alles will der Höchste zumal. (11.1–7)

> And there's no harm if some of it
> Is lost, and of the speech
> The living sound dies away,
> For the work of gods, too, is like our own,
> Not all things at once does the Highest intend.

This invites a Hegelian reading. Yet is it an answer? Or just an invitation to accept the place where God has cast us, destitute though it is? It is not much consolation to someone mourning the death of a loved one that what really mattered remains *aufgehoben,* canceled and preserved in memory. And it is not much consolation to tell someone struggling with the death of God that what really mattered remains *aufgehoben,* canceled and preserved in memory. As Hölderlin says of the disciples, it is difficult to accept such destitution and to live in the night. In the second part of this stanza, beginning with

> Zwar Eisen träget der Schacht (11.11)
>
> The pit bears iron, though

the language accelerates as there is a suggestion that the poet might be rich enough to form an image of Christ as he was; this breathlessness continues into the next stanza, but instead of coming to an end, the sentence breaks off, and separated from it by a hyphen appear the warning words:

> Im Zorne sichtbar sah' ich einmal
> Des Himmels Herrn, nicht daß ich seyn sollt' etwas, sondern
> Zu lernen. (12.5–8)
>
> In anger visible once I saw
> The Lord of Heaven, not that I should be something, but
> To learn.

The suggestion that the poet might be rich enough to create an image of God that would once again render him visible, present, is rejected. When, impatient, he tries to fashion such an image, another Golden Calf, falsehood reigns and humanity is lost.

The rest of this and the following stanza express an eschatological hope. The present night will come to an end, although we humans lack the strength to bring this about. Once again there will be those able to see and to name the Highest. But we cannot will this into reality:

> Denn sie [die Menschen] nicht walten, es waltet aber
> Unsterblicher Schicksaal und es wandelt ihr Werk
> Von selbst, und eilend geht es zu Ende.
> Wenn nemlich höher gehet himmlischer
> Triumphgang, wird genennet, der Sonne gleich
> Von Starken der frohlockende Sohn des Höchsten (12.10–15)
>
> For they do not govern, the fate
> It is of immortals that governs, and their work
> Proceeds by its own force and hurrying seeks its end.
> For when heavenly triumph goes higher
> The jubilant son of the Highest
> Is called like the sun by the strong.

This relates to the earlier statement:

> Denn wiederkommen sollt es
> Zu rechter Zeit (8.7–8)

> For it was to come back when
> The time was due

Yet this day belongs to an indefinite future. Until it arrives we have to wait:

> Es warten aber
> Der scheuen Augen viele,
> Zu schauen das Licht. (13.5–7)
>
> But many timid eyes
> Are waiting to see the light.

Willing to wait, they save themselves from destructive lightning:

> Nicht wollen
> Am scharfen Strale sie blühn (13.5–7)
>
> They are reluctant to flower
> Beneath the searing beam

Content with what has been established, they entrust themselves to the mediation of Holy Scripture (13.13; 14.11).

The fourteenth stanza addresses the landgrave of Homburg, to whom the poem is dedicated, as to someone more beloved by the Heavenly ones than the poet.

> Denn Eines weiß ich,
> Daß nemlich der Wille
> Des ewigen Vaters viel
> Dir gilt. Still ist sein Zeichen
> Am donnernden Himmel. (14.4–8)
>
> For one thing I know:
> The eternal Father's will
> Means much to you. Now silent is
> His sign on thundering heaven

The silent sign in the thundering sky is of course the rainbow, sign of the covenant between God and mankind, following the Deluge, but also the rainbow that in the Book of Revelations rises above the throne of the judge, that rises also, despite Hegel, and quite irrationally, above the throne of the Absolute Spirit which, appropriating the biblical text, Hegel names to end the *Phenomenology*.

The landgrave, himself committed to pietism, had asked the old Klopstock to write an ode against the critical reading of the Bible advanced by such representatives of the Enlightenment as Reimarus and Fichte.[53]

---

53. See Schmidt, *Hölderlins geschichtsphilosophische Hymnen*, pp. 187–90.

Does the conclusion of the Book of Revelations not warn in the most explicit way against such liberal interpretations: no one should add or take away any of its words (Rev. 22.18–19). Klopstock declined the request, but it was answered by Hölderlin. In this penultimate stanza Hölderlin once again asserts the presence of the divine, indeed of Christ, even in this age.

> Und Einer stehet darunter
> Sein Leben lang. Denn noch lebt Christus.
> Es sind aber die Helden, seine Söhne
> Gekommen all und heilige Schriften
> Von ihm und den Blitz erklären
> Die Thaten der Erde bis itzt (14.12–13)

> And there is one who stands
> Beneath it his whole life long. For Christ lives yet.
> But all the heroes, his sons,
> Have come, and holy scriptures
> About him, and lightning is explained by
> The deeds of the world until now

Though invisible and with his temples seized and his glory blown away by the storms of time, Christ still lives. And in the thundering sky stands the rainbow of hope.

The last stanza offers a final determination of the task of the poet; at the same time it states in what sense God can be grasped today. Its first two lines once again characterize this age as an age of need:

> Zu lang, zu lang schon ist
> Die Ehre der Himmlischen unsichtbar. (15.1–2; cf. 10.10–11)

> Too long, too long now
> The honour of the Heavenly has been invisible

And since we cannot see and thus describe them, they have to seize us:

> Denn fast die Finger müssen sie
> Uns führen und schmählich
> Entreißt das Herz uns eine Gewalt. (15.3–5)

> For almost they must guide
> Our fingers, and shamefully
> A power is wresting our hearts from us.

Pagan rather than Christian is the insistence on the Heavenly Ones, who do not want to be neglected. To each divinity we owe proper sacrifice and service. But the poet's own service, first to the earth, to nature, and then to the light of the sun, to reason, is now judged inadequate, because too one-sided.

> Wir haben gedienet der Mutter Erd'
> Und haben jüngst dem Sonnenlichte gedient,
> Unwissend, der Vater aber liebt,
> Der über allen waltet,
> Am meisten, daß gepfleget werde
> Der veste Buchstab, und Bestehendes gut
> Gedeutet. Dem folgt deutscher Gesang. (15.9–15)

> We have served Mother Earth
> And lately have served the sunlight,
> Unwittingly, but what the Father
> Who reigns over all loves most
> Is that the solid letter
> Be given scrupulous care, and the existing
> Be well interpreted. This German song observes.

The poet here distances himself from both the Greek gods and the Enlightenment. Poetry must serve what previous words have established. The reference to the *veste Buchstab* recalls Protestant insistence on the firm letter of the Bible. But that letter, while firm, needs to be well interpreted. This is the task of poetry. To refuse this modest hermeneutic function is to run the risk of letting go of what has been established without putting anything in its place.

There is thus a sense in which "Patmos" still addresses the demand of the "System-Programme" for a "Monotheism of reason and heart, for a polytheism of imagination and art." What the father loves most must be balanced against what is called for by the statement that every divinity demands sacrifice and service, where such balance is shadowed by God's presence as destructive time. But over the destructive waters of time rises the rainbow, prefigured in the poem by the lightly built bridges that allow the sons of the Alps to walk fearlessly across the abyss.

8 The Idealism of the German Romantics
KENNETH L. SCHMITZ

Three introductory comments will serve to clarify the manner in which I will approach the topic. First comment: The general theme places emphasis upon the emergence and character of German idealism. Now, the term "idealism" is associated most properly with philosophy, and the philosophical idealism most associated with the German romantics is the metaphysical idealism of the great post-Kantian philosophers. This invites a comparison, but it is one marked by a certain imbalance between the parties of such a comparison. For a major difficulty lies not with the idealist philosophers but with the romantic literati. By the very nature of the two enterprises the former sets considerable stock in striving for conceptual explicitness and systematic order, even if it does not always realize that ideal. On the other hand, the very character of romantic literature, poetry, and drama, as well as the critical essays written in the romantic spirit, are more varied, less explicit, and less persistent in the pursuit of conceptual definition, even if they are for that very reason often more charming. To see the marked difference, one has only to compare the treatment of the "irony of irony," an important theme with Friedrich Schlegel, and Hegel's criticism of Schlegel's treatment of the term in the *Ästhetik*. The philosopher's complaint is that the poet lacks both method and depth.[1]

1. What displeased Hegel about the romantics generally was not, of course, the elements they held somewhat in common, even if uneasily, such as a nonabstract sense of the whole—organic for the romantics, concretely universal for Hegel. It was rather the romantics' lack of a rational, or more precisely, speculative method and genuine philosophical depth. And, indeed, measured by the conceptual standard of philosophy, their ideas seem undeveloped and unfinished, more images and themes than ideas or concepts in the philosophical sense. Thus, for example, Hegel criticizes Friedrich Schlegel (1772–1829) for his insistence on detailed accuracy in presenting the (medieval) past, because he overlooks the higher truth that we moderns possess, and which Hegel recognizes in his own concept of objectivity (*Ästhetik*, 2 vols. [Frankfurt, 1966, based on the 2d ed., 1842], 1.264). Or again, Hegel criticizes Schlegel's overextension of the category of the symbolic because it remains vague (1.307, 388). And he complains that Schlegel's attempt at a sort

There is no "typical" romantic, anymore than there is a "typical" philosopher. I have drawn my characterization of romanticism from very different romantic authors, but the pertinent traits for a comparison with idealism include the following: the free play of the imagination in a world where the unexpected is to be expected, where identities may undergo sudden and surprising transformations; a rich tapestry of images, events, feelings, and moods; a loosening of the distinctions fixed by ordinary understanding between the real and the ideal, between the factual and the fictional; a conviction of the interrelatedness of things; the sense of a certain emptiness or absence in the present time; and a longing for the infinite.

The second comment: The role played by romanticism in the formation of German idealism may not best be grasped as a determinate genetic connection from a particular romantic author to a particular idealist philosopher. Indeed, there is a good deal of interchange of an indefinite sort. I say "indefinite," because there is very little reference to specific romantic authors in the philosophical accounts. What is more, the connection between, say, Fichte's notion of the productive imagination and the romantic employment of it by a poet such as Friedrich Schlegel reverses the sequence and dependence, since the origin of some romantic themes may seem to be found first in the philosophers, rather than idealist philosophy being prefigured by the poets. I say "may seem to be found," since I am not sure but that the relationship is grounded in a still deeper common cultural current, a groundswell and, so to speak, Zeitgeist that embraces both the poet and the philosopher even as it receives varied expression through them.[2]

---

of poetry of poetry ends in being the flattest prose (1.289). On the other hand, Hegel's evaluation of romanticism is not unnuanced. Thus, he finds that Karl Wilhelm Ferdinand Solger (1780–1819), unlike Ludwig Tieck (1773–1853), did penetrate to the philosophical depth of infinite absolute negativity (*unendliche absolute Negativität*) through which the infinite passes over into the finite, although he did not get beyond the point of negativity (1.7).

My own references to the romantics in what follows are not intended to be entirely representative. Variety is the very spice of the movement and only a comprehensive anthology and history of the movement can be at all adequate. The references do intend, however, to *illustrate* parallels in several key themes and ideas of especial import to philosophy—even convergences that are not accidental but rather show a deep affinity between the imagination of the romantics and the conceptuality of the post-Kantian philosophers. This is no surprise in respect to Schelling's philosophy, but suggests a closer affinity of spirit than Hegel would have cared to concede.

2. So that, even in the face of Hegel's protest and evident lack of sympathy with the literary expressions of the romantic spirit, the import of my argument leads to a point at which I dare to say that the title "The Idealism of the German Romantics," if not precisely convertible with, is nonetheless supplemented by, the title "The Romanticism of the German Idealists."

Third comment: On the philosopher's side, it is necessary to clarify the precise sense of the term "idealism," since there are so many of them. It is perhaps satisfactory initially to call the idealism "metaphysical," though here too one must be clear about the precise nature of the metaphysics that is married to idealism. Nevertheless, despite the scope of the field under consideration, even perhaps because of it, the topic is a rich one and promises to cast light upon both terms of the comparison—a comparison that I will argue is more than a comparison and is, in fact, a relation.

In approaching the topic, then, it will help to set the four points of the compass that will guide us along a current from romanticism to metaphysical idealism, a current that sometimes reverses its flow and in which the contrary waters mingle with one another. The four points of the compass are: (1) the idea or symbol of the *whole*, of the whole that is more than an external framework; (2) the *part* that is not just a part, but is in collusion with the whole; (3) the creative *power* that makes worlds by fusing the real and the ideal; and (4) the *oneness* of all things real and ideal, *hen kai pan, eins und alles*.³

It is fitting that with this figure I have written as a poet, even if a bad one; but I must now think as a philosopher. (1) The whole that is more than a frame is an organic whole, an interpenetrative totality that finds in nature its immediate embodiment. (2) The part that is not just a part is the singular that is no longer simply a particular nor even an individual, but is rather each feeling and imagining human subjectivity.⁴ (3) The power that fuses the real and the ideal, the actual and the

---

3. *Athenäum-Fragment* 116 signals the agenda of the early romantics of the Jena circle. The *hen kai pan* became a slogan for the young Hölderlin, Schelling, Sinclair, Hegel, and others. See H. S. Harris, *Hegel's Development: Night Thoughts (1801–1806)* (Oxford: Clarendon Press, 1983), pp. 57–59, 79, 5; also see *Hegel's Development: Toward the Sunlight (1770–1801)* (Oxford: Clarendon Press, 1972), pp. 97–99.

It was the enthusiasm for a certain reading of Spinoza that contributed to the charge of pantheism and that left not only the romantics, but also such diverse figures as Lessing and Goethe under mild suspicion in the aftermath of the *Pantheismusstreit*. This sense of organic unity was given theological expression by the young Friedrich Schleiermacher (*Über die Religion* [1799]):

Die Religion lebt ihr ganzes Leben auch in der Natur, aber in der unendlichen Natur des Ganzen, des Einen und Allen; was in dieser alles Einzelne und so auch der Mensch gilt und wo alles und auch er treiben und bleiben mag in dieser ewigen Gärung einzelner Formen und Wesen, das will sie in stiller Ergebenheit im Einzelnen anschauen und ahnden.

4. Recall the remark of Goethe (*Zahme Xenien* 5), who was neither *Aufklärer* nor *Romantiker*, nor even a "mere" philosopher, a remark that gave concrete expression to the unity of the universal and the singular and which Hegel would term the concrete universal: *"Ich bin Weltbewohner, Bin Weimaraner"* (*Goethes Werke*, ed. Heinrich Kurz [Leipzig and Vienna], 1.502).

imaginary, the factual and the fictional, is the creative imagination of the genius, and even of the merely talented artist.[5] But the power is also that of the speculative philosopher who sublates the fixed distinctions between the finite and the infinite, the inner and the outer, the real and the ideal. (4) The oneness of all things real and ideal is the unity that can only be expressed by the poet in and through a singular vision of the whole that is touched sometimes by nostalgia, sometimes by comedy, sometimes by melancholy, sometimes by irony, sometimes by the fantastic, sometimes by the grotesque, and at exalted moments by the sublime.[6] But it is also the achievement of the speculative philosopher who brings together all things in the unity of the absolute system. Moreover, it is the unity that transcends the older "dogmatic" metaphysics' preference for things over thoughts, for what is made over what is to be made.

I

The compass is meant to direct us toward the metaphysical idealists and their vision of the whole; for it is this vision, expressed by the poets in various and even chaotic ways, that also leads the philosophers to write—no longer the *Kritik der reinen Vernunft*, critiques of pure and practical reason, nor even the several Introductions to the *Wissenschaftslehre*—but to trace out instead the odyssey of *Spirit*. Indeed, the odyssey is so new that, moved in their own conceptual way by the sensibility and

---

5. Cf. Hegel's discussion of the productive activity of the *Phantasie* (as distinct from the passive *Einbildungskraft*) in the forms of *Talent* and *Genius*, the latter possessing the productive energy of a great soul and achieving universal import (*Ästhetik*, 1.275ff.).
6. It would be artificial to identify each of these moods and manners with one or another romantic author, since they are often to be found side by side in the same author. Hans Robert Jauss remarks that "*das Ungenügen an der eigene, unvollendeten Gegenwart ist der gemeinsame Nenner der konservativen wie der progressiven Romantiker*" (cited by Hans-Jürgen Schmitt, in *Die deutsche Literatur in Text und Darstellung: Romantik I* [Stuttgart: Reclam, 1974], p. 12). Heinrich Heine, no friend of the romantics, to be sure, writes of Friedrich Schlegel that "he hated the present, the future frightened him and his inspired prophetic gaze penetrated only into the past, which he loved" (*The Romantic School and Other Essays*, ed. Jost Hermand and Robert C. Holub, trans. Helen M. Mustard [New York: Continuum, 1985], p. 47; reprint from *Heinrich Heine: Selected Works*, ed. Helen M. Mustard [Random House, 1973]). Others insist that the romantics were very much in tune with their age. I see no contradiction in holding both positions: they were disaffected by what they took to be the lifeless dessication of the present condition, which was the late product of the *Aufklärung* (cf. A. W. Schlegel's critique in *Vorlesungen über schöne Literatur und Kunst*, nos. 5 & 6); but they nonetheless were actively engaged in attempting to reshape the present and the immediate future. One need only recall Novalis's famous demand: *Die Welt muss romantisiert werden;* and Friedrich Schlegel's promotion of *eine progressive Universalpoesie* (*Athenäum-Fragment* 116). This was of vital importance, given his conviction that "*alle Philosophie ist Idealismus, und es gibt keinen wahren Realismus als den der Poesie.*"

sublimity that moved the poets, the philosophical narrators find themselves constrained to give the hero of the story a new and more fitting name. For it is no longer the labor of *Verstand,* nor even of *Vernunft;* it is no longer reason, but *Geist,* the Germanic Spirit, that undertakes this new journey.

The German sense of *Geist* does not take its measure from the technical philosophical sense of the Greco-Latin *spiritus.*[7] The Latin term *spiritus* carries with it a distinction of form and matter, which finds its origin in the Greek philosophical notions of *eidos* and *hyle.* In this technical sense, *forma* is a specifying principle of each individual substance or entity, and as pure form it is *spiritus.* The philosophical sense of *Geist,* on the other hand, has its origins in part from the particular conditions of eighteenth-century German national life. I say "in part," since much that is continuous with the Greco-Latin intellectual heritage survives in a transformed way in the German *Geist.* Nor is this surprising, for, after all, the later culture had drunk from the ancient springs of Hellas and the aqueducts of Rome. The transformation, however, is more than a terminological one, more than a transliteration; it is a radical cultural translation.[8] Schelling is aware of the inadequacy of spirit understood as form when he writes that works of art that arise out of the composition or combination even of beautiful forms would still be without beauty, since

---

7. I have contrasted the two terms elsewhere at more length, most recently in "The First Principle of Personal Becoming," *Review of Metaphysics* 47 (June 1994): 757–74, esp. 757–60.

Indeed, *Geist* is not the only German term that has no direct equivalent in the Latin philosophical tradition. *Wirklichkeit* does not translate *actualitas,* nor does *Wesen* render *essentia,* even if translators are driven by the incommensurability of the languages to accept these obscure compromises. In general, the Latin philosophical tradition works off of present participles and intransitive verbs, whereas in key terms the German works from past participles and from transitive verbs.

8. Hans-Jürgen Schmitt (*Die deutsche Literatur,* p. 12) cites the not wholly implausible claim made by Hippolyte Taine that from 1780 to 1800 the German cultural nation had produced all the ideas of that age. Perhaps because the Germanic peoples were without a firm political unity that matched the breadth of their cultural ingenuity and their linguistic space, they were able to draw upon the implications of a broad and deep movement not wholly alien to Mediterranean culture. They drew upon it above all in music, science, and philosophy, and so the Greece they recovered—a Greece, if you will, that never was—is the Greece of the artists and philosophers. These are precisely those dimensions of the human spirit that are least directly and immediately affected by the strong hand of sociopolitical unity and power. Perhaps, too, this is why German intellectuals, fired by Winckelmann's panegyric, turned with such enthusiasm and sense of affinity to the Greeks who had also failed to win political unity, unlike the English in the sixteenth century who had turned with an imperial eye upon the Roman literary and legal tradition. This may catch, too, the excitement expressed by Hegel at the beginning of the *Science of Logic* when he makes the extraordinary observation that, with the abolition of the Holy Roman Empire, even logic and ontology have to be rethought! It is as though the promise of the unification of the Germanic peoples represented the culmination of the labor of *Geist.*

that whereby the work of the whole is beautiful can no longer be form. "It lies beyond form, is essence, the universal, has the look and the expression of the indwelling spirit of nature."[9] That spirit of nature is, of course, *Geist*.[10]

We today may appreciate the sense of *Geist* more easily from the music of the period—say, in listening to one of Beethoven's symphonies, none better perhaps than the *Pastoral*. *Geist* gathers all things into itself in the wake of a great storm, to be followed by a calm in which all things bask in the stillness of a waking dream.[11] Then again it is playful, almost skittish, and suddenly threatening, even hostile, a destructive force that is so inevitable, so compelling, that it is acceptable, even forgivable. That is how so many of the romantic poets and authors felt the moving force of *Geist* within their own works and lives. And that is why they could so easily draw nature up into the free power of *Geist*. For if the Latin *spiritus* laid emphasis upon form and its consequent order, *Geist* brought forward the element of life as profligate power. Whereas *spiritus* brought order to form, *Geist* caught up matter into the giddy swirl of its all-encompassing dance.

Friedrich Schlegel tells us that the essence of romantic poetry is that it is forever becoming (*ewig nur werden*).[12] The romantic authors find the proper medium for the expression of this living power to be the spoken and written word—in poetry, drama, legend, and novel. The philosophers, caught up in the same maelstrom, are more sober, and in the author of the *Phenomenology of Spirit* we even catch something of Fichte's

---

9. *Über das Verhältnis der bildenden Künste zu der Natur* (1807).

10. The sense of dynamic cultural unity found expression also in the national *Volksgeist*, given literary expression in the works of the Brothers Grimm (e.g., *Kinder-und Hausmärchen* [1812–1815]), Joseph Görres (*Die teutschen Volksbücher* [1807]), the collection of *Volkslieder* by Achim von Arnim and Clemens Brentano (*Des Knaben Wunderhorn* [1808]), and the writings of Ludwig Tieck and others.

11. Cf. these lines by Joseph von Eichendorff (1788–1857): "*Schläft ein Lied in allen Dingen, Die da träumen fort und fort, Und die Welt hebt an zu singen, Triffst du nur das Zauberwort.*"

12. In the *Athenäum-Fragment* 116 he writes:

Die romantische Dichtart ist noch im Werden; ja das ist ihr eigentliches Wesen, dass sie ewig nur werden, nie vollendet sein kann. Sie kann durch keine Theorie erschöpft werden. . . . Sie allein ist unendlich, wie sie allein frei ist and das als ihr erstes Gesetz anerkennt, dass die Willkür des Dichters kein Gesetz über sich leide.

Romantic poetic art is still coming into being; indeed, that is its proper essence, that eternally it is only coming to be, that it can never be finished. It can be exhausted by no theory. . . . It alone is endless [*unendlich*], just as it alone is free, and it recognizes as its first law, that the will of the poet suffers no law above it.

This is a poetic expression of Schlegel's appropriation of Fichte's *ego* as *ein unendliches Streben*.

ethical earnestness, now transformed beyond morality into the labor of a Spirit tinged with gray, in which playfulness has given way to striving—and perhaps a certain sadness.[13]

If *spiritus* as *forma* is the principle of an individual entity, *Geist* is the dynamism whose work may be called *Gestalt*, the figured whole, the integral totality. Much has been written about Fichte's and Schelling's influence upon many of the romantics, and quite rightly; but it is Kant, the father of German philosophy, who sets the contours of the concept of *Totalität*, though he does it in the name of reason (*Vernunft*). At the end of the First *Critique* Kant sets forth the ideal of philosophy as totality. In so doing he catches up and transforms the modern notion, one might even say the Enlightenment ideal, of *System* and sets it on the path toward the absolute systems of his own successors. Kant tells us that the ideal of philosophy is to realize the architectonic system, in which all the essential needs of transcendental reason are satisfied: the need to know, to do, and to hope. Now this couplet of *Vernunft* and *Totalität* (or transcendental system) prepares the way for that couplet which I have called *Geist* and *Gestalt*. And prepares the way for the emergence of the notion of the Absolute out of the concept of totality, when, against Kant's restriction to the finite, the concept of totality is taken to incorporate the infinite within itself.[14]

In contrasting the architectonic system with the partiality and contingency of what Kant calls "mere Scholastic systems," Kant stresses the transcendental necessity that binds the elements of the truly philosophical system together. For these essential needs are related within the very structure of reason itself. This sense of transcendental interrelationship becomes even more pronounced in Fichte's *ego* and its productive imagination. And among the romantics the sense of inwardness binds the various facets into a diffuse organic whole.

And yet, to the minds of the philosophers of absolute idealism who follow—Hegel even more than Schelling—the relations seem still too external, too contingent, and in their finitude too partial. The philosophers put the stress not so much on necessity, however, as on the internal character of the relations that bind the factors into an organic whole, and from which the necessity arises. For among the philosophers the

---

13. I have in mind, of course, the use to which Hegel puts Schiller's lines at the close of the *Phenomenology*—lines, moreover, that express the spirit of the whole work, and—if we are to believe Hegel—the spirit of the age.

As to the sadness, it is explicit at the end of the Berlin *Lectures on the Philosophy of Religion*.

14. This seems to be the case even in Fichte's development in which the unlimited activity of the *ego* is transformed in his later works into a sort of nonpersonal Absolute that is more ultimate even than the activity of the *ego*.

character of the necessity becomes more systemic with the inclusion of the infinite in the form of the Absolute.[15] But a deep sense of longing for the infinite had already been expressed before the turn of the century in the works of many romantics, a feeling that is the source of such moods as melancholy, nostalgia, and irony.[16] It was the overemphasis upon the finite in the rationalism of the age and the absence of an acknowledgment of the infinite that moved many of the poets to turn to the medieval past and its symbolic awareness of the infinite.

But while the philosophers strove to make more explicit the systemic necessity of the bonds, they still shared with the poets the inner character of those bonds, felt by the poets and conceptualized by the philosophers; so that both endorsed a totality in which inner unity is heightened by the disparate variety and contingency within its embrace. It was, of course, the young Schelling who drew the understanding of nature as totality and as art into the central place of his early system.[17] Nevertheless, it is already Kant's conception of the architectonic system and the notion of *Totalität* that finds expression in both the romantic literati and the post-Kantian philosophers.

The modern notion of system had been emerging in pre-Kantian philosophy under the aegis of an epistemologically oriented idealism initiated by Descartes. In distinguishing the absolute idealisms of the post-Kantian philosophers from the pre-Kantian idealisms, however, we must once again take notice of the idealism that in Kant was at once transcendental and critical, and precisely critical because it was transcendental. It was, so to speak, the gateway idealism; and its transcendental turn was not lost upon the metaphysical idealists who followed Kant. But neither did it go unnoticed by many of the romantic poets and literati as well; so that the transcendental turn entered into the German intellectual culture quite generally, and after 1783 quite quickly to judge by the enthusiasm for Kant, if not always the understanding of Kant, that reached

---

15. Although Schelling's works at the turn of the century made Nature their principal theme, nevertheless a precocious work took up the theme *Ueber Mythen* (1793), and decades-long preoccupation with religion received posthumous publication in *Philosophie der Offenbarung* and *Philosophie der Mythologie*. In *Philosophie und Religion* (1804) he clarifies the character of the Absolute as an absolutely simple infinite.

16. In *Art and the Absolute: A Study of Hegel's Aesthetics* (Albany: State University of New York Press, 1985), William Desmond comments upon the perceived sense of absence by quoting A. W. Schlegel: "The poetry of the ancients was that of possession, ours is that of longing" (p. 109).

17. Mention need only be made of *Ideen zu einer Philosophie der Natur* (1797), *Von der Weltseele* (1798), *Erster Entwurf eines Systems der Naturphilosophie* (1799), *Einleitung zu dem Entwurf eines Systems der Naturphilosophie oder über den Begriff der spekulativen Physik* (1799), *Ueber den wahren Begriff der Naturphilosophie* (1801), and *Bruno, oder über das göttliche und natürliche Prinzip der Dinge* (1802).

popular levels among the educated after Reinhold's presentation of the main lines of the Kantian philosophy.

On the previous side of Kant, the earlier versions of epistemological idealism, stemming from Descartes, are a necessary counterpoint in any consideration of romanticism. For the earlier idealism had underwritten the forms of mechanistic science, the utilitarian technology of the *Encyclopédie*, and the neoclassical formalisms of literature, art, and theater.[18] Romanticism was quite clearly a reaction to such epistemological idealism. August Wilhelm Schlegel complained that the narrow epistemologies of such as Descartes, Malebranche, Leibniz, and Spinoza, as well as Locke, had led many to judge that appearances that fall outside the limits of sensory reception are taken to be symptoms of illness and have been given the names *Schwärmerei* and *Wahnsinn*, which I suppose we might render as "moonshine and madness."[19]

2–3

I have gone on at some length about the transcendental notion of the *whole* and its relation to both the romantic poets and the idealist philosophers, stressing the reaction to the earlier idealisms and the formative influence of Kant. I must now say something about the *part and the power*. We have before us a parade of idealisms: the epistemological or methodological idealism[20] initiated by Descartes, the critical idealism

---

18. To be sure, the actual history calls for qualification of such a sweeping statement. Leibniz transformed the nominalism so explicit in mechanism into nonquantitative "windowless" monads; and Spinoza certainly did not promote the garden-variety utilitarianism associated with the *Encyclopédie*. But in the main and popular stream the statement holds.

19. *Vorlesungen über schöne Literatur und Kunst*, Lectures 5 & 6 (1801–1804); cited by Schmitt, in *Die deutsche Literatur*, p. 33. The phrase "*die über die Grenze der Empfänglichkeit ihres Sinnes hinauslagen*" could be taken to mean "those impressions that lie beyond the bound of their sense," i.e., of their criteria for what has meaning. The "rights of imagination" are also defended. Speaking of these same philosophers, he writes: "*Sie verkannten durchaus die Rechte der Fantasie und hätten, wo möglich, die Menschen gern ganz von ihr geheilt.*"

We ought not to forget, either, the other background forces that prepared the way for the romantic movement, such as, for example, the gothic revival, in which such authors as Klopstock, young Wieland, Hamann, and Herder played a prominent role. W. D. Robson-Scott, in *The Literary Background of the Gothic Revival in Germany* (Oxford: Clarendon Press, 1965), argues that the publication of the young Goethe's *Baukunst* essay in Herder's *Von Deutscher Art und Kunst* (1793) could be said to mark the beginning of the romantic movement in Germany. Christopher Dawson took up an even broader perspective (in *Mediaeval Religion and Other Essays* [New York: Sheed & Ward, 1935]), by arguing for a remote beginning in Arabic sources, through the troubadors—influences that reached down to Herder. He insisted upon the difference between the stress on sentiment in Rousseau and the feeling for the Middle Ages that characterizes the German romantics. Nevertheless, it would be hard to deny all French influence upon them.

20. The term "methodological" designates the procedure, whereas the term "epistemological" designates the goal, which is the attainment of certitude.

turned out by Kant, and the metaphysical idealisms of Schelling and Hegel. Not surprisingly, the post-Kantians are transcendental and not merely epistemological idealists. It is to the transcendental character that we must turn to appreciate the role of the part and the power in romanticism, and in order to take the measure of the metaphysical idealisms of Schelling and Hegel. To see that, however, we must first pay due notice to the role played by Kant and Fichte in providing a certain philosophical support for the prominence of the creative imagination in romanticism.

Scholars rightly stress the contribution of Fichte to the romantic movement, but the roots of that contribution lie in Kant's Third *Critique*. Of course, the boldness of the romantics is not to be found there, for Kantian principles would have condemned it as extravagant. Nevertheless, there is in the Third *Critique* the affirmation of the absolute superiority of the moral reason in the face of the dynamically sublime: the aesthetic fear awakened in us by the enormity of powers of nature is not the terror of actual physical injury, but rather a particular fear coupled with the consciousness of our physical safety. Such a combination of "secure danger" leads us to recognize the power of the imagination to *valorize* the ideal over against the empirically real and thereby to achieve a certain inner freedom.[21]

With Fichte this inner freedom becomes a constitutive freedom, but not an arbitrary one. The finite *ego* in and through the productive imagination engages in the constitution of the world as a field for moral action. But with Fichte there were two limiting conditions inherent in this unlimited activity of the *ego*. The first was that it was not conscious, and was only available through transcendental reflection; it followed, secondly, that it was not open to creative modification by the conscious will. It was quite other with the romantics who raised the productive imagination to free-ranging consciousness. The most extreme adoption of Fichte's productive imagination was undoubtedly the "magical idealism" of Novalis, for whom nature was "*rein poetisch.*"[22]

---

21. I deliberately say "valorize" because Kant's First *Critique* is not to be understood as constructing a phenomenal world, as though the human reason is a demigod; but rather as giving noetic validity and authority to the theoretical project of reason, once it is freed of its metaphysical dogmatism and has attained the critical attitude. This much at least of the earlier epistemological idealism remains in Kant's critical idealism.

22. Speaking of *Märchen*, Novalis insists that

die ganze Natur muss auf eine wunderliche Art mit der ganzen Geisterwelt vermischt seyn. Die Zeit der allg[emeinen] Anarchie — Gesetzlosigkeit — Freyheit — der Naturstand der Natur — die Zeit vor der Welt. Diese Zeit vor der Welt liefert gleichsam der zerstreuten Züge der Zeit nach der Welt — wie der Naturstand ein sonderbares Bild des ewigen Reichs ist. Die Welt des Märchens ist die durchausentgegengesetze Welt der Welt der Wahrheit (Geschichte) — und eben darum ihr so dur-

The Fichtean influence is, if more sober, no less strong in the young Schelling, who turned the productive imagination toward art and nature. But even more important, for Schelling the world of nature is not the objectification of the absolute *ego*, but rather the immediate manifestation of the infinite Absolute. He writes: "The objective world is only the original, still unconscious poetry of the Spirit. The universal organon of philosophy—and the keystone of the whole arch—is the philosophy of art," since it alone could read the unconscious poetry of *Geist*.[23] Now the creative imagination of the artist is a "free" expression which, with Schelling, has taken on a metaphysical significance. The poet, on the other hand, not necessarily heeding or even wanting a metaphysics, could nonetheless appreciate the philosopher's celebration of artistic freedom, even if the philosophical celebration remained merely cerebral. But artistic freedom is a curious sort of freedom. It is not the freedom of the citizen under the laws, nor the freedom of choice experienced in ethical conduct. And yet it is a creative power.

What, precisely, then, is the meaning of this new sense of creativity? Here it will help to go back several centuries to consider the status of *things* in premodern thought; I mean the things that are experienced as *real* in ordinary experience insofar as it is untouched by Kant's critical "Copernican" Revolution. Already prepared for by the pre-Kantian idealisms, the transcendental turn puts the nail in the coffin of the older sense of the reality of *things*. For it rejects the older understanding of causal power. That older project understood causal power as the communication of being, a communication that originated in the very *creation* of being. The transcendental turn moves away from creation and toward creativity. The movement from method to critique sees metaphysical causality replaced by the task of the vindication of reason. In

---

chaus ähnlich — wie das Chaos der vollendeten Schöpfung. (Novalis, *Schriften*, ed. R. Samuel [Stuttgart: Kohlhammer, 1960], 3.280–81)

Less extreme and somewhat more philosophical, Friedrich Schlegel saw in Fichte's *ego*, expanded by his own sense of the productive imagination, an infinity of meaning and inwardness.

23. *System des transzendentalen Idealismus (1800)*, in *Werke*, 6 vols., ed. M. Schröter (Munich, 1927–1928), 2. 349; cited by F. Copleston, *A History of Philosophy: 5.7, Fichte to Nietzsche* (Westminster, Md.: Newman, 1963), p. 119. Schelling's conception of the infinite Absolute as the indifference and identity of the subjective and the objective bears affinity with the romantic tendency to fuse the real and the ideal, especially when one recalls his doctrine of aesthetic intuition as the medium in which the Absolute is apprehended.

On seeing nature as totality in the form of art, Wilhelm Heinrich Wackenroder (1773–1798) wrote: "*Gott wohl die ganze Natur oder die ganze Welt auf ähnliche Art, wie wir ein Kunstwerk ansehen möge*" (*Herzengiessungen eines kunstliebenden Klosterbruder* [1797], in *Sämtliche Werke und Briefe: Historisch-kritische Ausgabe*, ed. S. Vietta [Heidelberg: C. Winter, 1991], 1.100).

the practical concerns of Kant, and indeed, of Fichte, that vindication was still restricted to the epistemological and moral orders.[24] Now, the resolution of that task in their philosophies purchased a certain inner freedom, whose character was deontic.[25] With the romantics, however, that freedom becomes something more: not quite the freedom of a creator of being ex nihilo, but not simply a deontic moral freedom either. It is instead a new kind of freedom that hovers in between (*in der Schwebe*), less than *creatio ex nihilo* but *more than epistemological validity or moral autonomy*. It becomes the free exercise of the creative imagination in which the passive acceptance of the real is transgressed and the real is fused with the ideal.[26]

We will have to ask: What kind of metaphysics will support such a freedom? It cannot be a metaphysics of creation, but a metaphysics of

24. The theme of the primacy of the moral order in Kant is most often thought of in terms of obligation and duty; but it is found too in aesthetic experience, precisely in the treatment of the sublime. The theme of moral superiority is developed in greater completeness by Schiller in the two essays *Vom Erhabenen* ("On the Sublime") and *Über das Erhabene* ("Concerning the Sublime"). In the first essay he writes:

> We call an object sublime if, whenever the object is presented or represented, our sensuous nature feels its limits, but our rational nature feels its superiority, its freedom from limits. Thus, we come up short against a sublime object *physically*, but we elevate ourselves above it *morally*, namely, through ideas.

And in the second he writes: "The will is what distinguishes the human race, and reason itself is nothing but the will's everlasting rule." See *Friedrich Schiller: Essays*, ed. Walter Hinderer and Daniel Dahlstrom (New York: Continuum, 1993), pp. 22, 70.

25. Rudolph A. Makkreel (in *Imagination and Interpretation in Kant: The Hermeneutical Import of the Critique of Judgment* [Chicago: University of Chicago Press, 1990]) contrasts the determinant judgment in Kant with the reflective: "The reflective judgment, however, is more free from external controls and allows the imagination to create its own ideas for organizing experience as a formally purposive system" (p. 3; cf. p. 67). We see in Kant the possibility of a certain free range for the imagination that, coupled with the role given to the productive imagination by Fichte, will turn to phantasy in many romantics.

In his consideration of romantic art, Hegel adopts the term *Phantasie* on the grounds that the term *Einbildungskraft* is too passive. The opening for such creative freedom has its root in Kant's understanding of an aesthetic judgment (without concept) as distinct from a determinant judgment which is bound to the constitution of objects in accordance with the necessity of the categories. And so, though the transcendental imagination is assigned an important role in the schematism of the First *Critique*, it attains to a certain freedom only in the aesthetic judgment.

26. Both the poets and the philosophers show how clearly they stand on the other side of the strict Kantian divide between passivity and activity—the poets fusing the real and the ideal, the philosophers transcending the categories of passivity and activity. In his famous essay *What Is Enlightenment?* Kant places mature freedom (in the form of autonomy) clearly on the side of activity. It was this sharp divorce (a heritage from Cartesian dualism) that prompted Gabriel Marcel (*The Mystery of Being*, 2 vols. [Chicago: Regnery, 1951]), who credits his early study of Schelling for an important though not definitive phase in his development, to develop what he took to be a more adequate category, his own sense of a nonpassive receptivity (*disponibilité*).

elevated moral autonomy will not suffice either. It must be a metaphysics of creativity, and this the metaphysical idealisms of Schelling and even of Hegel are equipped to support.

It is often said that the classical German idealist tradition has made freedom its principal value; but it is a freedom quite different from the freedom of choice so prominent in English and French writings, and even in the *liberum arbitrium* of the older Latin tradition. In place of a creator God or a moral hero, a transcendental subjectivity, grown beyond the finitude to which Kant and Fichte had confined it, has taken shape as *absoluter Geist;* and it is this Spirit that carries this distinctive freedom within itself as a cosmic force. It is not strong enough to bear the weight of creation strictly taken, *creatio ex nihilo*, but it claims for itself more than the field of moral action. It first finds the new cultural space in the power of the creative imagination exploited by the poets. How was it with the philosophers? They could not—or so they thought—revisit *creatio ex nihilo* (Hegel pronounced the notion to be without meaning), nor could they be content with Kant's elevated morality. But they sought their conceptual ground also in *absoluter Geist*. Not satisfied with moral freedom, the new freedom was given expression in literature as romanticism, and in philosophy as metaphysical idealism.

What, then, is the character of this new freedom? It is essentially the freedom to make, to shape, that is, to "create" in the modern meaning of that word. Now the romantics had already met with the productive power of the imagination in Fichte, and with Schelling's identification of nature with an Absolute whose own identity overcomes the distinction between objectivity and subjectivity. And it is not surprising that romantic freedom takes on the character of world building. The older metaphysics of being had reserved creation to the supreme being,[27] but this no longer tempered the artistic taste, nor fitted the philosophical tongue. The new sense of freedom, on the other hand, welcomed the fusion of the real and the ideal as having all the validity that artistic expression can attain, all of what was called *Realidealismus*.[28] In the *Athe-*

---

27. The art historian Tatarkewicz observes that the term "creatio" was first applied to human artistry by Vasari in describing the overwhelming power and beauty of Michelangelo's Sistine Chapel. (Cf. a similar reserve in the use of the term *Brt* in *Genesis*.)

28. F. Copleston, S. J. (in *A History of Philosophy*, vol. 7: *Fichte to Nietzsche* [Westminster, Md.: Newman, 1963], p. 125), sums up the matter thus:

> In Schelling's opinion the theory of identity enables him to transcend all disputes between realism and idealism. For such controversy assumes that the distinction made by empirical consciousness between the real and the ideal can be overcome only by subordinating or even reducing the one to the other. But once we understand that the real and the ideal are one in the Absolute, the controversy loses its point. And the system of identity can thus be called real-idealism (*Realidealismus*).

näum-Fragment (116) Friedrich Schlegel claims the crown of the new freedom for poetry and draws this strong conclusion: "Romantic poetry is a progressive universal poetry. Its character is not merely to reunite all the disparate kinds of poetry and to put poetry in touch with philosophy and rhetoric. . . . All philosophy is idealism, and there is no true realism other than poetry."[29] Schelling held that the identity of the real and the ideal in the Absolute put *Schluss* to the controversy between the idealists and the realists.[30]

It is clear enough that romanticism has not escaped idealism; nor does it seem to have much cared to; but it has also claimed for itself some sort of realism. As to the philosophers, it is not unfashionable today to reject the name "idealist" when referring to Schelling's and Hegel's philosophies, and to claim for their philosophies a recovery of reality temporarily lost by Kant's phenomenalism. It remains to ask what sort of philosophical idealism and what sort of realism best describes the post-Kantian situation. And that returns us once again to Kant.

4

Let me summarize. In Part 1, I sought to establish the nature of the development of the whole as it shifted from architectonic system (*Totalität*) to integral configuration (*Gestalt*), no longer under the sponsorship of *Vernunft* but of *Geist*. In the combined Parts 2 and 3 I pointed to the aesthetic imagination as the new power that changed the character of freedom. Both of these transformations begin with Kant's critical idealism and end in metaphysical idealism. At each moment we encounter Kant.

In this fourth and final part I wish to conclude with a reflection upon the *critical attitude* effected by Kant's transcendental turn. For it is through the critical attitude that imagination and reason are redefined in their character and role to become the imagination celebrated by the poets and the reason exploited by the philosophers.

Of course, by "critical attitude" I do not mean merely human reason alert to the possibility of error. It is good to have a critical attitude toward that which deserves criticism. Aristotle had his share, and Plato too, and Thomas Aquinas insisted that authority in matters reasonable was the

---

29. "*Die romantische Poesie ist eine progressive Universalpoesie. Ihre Bestimmung ist nicht bloss, alle getrennten Gattungen der Poesie wieder zu vereinigen und die Poesie mit der Philosophie und Rhetorik in Berührhing zu setzen. . . . Alle Philosophie ist Idealismus, und es gibt keinen wahren Realismus als den der Poesie.*"

30. As always, Hegel is more muted in his enthusiasm for the new creative power, but in the *Science of Logic* even he transcends the fixed distinction between the world as appearance and the world as reality.

weakest of validations. Gilson used to say that the keen principle of economy we call "Ockham's razor" was an overly sharp implement and successor to an earlier model that Aristotle had already used for many a shave.

The Kantian critical attitude, however, is something quite specific. And it is in the retention of that attitude by the post-Kantian idealists, transformed, of course, that I find the *specific difference* between post-Kantian and pre-Kantian metaphysics. For while the Kantian criticism differs from the critical use of reason in the epistemological metaphysics of the early modern period, its major target was the ontological metaphysics of the ancient and medieval kind. It should be remarked, however, that the modern pre-Kantian epistemological metaphysics prepared the way for the Kantian critical attitude.

Everyone recognizes that there is a difference between the various pre-Kantian metaphysics and the post-Kantian metaphysical idealism. But precisely *how* does the *idealism* of the metaphysical idealists differ from other idealisms? And *how* does the *metaphysics* of the metaphysical idealists differ from other metaphysics? It is somewhat easier to answer the question about the difference among the idealisms: thus, the pre-Kantian idealisms are principally methodological; Kant's critical idealism clings to the *Ding-an-sich*, the post-Kantians reject it; Kant rejects a metaphysical intuition, while in their early phase the post-Kantians accept it.[31] Indeed, it seems to me that historians of modern philosophy have concentrated mostly on just such differences.

When we ask how their metaphysics differ from other metaphysics, however, the root of that difference is not so easily isolated. We recognize that there is a radical difference. The metaphysical idealists no longer rest content with Kantian phenomena, for they lay claim to the whole of reality.[32] Yet they do not return to the entities of traditional metaphysics. The transformation of reason by Kant's critical idealism signals, for Schelling and Hegel, a change of direction from which they cannot— nor do they wish to—turn back; the designation "post-Kantian" applied to them is more than chronological. Kant's critical idealism is a gateway through which they pass, and that passage marks their own metaphysics as specifically different from all pre-Kantian metaphysics.

A certain emancipation of the imagination and the reason receives legitimation through the critical attitude. That emancipation can be seen to unfold in three steps: first, the attack upon dogmatism; second, the twofold inversion of orders; and third, the expansion of the whole

---

31. To be sure, Hegel moved away from the notion of a metaphysical intuition, but did not return to the Kantian grounds for rejecting the notion.

32. Indeed, their critics say "the whole of reality and something more," and mean by that "more" obscure nonsense.

from an architectonic to an absolute system through the inclusion of the positive infinite. In short: dogmatism, inversion, and expansion.

First, then: In what precisely does Kant's attack upon dogmatism consist? It is usual to mark the difference between the critical idealism of Kant and that of his successors by the different status accorded to the thing-in-itself. Kant had posited it as unknowable yet necessary for thought; Fichte had rejected it in the name of the unlimited activity of the ego; and the metaphysical idealists thought themselves entirely free from it as from a chimera. But it seems to me that in asking what sort of idealism and realism we are concerned with here, it is not simply a question of how one stands with respect to the *Ding-an-sich;* or whether one accepts or rejects Kant's ostracism of it from the sphere of possible cognitive experience.[33] For the Kantian "Copernican Revolution" is not simply an affair of the unknowability of the thing-in-itself, as though one escapes the critical attitude by rejecting that doctrine. Indeed, the critical attitude does not consist primarily of a quarrel about things and their status; it is above all a disagreement about *reason* and *its* character. This is the issue of dogmatism, the theme of the matter is primarily not things but reason and its claims.

It is, then, the concern to refute dogmatism that is decisive. Kant saw this in focusing upon a critique of reason, and Schelling gave expression to it in his *Philosophical Letters on Dogmatism and Criticism* (1795). Of course, in rejecting dogmatism, neither Schelling nor Hegel simply subscribe to the Kantian or Fichtean forms of criticism, since the former is left with several dualisms and the latter with a one-sided subjectivism, and hence an even deeper unresolved dualism.[34]

---

33. We know the fate of the *an sich* in Kant: it is the unknowable *Ding an sich.* But what of it in Hegel? It appears in the notion of the *Ansichsein.* Now it can be said that the *an sich* plays a role in Hegel's dialectical philosophy somewhat parallel to the role played by *dunamis* or potency in Aristotle. But then one must stress the "somewhat," since the disanalogy is great. One must maintain the distance between what, for Hegel, would be a premodern, precritical sense and his own postcritical (yet somehow critical) sense. What, then, is the Hegelian *an sich*? It is the implicit being situated within the primacy of an absolute subjectivity. Whereas in Aristotle *dunamis* is in the service of the development of entities, in Hegel the *an sich* is in the interest of developing a transcendental subjectivity that has become *absoluter Geist.* One might say, then, that the *differentia specifica* of the new metaphysical idealism is precisely its indebtedness to Kantian critique.

34. When Hegel returns to religion to rescue it from its confines in Kantian morality, his attack upon the *Reflexionsphilosophie* does not release him from the grip of the critical attitude. The Hegelian *an sich* bears, transformed within it, the patrimony of the critical attitude; for it serves the absolute system, whereas Aristotle's *dunamis* plays out its role in the formation of entities. So, too, the critical attitude actively inspires his insistence that philosophy have the last word, since if it does not we will fall back into dogmatism. It is the critical attitude that drives Hegel on from the mere love of wisdom, *philosophia,* to philosophy become absolute science.

To repeat: It is the conception of reason itself that is at issue and not simply the fate of things. It is in the charge of *dogmatism* and Kant's resolution of it that the decisive step forward is taken. Now, as already indicated, dogmatism is first of all an attitude toward the claims of reason and not an assertion about things. And yet we must ask: What was it in things that made them the victim of the attack upon dogmatism, when the attack was directed against what was perceived to be a fault of reason? That question brings us closer to the issue; and to answer it moves us on to the second step: the twofold inversion of orders.

The twofold inversion of orders comes about first under the sponsorship of epistemology. It is the inversion of the order of cognition and the order of what is cognized; or more properly, the inversion of thought over being. Kant's famous passage in the Preface to the second edition of the First *Critique* gave it definitive expression: Reason was to approach nature in the manner of a judge, not listening to everything nature has to say, but constraining nature to answer questions of reason's own devising, drawn up a priori after a plan of its own.

There is no doubt that this first inversion was able to come about more easily and more credibly just because Kant thought he faced a nature already denuded by epistemological idealism, an impoverished nature reduced to the state of mere objectivity. That ontological reduction brought about a near-vacuum that called for the empowering of subjectivity—a subjectivity no longer simply opposed to objectivity but superior to it. That is the first inversion: if you will, the inversion of knowing over being.

But there is a further and deeper inversion that occurs in Kant's Third *Critique:* it is the inversion of cognition and freedom. A new sense of freedom finds new strength in the encounter with the sublime, for, as we have seen, that confrontation discloses the deontic superiority of a moral freedom over the world of nature. The new freedom is no longer directly and dogmatically tied to things; and given the emptying out of things and the empowering of subjectivity, that freedom is about to take itself as the ground of more than its moral life. In sum, there is a twofold inversion and priority: the subjectivity of knowing is empowered to preside over the objectivity of the known; and then, on that basis, freedom has taken priority over cognition.

If, as I am arguing, the critical attitude is definitive for the metaphysical idealists and indirectly for the romantics, both are closer to the Enlightenment ideal of autonomy than might at first appear. For what was rejected by the philosophers and poets was not the freedom of the Enlightenment as such and its ideal of autonomy—an ideal that Kant's critical attitude had exalted in the essay *What Is Enlightenment?* Rather, the philosophers and poets rejected the confinement of autonomous freedom to an abstract and utilitarian form of rationality and individuality.

The new sense of freedom called for a redefinition of creativity and of reason. The romantics thought that it was a matter of restoring sensibility and imagination, but the philosophers knew that it required a reformulation of reason as *Geist*. The issue, then, is not between minds and things, or between subjects and objects, but between two contending forms of reason. The older notion of reason, allegedly dogmatic, had found itself already inserted into a context of beings that has a source other than itself, and had found its knowledge through participation in that context of being; but that participation was now condemned as a lack of freedom, the essence of dogmatism.[35]

The Kantian and post-Kantian critical notion of reason found (and founded) the world in and through its own actualization of what was initially the superiority of moral freedom, a superiority that became an expanded freedom. For it is important to recognize that the critical attitude comes to completion not by way of cognition itself but by way of the new experience of freedom. The concrete world does not come back by virtue of a new cognitive relationship. The richness comes back through the freedom of absolute Spirit. Schelling had already seen this when, echoing Fichte, he insisted that the initial relation of consciousness to the world was to be practical rather than theoretical. Even Hegel accomplishes only a partial restoration of the theoretical—partial because restored on the basis of the new sense of freedom.

Indeed, the richness of the world did come back—its beauty, its concrete variety, its religious symbolism, its transphenomenal character. One has only to compare the moral treatment of religion in Kant's *Religion within the Bounds of Reason* with Schelling's later lectures on religion and mythology or Hegel's treatment of determinate religions in the Berlin *Lectures on the Philosophy of Religion*. Moreover, in order to address this concreteness the metaphysical idealists employed dialectic in a sense more open and flexible than Kant's limited use of it in the antinomies and in the second part of the *Kritik der reinen Vernunft*. Since the recovery encompassed the concrete forms of life, it was seen as the work of *Geist*

---

35. In the universe articulated by the older metaphysics, things qua creatures found their source in, dependence upon, and return to the creator. Nevertheless, the attack upon the alleged dogmatism did not call for atheism—only in the early Fichte. A role could be found for God, who could be honored in others ways than as creator ex nihilo: in Kant's reverent postulate, as Schelling's turbulent Absolute, or in Hegel's self-determining Trinitarian Absolute.

and no longer merely that of *Vernunft*. Having appropriated all that is, *Geist* can now make an all-encompassing claim to be a realism as much as an idealism.

Now, if these speculations have any merit, it remains to say on what grounds and by what process the metaphysical idealists were able to expand the scope of consciousness to include the infinite.[36] For this is the third step in the passage from critical idealism to metaphysical idealism. Once *Geist* has achieved infinitude, it can claim to be self-grounding and absolute. With the incorporation of the infinite, it is itself infinite, encompassing all things, real and ideal.

It remains to ask, then, How could such an appropriation and inclusion of the infinite come to appear credible? The thesis I have been arguing for is this: The absolutization of Spirit achieved such widespread acceptance precisely because it followed through the implications of the critical attitude with its attack upon dogmatism; and it did this by means of the twofold inversion from which emerged the primacy of a confident and creative freedom. Bear in mind the twofold inversion within the critical attitude in its attack upon dogmatism: the inversion of thing and cognition, followed by the inversion of cognition and freedom, with freedom emerging as victor over both cognition and thing. Now metaphysical idealism could recover the richer world for rationality, and romanticism could display it in imagination and art only by redefining the character of the world; and that could be achieved only with a new sense of the power of creative imagination, on the one hand, and the spirit of reason as *Geist*, on the other. I realize that this puts the Hegelian sublation of dogmatic distinctions much closer to the romantic creative power of transformation than Hegel would have found acceptable.

I have recently written about the lack of depth and interiority in being that has occurred since the seventeenth century with the emptying out of the older nexus of causes and principles that constituted each being, for they gave to each entity its own interiority and depth.[37] My present thesis is that, prepared for by the reduction of the natural world to pure objectivity in the seventeenth and eighteenth centuries, Kant's critical idealism completed the loss of ontological *weight* in the things known. For the Kantian attack upon dogmatism tore the older metaphysical being from its complex of ontological causes and principles and dissected it into phenomenal objects, on the one hand, and the thought of the unknowable *Ding-an-sich*, on the other.

36. The earlier *Pantheismusstreit*, occasioned by a pantheistic reading of Spinoza, had brought to the fore fresh speculations on the infinite.
37. See note 7 above.

What must be noticed here is that this was done in the name of an attack upon dogmatism. Why did the ontological weight of things come to appear as unwarranted dogmatism? My conclusion is that their ontological weight imposed itself upon the new sense of freedom, seeming to make it captive to things. This is not to say that the new freedom was arbitrary, despite the antics of some of the poets, but rather that it had to find new sources of order within itself: in moral duty and ethical earnestness in Kant and Fichte, in the discipline of artistic creativity in Schelling and many of the romantics, and in the dialectical movement of the Spirit in Hegel.

Now, it is easier to subvert phenomena than things. The lightness of things in the critical idealism of Kant came about by lifting the weight attributed to them by the old metaphysics and already mostly lost.[38] That weight was taken from the scales as no longer providing the measure for a reason armed with the critical attitude and the new sense of freedom. That weight was not restored by the rejection of the unknowable *Ding-an-sich*, nor by the metaphysical idealists, since it was still perceived to be a dogmatic weight—a weight that brought freedom into an unwarranted dependency. Phenomena replace things in Kant, but the lightness of the being of phenomena persists in the metaphysical idealists even after the restriction to appearances is withdrawn. Even though the *Ding-an-sich* was rejected, the weight with which things seemed now to press upon consciousness was not restored. Among the poets the lightness gave full room to the play of the imagination, which needed to defer no longer to the restraint that the weight of things had put upon it. Even the so-called heavy moods—nostalgia, melancholy, and the grotesque—were heavy only as moods, mood-heavy not thing-heavy. Irony disclosed their true condition, their lightness of being.[39]

As for the philosophers, reason had found new scope, incorporating the infinite, and opening out onto absolute knowing and absolute system. Emboldened by its new power, it crossed the threshold to the infinite.[40] Once the positive infinite was incorporated, no reality was left out. The older metaphysics of the Aristotelian kind had sought to confirm

---

38. The root of the charge against dogmatism did not lie precisely in the externality of the relation between consciousness and things and the apparent failure to achieve a total and systematic unity in our knowledge. The failure to achieve the unity of totality lay rather more in the residual weight of things (as construed by the older metaphysics of creation). It was their ontological weight that seemed alien to the new creative freedom.

39. Hegel criticized the poets' irony (esp. that of Friedrich Schlegel) because, lacking method and depth, it was unserious.

40. It is possible to view Schelling's move from negative to positive philosophy as an attempt to recuperate a richer infinite through religion and mythology.

the reality of its knowledge by a noetic encounter with things. Metaphysical idealism, on the other hand, confirms the scope of its thought by inclusion, that is, by expanding the horizon of its concern, and thereby assigning to reason a new scope, role, and power.[41]

Now, the romantics played out their role in expanding the scope of the human quest, and if they did not use the reshaped tools of transcendental philosophy explicitly, nevertheless they took up its spirit. They dared—usually without rational method—to give over to philosophy-become-poetry the new quest for truth in the form not only of beauty, but of beauty touched by the sublime, a beauty that could in its freedom find its meaning as easily in fantastic shapes and devils' dances as in nostalgic images of folktales and medieval sagas.[42] For if the romantics did not take up Kant's transcendental reason in its pure form, or his critical attitude as such, the poets did take up its effects, and they did take up the transcendental imagination and the experience of the sublime. And if they distorted Fichte's ethical productive imagination, slipping the tight bonds of ethical earnestness, they increased the power and import of the creative imagination.

The ground of the romantic emphasis upon art must be traced back to the role of the imagination, pointed out by Kant and developed by Fichte. The romantics reaped the harvest of Kantian and Fichtean transcendental critique, which had freed the imagination and prepared the way for a new freedom for Reason. The romantics did not pay Kant's and Fichte's price, which was the restriction to finite subjectivity and the field of moral freedom. They thought they had direct access to a larger world in which the real and the ideal were fused in coequal oneness.

The creative self of the romantic artist was a part that is not just a part, in a whole that is not just an architectonic shell. The poet was armed with a creative power that called for the loosening of fixed distinctions between reality and appearance, between self and world. Creativity so overwhelmed the other aspects of the poet—especially in genius—that the fantastic itself was given an even playing field in the expression of truth. The fantasies of the romantics were not quite fictions; or rather, fiction itself opened the way to a higher and deeper truth.[43] Freedom,

---

41. It seems to me that transcendental Thomism *identifies* Being with that expanded horizon, thus adopting the critical attitude, wittingly or unwittingly; but that is another argument.

42. The cultivation of the fantastic is to be seen in Ludwig Tieck, Wilhelm Heinrich Wackenroder, Clemens Brentano, and Ludwig Achim von Arnim; and somewhat removed, in Heinrich von Kleist and E.T.A. Hoffmann; and in a still more detached way in the strange world met with in the *Märchen* of the Brothers Grimm.

43. A great deal could be said of the influence of Rousseau upon the German roman-

too, took on a new form and power, or rather a new self-forming power that pervaded the world. The productive imagination under the creative power of the artistic genius could lead us to new visions, to an inner world, or rather to an outer world characterized by interiority. Despite the nostalgia, the world of the romantics is not at all the older interiority of ontological principles and causes, it is no longer the interiority of metaphysical being. Instead, it is an interiority provided by infinite subjectivity, the interiority of spirit, a world in which magic and myth are as real and as truth bearing as the more rational truths that breathed for the philosophers with the same freedom of *Geist*.

---

tics, precisely in this blurring of fact and fiction, as in the *Confessions* and *Reveries*, which implies a revolutionary break in the theory of meaning.

PART V
THE MORAL BEGINNINGS: SCHELLING AND HEGEL ON THE KANTIAN POSTULATES

9 The Reception of Kant's Doctrine of Postulates in Schelling's and Hegel's Early Philosophical Projects

KLAUS DÜSING
Translated by Daniel O. Dahlstrom

Kant's theory of postulates of practical reason is of particular significance for the beginnings of German idealism. In the earliest drafts of their philosophies, the idealists sought to develop their own conceptions and to formulate their own positions principally by taking up and critically engaging Kant's doctrine of postulates. In this way they took their start from a problem, namely, the problem of a metaphysics founded on a practical basis, a problem that managed to take shape within the structure of Kant's system only toward the end, that is to say, after the principles for theoretical and practical reason had been established and legitimated. The actual discussion and critique of Kant's foundational principles essentially took place only in the wake of the reception of the doctrine of postulates. This holds, in the first place, for Fichte, whose very first work, *Attempt at a Critique of All Revelation*, goes back to Kant's doctrine of postulates. But it is also the case, as is to be discussed below, for Schelling and in particular measure for Hegel. The aim of the following study, then, is to show that Schelling and Hegel in different ways critically unpacked Kant's doctrine of postulates and the Kantianizing theology taught at Tübingen, and that in this critical process they developed their own ethical theories, theories occasionally diverging from one another. In the course of pursuing this aim, attention is initially diverted from the "Earliest System-Programme of German Idealism" and the question of its author. Only after the issues indicated above have been clarified is an attempt made to examine the conception of the postulate-doctrine and of the ethics contained in the "System-Programme" and to compare that conception with Schelling's and with Hegel's practical philosophy.

I

Kant established the assumption of the postulates of practical reason by claiming that they are indispensable presuppositions for the representation of the possibility of the highest good. (What is involved in this establishment of the assumption of the postulates can only be sketched here very briefly.) "The highest good" in this context is not merely the ideal of the perfection of a person; it is to be considered as a world in which the ethical life and the happiness of a rational entity are in accord with one another. For a finite will that can act only after entertaining purposes, the highest good is necessarily the final goal or the ultimate purpose of all its ethical efforts. Kant's mature, definitive theory of the highest good, as he first presents it on the basis of the *Critique of Practical Reason*, is no longer a constitutive part of the foundation of moral philosophy. Instead, the clarification of the principles of moral philosophy is presupposed. The doctrine of the highest good, nevertheless, results from the application of the principles of an ethical life to a finite will, acting according to purposes.[1] Since an individual with a finite will is supposed to cooperate in realizing the ultimate ethical purpose, but cannot perfectly attain the ultimate purpose on his own, he must make additional assumptions, that is to say, he must set up postulates, in order to be able to think for himself the possibility of the highest good in general. By a postulate of pure practical reason Kant understands a "*theoretical, but as such indemonstrable proposition* [*Satz*] . . . , *insofar as it is inseparably linked to a practical law that is unconditionally valid a priori.*"[2] Postulates are thus theoretical assumptions, the necessity of which, however, is to be established only on practical grounds. These postulates are (1) the assumption of the immortality of the person, (2) the assumption of freedom in a positive sense as the determining feature of an entity existing in the intelligible world, and (3) the assumption of the existence of God as the moral cause of the world.[3] Thus, by means of the postulates, as Kant explains, the highest good is thought to be possible, but not objectively known to be possible. The possibility of the highest

---

1. In regard to this point, compare above all the note from the preface to the first edition of Kant's work on religion; cf. *Religion innerhalb der Grenzen der bloßen Vernunft* in *Kant's gesammelte Schriften*, volume 6 (Berlin: de Gruyter, 1968), pp. 6ff.n.; see also *Kritik der Urteilskraft* in *Kant's gesammelte Schriften*, volume 5 (Berlin: de Gruyter, 1968), p.471n. (The note is on page 461 of the 1793 edition).

2. *Kritik der praktischen Vernunft* in *Kant's gesammelte Schriften*, volume 5 (Berlin: de Gruyter, 1968), p. 122 (page 220 of the 1788 edition) (hereafter = 'KpV'). See also footnote 29 below.

3. The problem that emerges from the fact that freedom is both the condition of the possibility of the highest good and also the *ratio essendi* of the moral law probably has its basis in the history of the development of Kant's practical philosophy.

good is only a subjectively practical presupposition conceived by someone with a finite will for the sake of projecting and carrying out ethical purposes, a presupposition by means of which that individual assumes that these purposes can also be successful in the world and produce happiness or better conditions, thus a presupposition that his ethical endeavor is not, from the very outset, senseless and in vain.

Kant has worked into his theory of the highest good a series of Christian images (*Vorstellungen*) but then transformed their significance fundamentally in the context of his moral philosophy. Thus, for example, several times in the *Critique of Practical Reason* he designates the highest good also as the "kingdom of God."[4] In his work on religion, Kant understands by the "kingdom of God" a purely ethical community as the supreme communal good of all human beings.[5] Already in the *Tübinger Stift* the "kingdom of God" became a guiding image for the three mutual friends, Hegel, Schelling, and Hölderlin; indeed, it was an image in which they wanted to recognize one another after all the "metamorphoses" of life.[6] Indeed, prompted by the interpretation of the image in Kant's moral philosophy, they considered it as the actuality of reason and freedom and demanded of each other that they contribute to the practical realization of this kingdom.

In the following years, however, Schelling's and also Hegel's reception of the Kantian doctrine of the highest good and of the practical postulates was influenced by their common battle against the orthodox teachers in Tübingen who were once again in a position of strength. Implicitly with his doctrine of postulates and explicitly with his work *Religion within the Limits of Reason Alone,* Kant had made his entrance into the eighteenth-century discussion about the relation of natural to revealed religion. Storr, the Tübingen theologian, composed his *Annotations* to Kant's work on religion immediately after its appearance; they appeared a year later in German translation as *Remarks on Kant's Philosophy of Religion* with a comprehensive appendix by the translator, Süskind, on Fichte's *Attempt at a Critique of All Revelation*. Storr, the theological teacher of the three friends at the Stift, and Süskind, his successor, sought to defend the religion of revelation by means of the Kantian doctrine of postulates. They weakened and falsified the concept of the practical postulate in that they declared every possible claim containing theoretical,

---

4. *Kritik der praktischen Vernunft*, 127ff, 130 (pages 230, 232, 235 of the 1788 edition).
5. *Religion innerhalb der Grenzen der bloßen Vernunft*, 97f, 139.
6. See Hölderlin's letter to Hegel, July 10, 1794, in *Briefe von und an Hegel*, volume 1, ed. J. Hoffmeister (Hamburg: Meiner, 1952), pp. 9, 18; see also *Dokumente zu Hegels Entwicklung*, ed. J. Hoffmeister (Stuttgart: Frommann, 1936), pp. 180f. On the concept of the kingdom of God in Hegel, see, e.g., Adriaan Peperzak, *Le jeune Hegel et la vision morale du monde*, 2d ed. (The Hague: Nijhoff, 1969), pp. 6–11.

even empirical, representations to be a postulate of practical reason merely insofar as a moral-practical interest or need was served thereby. Christian revelations and teachings, for example, the effects of grace or Jesus' miracles, were in this way supposed to be identified as practically possible and their assumption grounded in a practical need.[7] This justification of the religion of revelation, which apparently was also taught from the lectern at the University of Tübingen, is probably to be understood as a response to the vehement attacks on the Christian religion, launched at the beginning of the 1790s among those in the Stift, especially by Dietz who was a friend of Süskind and a "Repetent," a teacher who helped students prepare for exams during the time Hegel, Hölderlin, and even Schelling were at the Stift.[8] During his time at Tübingen, then, Hegel already takes up Kant's doctrine of the postulates, as is yet to be elaborated. But apparently it is first in Bern that the claims and procedure of the Tübingen school, about which he learns in greater detail from Schelling's letters, provide him with the occasion—or the occasion along with other things—to turn anew to the Kantian doctrine of postulates, though, indeed, more thoroughly than before and with an expanded horizon of inquiry.

Hegel was probably spurred on to the critical engagement with the Tübingen school through Schelling's reports in particular, which had for him the value of original information, and he was also in part influenced by Schelling's thoughts on the matter. For this reason, attention is focused here first on Schelling's treatment of the Kantian doctrine of postulates and the orthodox transformation of their meaning. In any case, since Schelling was still in the Stift at this time (that is, until 1795), he was more immediately disturbed than Hegel was by the orthodox attempts at justification. His first writings and his letters are filled with covert or even open, vehement critique of the Tübingen school. Thus, for example, he writes to Hegel on January 6, 1795: "All possible dogmas have now already been stamped as postulates of practical reason and where theoretical-historical proofs never suffice, the practical (Tübingen) reason hacks away the knots. It is bliss, to look upon the triumph

---

7. For the status of this first Tübingen school, which is also called the "Storr school," in the history of theology, see H. Hermelink, *Geschichte der evangelischen Kirche in Württemberg von der Reformation bis zur Gegenwart* (Stuttgart and Tübingen: R. Wunderlich, 1949), pp. 301–10. From the standpoint of the history of theology, the Tübingen "orthodoxy" was probably not entirely as reactionary as Schelling and Hegel made them out to be.

8. On this matter, see Dieter Henrich and Johann Ludwig Döderlein, "Carl Immanuel Dietz," *Hegel-Studien* 3 (1965): 276–87. Cf. Martin Brecht and Jörg Sandberger, "Hegels Begegnung mit der Theologie im Tübinger Stift," *Hegel-Studien* 5 (1969): 58–60, where it is shown that there were still broader engaged Kantians among the "Repetents" at that time.

of these philosophical heroes."⁹ To be sure, in his writings Schelling expresses himself less definitely. Yet it is still clear enough to recognize that in those writings, with the uncovering of the misinterpretations of practical reason and the practical postulates, he is opposed to the Tübingen orthodoxy in particular. Criticism of such deficient interpretations and the presentation of the genuine critical philosophy (*Kritizismus*), as Schelling understood it, became a central theme in the *Philosophical Letters on Dogmatism and Critical Philosophy*. The immediate occasion for the composition of these *Philosophical Letters* was, as Schelling says, the attempt at that time "to erect a new system of dogmatism from the casualties of the critical philosophy."¹⁰ According to Schelling, this dogmatism that put itself forth as critical philosophy became possible precisely in the way that the critical philosophy first appeared, namely, in Kant's *Critique of Pure Reason*. The critical philosophy proceeded from a critique of cognitive faculties; it showed that things in themselves are unknowable by theoretical reason. This was interpreted, then, as a weakness of reason. To be sure, according to Schelling, weakness and deficiency are a merely contingent, quantitative limitation; but people did not probe behind the limitation of our rational faculty, they did not ground it in the original essence of subjectivity. What is theoretically unknowable on the basis of the weakness of reason, namely, the things in themselves, is now supposed to be held as true in a practical faith. Similar to what was said in the already cited letter to Hegel, it is stated: "What you could not prove, you fix with the stamp of practical reason."¹¹ But even this practical faith is, according to Schelling, really dogmatic, since it makes itself dependent upon things-in-themselves.

With his doctrine of postulates Kant had, in Schelling's view, left the field wide open for dogmatic philosophy (*Dogmatismus*). For dogmatic philosophy and not only critical philosophy takes account of a practical philosophy and is able to make use, as Schelling puts it, of the "method of the practical postulates."¹² The very same dogmatic philosophy, then, that disguises itself as critical philosophy, believes in the supersensible that is in itself, because it regards reason as too weak to know it. Schelling is referring to the fact that holding something to be true in this way is "*theoretical* as far as its form is concerned."¹³ For example, the existence

---

9. *Briefe von und an Hegel*, 1.14.
10. Schelling, *Sämtliche Werke*, 14 vols., ed. K.F.A. Schelling (Stuttgart and Augsburg: J. G. Cotta, 1856–1861), 1.283 (hereafter referred to in short form as "Schelling, *Werke*, 1.283").
11. Schelling, *Werke*, 1.292.
12. Ibid., 1.300f., and frequently elsewhere.
13. Ibid., 1.287.

of God is accepted, to be sure, on the basis of practical need, but is still held to be true theoretically in belief, that is to say, it is presupposed objectively.[14] But genuine critical philosophy, as Schelling stresses, may not let itself be demeaned into this "hiding place of superstition."[15] In elaborating these points, Schelling is apparently thinking of the Tübingen orthodoxy and its "method" of erecting practical postulates. In the essay *On Revelation and Instruction of the People* (1798), Schelling already has at his disposal his own, new concept of the practical postulates. But even in this essay, in the course of discussing something written by Niethammer, he explicitly declares that the concept of revelation may not be regarded as a postulate of practical reason, as orthodoxy attempts to regard it, and that in this way orthodoxy completely fails to appreciate the essence of practical postulates.[16]

In the *Philosophical Letters*, then, this dogmatic philosophy (*Dogmatismus*) that would be critical philosophy (*Kritizismus*) is distinguished from, on the one hand, the "dogmatizing philosophy" (*Dogmatizismus*) that claims to know things-in-themselves theoretically, that is to say, the dogmatic metaphysics that Kant's critique is directed against and, on the other hand, the thoroughgoing dogmatic philosophy (*Dogmatismus*) that reaches its perfection in Spinoza's *Ethics*.[17] According to Schelling,

---

14. See Schelling, *Werke*, 1.333n., 202, 476f. Schelling sees in this belief a contradiction of the claim of reason's frailty (see Schelling, *Werke*, 1.287), a rather misfortunate objection, disputing the theory of the thinkability of God; however, the objection is not later raised by Schelling. A similar argument was once used by Flatt; see J. F. Flatt, *Briefe über den moralischen Erkenntnisgrund der Religion überhaupt und besonders in Beziehung auf die Kantische Philosophie* (Tübingen, 1789), pp. 78f. Nevertheless, Schelling's critique of the orthodox understanding of the doctrine of postulates as a whole is not dependent upon Flatt; indeed, it is directly opposed to the conception on the basis of which Flatt criticizes Kant's doctrine of postulates, namely, a conception holding fast to theoretical proofs of God's existence and revelation. Flatt's criticism of Kant was in place before the Tübingen school attempted to take up the Kantian doctrine of postulates in a positive way into orthodoxy.

15. Schelling, *Werke*, 1.292.

16. See Schelling, *Werke*, 1.474ff. In the literature there already are some indications that Schelling polemicized in the *Philosophical Letters* against the Tübingen orthodoxy, though, to be sure, without investigating this question more closely. See Schelling, *Briefe und Dokumente*, 3 vols., ed. H. Fuhrmans (Bonn: Bouvier, 1962), 1.32; Dieter Henrich and Johann Ludwig Döderlein, "Carl Immanuel Diez," p. 278; and Hermelink, *Geschichte der evangelischen Kirche*, p. 307. However, it still remains an open problem how, then, Schelling's relationship to Kant's doctrine of postulates itself is to be assessed.

17. See Schelling, *Werke*, 1.302. Schelling introduced this distinction between "dogmatic philosophy" (*Dogmatismus*) and "dogmatizing philosophy" (*Dogmatizismus*) in the fifth letter, after "dogmatizing philosophy" (apparently instead of "dogmatic philosophy") regularly was printed in the first four letters and even in the title through the arbitrary interference by the editor of the "Philosophical Journal for a Society of German Scholars" (in which Schelling's *Philosophical Letters* appeared in several parts). The editor subse-

then, the dogmatic philosophy that regards itself as critical philosophy, namely, that of the Tübingen school, proceeds from an inadequate concept of critical philosophy (*Kritizismus*) that Kant's critical philosophy (*kritische Philosophie*) clarified. According to Schelling's presentation of it, Kant's critique of the cognitive faculties with its demonstration of the weakness of reason in theoretical knowledge has only refuted the "dogmatizing philosophy" (*Dogmatizismus*), the dogmatic metaphysics of the eighteenth century, but not the thoroughgoing dogmatic philosophy that sets up practical demands with regard to the absolute and unconditioned. To be sure, as Schelling acknowledges, Kant already had his eyes on the first and unified principle of our essence, the activity of the I, but he never explicitly developed this. Thus, for Schelling, Kant's critique actually belongs neither to dogmatic nor to critical philosophy exclusively, but rather represents the possibility of a system in general; accordingly, even the doctrine of the postulates leaves open both possible applications.[18] In accordance with the spirit of the time, this doctrine of postulates had first been applied dogmatically.

Schelling's critique, as discussed up till now, of both the use of the doctrine of postulates and the grounding of this doctrine in the claim about the "weakness" of reason is valid. It is valid, above all, insofar as it is directed at the dogmatic philosophy that puts itself forth as critical philosophy, that is, the Tübingen orthodoxy and its "hiding place of superstition."[19] Schelling does not express himself with any clarity regarding whether these objections are also supposed to obtain in regard to Kant. Several times he declares himself only against the interpreters of the Kantian philosophy and does not intend "to lay the burden of the blame for those misinterpretations on the critique of pure reason itself, though"—as a mere critique of cognitive faculties—"it did give *occasion* for those misinterpretations."[20] On the other hand, Schelling is of the opinion that Kant himself applied his doctrine of postulates "rather to the *newly* grounded system of dogmatic philosophy."[21] Thus, Schelling can also make the charge against Kant that his system is a "system of

---

quently took sole responsibility for this interference (see *Philosophical Journal*, vol. 3, no. 2, p. 175n.). See also Schelling, *Briefe und Dokumente*, 1.59. The edition of the *Werke*, which discusses this state of affairs only imperfectly, does not always pay attention in a precise way to this distinction between "dogmatic philosophy" and "dogmatizing philosophy" from the fifth letter on. Thus, for example, it should not read "blind dogmatic philosophy" (line 5 from the bottom in *Werke*, 1.314), but rather, in conformity with the original printing, "blind dogmatizing philosophy."

18. See Schelling, *Werke*, 1.301–5.   19. Ibid., 1.292.
20. Ibid., 1.293; see also 288n, 289f., 298n.
21. Ibid., 1.304.

accommodation"[22] that, in spite of its novel motifs, adapted itself to the intuitions of the age. In any case, there is no passage in which Schelling takes the trouble to demonstrate more precisely the substantial differences between the doctrine of postulates of the Tübingen school's ostensible critical philosophy and the doctrine of postulates as it was established and developed by Kant himself. The basis for his refutation of the Tübingen orthodoxy is not the theory presented by Kant but rather the "spirit" of critical philosophy, and he concedes that the orthodox, dogmatic application of the doctrine of postulates is quite possible, as far as the "letter" of the Kantian presentation is concerned.[23]

The result of all this is that Schelling, who indeed was still at the Tübingen Stift until 1795, took up the doctrine of the postulates of practical reason from the outset in view of the perspective of the Tübingen school and that he criticized this doctrine not through recourse to Kant himself, but rather immediately from his own conception of the freedom of the I. From a systematic standpoint his own conception is naturally unthinkable without Kant's and Fichte's general doctrine of freedom. However, for the polemical direction of the thrust of his systematic starting point against orthodoxy, which Schelling carries out in convincing and uncompromising fashion, and even for certain systematic motives themselves, one could well suppose yet another model, namely, Lessing. As Jacobi, for example, reported, the orthodox concepts of divinity no longer had any meaning for Lessing. Schelling himself brings up a long quotation from a letter of Lessing to his brother Karl regarding orthodox theology, in which it is stated (among other things): "Orthodoxy is, thanks be to God! finished."[24] In what, accordingly, was subsequently named *Essays on the Clarification of the Idealism of the Doctrine of Science*, Schelling's criticism of the orthodox conception of the postulates is even sharper. In the "Appendix" to the *Essays*, in which Schelling once again takes up the problem of postulates in philosophy, he rejects the concept

---

22. Ibid., 1.231n.; see also 210. The term "system of accommodation" probably has a theological background. People spoke in theology of a "hypothesis of accommodation" which said that, despite their novel views, Jesus and the Apostles were supposed to have adapted themselves to the prevailing images of the time. See Hermelink, *Geschichte der evangelischen Kirche*, p. 303. Moreover, this "hypothesis of accommodation," contested by Storr and his school, is not without significance for Hegel's theory of the origins of the positivity of the Christian religion as well.

23. See esp. *Briefe von und an Hegel*, 1.14.

24. Schelling, *Werke*, 1.478. The quotation, to be sure, is to be found first in *Über Offenbarung und Volksunterricht* from 1798. However, the source cited by Schelling concerns a "Biography" that appeared in 1793 and that Schelling had probably studied already during his time at the Stift; the text is *Gotthold Ephraim Lessings Leben, nebst seinem noch übrigen litterarischen Nachlasse*, volume 1, ed. K. G. Lessing (Berlin: Voss, 1793), pp. 350f. As for the systematic background, the "Spinozism" of Lessing, assumed by Schelling, see note 94 below.

of the practical postulate in the sense discussed above. From this point on he wants to construe postulates in philosophy in strict analogy with postulates in geometry, namely, as demands for actions of construction.[25] Thus, after mentioning Kant's practical postulates, Schelling says: "As far, moreover, as what concerns those postulates of practical reason itself, for some time now they will have, I think, played out their role in philosophy."[26]

Thus, from the beginning Schelling's stance toward the doctrine of postulates, in the form at least in which they were proposed to him, was one of rejection. Nevertheless, the critical engagement with this doctrine was fruitful for Schelling's own philosophizing. He gave new interpretations of the doctrine of the highest good and of the practical postulates on the basis of the "spirit of critical philosophy" and thereby developed the basic features of an ethics which, according to Schelling's plans at that time, was supposed to present a "counterpart to Spinoza's *Ethics*."[27] In the work *On the I*, Schelling seizes upon the Kantian concept of the highest good, namely, the representation of the attunement of morality and happiness, and criticizes the empirical concept of happiness contained therein. Empirical happiness is a morally contingent agreement of objects with the finite I, an agreement produced by nature, and cannot even be intended on moral grounds. With this consideration Schelling also turns against the representation of happiness as a reward that can have significance only for the empirical, sentient subject and, in this way, at the same time criticizes the orthodox theological implications of this concept. Instead, in the highest good only a "pure happiness" is to be considered, which is either already identical with the ultimate purpose of the I or—in accord with morality—progressively leads to it. Schelling believes that Kant, in his concept of the highest good, could only have meant this concept of pure, nonempirical happiness.[28]

---

25. Kant himself had explicitly distinguished the geometrical from the practical postulates; see *Kritik der praktischen Vernunft*, 11n (page 22n of the 1788 edition).
26. Schelling, *Werke*, 1.451; see also 447.
27. Ibid., 1.159.
28. Ibid., 1.196f., 197n., 322f., as well as 240, 328. In this context Schelling also polemicizes against Christian theology and probably in particular against the Tübingen school. In the interest of historical fairness it may be mentioned that Storr and Süskind in the *Bemerkungen über Kants philosophische Religionslehre* speak, to be sure, of happiness as a reward, but also elevate happiness to the highest good above all experience (see the *Bemerkungen*, pp. 167, 176ff., 39f., 45). See also Flatt, *Beiträge zur christlichen Dogmatik und Moral und zur Geschichte derselben* (Tübingen: Heerbrandt, 1792), pp. 100ff. Schelling was, of course, well aware of Kant's synthetic connection of morality and happiness in the highest good, quite independently of the doctrine of postulates, but at the same time he gave that connection a revised interpretation in his own sense.

The relationship to Kant's philosophy itself on this question is difficult, to be sure. Kant developed the familiar, later theory of the highest good from the *Critique of Practial Reason* onward, a theory that no longer belongs to the doctrine of the principles of morality. In this theory, happiness is regarded as an effect in the world of the senses, produced by a cause of a different sort, an intelligible cause, that is to say, it is regarded—in contrast to Schelling's view of Kant—as empirical happiness. Nevertheless, this theory is a later one, preceded in Kant by another theory of the highest good, which apparently still obtained even in the *Critique of Pure Reason,* without, however, being further elaborated there. According to this theory, the highest good still belonged to the question of the principles of ethics. At the same time, in the thought of the highest good there was also the concept of a happiness a priori, that is to say, the pure happiness demanded by Schelling. Kant had reasons for changing this theory, which Schelling, of course, could not have known.[29]

Schelling, however, criticizes not only the empirical concept of happiness, but also the concept of morality as a constitutive part of the idea of the highest good. For morality always presupposes a limitation of the I by the Not-I; the moral law is valid as a law of the ought (*Sollen*) only for the finite I that ought to strive forward beyond its respective limits. Kant's concept of the highest good as the ultimate purpose of practical reason accordingly still contains limitations and finitudes; thus, according to Schelling, the harmony of morality and pure happiness can in every case be regarded as preparation for the true ultimate purpose of the I's striving. The true ultimate purpose must, however, be determined otherwise, namely, as the elevation of the I above the sphere of finitudes, as the attainment of the being of the infinite, absolute I. On the basis of this concept of the ultimate purpose, one can then make the attempt to reconstruct the basic features of an "ethics à la Spinoza," planned but not carried out by Schelling.[30] In other words, on the basis of Schelling's suggestions, the conception of an idealistic ethics that is thoroughly his own, derivable neither from Kant nor from Fichte, can be recognized,

---

29. For an explanation of these theses regarding Kant's doctrine of the highest good, see Klaus Düsing, "Das Problem des höchsten Gutes in Kants praktischer Philosophie," *Kant-Studien* 62 (1971): 5–42.

30. *Briefe von und an Hegel,* 1.15. In January 1795 Schelling hoped that the planned ethics should "be finished next summer" at the latest (ibid.). See Schelling, *Werke,* 1.159. Yet on January 22, 1796, he still writes to Niethammer: "The next thing that I undertake is a system of ethics (a counterpart to Spinoza, a work, the idea of which has excited me already for some time and which is already begun)" (Schelling, *Briefe und Dokumente,* p. 61). The "system of ethics" did not come to completion. Yet basic features of this plan are to be found in Schelling's correspondence with Hegel from this time, as well as in his works *On the I* and especially the *Philosophische Briefen über Dogmatismus und Kritizismus.*

though it was never built up into a complete theory. Up until now such an attempt at reconstruction was, in my view, not undertaken, in part perhaps because people from the time of Rosenzweig wanted to see or even to develop Schelling's early ethics in connection with the "Earliest System-Programme of German Idealism."[31]

The ultimate purpose of all striving by the finite I is the attainment of the infinity of the absolute I. Harkening back to Spinoza, Schelling thinks of the absolute I as the sole, absolute substance and attributes to it the attributes of this absolute substance: pure being, absolute power, absolute freedom, and so forth. Schelling is consistent enough and bold enough to regard this absolute I as God.[32] Such metaphysical reflections have justification only in an ethics. Schelling alludes to this thought several times in the work *On the I;* and in the *Philosophical Letters* it is explicitly justified. Along the way, Schelling recalls that even Spinoza gathered his metaphysics under the general title of an "ethics."[33] Since, according to the *Philosophical Letters,* the dispute between dogmatic philosophy and critical philosophy cannot be decided theoretically, the authentic domain of philosophy is practical philosophy with its principles. The consistent dogmatic philosophy, like the consistent critical philosophy, also develops an ethics. Only in the latter can the relation of the finite I to the absolute I be made evident and clarified.[34] According to Schelling,

31. Without having an acquaintance yet with the "System-Programme," Metzger discusses Schelling's drafts about ethics in the *Philosophical Letters,* but he principally establishes instances of its unfinished character and contradictions; see *Die Epochen der Schellingschen Philosophie von 1795 bis 1802* (Heidelberg: Winter, 1911), pp. 37ff. F. Meier, who, of course, does not make the systematic conception a problem at all, also discusses the "ethical viewpoints" in the *Philosophical Letters,* likewise without regard to the "System-Programme"; see *Die Idee der Transzendentalphilosophie beim jungen Schelling* (Winterthur: Keller, 1961), pp. 24–30. Rosenzweig was the first to attempt to interpret the "System-Programme" as the culmination of Schelling's ethics at that time, the result of his earlier efforts; see *Das älteste Systemprogramm des deutschen Idealismus* (Heidelberg: Winter, 1917), pp. 11ff. Even L. Strauß saw the development of Schelling's ethics as emerging from the "System-Programme"; see "Hölderlins Anteil an Schellings frühem Systemprogramm," *Deutsche Vierteljahrsschrift für Literaturwissenschaft und Geistesgeschichte* 5 (1927): 710–13. Hollerbach sees in the "System-Programme," which he likewise acribes to Schelling, the projection of an "ethics à la Spinoza." However, in Schelling's early writings, according to Hollerbach, this ethics is flimsy and abstract and leaves the relation of the abstract I to the empirical I undetermined; see *Der Rechtsgedanke bei Schelling* (Frankfurt am Main: Klostermann, 1957), pp. 85–94. Wieland explicitly seeks to justify the view of the practical postulates in the "System-Programme" as the consistent formulation of Schelling's conception of ethics; see "Die Anfänge der Philosophie Schellings und die Frage nach der Natur," in *Natur und Geschichte: Karl Löwith zum 70. Geburtstag* (Stuttgart: Kohlhammer, 1967), pp. 408–12.

32. See Schelling, *Werke,* 1.201, 210, and Schelling's letter to Hegel of February 4, 1795, in *Briefe von und an Hegel,* 1.22.

33. See Schelling, *Werke,* 1.305, 325, 317n.

34. The terminological difference between ethics and morals, introduced by Schelling in his *Neue Deduktion des Naturrechts* (see Schelling, *Werke,* 1.252ff.), is not considered here.

then, the absolute I or God is considered only because the ultimate purpose of moral endeavor by the finite I is sought in the attainment of that pure infinity and that absolute freedom of pure being. Through the ethical significance of these ideas the determination of the condition of the divine I also proves to be important for Schelling, a determination for which he likewise appeals to Spinoza. The activity of the divine, intellectual intuition of the self signifies a condition of the highest blessedness, a blessedness that never ceases.[35] Kant's concept of the highest good as the accord between morality and happiness is reinterpreted by Schelling as an original unity of absolute freedom and supreme blessedness, as it is possible only in God as the absolute I.[36]

In the more detailed elucidation of the ethical significance of these ideas, Schelling latches on to the alternatives of Stoicism and Epicureanism, which Kant had set up in the *Critique of Practical Reason* in regard to the problem of the highest good.[37] Both the Stoic and the Epicurean strive to attain the highest good. According to Schelling, the Stoic seeks to make himself independent of objects and to find absolute freedom and blessedness in his own autonomy. The Epicurean, on the other hand, gives himself completely up to the world and nature in the satisfaction of all his needs, in order to attain tranquility and blessedness by this means. In these ancient theories Schelling apparently sees precursors of critical and dogmatic ethics. Dogmatic ethics and critical ethics do not differ in the goal of reaching the ultimate purpose or the highest good, but rather in the fundamental direction of moral striving, for which, indeed, the practical interest of the acting, finite I in particular is telling. It is Schelling's thesis that the activity or causality of the finite I is not qualitatively different from the activity or causality of the absolute; instead it differs only through its restrictiveness, through its limitation. The finite I thus has the same qualities as the absolute I or God, only in a limited way. The ethics of dogmatism requires, then, that the ultimate purpose be attained by nullifying the finite I's own causality, by becoming passive and removing boundaries, by surrendering oneself in the love of the infinite, and by entering into the perfect tranquility and blessedness of the Absolute.[38] Critical philosophy's ethics, on the contrary,

---

35. See Schelling, *Werke*, 1.317 and 317n., 322.
36. See ibid., 1.324, 328.
37. See ibid., 1.329, 325; see *Kritik der praktischen Vernunft*, 111ff, 115f, 126f (pages 200ff., 208f., 227f. of the 1788 edition). Nevertheless, the mistake made by these ancient theories was, according to Kant, to assume an analytic unity of virtue and happiness in the highest good. Schelling does not enter into this argument.
38. In this regard Schelling constantly has his eyes on Spinoza and his thoughts of the being of the soul in God; see Schelling, *Werke*, 1.316f. However, he also refers to a passage in Kant where Kant speaks of the highest good of Chinese philosophers as nothing (see

consists in the demand of approaching absolute freedom and blessedness by intensifying one's own activities to an ultimate degree and overcoming the limitations of finite freedom. Schelling gives the edge to critical philosophy's ethics. For in the first place it takes into account the I's intellectual intuition which must be posited at bottom as the ultimate purpose in every instance of representing absolute freedom and blessedness and which dogmatic philosophy disregards. In the second place—something that Schelling does not explicitly state, but is certainly a decisive argument—only the critical or idealistic ethics does justice to the fact, obtaining as certain, of the freedom of the finite I, which is essentially the same as the freedom of the Absolute and only different from it through limitation.

Schelling characterizes this distinction between dogmatic and critical ethics, then, also by means of the diverse "spirit" in which the practical postulates are understood.[39] In Schelling's own project of ethics, the practical postulates accordingly acquire a completely new significance. Their significance is connected with the establishment and structure of Schelling's ethics, which depart in principle from those of Kant and Fichte. This should be shown in particular in Schelling's outline of a critical or idealistic ethics. At least from the time of the *Critique of Practical Reason,* as already mentioned, Kant completely eliminated the doctrine of the highest good and of the postulates of practical reason from the problematic of the foundation of an ethics and he presupposed this foundation of principles for the development of practical metaphysics. In these years even Fichte's ethical doctrine of principles is independent of the concept of the highest good and the practical postulates. Yet, for Schelling, it is the other way around; the basic concepts of morality first acquire sense and reference through the concept of the final purpose of our striving. Morality has "itself no reality without the higher final purpose."[40] The moral law "itself still has no sense and reference, if it does not set up the infinity of the I as the final purpose of all striving."[41] The moral law is thus grounded in the representation of the final purpose: the supreme freedom which is, at the same time, the perfect blessedness. Therein consists the being of the absolute I. The law of this be-

---

Schelling, *Werke*, 1.326; *Kant's gesammelte Schriften*, volume 8 [Berlin: de Gruyter, 1968], p. 335). To be sure, Kant calls the Nothing (*Nirvana*) as the final purpose a "monster." This thought of a dogmatic philosophy that cannot be refuted theoretically by critical philosophy and forms an ethics of its own was "contradicted" by Fichte—see Fichte's letters to Schelling for May 31 and August 7, 1801—in the *Erste Einleitung in die Wissenschaftslehre* in which he at first seems to enter into Schelling's concept of dogmatic philosophy, but then sharply distances himself from it.

39. See Schelling, *Werke*, 1.301, 332ff.   40. Ibid., 1.196.
41. Ibid., 1.198.

ing, however, is the Absolute identity that is still free from plurality as its opposite. Since the finite I finds itself in the midst of the manifoldness of the world, interpreted by Schelling categorially as plurality, the law of identity can be for it no law of being, but rather only of the ought, that is to say, a command, the content of which is "Be identical!" The unity of practical self-consciousness is thus not simply given, it is a task: finite self-consciousness that consists and develops solely in opposition to plurality ought to prevail in practical, free action; to appropriate the many to the unity of self-consciousness; and thereby to approach the totality. This moral law and, with it, all morality is thus understandable for Schelling only under the supposition of the law of being, namely, of the identity of the absolute I or God. The attainment of this identity is the final purpose of moral action, which can nevertheless only be realized in endless approximation.[42]

With this doctrine Schelling completely altered the sense of the postulate of God in opposition to the Tübingen school as well as in opposition to Kant. He does not postulate the existence of a divine creator of the world, but rather demands the striving for realization of the divinity in the finite I. He transforms the postulate of immortality just as much. Since the finite I must act in time and can only approach the final purpose endlessly, without ever being able to attain it, it must strive for endless progress; it must make immortality in itself into the object to be realized. God and immortality, therefore, may not be regarded as something outside the I.[43] Instead, the moral law demands of the finite I that it realize them in itself.

In this way Schelling decisively transformed Kant's concept of the highest good and the practical postulates in his ethics which he regards as the "counterpart" to Spinoza's ethics. Above all, the basic conception is different; Schelling grounds his ethics on the concept of the final purpose or the perfection of being, and from this vantage point determines the moral law and the criteria of morality. However, the final purpose and the way to its realization, namely, the being of the absolute I or God and immortality, are only determinable metaphysically. On the other hand, metaphysics itself is only possible as ethics; it alone contains the supreme concepts of the latter. For the relation of the finite, limited I to the absolute can be understood, not in a theoretical philosophy, but only

---

42. In regard to this point, see Schelling, *Werke*, 1.198ff., where Schelling elaborates on further details of this point of departure and inverts, for example, Kant's "typic of pure practical judgment"; the moral law, according to Schelling, is the "schema" of the natural law, i.e., of the law of being of absolute identity. See also Schelling, *Werke*, 1.206f., 247, 335.

43. See ibid., 1.200f., 333f.n., 335. See also Schelling's letter to Hegel, February 4, 1795, in *Briefe von und an Hegel*, 1.22: "There is no supersensible world for us other than that of the absolute I."

in an ethics, as Schelling argues especially in the *Philosophical Letters*. In this regard Schelling proceeds from the presupposition that he finds already sketched in Jacobi's presentation of Spinoza and that he at the same time applies as a critical restriction on theoretical knowledge, namely, that no system can explain and realize the transition from the infinite, the absolute, to the finite. The transition from the finite to the infinite is, on the contrary, itself immanent to the finite I as a tendency, a practical drive. Hence, metaphysical concepts are necessarily constitutive parts of an ethics that proceeds from the final purpose, the perfection proper to the infinite.[44] In the system of identity (from 1801 on), by contrast, Schelling discusses the transition from the infinite to the finite in a metaphysics independent of ethics.

In the course of the reconstruction of this ethics which Schelling conceived in a critical engagement with Kant's practical metaphysics as well as with Spinoza's ethics and with dogmatic philosophy, the "System-Programme" has been consciously set aside. It is, perhaps, first by this means that the specific and characteristic moments of this project may be more precisely characterized. To be sure, it is possible to find in a modified way in the "System-Programme" some of the basic conceptions of this ethics, though by no means all of them. But from this fact, without adding much more, it cannot be concluded that, for this sphere of problems, Schelling is the actual author of the "System-Programme." Instead, as is to be shown later, the fact of this partial agreement can also be explained—and probably better explained—by the fact that, through his correspondence with Schelling and through Schelling's first writings, essential considerations of his younger friend went into Hegel's reception of the Kantian doctrine of postulates and into his conception of the significance of these practical postulates for an ethics. The way in which Hegel takes up the Kantian doctrine of postulates and modifies them through the influence of Schelling as well as Hegel's ordering of the practical postulates in his own project of ethics and religion is, however, also to be first discussed independently of the "System-Programme."

2

Mention of Kant's concept of the highest good and Kant's moral theology can already be found in Hegel's excerpts of 1788. Hegel excerpts the review of A. W. Rehberg's book, *On the Relation of Metaphysics to Religion* (published at Berlin in 1787), in which Rehberg is criticized from

44. See Schelling, *Werke*, 1.314f., also 313. Regarding the thought mentioned, which stands in a different systematic connection for Jacobi, see Jacobi, *Werke* (Leipzig: Fleischer, 1812ff), 4.1.56.

Kant's standpoint.[45] Hegel's own drafts contain the first references to Kant's doctrine of the highest good and of the postulates of practical reason in the so-called Tübingen Fragments of 1792–1793 on the theme "Folk Religion and Christianity." Hegel reveals here an acquaintance with the individual problems treated by Kant that is more precise than Schelling's; apparently he did not take over this doctrine in the perspectival shift of any sort of intermediary; instead he took it up immediately as it is to be found in Kant himself. In one passage he says, for example: "In order to be able to hope that the highest good becomes actual in the entirety of things, a good the realization of a part of which is imposed on us as a duty, practical reason demands belief in a divinity—in immortality."[46]

At first Hegel takes up Kant's doctrine without making any criticism. At the same time, however, already in the Tübingen Fragment and then later in his Bern drafts, he attempts to make this theory fruitful for his own problematic and to apply it to the relation between subjective and objective religion. For Hegel, as for Kant, the doctrine of the postulates is not scientific and metaphysical, that is to say, objective knowledge, but rather belongs to moral religion as a necessary, constitutive part of it.[47] In contrast to the dogmatic religion of the theologians, this moral religion is for Hegel the genuinely living, subjective religion.

Up until now the fundamental distinction between subjective and objective religion and the emphasis on subjective religion have always been regarded as Hegel's distinctive interest and his distinctive accomplishment in these early fragments.[48] The distinction itself is, to be sure, not

---

45. See *Dokumente zu Hegels Entwicklung*, pp. 158f., 165f.

46. *Hegels theologische Jugendschriften*, ed. H. Nohl (Tübingen: Mohr, 1907), p. 9. On the theme of the young Hegel's reception of Kant, see D. Henrich, "Some Historical Presuppositions of Hegel's System," in *Hegel and the Philosophy of Religion*, ed. D. E. Christensen (The Hague: Nijhoff, 1970), pp. 25–44. Henrich distinguishes two conceptions of moral theology in Kant: the earlier theory, influenced in his view by Rousseau, is carried on by orthodoxy; the later, supposing the principle of autonomy independent of theology, is taken up by Schelling and Hegel, in the course of which Hegel also reaches back to Rousseau's ethics of feelings. Our inquiry is similar to Henrich's and, in regard to the presupposition of Kantian ethics on the problem of principles (the distinction of *principium diiudicationis* from *principium executionis*), our inquiry takes Henrich's essays on Kant's ethics as its point of departure. As one may surmise from the following, at times the solutions presented here diverge from his solutions. On this theme, see also H. S. Harris, "The Young Hegel and the Postulates of Practical Reason," in *Hegel and the Philosophy of Religion*, pp. 61–78.

47. See *Hegels theologische Jugendschriften*, p. 8. Since Hegel, in Tübingen, takes up the Kantian doctrine of postulates in a positive way, Flatt's criticism of this doctrine (see note 14 above) apparently is not meaningful in his view. On Hegel's readings of Kant, see also the undoubtedly correct remarks by Rosenkranz, in *Hegels Leben* (Berlin: Duncker und Humblot, 1844), pp. 40, 86.

48. See, e.g., Theodor Haering, *Hegel. Sein Wollen und sein Werk*, 2 vols. (Leipzig and Berlin: B. G. Teubner, 1929), 1.63, 78f., and elsewhere; Paul Asveld, *La pensée religieuse du*

new. Hegel traces it back to the Reformation and declares that people have tried in vain to give it adequate consideration in "compendiums."[49] In *Remarks on Kant's Philosophical Doctrine of Religion,* Storr and Süskind speak of objective and subjective religion in a way that shows that this distinction is quite familiar to them.[50] The distinction is also to be found in the compendium by Sartorius that was basic in the Tübingen Stift.[51] The latter must have been the actual source and the motivation for reflecting upon and determining anew the relationship between objective and subjective religion. At first, then, Hegel took an internal theological problematic as his point of departure and attempted to reinterpret the concept of subjective religion by means of Kant's doctrine of postulates and Fichte's *Attempt at a Critique of All Revelation.*[52] Even Süskind, in the Appendix to his *Remarks,* took this path and arrived at a determination of the relation between objective and subjective religion that came very close to Hegel's.[53] But Süskind's purpose thereby was the justification of orthodox theology; even the moral religion of reason was supposed to be built into the system of orthodox theology. Hegel's intention was, to the contrary, as shown more clearly in his later drafts, the establishment of an ethics in which moral religion occupied a constitutive function.

Hence, independently of Storr's and Süskind's efforts, Hegel applied Kant's concept of the highest good and doctrine of postulates to his own, new conception of subjective religion. To be sure, Hegel also once gives

---

jeune Hegel (Louvain: Publications universitaires de Louvain, 1953), p. 40; Adriaan Peperzak, *La jeune Hegel,* pp. 19ff.; also Martin Brecht and Jörg Sandberger, "Hegels Begegnung mit der Theologie," pp. 73f., 78.

49. See *Hegels theologische Jugendschriften,* p. 356.

50. See Storr, *Bemerkungen,* pp. 43, 52, 132.

51. *Sartorii Compendium Theologiae dogmaticae* (Positiones A. 1764 editas retractatas exhibens Tubingae 1777). There, in § 1, it reads: "*Theologiae* vox ecclesiastica est. Hodierno loquendi usu, *objective* sumta notat *doctrinam de Deo* et religione: cum vero *subjective* accipitur, intelligi solet *cognitio* religionis, eaque accuratior et docta." He expresses himself more precisely in § 2 regarding subjective religion: "*Religio* (subjective sumta) est *studium colendi Deum, cum spe obtinendi et conservandi favorem Ipsium beneficum.*" The later edition of 1782 diverges from this somewhat. To whom Sartorius himself in turn goes back need not be further discussed here. Even Brecht and Sandberger do not cite this passage. They speak only of various "loci" that Sartorius's compendium and other writings treat at the systematic place which Hegel understands as subjective religion. Otherwise they correctly refer to the fact that Sartorius's was the compendium studied in the Tübingen Stift at that time. See Brecht and Sandberger, "Hegels Begegnung mit der Theologie," p. 73. Ansveld and Peperzak assume Fichte's and Rousseau's influence; see Ansveld, *La pensée religieuse,* pp. 39f.; and Peperzak, *Le jeune Hegel,* pp. 19f., 29.

52. On the relation to Fichte, see *Hegels theologische Jugendschriften,* p. 355. In Fichte's case it was just as much a matter of the highest good and moral theology.

53. Süskind, *Bemerkungen,* Appendix, p. 132: "Der Inbegriff dieser praktischen Sätze (sc.: Vernunftpostulate) oder Wahrheiten heißt *Religion* in *objektiver* Bedeutung. / Anerkennung dieser praktischen Wahrheiten, verbunden mit wirklichem praktischen Einfluß derselben auf unsere Willensbestimmung, heißt *Religion* in *subjektiver* Bedeutung."

the name of "objective religion" to the "system" of the highest good and the postulates.[54] But in this case it referred to the practical-moral vitality and impetus of religion that in this regard is then called "subjective." By "objective religion," then, Hegel here does not mean, as usual, positive religion, the dogmas of which are only a matter of understanding and memory, but instead a theory of pure reason with a view toward practice. The final purpose of practical reason and the postulates must, to be sure, be gathered into a "system" and set up as a philosophical theory. But their practical effect is that of "strengthening the motivations of morality."[55] These motivations are feelings that induce human beings to carry out and realize the moral law. Particularly in the Tübingen Fragment Hegel gives a more exact description of the "web of sentiments" that is animated by "ideas of reason,"[56] and seeks to show that the interest of the "heart" is awakened by these ideas. This inner presence and immediate liveliness of religious, moral ideas in feeling, by means of which the moral character of a subject determines itself, is for Hegel "subjective religion."[57] With this he employs experiences and descriptions of the ethics of feeling—Shaftesbury and Rousseau are named[58]—in order to unpack details of his concept of subjective religion. The idea of the highest good and, among the postulates, the idea of God above all, are, accordingly, so interwoven into the totality of sentiments that the human being feels himself determined to act morally and his feelings become moral motivations. But, indeed, by definition, morality must contain motivations to actual actions in the world and, hence, to this extent, subjective religion is morally necessary.

Moreover, without knowing it, Hegel stands thereby closer systematically (though not in the particular elaboration) to Kant's earlier doctrine of the highest good, of God and immortality, than his better known later theory. In the *Critique of Pure Reason* the "ideas of morality" and the moral law are still, to be sure, "objects of approval and amazement"; they contain the criteria of moral evaluation of actions. But they are first "motivations of design and execution" by virtue of the idea of the highest

---

54. *Hegels theologische Jugendschriften*, p. 48.
55. Ibid., p. 61; see also pp. 3, 5, 7, and elsewhere. Hegel thereby presupposes that the moral law itself as a principle of reason is independent of theology and religion, in accordance with the doctrine of Kant's ethical law as a principle for the evaluation of actions.
56. Ibid., p. 4. 57. Ibid., pp. 6f., 48, and elsewhere.
58. Ibid., pp. 51, also 8. Peperzak refers to the aesthetic character of virtue in Hegel's views at this time and identifies the Greeks as background for this (see *Le jeune Hegel*, pp. 21ff.). One must certainly also consider this relation along with the others, a relation that already was present, for example, in Shaftesbury.

good and the assumptions of God and immortality.[59] Hegel was not familiar with this earlier theory of the highest good. Nevertheless, as far as the content is concerned, his own conception of subjective religion is related to it.[60] Hegel also recognized the necessity of having to demonstrate the relation of the moral ideas to feelings as motivations, and he sought to comply with this requirement by means of closer descriptions of the ethically relevant feelings.

To be sure, on the question of feelings as motivations, a difficulty presents itself for Hegel. Namely, during his time in Bern especially, Hegel also takes over Kant's theory of respect as the sole ethical motivation known by us.[61] However, respect does not immediately lead to subjective religion. Kant's theory of respect as the ethical motivation was bound up with a fundamental revision of his (already mentioned) earlier theory of the highest good. Hegel tries to tie together conceptions distinguished in Kant and to unite the doctrine of respect as a motivation with his concept of subjective religion as a motivation, that is, as realization of the ethical. If, however, respect is recognized as the motivation for ethical actions in the world, then only an "intensification" of ethical motivations can still fall to subjective religion.[62] Yet this modest function of an "intensification" of moral motivation does not genuinely correspond to the central position that Hegel wants to attribute to subjective religion in the ethical life of the individual and an entire people. Rather, already from the time of the Tübingen Fragment onward, Hegel takes the trouble to elaborate more closely the actualization of the ethical, above all, in terms of Greek religion and its specification and formation of the entire life of the community. According to Hegel's starting point at that time, this consideration which treats the religion of a people as a historically cultural phenomenon—in the aftermath of Herder—is systematically and principally grounded in the fact that subjective religion is being appealed to as the force of realizing ethical principles, that is, as moral motivation. In this way, then, the relation of respect as motivation to Hegel's concept of subjective religion remained unclarified. Even in

59. KrV A813/B841. See also note 29 above.
60. The opposition, construed by Haering, between a pure, moral religion and the living, subjective religion apparently rests as much on a misunderstanding of Kant's practical philosophy as on an irrational prejudice against the Enlightenment. See esp. *Hegel. Sein Wollen und sein Werk*, 1.66.
61. See, e.g., *Hegels theologische Jugendschriften*, p. 212. Even in the Tübingen Fragment he already speaks of the "pure respect for the law," which in the course of coming closer to morality must, nonetheless, be supported by other moral feelings as they are analyzed by the ethics of feeling; see ibid., p. 18.
62. See ibid., pp. 61, 48, 18. Hegel appears here, not entirely in the sense of Kant, to conceive respect as a quite distinctive, yet still a particular moral feeling next to others.

his time at Bern, especially in regard to the religion of the Greeks as he understood it, Hegel clung at bottom to the "holy sentiments" and to the free interest of the "heart"—in combination with fantasy—as the vitality of religion and the effective power of the ethical.[63]

Among the friends at Tübingen, only Hegel can be credited with setting the doctrine of the postulates, and the practically significant ideas contained in them, into the contexts of rational religion in this way. A specific concept of ethical life lies at the bottom of this arrangement. This theme and this conception are not contained in Schelling's reinterpretation of the postulates within his draft of ethics.

Yet Hegel does more than take up Kant's doctrine of postulates and bring it into the context of his own problematic. Provoked by Storr's "Contradictions ... against Kant's Doctrine of Religion"[64] and Schelling's reports from the Tübingen Stift, and perhaps also by Fichte's *Attempt at a Critique of All Revelation* and Süskind's appeal to this writing for orthodoxy, Hegel also criticizes the misinterpretations of the doctrine of the postulates by the Tübingen theological school. Just like Schelling, he criticizes the claim about "reason's inability" that leads to the assumption that the human being, in leading an ethical life, is dependent upon an entity outside himself, namely, an objective God.[65] Once this is conceded, people can even declare dogmas such as the forgiveness of sins to be "postulates of practical reason,"[66] they can again develop the properties of the objective God dogmatically from his essence. In the "postulate" of the harmony of morality and happiness, the thesis of reason's frailty at the same time implies the image of a sensuous happiness.[67] According to Hegel, however, such happiness is not able to be combined with genuine morality. As a counterexample he sets up the ancient sort of republican who fought and died for a "free constitution" of the "fatherland," without hoping for happiness.[68] With these reflections Hegel obviously turns against the positive Christian religion and their theoreti-

---

63. Ibid., pp. 229, 219ff. On the developing historical changes and nuances of Hegel's "Kantianism" and his conception of the Greek religion in the drafts of this year, see O. Pöggeler, *Hegels Jugendschriften und die Idee einer Phänomenologie des Geistes* (unpublished Habilitation, University of Heidelberg, 1966).
64. See Hegel's letter to Schelling, December 24, 1794, in *Briefe von und an Hegel*, 1.12.
65. *Hegels theologische Jugendschriften*, p. 235.
66. Ibid., pp. 156, 64. The closeness to Schelling's thoughts and formulations in his letter to Hegel of January 6, 1795, is striking; see *Briefe von und an Hegel*, 1.14.
67. See *Hegels theologische Jugendschriften*, pp. 237ff. Hegel also sought (around 1794) to grasp happiness, insofar as it is a constitutive part of the highest good, as moral philosophy's interpretation of the Christian idea of blessedness; see ibid., pp. 62, 68. Yet he also expresses criticism of this Christian idea; see ibid., p. 59.
68. Ibid., pp. 362, 238f., 222, 223.

cians, the orthodox theologians.[69] He raises no objection against Kant, although this would have been possible, as far as the matter itself is concerned, in regard to the empirical concept of happiness in Kant's later doctrine of the highest good. But, already in his work *On the I*, Schelling wanted to except Kant from this objection.[70] The Tübingen orthodoxy, by contrast, belongs for Hegel to positive religion which plays even with politics "under *one* roof."[71] Like Schelling, Hegel makes this combination of orthodoxy and politics responsible for the lack of political and religious freedom at that time.

Nevertheless, this way of proceeding, proper to orthodoxy, which in alliance with the political powers only feigns the recognition of critical and free reason, is more clearly distinguished by Hegel than it is by Schelling from Kant's own doctrine. Probably in connection with the criticism of the Tübingen school, Hegel takes up the study of Kant's doctrine of postulates once again.[72] In his letters to Schelling he emphatically repudiates the claims of the Tübingen orthodoxy as well as those of the *Attempt at a Critique of All Revelation*, by means of which Fichte has "reintroduced the old manner of demonstrating in dogmatics."[73] In an appendage to this critique Hegel then suggests his own plan, which takes its start approvingly from the doctrine of postulates and practically based metaphysics as Kant developed them in connection with his teleology in the *Critique of Judgment*. He says:

If I had time, I would seek to determine more precisely how far, after the establishment of moral belief, we now, looking backwards, need the legimated idea of God, for example, in the explanation of the relation of purpose and so forth, how far we are permitted to take it with us now from ethico-theology to physico-theology and manage then with it there.

To be sure, people already take this "path" in the course of explaining "Providence," "miracles," and—like Fichte—"revelation."[74] However, one thereby oversteps the boundaries of human reason. Thus, leaning

69. Ibid., p. 234f. On this critique of the doctrine of postulates, see Asveld, *La pensée religieuse*, pp. 108ff., and Peperzak, *Le jeune Hegel*, pp. 110ff. Peperzak also considers whether Hegel intended to target only the Tübingen orthodoxy but not Kant.

70. See note 28 above. It is in Frankfurt in connection with the new philosophical draft of antinomy and unification in "believing and being" that Hegel first parallels Kant's philosophy with positive religion; see *Hegels theologische Jugendschriften*, p. 385.

71. See Hegel's letter to Schelling of April 16, 1795, in *Briefe von und an Hegel*, 1.24, 16.

72. Ibid., 1.16, 24.

73. See Hegel's letter to Schelling from the end of January 1795 in *Briefe von und an Hegel*, 1.17.

74. Ibid. For an interpretation of the correspondence between Hegel and Schelling, see also Haering, *Hegel. Sein Wollen und sein Werk*, 1.196–210. Nevertheless, in some details he comes to different conclusions.

on Kant, Hegel asks for the justification of this way of proceeding and "how far" it may be taken, that is to say, he asks for the purely philosophical foundation.

As Hegel, in close adherence to Kant, puts it in a fragment from this period, physicotheology or, more precisely, consideration of nature as critical natural teleology does not of itself make belief in God possible.[75] Belief in God is made possible only by practical reason which, along with willing the ethical final purpose, accepts the conditions of the possibility of this final purpose. But after the establishment of ethicotheology through practical reason, nature still must also be able to be considered with moral belief, since God, the moral creator and ruler of the world, is regarded as producing it and acting in it. Hegel thereby naturally rejects the vulgar physicotheology that looks everywhere for things physically useful to human beings.[76] Instead, like Kant in the concluding part of the *Critique of Judgment*, he poses to himself the question whether one might not be able to see the purposiveness of nature on the basis of moral interest, whether physical teleology in this moral consideration of the world is not to be represented as a precondition of the possibility of the final purpose in the world.[77] Without the purposiveness of nature, namely, one cannot think the final purpose, the highest good in the world, as accomplishable even by way of approximating it. Since, however, according to the doctrine of postulates, only God guarantees the complete realization of the final purpose in the world, the purposiveness of nature, following the establishment of ethicotheology, may also be ascribed to the moral creator, maintainer, and ruler of the world. Hegel probably means by this the "use of the legitimized idea of God" in "physicotheology." He is not thereby speaking of particular instances of purposiveness that would have their basis in particular divine purposes. Miracles wrought by God should neither be explained by the understanding nor justified by reason; according to Hegel, they are rather products of free imagination.[78] The modality of holding something to be true, by means of which God and a general purposiveness of nature, produced by him, are assumed in order to entertain the possibility of the final purpose, is not knowledge for Hegel, not even practical knowledge, but rather a rational belief on the basis of moral interest. He takes pains to distinguish the subjectivity of this assumption on the basis of rational

---

75. See *Hegels theologische Jugendschriften*, p. 361.
76. See *Dokumente*, pp. 234f.
77. See, e.g., *Kritik der Urteilskraft* 447f., 443f., 458f., as well as 175f., 195f. (pages 419f., 413, 439, as well as xixf, lv of the 1793 edition).
78. See *Hegels theologische Jugendschriften*, pp. 231f.n. Such products of the imagination belong to a historical form of religion.

grounds as well as the subjectivity of the necessary, teleological maxims in the evaluation of nature from the modality of the merely subjectively necessary—though not on the basis of rational grounds—judgment about miracles, which have a meaning only for the imagination.[79]

From this foundation of moral belief it is also possible to obtain a morally purified concept of Providence. Hegel here seeks to reinterpret, with the help of Kant's *Critique of Judgment*, the concepts that belong to *providentia* (*conservatio, concursus, gubernatio*, etc.) as he found them already in Sartorius's compendium.[80] He criticizes the orthodox concept of Providence; according to Hegel, it is neither possible to indicate the way Providence prevails for specific purposes in the world nor reasonable to think of Providence as the effectiveness of an "objective," alien God for the sake of our physical happiness.[81] Thus, a Divine Providence that acts on the basis of moral reasons can in general only be believed as the cause of the purposiveness in the maintenance and direction of the course of the world. For such a purposiveness is a presupposition of the possibility of the final purpose in the world.[82] A letter of Hölderlin to Hegel proves that Hegel, in the course of moving from the ethicotheology back to the physicotheology, intended to discuss "the concepts of religion" and to treat the concept of Providence in a way "completely parallel with Kant's teleology." Hölderlin continues: "The way in which he [namely, Kant] unites the mechanism of nature (and thus also of fate) with its purposiveness appears to me actually to contain the entire spirit of his system."[83] In correspondence with Hölderlin, Hegel must have written about such projects as what he was planning, projects which correspond to what Hegel announces in a letter to Schelling (from the end of January, 1795).

Hence, with the critique of orthodox theology, Hegel seeks at the same time to develop his own concepts of religion, indeed, in particular

---

79. See *Hegels theologische Jugendschriften*, p. 364. Hegel intends such a distinction although he arrives at no definitive clarification of it. By contrast, Süskind explicitly denies such a distinction. See Storr, *Bemerkungen*, Appendix 228f.

80. *Sartorii Compendium*, § § 104ff.

81. See *Hegels theologische Jugendschriften*, pp. 22, 58, 227, 234.

82. See ibid., pp. 362, 20; also see 75, 375. Hegel's attempts at achieving a rational concept of Providence are, to be sure, still probing. He characterizes the problem, for example, with the proposition: "In his governing of the world God does not alter the laws, only the course of nature" (ibid., p. 364); nevertheless, he does not formulate a clear solution. Compare also Kant's determination of diverse concepts of Providence and the establishment of a moral concept of Providence in the work *Zum ewigen Frieden* (in *Kants gesammelte Schriften*, volume 8, pp. 361fn), with which Hegel could have been acquainted from 1795 on. Compare also Lessing's concept of Providence, e.g., in *Erziehung des Menschengeschlechts* (§ 91).

83. Hölderlin's letter to Hegel of January 26, 1795, in *Briefe von und an Hegel*, 1.20.

the concept of Providence, in connection with Kant's moral theology in the *Critique of Judgment*. Thereby he intends, apparently in terms of moral theology, to resolve Kant's problem of making possible the transition from the concepts of nature to the concepts of freedom by means of the concept and the principle of the purposiveness of nature. The moral belief in God turns back to nature and the world as the effective field of human freedom, a field in which the final purpose, demanded from a practical point of view, must be possible, a field in which purposive presuppositions must, therefore, in general be assumed for a realization of the final purpose.

However, in Bern the renewed study of the Kantian doctrine of postulates probably stirred Hegel to yet a further plan. He writes to Schelling: "I once had in mind making clear to myself in an essay what it could mean to come nearer to God and believed that I found therein a satisfaction of the postulate that practical reason commands the world of appearances and the remaining postules."[84] Hegel's formulation is not completely clear. Supposedly, he poses to himself as a theme the religious question, What does it mean "to come closer to God"? That is, indeed, the question of the genuine divine service, and Hegel seeks to clarify it through Kant's doctrine of postulates. The satisfactory solution to this question consists for him, then, "in this . . . , that practical reason commands the world of appearances." In a fragment from this period Hegel declares: if the "drive" in Fichte's sense, which is determined by the moral law, "commanded the world of appearances," it would be "worthiness in a lawful way (in a morally actual way)."[85] The execution of the moral law through the inner, moral determination of motivations, by means of which practical reason commands the world of appearances in us, is thus the worthiness of being happy. As Hegel expresses himself in the fragment, it is no renunciation of the "rights" that reason can validate in regard to a happiness corresponding to morality, but rather precisely the necessary condition for attaining the highest good. The moral disposition is, therefore, the true manner of coming closer to the highest good and, with that, also of "coming closer to God." On the basis of this moral disposition as the first and indispensable component of the highest good, Hegel apparently intended to make it understandable how the other concepts belonging to a rational religion are postulates.[86]

---

84. Hegel's letter to Schelling of August 30, 1795 in *Briefe von und an Hegel*, 1.29.
85. See *Hegels theologische Jugendschriften*, pp. 361, 362.
86. According to this interpretation the expressions "darin . . . daß" in the cited example (see note 84 above) belong together, while "satisfaction of the postulate" would mean the satisfactory resolution of the postulate, namely, "coming closer to God." Hegel would then have grasped this religious question by means of the moral concept of free-

In this question of the genuine divine service the concept of the rational, subjective religion probably had played a central role.

Hegel did not carry out these plans which he apparently still had at the beginning of 1795, plans that take Kant's doctrine of postulates as their point of departure. He is then considerably influenced by Schelling's reinterpretation of the doctrine of postulates and his conception of Kant. Hegel acknowledges that he himself had only "glimpses" of what Schelling clearly elaborated to him first in a letter (which already contained the basic thoughts of the work *On the I*) and then in this work itself.[87] Prepared, of course, by his own reflections, he obviously takes over from Schelling the insight that the supersensible world, God, and immortality are only to be found in the I and its absolute freedom.[88] He likewise apparently accepts Schelling's thesis that Kant's philosophy must still be completed, that its first and supreme principles are still lacking. Up to this point Hegel had not uttered such a critique of Kant.[89] Just then he first becomes acquainted with Reinhold and Fichte, and from Schelling he learns that the completion of philosophy still lies before them. Thus, Hegel then expects "from the Kantian system and its full completion . . . a revolution in Germany."[90]

Schelling had announced that he would provide the premises—as he construed them—that Kant's philosophy still lacked and would establish the supreme principles of philosophy.[91] The supreme principle, however, or the idea of the unconditioned is, according to Schelling, God or the absolute I. Hegel then tries to take over from Schelling this identification of God with the absolute I. Thus, he writes to Schelling that "the idea of God as the absolute I" will always be a part of what remains an esoteric philosophy.[92] Yet discussion of a philosophical concept of God extends through the entire correspondence of Hegel with Schelling in these years. At the beginning of the discussion Hegel represents the posi-

---

dom. One could also quite naturally understand the sentence differently ("darin" to refer to "sich Gott zu nähern" and the "postulate" combined with the "daß"-sentence); yet, then, the religious theme "coming closer to God" would be an interpretation of the Kantian postulates that is less probable, given the history of Hegel's development. Harris, for example, translates the sentence in this sense. Moreover, in the postulate, so understood, he sees Providence. See Harris, "The Young Hegel," p. 69.

87. *Briefe von und an Hegel*, 1.24, 29. For what follows in the text, see also Asveld, *Le pensée religieuse*, pp. 75–99, and Peperzak, *Le jeune Hegel*, p. 108f.n. Peperzak assigns less significance than Asveld does to the influence of Schelling on Hegel.

88. See, e.g., *Hegels theologische Jugendschriften*, pp. 224, 225, 227f.

89. See, e.g., ibid., p. 211.

90. Hegel's letter to Schelling of April 16, 1795, in *Briefe von und an Hegel*, 1.23.

91. Cf. Schelling's letter to Hegel of January 6, 1795, in *Briefe von und an Hegel*, 1.14; also Schelling, *Werke*, 1.152.

92. Cf. *Briefe von und an Hegel*, 1.24; *Hegels theologische Jugendschriften*, p. 75.

tion of the Kantian postulate of God according to which God is to be thought as the moral creator of the world, distinct from the world.[93] Schelling, by contrast, criticizes this standpoint of moral theism. He is thinking, of course, principally of orthodox theology when he says (in a word-play on an assertion by Lessing, conveyed by Jacobi): "For us, too, the orthodox concepts of God are no more."[94] With this remark he refers Hegel, of whose familiarity with Lessing he was well aware, to Lessing's critique of the orthodox concept of God. Yet Hegel apparently understood Lessing as the representative of a rational religion that was compatible with Kant's moral theology. Schelling appealed, by contrast, to Lessing's Spinozism as presented by Jacobi in the latter's *Letters on the Doctrine of Spinoza*. Schelling declares that he himself has become a "Spinozist"; nevertheless, according to Schelling, Spinoza's God, the sole substance or even the *"Hen kai pan"*, may not be regarded as an absolute object, but instead must be regarded as an absolute I. The absolute I lies beyond the determinations of personality and self-consciousness, which are contained as features in the orthodox concept of God.[95]

At first Hegel goes along with Schelling's program of regarding God as the absolute I. Nevertheless, in a later letter he utters a cautious critique precisely of Schelling's "Spinozism." Hegel thereby points up the decisive difference between Schelling's idea of the absolute I as the sole, divine substance and Fichte's systematic consideration in *Foundation of the Entire Wissenschaftslehre*, in which the absolute I of the first principle is distinguished from the derivative category of substance. To be sure, Fichte already says: "It is originally only one substance, the I."[96] But this I, according to Fichte, encompasses all realities and is the sole substance only insofar as it limits itself and posits a definite, restricted reality in itself as accident. Substance is a category of relation that sets up the relation between I and not-I in a definite way as a condition of the possibility of finite self-consciousness. Hegel puts forth this Fichtean doctrine of categories as the basis for this objection to Schelling's identification

---

93. See Hegel's letter to Schelling from the end of January 1795, in *Briefe von und an Hegel*, 1.18.

94. Schelling's letter to Hegel of February 4, 1795, in *Briefe von und an Hegel*, 1.22. See Jacobi, *Werke*, 4.1.54: "Die orthodoxen Begriffe von der Gottheit sind nicht mehr für mich.... 'Hen kai pan! Ich weiß nichts anders." Hölderlin also noted this passage for himself.

95. See Schelling's letter to Hegel of February 4, 1795, in *Briefe von und an Hegel*, 1.22, and in Schelling, *Werke*, 1.192f. With these remarks Schelling seeks to target the "so-called natural religion" and the moral concept of God as well. See *Briefe von und an Hegel*, 1.14.

96. Fichte, *Gesamtausgabe*, Division 1, volume 2, ed. R. Lauth and H. Jacob with the assistance of M. Zahn (Stuttgart-Bad Cannstadt: Frommann, 1965), p. 300.

of the absolute I with Spinoza's divine substance.[97] Hegel thereby upholds, to be sure, the distinction of the absolute I from finite self-consciousness, but apparently does not want to regard the absolute I as the one absolute substance, that is to say, as God in Spinoza's sense. Yet Hegel's actual motive for his objection to Schelling may not be so much Fichte's systematic consideration, which he is just then appropriating. Instead, his motive may be his resistance to a metaphysical concept of God as he sees it in the work *On the I* and his insistence on a moral concept of God which he himself is still not yet capable of explicating on his own, but the significance of which is prefigured for him in Kant's postulate of God. Hence, under the influence of Schelling's first writings and letters, Hegel tries to reinterpret Kant's doctrine of postulates, though without taking over Schelling's conception of Spinozism on the basis of the absolute I.[98]

Up to this point it has been discussed how Schelling and Hegel took up the Kantian doctrine of postulates in different ways and how, in connection with this, they set up diverse systematic conceptions of ethics. The problem of the relation between ethics and metaphysics lay at the bottom of the philosophical projects of both. With regard to this question, in particular what concerned philosophical theology, Hegel was influenced in part by Schelling's first works and letters, without, of course, surrendering his own position, which one could identify as the constitutive significance of moral "subjective religion" and all its concepts for an ethics.

3

The "Earliest System-Programme of German Idealism" has not yet been drawn into the accounts given up to this point. Nevertheless, for the history of the development of the theories of early German idealism and for the network of communication among the young idealists, this text is significant and highly instructive. During the 1920s the debate about its authorship seemed to have been ended by Ludwig Strauß with a decision in favor of Schelling and against Hölderlin.[99] In the after-

97. Cf. Hegel's letter to Schelling of August 30, 1795, in *Briefe von und an Hegel*, 1.32. To be sure, the further assertion—only the empirical I can properly be substance—does not correspond completely to Fichte's theory.

98. Hegel's apparently approving judgment of Schelling's *Philosophische Briefe über Dogmatismus und Kritizismus* in a letter to Schelling has unfortunately not survived. See Schelling's letter to Hegel on June 20, 1796, in *Briefe von und an Hegel*, 1.37.

99. L. Strauß, *Hölderlins Anteil an Schellings frühem Systemprogramm* (see note 31 above). Rosenzweig had first edited the "System-Programme" and named Schelling as the author;

math, Schelling research made use of the "System-Programme" for the interpretation of the early Schelling without further investigation of the question of the author. Some years ago Otto Pöggeler first made the attempt to prove that the "System-Programme" was not only written down, but also composed by, Hegel.[100] At odds with the claims of F. Rosenzweig,[101] it must be philologically accepted that no certain criteria, indeed, not even hints or indications of a transcript, are to be gathered from Hegel's manuscript. The supposed basis for Hegel's transcript remains unknown today. On the grounds of this finding, the first task that presents itself is that of investigating, in a separate, historical interpretation, whether or not this text may be given a place in the history of the young Hegel's development. On the basis of handwriting analysis, we know that Hegel wrote it either from the middle to the end of 1796 or at the beginning of 1797; thus, in the latter case, which is quite possible, he wrote it first in Frankfurt.[102] Only if it is possible to show incongruities or contradictions between the "System-Programme" and Hegel's thinking at this time, can one pose the question whether another author comes into consideration. Yet even then Schelling would be able to be considered the author of the "System-Programme" in any case only with a degree of probability, but never with certainty, even if the thoughts and formulations of the "System-Programme" obviously may be given a fitting place in the context of his drafts at that time.[103]

In what follows, only the reference in the "System-Programme" back to the Kantian doctrine of postulates and to the *Critique of Judgment* as well as the project in it of a metaphysics as morals or, better, ethics are to be treated and compared with Schelling's and Hegel's theories and plans for these themes at this time. The text begins in a fragmentary way with the words: "an ethics." The preceding page and the beginning of

---

see his *Das älteste Systemprogramm des deutschen Idealismus* (Heidelberg: Winter, 1917). W. Böhm sought to demonstrate that Hölderlin was the author; see his "Hölderlin als Verfasser des 'Ältesten Systemprogramms des deutschen Idealismus,'" *Deutsche Vierteljahrsschrift* 4 (1926): 339–426. Strauß opposed Böhm's thesis and gave his approval to Rosenzweig's view by bringing up at the same time a series of new arguments.

100. See O. Pöggeler, "Hegel, der Verfasser des ältesten Systemprogramms des deutschen Idealismus," *Hegel-Studien* 4 (1969): 17–32.

101. Rosenzweig, *Das älteste Systemprogramm des deutschen Idealismus*, pp. 8–11.

102. See Pöggeler, "Hegel, der Verfasser des ältesten Systemprogramms," p. 18. In this essay, for the first time the basic lines are drawn for the inclusion of the "System-Programme" in the history of Hegel's development, and from this it is concluded that Hegel very probably first wrote the "System-Programme" in Frankfurt.

103. Despite the presupposition that it is a matter of a transcription and despite the clearly recognizable influences of Hölderlin on the elaborations of beauty and aesthetics in the "System-Programme," Hölderlin's authorship was already rejected by L. Strauß with justification, on account of the other parts of this draft (see note 99 above).

the entire text have not survived. With the start of a new page the author appears to have passed over to the problem of ethics, the outline of which he then develops. "Since the whole of metaphysics in the future falls under *morality* (of which Kant with his two practical postulates has given us merely one *example*, and not by any means *exhausted*), this ethics will be nothing else but a complete system of all ideas or, what is the same, of all practical postulates." The author thus takes Kant's doctrine of postulates as the point of departure. By the "two practical postulates," the postulate of immortality and the postulate of the existence of God are probably meant. Yet Kant's philosophy must be completed; metaphysics as ethics may not merely set up two postulates, but rather must set up "a complete system of all ideas." Already from these remarks it may be gathered that the relationship of ethics to metaphysics has changed decisively relative to Kant's *Critique of Practical Reason* and Kant's *Critique of Judgment*. The practical grounding of metaphysics no longer presupposes, as it does for Kant, principles of ethics developed independently of metaphysics; metaphysics no longer contains merely postulates as conditions of the possibility of the highest good that is, to be sure, the ultimate purpose but not the principle of our moral will. Instead, metaphysics is as such ethics, that is, a "complete system of all ideas." For the author of the "System-Programme," an idea signifies only "what is an object of *freedom*." However, so understood, the idea has for him the same meaning as a practical postulate. Thus, in contrast to how it is for Kant, ethics consists of a system of all ideas or practical postulates.

This way of taking up Kant's doctrine of postulates is characteristic only of Hegel at this time. From the outset Schelling had contested the conception of postulates in the Tübingen orthodoxy and never distinctly distinguished this conception from Kant's theory itself. He ultimately demanded, as was shown, that postulates be permitted in philosophy only in strict analogy with postulates in geometry, thus at odds with Kant's determination of the concept in the *Critique of Practical Reason*, and he rejected the postulates of practical reason altogether. Hegel, on the other hand, was receptive to the doctrine of postulates as Kant himself had presented them and he sought to apply them for the clarification of his own problems. During his time in Bern he critically unpacked this doctrine once again and, under Schelling's influence, endeavored to combine it with the thought of the absolute I. The doctrine of postulates remained for Hegel a theory with which one, to be sure, cannot be satisfied as it stands, but from which one must take one's bearings. To the question of how one could reinterpret Kant's doctrine of postulates in an ethics, on the basis of the principle of the absolute freedom of the

I, Hegel probably still found no sure answer in his correspondence with Schelling and in his Bern fragments. In further elaborations of the "System-Programme," however, a solution is at least suggested.

The immediate continuation of the cited passage in the "System-Programme" leads at first, to be sure, to the problem of the relation of freedom and nature:

> The first idea is naturally the representation *of me myself* as an absolutely free entity. With this free, self-conscious entity there emerges at the same time an entire *world*—out of nothing—the only true and thinkable *creation out of nothing*—Here I shall descend to the fields of physics; the question is this: how must a world be constituted for a moral entity? I would like to give wings again to our physics that plods so slowly and with such difficulty by experiments.

The idea of the absolute freedom is thus contained in the "representation of *me myself*," that is, it is the content of the consciousness of the self-conscious entity that represents its very self. Hence, here this idea is not to be ascribed as an attribute to the absolute I. Since Schelling, as well as Hegel, knew to distinguish the absolute I from the self-consciousness that is always finite (in which case Hegel follows Schelling's drafts),[104] one must try to bring the expressions of the "System-Programme" into accord with that theory of the distinction between the absolute I and self-consciousness. To be sure, here the absolute I and its absolute freedom might be permitted to remain in the background. However, absolute freedom is no theoretically metaphysical idea, but rather the first idea of the ethics of a self-conscious entity. It signifies the capacity of acting on the basis of unconditioned spontaneity. As in Schelling's *Philosophical Letters on Dogmatism and Criticism*, with which Hegel was indeed acquainted, the ideas have significance—and as the first, the idea of absolute freedom has significance—only for a practical self-consciousness that, as one might suppose, recognizes as its moral task the continuous, active overcoming of the limits of the finite. It thereby possesses the certainty of being different from the absolute I not qualitatively, but rather only quantitatively, that is, through limitation somehow of its possibility of having an effect. To this extent, then, absolute freedom can be the content of the representation of the finite entity, conscious of its very self. Schelling's project of an ethics in the *Philosophical Letters* probably underlies this systematically. Hegel apparently agreed with this project[105] since it confronted his own problems so much and at the same time dispelled his doubts regarding a purely metaphysical determination of

---

104. See Hegel's letter to Schelling of August 30, 1795, in *Briefe von und an Hegel*, 1.32, and in *Hegels theologische Jugendschriften*, p. 361.

105. See Schelling's letter to Hegel, in *Briefe von und an Hegel*, 1.37.

the absolute I as the sole substance. This thought of the "System-Programme" thus inserts itself seamlessly into Hegel's historical development. That the author speaks of finite self-consciousness is evidenced above all by the formulation of "an entire world" emerging "with," not "out" of, free self-consciousness. The finite self-consciousness can understand itself only in the distinction it makes between its own subjectivity and the world of objects. Fichte's and even Schelling's theories of the finite subject are hereby presupposed. The indication, this is "the only true and thinkable *creation out of nothing*," is a criticism of the orthodox and theistic concept of God. This thought is to be found in Schelling; similar formulations also appear in the latter's writings.[106] But the problem of *creatio ex nihilo* which Spinoza, for example, disputed (as Jacobi had shown),[107] was naturally also known to Hegel. In his discussion of a philosophical concept of God in his correspondence with Schelling, he indeed proceeds at first from Kant's concept of the moral creator of the world, but then arrives at an alteration of this Kantian concept of God. Thus the polemic against the divinely produced creation out of nothing can very probably also be a result of this critical engagement.

The ensuing problematic of the "physics" has often been connected with the emergence of Schelling's philosophy of nature.[108] But the basic question which in the "System-Programme" is supposed to make a new philosophy of nature and physics necessary, namely, "How must a world be constituted for a moral entity?" is clearly a question of Hegel's, but hardly a motive of Schelling's for his philosophy of nature. In the *Critique of Judgment* Kant had already posed the question in connection with the systematic problem of the transition from nature to freedom and put forth the maxims of the purposiveness of nature as the necessary condition under which the moral final purpose of practical reason in the world can be thought as possible. Hegel took up this problem of Kant's and planned to investigate the teleological determinations of nature when it is considered on the basis of moral-theologically grounded faith and on the basis of moral interest. The "physics" projected in the "System-Programme" was apparently supposed to proceed from this ethical motivation and supposedly also to be grounded in the teleological maxims of the morally interested consideration of the world.

---

106. L. Strauß has already shown this; see *Hölderlins Anteil an Schellings frühem Systemprogramm*, p. 697.
107. See Jacobi, *Werke*, 4.1.56.
108. See Rosenzweig, *Das älteste Systemprogramm*, pp. 15ff.; Strauß, *Hölderlins Anteil an Schellings frühem Systemprogramm*, pp. 714f.; Wieland, *Die Anfänge der Philosophie Schellings und die Frage nach der Natur*, pp. 411ff.

To be sure, in a letter to Niethammer, Schelling also announced an interpretation of the *Critique of Judgment* according to his own principles.[109] But mention of the Kantian teleology in the work *On the I*, and in the Introduction to the *Ideas for a Philosophy of Nature* (1797), does not yet indicate this purely moral grounding of the consideration of nature.[110] Thus one cannot explain the emergence of Schelling's philosophy of nature on the basis of the "System-Programme." The actual grounds for the development of a philosophy of nature in Schelling's case are to be identified here only briefly in a thesis. The initial seeds of a philosophy of nature are to be found in the *Essays toward the Elucidation of the Idealism of the Doctrine of Science*.[111] There Schelling drafts a transcendental-philosophical history of self-consciousness in analogy with Fichte's "pragmatic history of the human spirit" in the *Foundation of the Entire Wissenschaftslehre*. But in contrast to Fichte, this history of self-consciousness is expanded around the various preconscious stages of the actions of the human spirit, which on account of their unconsciousness appear external to self-consciousness, that is, they appear as nature. At the same time, with this, the problem of the reality of the external world is supposed to be clarified. Decisive for Schelling in this regard is the intuition that alone guarantees reality and on which every self-consciousness also rests. The products of its unconsciously productive activity in the various stages are, for self-consciousness, various stages of nature. Only by taking up into transcendental philosophy the Leibnizian theory of unconscious representations and the monads' ladder of stages was Schelling able to conceive this expansion of transcendental philosophy to include a part that is natural philosophy. For the part that is natural philosophy not only contains the concepts of the object in general, but at the same time discusses the various particular domains and series of stages of nature. Schelling may well have had in front of him the Leibnizian ladder of the stages of nature, in Herder's interpretation, when

109. See Schelling's letter to Niethammer of January 22, 1796, in *Briefe und Dokumente*, 1.61.
110. See Schelling, *Werke*, 1.241–42; 2.47ff. and 3f.
111. Strauß maintained that the origin of Schelling's philosophy of nature is already to be observed in the turn to nature at the end of the *Philosophical Letters on Dogmatism and Criticism*. The claim, which since then has been often repeated, is inaccurate. In this case the multiple senses of the term "nature" are probably the source of a deception. Schelling turns from arduous speculation, that is to say, intellectual argumentation, and returns to the consideration of our own original nature and our life. Here nature as human nature is probably to be taken in terms of the model of the understanding of the Greeks at that time or even in Rousseau's sense. Such a concept of nature does not make the emergence of Schelling's philosophy of nature understandable, a philosophy that has as its object the possibility of the conceptual core of the things of experience and their division and thereby also the possibility of the external world. For Strauß's view, see *Hölderlins Anteil an Schellings frühem Systemprogramm*, p. 714.

he (Schelling) speaks of the "productive power," the "universal spirit of nature," and the "eternal original form" (*ewiges Urbild*), approached by all the formations of nature, from raw matter to ever higher organizations up to self-consciousness.[112] With that it became possible to develop a concrete philosophy of nature within transcendental idealism as a history of self-consciousness.[113] Hence, Schelling's initial conception of the philosophy of nature, which presented an extension of transcendental idealism, had other systematic grounds and other historical presuppositions than the grounding of "physics" by way of moral philosophy within the "System-Programme."

After the transition from nature to the world of the human being and after the mention of the idea of humanity as well as the naming of "subordinate" ideas, for example, the idea of "eternal peace," the author of the "System-Programme" once more plays on Kant's doctrine of postulates and sketches his own transformation of the significance of this doctrine:

Finally come the ideas of a moral world, divinity, immortality—overthrow of all superstition, pursuit, by reason itself, of the priesthood that nowadays puts on airs of being reasonable.—Absolute freedom of all spirits who bear the intellectual world within themselves and do not permit themselves to look for either God or immortality *outside themselves.*

The idea of a "moral world" is probably taken from the *Critique of Pure Reason*, in which Kant mentions it several times in connection with the doctrine of the highest good espoused by him there and with the idea of the intelligible world.[114] In the "System-Programme" it apparently has the same meaning as the "intellectual world." The ideas or practical postulates of divinity and immortality are likewise mentioned. Here, too, Kant's doctrine of postulates is taken up and then, in a vehement polemic, set off against the misunderstandings and "hypocrisies of reason" which are dissimulated as the right doctrines by the Tübingen orthodoxy and by every politically allied priestly class in the interest of maintaining

112. See Schelling, *Werke*, 1.386f., 382f., among others.
113. In *Schellings Verhältnis zu Leibniz* (Augsburg: Schoder, 1937), Brenner presents, to be sure, several passages in which the young Schelling mentions Leibniz. But what is not shown are the connections among the problems in which Leibniz became important for Schelling's *Abhandlungen* and what systematic significance Leibniz had for him there.
114. See KrV A808ff./B836ff. In later years (before 1797) Kant speaks no longer of the moral, but rather only of the intelligible world or of the world of the intellect (*Verstandeswelt*). This expression is to be found already in Hegel's excerpt from the review of Rehberg's *Über das Verhältnis der Metaphysik zu der Religion*. There the expression was already taken up from the KrV (see *Dokumente*, p. 163; cf. also note 45 above). In regard to the expression, however, see also Reinhold, *Versuch einer neuen Theorie des menschlichen Vorstellungsvermögen* (Prague and Jena: C. Widtman und I. M. Mauke, 1789), p. 576; Schelling, *Werke*, 1.252, 255 (in the *Neue Deduktion des Naturrechts*).

the absence of freedom. For the author of the "System-Programme," on the other hand, the true interpretation of the Kantian postulates forms the programmatic demand for the "absolute freedom of all spirits." On the basis of "absolute freedom," every spirit belonging to the intelligible world has God within itself and is immortal. This transformation of the significance of the doctrine of postulates is unthinkable without Schelling's project of the perfected freedom of the absolute I as the principle and the ultimate purpose for moral self-consciousness. But even in this passage of the "System-Programme" the idea of the absolute I or the Absolute remains in the background. Instead, the "absolute freedom of all spirits" is explicitly named as the basis for the novel understanding of the Kantian postulates; for this freedom alone can be the first idea of an ethics of self-conscious entities. The pluralism of free entities is thereby presupposed. Yet with this presupposition the author of the "System-Programme" continues to be much closer to Kant than does Schelling in *On the I* and in *Philosophical Letters*. He does not look for the allegedly still missing premises, namely, the supreme principles for Kant's results, but rather takes his start from the cornerstone of the system of pure reason and the *principium essendi* of the moral law: freedom. He, too, wants to go beyond Kant by positing absolute freedom. The absolute freedom, on the basis of which finite self-consciousness first grasps its moral task, justifies its understanding of itself, that it is intelligible and thereby divine and immortal. Here, there is naturally no longer an inference, as is the case with Kant, from consciousness of the moral law to freedom as a necessary presupposition. Rather, the evidence and reality of freedom are apparently themselves made into the foundation of moral consciousness and its practical self-certainty. Freedom is thereby absolute as the unconditioned principle of acting morally, but at the same time also as the perfection of existing morally, toward which finite self-consciousness is supposed to strive, that is to say, as the ultimate purpose. Thus, self-consciousness already understands its existence qualitatively as absolute freedom, that is, as the capability of acting in an absolutely spontaneous way. But it ought, through acting morally, to overcome the quantitative limitations not essential to it in order to attain the actual perfection of absolute freedom. In the "System-Programme" this absolute freedom is conceived intersubjectively. Such a conception of the ethical significance of metaphysical ideas on the basis of absolute freedom corresponds to Hegel's reflections, which he developed while appropriating and criticizing Schelling's early philosophy; in addition, it probably contains the resolution, not yet formulated by Hegel in Bern, of the transformation of the meaning of the Kantian postulate of God. How this project in the "System-Programme" can be brought into accord with the idea taken up by Hölderlin, the idea of beauty that "unites" all ideas in itself, is, to be sure, another question.

In the "System-Programme," following the ruminations about poetry and aesthetic sense, yet another problem is broached that is connected with Hegel's reception of the Kantian doctrine of postulates and rational religion: "Monotheism of reason and the heart, polytheism of the imagination and art, this is what we need!" The idea that, on the basis of absolute freedom, God can be sought only in ourselves, is not only a pure idea of reason, but also determines our "heart," that is to say, it determines feelings as motives for carrying out what is moral. By this means the notion of subjective religion is obviously furthered, a notion interpreted earlier by Hegel with the help of Kant's doctrine of postulates, the content of which was constitutive for grounding his project of ethics. Even in the "System-Programme" the problem of realizing what is moral in a community presents itself through religion. It is bound up with the "polytheism of the imagination," which Hegel in his Bern fragments described historically as the Greek religion of fantasy. This polytheism can be present once again in the modern era only in art, that is, aesthetically.

These reflections have, indeed, shown that, in view of the way that Kant's doctrine of postulates are taken up and their significance transformed, and in view of its outline of an ethics, the elaborations in the "System-Programme" may be inserted into the young Hegel's posing of problems (up to 1796–1797), which, to be sure, would not be possible without the discussion with Schelling. Nothing can be demonstrated that would be incongruent with or would contradict his thinking at that time; in the "System-Programme" one can even detect a solution, in part, of his earlier questions and a clarification of his Bern position. Insofar as no new facts become known and other themes in the "System-Programme" can in similar fashion also be successfully shown to fit into the history of Hegel's development—which one might well suppose—one must concede that the assumption with the greatest probability is the assumption that Hegel composed the "System-Programme."

With this conclusion it is possible also to gather from the "System-Programme," probably Hegel's last text containing this conception of ethics, that the early projects of the German idealists were concerned with taking up and transforming the Kantian postulates of practical reason and, in the process, determining anew the relation between ethics and metaphysics. They set up metaphysical ideas that were supposed to be valid only within an ethics, Schelling the idea of the absolute I as the sole substance or absolute, Hegel the idea of absolute freedom on the basis of which the intelligible world, God, and immortality were to be grasped. But the principle of the ethics of a finite self-consciousness was first able to be derived from the metaphysical ideas. The finite self-consciousness recognizes its own existence in the absolute I or the absolute freedom, and, at the same time, in the perfection of the latter, it recognizes the final aim of its action, that on this basis defines itself as moral. Ethics becomes thereby, in its foundation, metaphysics.

Both Schelling and Hegel soon take leave of this position again. But even later for Hegel, in contrast to Schelling, the critical engagement with Kant's doctrine of postulates remains of abiding importance.[115] In *Faith and Knowledge*, in any case, Hegel grants to the Kantian thought of the highest good the rank of an idea, an idea, to be sure, that is misunderstood and "poured into human form," but still at bottom a speculative idea.[116] The harmony of morality and happiness as finite determinations is, nevertheless, to be conceived actually as the identity of reason and nature. Such an alteration of the idea of the highest good, like Hegel's critique of practical faith and the doctrine of postulates in this passage, naturally already presupposes the principle of speculation as knowledge of the absolute. This critique of the Kantian doctrine of the highest good and of the postulates of practical reason is subsequently elaborated systematically in the *Phenomenology of Spirit*. In the case of the latter, to be sure, Kant's doctrine is transformed into the idealized form of consciousness labeled "moral worldview" with its dialectical "dissemblings," with the result that Hegel no longer critically engages Kant himself. According to Hegel, moral self-consciousness is aware of its absolute freedom; but since it contrasts with the morality of the actual world, it is capable of grasping the underlying unity of both only in thought, that is to say, it is capable only of postulating it. The critique of this incompleteness of moral self-consciousness is at the same time significant for Hegel's own conception of the absolute freedom of self-consciousness, in accordance with which the spirit as will grasps the world of actual things and of history as its own reality.[117] In conclusion, it may be mentioned that, even in the third edition of the *Encyclopedia*, Hegel is still critically engaging Kant's doctrine of postulates.[118] In this critique of

---

115. In Schelling's case it is possible to find only vague and fleeting plays on Kant's practical metaphysics later; see, e.g., Schelling, *Werke*, 6.17 and 10.88.

116. Hegel, *Gesammelte Werke*, ed. H. Buchner and O. Pöggeler (Hamburg: Meiner, 1968), 4.345.

117. See *Phänomenologie des Geistes*, ed. J. Hoffmeister (Hamburg: Meiner, 1952), pp. 424ff.; recently on this point, see M. Guéroult, "Les 'Déplacements' (*Verstellungen*) de la conscience morale kantienne selon Hegel," in *Hommage à Jean Hyppolite*, ed. Suzanne Bachelard (Paris: Presses universitaires de France, 1971), pp. 47–80.

118. *Enzyklopädie der philosophischen Wissenschaften im Grundrisse*, 3d ed. (Heidelberg: Osswald [C. F. Winter], 1830), § § 59f. and § 552n.

Kant's practically grounded metaphysics, a critique retained by Hegel in his later works, one must, indeed, at the same time see a self-criticism on Hegel's part, aimed at his own earlier projects that still took Kant as their point of departure and, that means, aimed at the first form of idealistic metaphysics, represented by him along with others, as ethics.

PART VI

LIBERATING THE ABSOLUTE FROM TRANSCENDENTAL PHILOSOPHY: ESSAYS ON SCHELLING

10 The Unconditioned in Knowing: I—Identity—Freedom

HANS MICHAEL BAUMGARTNER
Translated by Richard Polt

I

In 1794 Schelling enters into the philosophical discussion of his age with the essay "On the Possibility of a Form of Philosophy in General." Here he explicitly refers to Kant's *Critique of Pure Reason*, "in which, from the beginning, nothing seemed more obscure and difficult to him [Schelling] than the attempt to ground a form of all philosophy without somewhere laying down a principle which would ground not only the primordial form underlying all the individual forms, but also the necessary connection of this primordial form with the individual forms that depend on it."[1] Schelling is thus faced not only with the problem of the unity of philosophy as a supreme science, but also with the question of determining the supreme unifying principle of philosophy, a principle that—in accordance with its function—must unite in itself both the form and the content of all philosophy, and must serve as the material, no less than the formal, principle of all knowing. The foils for Schelling's reflections are—as, incidentally, they are for Fichte as well—the skepticism of Aenesidemus (Schulze), Reinhold's *Elementarphilosophie*, Salomon Maimon's *New Theory of Thinking*, and—in the further development of these reflections—Leibniz's conception of the principles of noncontradiction and sufficient reason. To be sure, in the foreground of the theme of "finally providing a solution to the *whole* problem *of the possibility of philosophy in general*" (*SW*, 1.88) there stood Kant's distinction between

---

This essay [The Unconditioned in Knowing: I—Identity—Freedom] originally appeared as "Das Unbedingte im Wissen: Ich—Identität—Freiheit" in *Schelling: Einführung in seine Philosophie*, ed. Hans Michael Baumgartner (Freiburg and Munich: Verlag Karl Alber, 1975).
    1. Friedrich Wilhelm Joseph von Schelling, *Sämmtliche Werke*, 13 vols., ed. Karl Friedrich August Schelling (Stuttgart and Augsburg: J. G. Cotta, 1856–1861), 1.87; henceforth cited as *SW*.

analytic and synthetic judgments, as well as his doctrine of the categories, to which Schelling attempted to give a unitary foundation with his proposal for a deduction.[2] However, Schelling's immediate point of departure and his intellectual as well as stylistic medium was Fichte's "On the Concept of the *Wissenschaftslehre,* or So-Called Philosophy" (1794), which had appeared shortly before Schelling's essay. Relying closely on Fichte, Schelling conceives of *philosophia prima* as the "theory (science) of all science," as "primordial science, or science κατ' ἐξοχήν" (*SW,* 1.92). Having taken over from Fichte the three principles of all knowing, Schelling develops not only the "primordial form of all science," which he formulates as "form of *unconditionedness* [First Principle], of *conditionedness* [Second Principle], and of *conditionedness determined by unconditionedness* [Third Principle]," but also the originally given content of all knowing, which—on the basis of the reciprocal relation between form and content—can be determined in accordance with the three principles as the I, the Not-I, and the product of both.[3]

2

Schelling's essay "On the Possibility of a Form of Philosophy" had attempted to found philosophy as the highest science on the concept of the I. For Schelling, this foundation seemed to open up "the prospect of finally attaining a unity of knowing, believing and willing—the ultimate heritage of humanity" (*SW,* 1.112); it seemed thereby to open up the possibility of "healing the woes of humanity" by means of philosophy, and of influencing "the destinies of our entire race" (*SW,* 1.112). The goal of his intended critique of previous philosophy thus transcended philosophical reflection for its own sake; this goal took its horizon and guideline from the early concept of history as a process of reason.[4] Now, with the principles that founded unity—the primordial form, unconditionedness, and the primordial content, the I—Schelling had laid out the general formal framework of a historically relevant philosophy. What was required next, then, was to explicate more accurately and make transparent the I as the principle of philosophy, that is, as the supreme, unconditioned condition of knowing in general. This was precisely the task that Schelling attempted to accomplish in the essay "On the I as the Principle of Philosophy; or, On the Unconditioned in Human Know-

---

2. Cf. *SW,* 1.103–10.   3. Cf. *SW,* 1.110.
4. Cf. Wilhelm G. Jacobs, "Geschichte als Prozeß der Vernunft," in *Schelling: Einführung in seine Philosophie,* ed. Hans Michael Baumgartner (Freiburg and Munich: Verlag Karl Alber, 1975).

ing," which appeared in 1795. Thus, the aim of this essay is to conceive of the unity of philosophy on the basis of the single principle, the ultimate ground of the unity and reality of all knowing, in a way that exhibits not only the sole possible philosophy, but also the true essence of the human being. Hence, the completion of critical philosophy appears to be bound up in a special way with the completion of true knowledge about the human being and with the completion of the historical process of humanity.

Schelling's reflections, which are essentially concerned with the relation between dogmatism and criticism, and thus with Spinoza, Kant, and Fichte, follow a line of argument that is to be sketched here only in its principal stages. Since knowing without reality is not knowing at all, there must be an "ultimate point of reality" (*SW*, 1.162), an "ultimate ground of the reality of all knowing" (*SW*, 1.163), which can be understood only as "the absolute" (*SW*, 1.163). This absolute can be given only through itself; it must be thought of as "something that is thinkable only through itself, i.e., through its being; something that is thought only insofar as it is; in short, *something in which the principle of being coincides with that of thinking*" (*SW*, 1.163). Insofar as this absolute is what conditions everything conditioned, and itself does not belong to the sphere of the conditioned, it itself is "not only unconditioned, but simply *incapable of being conditioned*" (*SW*, 1.164). Now, this unconditioned cannot be specified without an internal contradiction either as an absolute object or, in the sphere of empirical self-consciousness, as a conditioned object or a conditioned subject—that is, it cannot be specified at all in the sphere of objects and *things*. Hence, it can lie only in the "absolute I" (*SW*, 1.167), the reality of which cannot be "proved," but can be shown only in a "regress" (*SW*, 1.169) from the conditioned. But if the unconditioned in human knowing is to be conceived exclusively as the "absolute I," then one cannot maintain as a philosophical theory of the unconditioned either the complete dogmatism of Spinoza or the incomplete criticism of Kant and Reinhold—which is at the same time an incomplete dogmatism. Instead, what is required is a complete criticism, which begins neither with appearances nor with the thing-in-itself, but "with the absolute I, which excludes all that is opposed to it" (*SW*, 1.176). With this, Schelling has attained the point of departure and the fundamental specification that enable him to develop the further, already implicitly posited specifications of the I: pure identity (sameness with itself) as the primordial form of the I (§ 7), absolute freedom as the essence of the I in its self-positing (the form of its being-posited), and intellectual intuition as the sole possible form of its givenness (§ 8). In addition, Schelling "deduces," following the guidelines of the Kantian table of categories, the "subordinate forms of the I" (§§ 9–15) as well as "the forms of all that can be posited, which are grounded by the I" (§ 16).

In summary, we can assert that, relying on Fichte and looking back critically to both Spinoza and Kant, Schelling specifies the unconditioned in knowing as the absolute I, which he understands, beyond the self-consciousness that divides itself into I and Not-I, as pure undifferentiated identity and absolute freedom, so that the absolute I can be *given* only to a nonsensory, intellectual intuition. Thus, the being and essence of the human being, who according to his facticity is a finite self-consciousness, are determined by the absolute I: the human being's existence is the infinite and at the same time paradoxical task of eliminating the boundaries of finitude, that is, realizing pure identity and absolute freedom both theoretically and practically.[5]

3

A number of factors might lead us to assess Schelling's first explicitly philosophical writings as contributions to transcendental philosophy—to its problems and its self-comprehension: Schelling's philosophical intention, his relation to Kantian philosophy, his attempt to establish a deeper foundation for the results of critical philosophy, and his adoption of individual theorems from Fichte's *Wissenschaftslehre*. This impression becomes stronger when one considers—with regards to their con-

---

5. As regards this entire section, cf. Schelling's letter to Hegel of February 4, 1795, in particular the following passage:

> In the meantime, I have become a Spinozist!—Don't be amazed; you are about to hear in what way. For Spinoza, the world (the object pure and simple, as opposed to the subject) was *all;* for me, it is the *I.* It seems to me that the real difference between critical and dogmatic philosophy lies in the fact that the critical philosophy begins with the absolute I (the I which is as yet unconditioned by any object), and dogmatic philosophy begins with the absolute object, or the not-I. The ultimate consequence of the latter is Spinoza's system; of the former, the Kantian system. Philosophy must begin with the *unconditioned.* Now, the only question is where this unconditioned lies: in the I or in the not-I. When this question is decided, *everything* is decided.—For me, the supreme principle of all philosophy is the pure, absolute I, that is, the I insofar as it is a simple I, not yet conditioned by any objects at all, but rather posited through *freedom.* The alpha and omega of all philosophy is freedom.—The absolute I comprises an infinite sphere of absolute being; within this sphere, *finite* spheres take shape, which arise through the *restriction* of the absolute sphere by an object (spheres of *existence*—theoretical philosophy). In these there is nothing but conditionedness, and the unconditioned leads to contradictions.—But we *ought* to break through these boundaries; that is, we ought to emerge from the finite sphere and enter the infinite (*practical* philosophy). Thus, practical philosophy *demands* that finitude be destroyed, and thereby leads us into the supersensible world. (*Briefe von und an Hegel,* 3d ed., 4 vols., ed. J. Hoffmeister [Hamburg, 1969], 1.22.)

tent, their form of argumentation, and Schelling's self-understanding—not only the publications we have summarized, but also those that were to follow, for example, the "Essays Expounding the Idealism of the *Wissenschaftslehre*" (1796–1797) and the "System of Transcendental Idealism" (1800). All the same, we would do justice neither to Schelling, nor to the Kantian idea of transcendental philosophy, nor to Fichte's *Wissenschaftslehre*, if we were to sum up Schelling's early philosophical endeavors without further ado under the title "transcendental philosophy." In any case, important facts militate against such a move. A case in point is (1) the "Philosophical Letters on Dogmatism and Criticism" (1795), which appeared almost at the same time as the essay "On the I." Here both the Kantian critique of reason and the Fichtean *Wissenschaftslehre* are granted no greater significance than that of being general methodologies for philosophical systems; correspondingly, dogmatism and criticism are seen as philosophical systems that, from the perspective of theoretical philosophy, are equally justified and equally possible.[6] This point of view contradicts in principle Kant's self-understanding as well as that of Fichte. (2) Then there is Fichte's confrontation with Schelling, which concerns precisely the "Philosophical Letters"; the theorems of the "Letters" rightly permit Fichte to suppose that Schelling has misunderstood both Kant and his own *Wissenschaftslehre*.[7] (3) There is also the fact that in the course of his criticism of Tübingen orthodoxy and its attempt to found the theology of revelation on practical postulates, Schelling parenthetically rejects the Kantian doctrine of postulates as well.[8] (4) Finally and decisively, substantive points of view in the writings that one would want to assign to transcendental philosophy are in fact incompatible with the transcendental point of departure. There are, above all, three such incompatibilities. First, there is the ambiguous specification of methodological procedure in the search for the highest principle: in "On the I" this is conceived as a regressive procedure (*SW*, 1.169), while in the essay "On Possibility" the regress is rejected as unsuitable (*SW*, 1.96). Second, there is the conception of the unconditioned as strictly

---

6. Cf. *SW*, 1.225ff; cf. also Hermann Braun, "Philosophie für freie Geister, zu Hegels Manuskript: . . . eine Ethik," in *Das älteste Systemprogramm: Studien zur Frühgeschichte des deutschen Idealismus*, Hegel-Studien no. 9, ed. Rüdiger Bubner (Bonn: Bouvier Verlag Herbert Grundmann, 1973), pp. 17–33, esp. pp. 27ff.

7. Cf. particularly Reinhard Lauth, "Die erste philosophische Auseinandersetzung zwischen Fichte und Schelling 1795–1797," *Zeitschrift für philosophische Forschung* 21 (1967): 357, 366; and also, more recently, Ingtraud Görland, *Die Entwicklung der Frühphilosophie Schellings in der Auseinandersetzung mit Fichte* (Frankfurt: Vittorio Klostermann, 1973).

8. Cf. esp. Klaus Düsing, "Die Rezeption der Kantischen Postulatenlehre in den frühen philosophischen Entwürfen Schellings und Hegels," in *Das älteste Systemprogramm*, ed. Bubner, pp. 53–90, esp. pp. 60ff. An English translation of this article by Düsing is included in the present volume.

opposed to the sphere of self-consciousness, a conception that, on the one hand, makes it impossible to interpret the unconditioned in accordance with the categories—as Schelling nevertheless attempts to do in "On the I"—and, on the other hand, makes it no longer feasible to grasp the genesis of self-consciousness and to attribute to the supreme principle the function of a foundation for a deduction. Third, there is the reversal of the relationship between the "natural law of finitude" and the "moral law" (*SW*, 1.199), which contradicts both Kant and Fichte: this reversal conceives of moral law not as the ground of knowing the absolute, but rather as a moment derived from the now inexplicable fact of the empirical, conditioned I.[9]

It is thus correct to say that "Schelling's own philosophical origin ... essentially [differs] from that of Fichte, and this difference in the starting points of both thinkers ... already [plays] itself out in Schelling's early period."[10] "The young Schelling does not begin with a ... philosophy that reflects critically on the possibility of knowing [for finite consciousness] ... ; he presses toward an ultimate unity which, as the whole, contains everything."[11] "Schelling's original philosophical tendency is to elevate the idea of the unconditioned to the rank of the fundamental determination of all philosophy."[12] If we do not simply interpret this difference negatively and say that Schelling remained behind Fichte, then it seems appropriate to give up the lapidary title "transcendental philosophy" as a characterization of Schelling's philosophy from 1794 to 1797 or 1800. Rather, we should conceive of this first period of his publications as the opening phase of a philosophical reflection that employs transcendental concepts, arguments, and forms of reflection in order to do justice to the conception of the absolute in the theoretical-philosophical realm, be this conception that of Spinoza or that of classical metaphysics; meanwhile, from a practical and historical perspective, Schelling aims to produce precisely that philosophy that promotes universal history as a progression of reason toward itself—that philosophy that, as a philosophical science that has been completed and unified,

---

9. Cf. also *SW,* 1.232. Adolf Schurr has recently presented this point of view in a thorough interpretation of "Schelling's Early Writings in Transcendental Philosophy"; see his *Philosophie als System bei Fichte, Schelling und Hegel* (Stuttgart-Bad Cannstatt: Frommann-Holzboog, 1974), pp. 93–134, esp. pp. 97, 98ff.

10. Walter Schulz, introduction to *System des transzendentalen Idealismus*, by F.W.J. Schelling, 2d ed., ed. Ruth-Eva Schulz, Philosophische Bibliothek no. 254 (Hamburg: Felix Meiner, 1962), p. x; cf. also Görland, *Die Entwicklung der Frühphilosophie Schellings*, p. 1.

11. Schulz, introduction to *System des transzendentalen Idealismus*, p. xi.

12. Walter Schulz, introduction to *Fichte-Schelling Briefwechsel* (Frankfurt: Suhrkamp, 1968), p. 28. Cf. also Manfred Schröter, "Der Ausgangspunkt der Metaphysik Schellings," in *Kritische Studien: Über Schelling und zur Kulturphilosophie* (Munich: R. Oldenbourg, 1971), pp. 11–51, esp. pp. 17, 25, 27, 35, 49ff.

and has recognized the total connection of the actual within the absolute, can make the transition to action.[13] Thus, neither in its beginning nor at some later point is Schelling's thought simply transcendental philosophy—and this insight leads us not only to a different understanding of his philosophical development, but also to a different standard for judging his confrontation with Fichte. Rather, his thought begins with a philosophical theory of history and, in accordance with this theory, uses concepts and argumentative strategies that stem primarily from Fichtean transcendental philosophy. With this set of tools, he undertakes to base the historically required unity of all sciences on philosophy as the supreme science, by means of the concept of the absolute I and its corollaries: pure identity and absolute freedom. But at the same time, he undertakes to conceive of freedom as the supreme principle of reality, and thus to grasp the completion of knowing as a paradigm or guarantor of a self-completing human history. The following passage from the Preface to the essay "On the I," a passage that has not always received the attention due to it, may confirm this connection:

> It is hard to resist enthusiasm when one thinks the great thought that, just as all the sciences, the empirical sciences included, are forever pursuing the point of complete unity, in the end humanity itself will also realize the principle of unity as a constitutive law—a principle which, as regulative, lies at the basis of human history from its beginning. [This very thought has already exceeded the theoretical possibilities of a transcendental philosophy!] Just as all the rays of human knowing and the experiences of many centuries will eventually gather into one focal point of truth, and thus make actual the idea which has already dawned on a number of great minds, the idea that in the end, all the different sciences must become a single science—just so, all the different ways and byways that the human race has followed until now will finally run together towards a single point where humanity will once again be gathered, and will, as one perfected person, obey the same law of freedom. As distant as this point in time may be, as long as it may still be possible to burst out in haughty laughter at the audacious hopes for the progress of humanity, those who do not view these hopes as foolishness are still charged with the great task of preparing, at least, for that great period of humanity by means of communal work on the *completion* of the sciences. For all ideas must first have been realized in the domain of knowing before they are realized in history; and humanity will never become *one* until its knowing has attained unity. (*SW*, 1.158ff.)

4

The structure of Schelling's early philosophy that we have sketched can be verified in various ways. This structure is manifested in Schelling's understanding of his guiding fundamental concepts (the absolute, the

13. Cf. Jacobs, "Geschichte als Prozeß der Vernunft."

I, identity, freedom, intellectual intuition), each of which grasps an epistemic ground which, as infinite and incapable of being conditioned, absolutely transcends finite knowing and self-consciousness—the sphere of finitude. The structure we have presented also comes to the fore in the central problematic that motivates Schelling's various new beginnings; only the conception of the absolute that we have delineated can make intelligible how the absolute as such can be grasped by finite consciousness, and how it is possible to think of a transition from the absolute to self-consciousness, from the infinite to the finite, from theoretical to practical philosophy, without having the unconditioned, which is elevated above all difference and every opposition, lose its character of absoluteness.[14] Finally, the same structure is particularly in evidence in the argumentative strategy of the "Philosophical Letters," in which the theoretical inexplicability of the transition from the infinite to the finite becomes the basis of a practical striving of the finite toward the infinite, so that the required mediation between the absolute and the conditioned can be regarded only as the infinite praxis of a progressive self-surpassing of the finite human being toward the unity and freedom of the absolute. It is precisely in this concept that the teleological function of the absolute I becomes manifest, a function that binds philosophy and the historical process to each other: the absolute is the foundation and goal of theory—theory that completes and perfects itself in practice—but is thereby also the principle and completion of history itself.

5

The interpretive hypothesis we have indicated and sketched holds that Schelling's so-called transcendental philosophy[15] presents itself with its first public appearance, in the essay "On the Possibility of a Form of Philosophy in General," as a philosophy of the absolute that employs transcendental concepts and arguments. This interpretation includes the thesis that the writings of 1801 to 1806, which outline the so-called system of identity, as well as the steps toward a nature philosophy and "speculative physics" beginning in 1797, by no means signify a deviation from Schelling's original intentions; rather, they indicate how these intentions are progressively made more precise and realized. Thus, inso-

---

14. Cf. esp. Schulz, introduction to *System des transzendentalen Idealismus*, p. xii.
15. On Schelling's early philosophy as a whole, see esp. Christoph Wild, *Reflexion und Erfahrung: Eine Interpretation der Früh- und Spätphilosophie Schellings* (Freiburg and Munich: Verlag Karl Alber, 1968), and Harald Holz, "Die Struktur der Dialektik in den Frühschriften von Fichte und Schelling," *Archiv für die Geschichte der Philosophie* 52 (1970): 71–90. However, both Wild and Holz maintain—albeit with modifications—the characterization of the early philosophy as a transcendental philosophy.

far as Schelling maintains the specification of the absolute as identity, or indifference of the finite relation of subject and object, it seems to be the consistency of his intellectual development that is responsible for the fact that his reflections lead to a doctrine of the appearance of the absolute, with regard to both the objective content for a self-consciousness (nature) and an already constituted subjectivity (history, spirit). In that doctrine, the particular previous stages of the absolute are to be understood as various structural articulations of the relation between subjectivity and objectivity.[16] No break takes place between Schelling's transcendental philosophy and his philosophy of nature or identity philosophy, because, from the beginning, Schelling's philosophy was never transcendental philosophy in the strict sense. To be sure, there is still the question of whether the philosophical conception of a history of reason that precedes Schelling's philosophy of the unconditioned is not already due to the intentions that are conceptualized in the system of the identity philosophy, even though the latter no longer seems to be concerned with the initial projection of a philosophy of history. However, the fact that in his confrontation with Fichte, Schelling abruptly conceives of a "history of self-consciousness," a development of nature into intelligence, in contrast to Fichte's "pragmatic history [of the actions] of the human spirit,"[17] appears to indicate a connection between system and history that was already at work in Schelling's beginnings. Although up to now this connection has not been investigated more closely, it already leaves its mark, as we have shown, on the "Philosophical Letters" and on the Preface to the essay "On the I"; it is expressed in the peculiar parallelism between world history and the development of the sciences, as well as in the principle of unity or freedom that lies at the basis of both domains.

But as concerns the characterization of Schelling's early philosophy as transcendental philosophy, we must contradict not only some of his interpreters, but even the young Schelling himself. It is a peculiarly sig-

16. Cf. Holz, "Die Struktur der Dialektik," p. 82.
17. However, cf. on this point U. Claesges, *Geschichte des Selbstbewußtseins: Der Ursprung des spekulativen Problems in Fichtes Wissenschaftslehre von 1794–1795* (The Hague, 1974). Claesges interprets Fichte's first *Wissenschaftslehre*, particularly in regards to its two series of reflections, as a history of self-consciousness, and hence identifies Schelling's idea in the "Essays Expounding the *Wissenschaftslehre*" (1796–1797) with Fichte's "pragmatic history of the human spirit." The discussion provoked by this recently published book will no doubt be fruitful and interesting; it will have to clarify, first, whether concepts used in the context of a transcendental reconstruction—"result," "genesis," "action," "series of what is presented," etc.—may in any way be interpreted in terms of the process or study of history. Secondly, the discussion will have to clarify whether, in regards to Kant and Fichte, there is not a theoretical self-contradiction involved in taking the "history of self-consciousness" as "a particular form of transcendental philosophy" (p. 4).

nificant fact that while in the "System of Transcendental Idealism" (1800) he ranks transcendental philosophy side by side with nature philosophy, already in 1801–1802 and then again in 1806, in the "Exposition of the True Relation of Nature Philosophy to the Improved Doctrine of Fichte," he goes so far as to negate and reject transcendental philosophy as a philosophy of reflection, that is, as a philosophy of finite human consciousness and the facts about this consciousness. However, depending on one's preferred perspective, this fact appears as an indication that Schelling either had correctly appraised his relation to Kant and Fichte or had succumbed to a fundamental self-deception regarding the essence of transcendental theory and his early philosophical intention, which he had identified with transcendental philosophy. Both points of view confirm the interpretation we have presented, for it establishes the structure of a body of thought even in opposition to the author himself. However a philosophical author may, at a particular stage of his development, evaluate the earlier philosophical works that came from his pen by arranging and organizing them, however he may correspondingly understand the history of his development, in each instance a latter-day interpreter must take these self-interpretations into account; but whether the interpreter can follow him in this self-assessment is a question that must be decided by other criteria.

11 The Problem of Metaphysics
XAVIER TILLIETTE
Translated by Christopher Doss

For decades, especially during his own lifetime, Schelling was thought of as a pliable reed, ready to shift with the slightest wind. Today, however, his consistency and stability are usually affirmed.[1] Both assessments are exaggerated. There is perhaps no better demonstration of this than Schelling's attitude toward metaphysics, a subject with which he was constantly, albeit sporadically, preoccupied—even if this sounds somewhat paradoxical. Taking this paradoxical claim, we can obtain a "cross section" of his development, to use the terminology of Eduard von Hartmann.[2]

In his short dissertation, written under the inspiration of Dilthey, Manfred Schröter[3] has already shown that the metaphysical impulse is secretly at work even in the arid theorems of Schelling's first short piece, *On the Possibility of Philosophy in General* (1794). In the formal structure of the exposition, he hears, or believes that he hears, the timbre of the golden voice of the Absolute. This impression is, in any case, corroborated by Schelling's next, much more general book, *On the I as Principle*

This essay ["The Problem of Metaphysics"] appeared as "Schelling und das Problem der Metaphysik," in *Perspectiven der Philosophie: Neues Jahrbuch* 2 (1976): 123–43; it is reprinted as "Le Problème de la Métaphysique" in *L'Absolu et la Philosophie: Essais sur Schelling*, by Xavier Tilliette (Paris: Presses Universitaires de France, 1987), pp.143–61. The editors wish to thank Nicolas de Warren for help in final revisions to this translation.

1. Cf. Walter Schulz, *Die Vollendung des deutschen Idealismus in der Spätphilosophie Schellings* (Stuttgart: W. Kohlhammer, 1955), e.g., p. 135; Harald Holz, *Spekulation und Faktizität. Zum Freiheitsbegriff des mittleren und späten Schelling* (Bonn: Bouvier, 1970); Klaus Hemmerle, *Gott und das Denken nach Schellings Spätphilosophie* (Freiburg: Herder, 1968). Heidegger's course in the spring of 1936, in a complete reversal of the then-prevailing fashion, already emphasized the consistency of Schelling's thought (see Martin Heidegger, *Schellings Abhandlung über das Wesen der menschlichen Freiheit 1809*, ed. Hildegard Feick [Tübingen: Max Niemeyer, 1971]).

2. E. von Hartmann, *Schellings philosophisches System* (Leipzig: Hermann Hacke, 1897), p. v.

3. Manfred Schröter, *Der Ausgangspunkt der Metaphysik Schellings entwickelt aus seiner ersten philosophischen Abhandlung, Über die Möglichkeit einer Form der Philosophie Überhaupt* (Ph.D. diss., University of Jena, 1908).

of Philosophy. A genuinely metaphysical spirit surges forth from these enthusiastic, disordered paragraphs; after all, what is at stake is nothing less than metaphysics conceived as the recovery of freedom, and this in such a way that the question of metaphysics also functions as that of hermeneutics. In the following discussion, an attempt will be made to treat Schelling's initial works, up to the overt rupture of the *Exposition of My System* (1801), as a unity, in this way showing Schelling's consistency and integrity. The young Schelling was more prudent than his reputation suggests, never allowing himself to be dragged into the snare of impressions and opinions. This is not meant to suggest that he is always clear on what he was about; to the contrary, it is a time of questioning and orientation. It is particularly difficult to get a handle on his place in the middle of the Spinoza -(Jacobi)-Kant-Fichte triangle, because his relationship with Fichte oscillates between rapprochement and repudiation, and a clandestine—or perhaps an overt?—misunderstanding proceeded to insinuate itself between the two. It is precisely because of the opaque character of his relation to Fichte[4] that Schelling's intention remains virtually inscrutable. This is why the critics generally choose to cut the Gordian knot instead of untying it. Nevertheless, the fact remains that Schelling always wanted to preserve his autonomy. From this it follows that his constant discussion and grappling with Fichte scarcely influenced his attitude toward metaphysics.

In any case, it still seems odd that Kant's immediate successors, his admirers and imitators, that is, Fichte and Schelling, overlooked the result of the threefold *Critique* so easily: the challenge posed by critical philosophy was simply shunted aside. It is customary to consider Kant's work as a profound break in the history of philosophy, and with reason, if we ignore the great post-Kantians. However, the book *After Kant*[5] demonstrates that, despite the critical philosophy's example, the demand for metaphysics, under the name of science, flourished anew immediately. The honor of preserving the supreme *telos* must be accorded to Jacobi, the discoverer of the forgotten Saint Spinoza. But the future of metaphysics is mainly to be credited to Kant himself, in whom this renaissance had its origin. The title bequeathed to him by Max Wundt, "Kant the Metaphysician," has never been usurped. The "Moses of Our Na-

---

4. Noted by Fritz Medicus, Xavier Léon, and Martial Gueroult. See Xavier Léon, *Fichte et son temps*, 2 vols. (Paris: A. Colin, 1922–27), and Martial Guéroult, *Études sur Fichte* (Hildesheim: Olms, 1974). Cf. the detailed and considered judgment of Reinhard Lauth, in *Die Entstehung von Schellings Identitätsphilosophie in der Auseinandersetzung mit Fichtes Wissenschaftslehre* (Freiburg and Munich: Alber, 1975).

5. Valerio Verra, *Dopo Kant. Il criticismo nell'età preromantica* (Turin: Edizioni di Filosofia, 1975).

tion," as Hölderlin called him,[6] had sighted the promised land of metaphysics.

Nevertheless, the task of a critical philosophy properly understood was not forsaken. The vacuous nature of the preceding metaphysics (the ontology of Christian Wolff) had been laid bare.[7] But this destruction prepared a foundation. "Kant has swept everything away," declared Schelling in a letter to Hegel, so that a much more beautiful edifice could be built (the metaphor of the edifice characterizes Fichte's project).[8] According to Fichte, Kant had possessed the marvelous system of the human spirit, but was prevented by age or by fear from realizing the full extent of his discovery—a task reserved for Fichte himself.[9] Accordingly, the epigones who reduce Kantianism to a system of morality err and are disloyal to the master. This is the source of the merciless polemic that Schelling conducts against them in the famous *Letters on Dogmatism and Criticism*. It is, of course, true that Schelling also places an emphasis on morality, but "ethics in the style of Spinoza" is a system of freedom and (unlimited) action. The key to understanding both the developing thought of the young Schelling and his ambiguous relation to Fichte and Spinoza is to realize that *he considers freedom to be the content of metaphysics*. All in all, Schelling is still a disciple of Kant. This doesn't, however, controvert what we said earlier. If Schelling did, in fact, conduct his intellectual development in full public view, as Hegel and Steffens assert, it is also clear that the character of this development cannot be reduced to a simple, gradual progress (Metzger), or a mere set of preparatory "finger" exercises (Fuhrmans).

An unaccountable ambiguity remains. However, it concerns the choice of a philosophy and not the "metaphysical" tendency inherent in philosophical thought. When it came to the subject of freedom, Schelling took the example set up by critical philosophy very seriously. It animates the (sometimes confused) pages of *Vom Ich*. Metaphysics is reclaimed as freedom, the inalienable possession of man. The password is: I, absolute I; and freedom—the conception of freedom—serves as standard and measure. We need to become accustomed to Schelling's ambivalent assessment of metaphysics: metaphysics is, on the one hand,

6. To his brother, January 1, 1799, in *Hölderlin. Werke und Briefe*, 2 vols., ed. Friedrich Beissner and Jochen Schmidt (Frankfurt am Main: Insel-Verlag, 1968), 2.889.

7. *Aus Schellings Leben: In Briefen*, 3 vols., ed. G. L. Plitt (Leipzig: S. Hirzel, 1869), 1.73 (January 6, 1795).

8. J. G. Fichte, *Über den Begriff der Wissenschaftslehre oder der sogenannten Philosophie*, 1794, in *Werke*, 7 vols., ed. Fritz Medicus (Leipzig: Felix Meiner, 1919) 1.182; in *Sämmtliche Werke*, 8 vols., ed. I. H. Fichte (Berlin: Veit, 1845) 1.53.

9. Ibid., 1.158–59 (1.30–31).

the object of an historical investigation and, on the other, the soul and animating force of the philosophy sought. This, in fact, is part of the philosopher's habitual way of thinking. What then exactly is the problem of metaphysics? The legacy of Kant provides the decisive perspective, although Spinoza and Fichte are placed in the foreground, in a sort of tension. The phenomenon, the feeling of finitude, and the world of objects all determine the human situation, and the absolute I is the negation of the finite I; freedom is *transcendental* in its essence.[10] Access to the absolute is prohibited. The clarion call of the absolute I trumpets its victorious charge in vain, as it is impossible to disguise the fact that the I, encumbered by objects as it is, is not absolute. Mankind would not even know how to deceive itself about its Fate. The Kantian doctrine thus remains intact. But the famous question "How are synthetic a priori judgments possible?" immediately becomes transformed into a metaphysical question: "How can the absolute I oppose a not-I to itself (*Vom Ich*);[11] how can the Absolute move beyond itself and posit a world (*Letters*)?"[12] Answers are not immediately forthcoming, but are always referred to the original Fichtean doctrine of finite striving.

This only precludes the possibility that the Absolute might reveal itself, so to speak, with the help of intellectual intuition, as the unconditioned, as I. Schelling advances beyond the comments of Fichte, who had mentioned intellectual intuition three times in the critical review of *Aenesidemus*.[13] This is what makes possible the immediate discovery of the I in its freedom and identity. Neither Fichte nor Schelling, in this case, believe that they are betraying Kant. Nor does Kant give a univocal meaning to intellectual intuition.[14] In any case, it is undeniable that Schelling combines the absolute I with dangerously mystical expressions. He associates or conflates lived freedom and the intellectual world: here all is pure, all is absolute, all is intellectual. . . .[15] The Platonic and Jacobian line runs parallel to the pure motion and incomprehensible agility of Fichte. Similarly, Spinoza's knowledge of the third type exercises an undiminished seductive power. We might, however, be inclined to de-emphasize the contemplative moment and give the victory to active freedom and the energy of the I. The absolute I effects the *infinite* and continual expansion of the barriers of the finite.[16] The "system of activity" subsumes the "system of knowledge." In a word, the description of the

---

10. F.W.J. Schelling, *Schellings Werke*, 6 vols., ed. Manfred Schröter (Munich: C. H. Beck, 1958), 1.235–36.
11. Ibid., 1.175.   12. Ibid., 1.296.
13. *Fichtes Werke*, 1.50 (1.22), 1.44 (1.16).
14. Ibid., 3.55–63 (1.471–79), and cf. 3.48 (1.464); *Schellings Werke*, 1.181–82.
15. *Schellings Werke*, 1.215.   16. Ibid., 1.238–39.

world of intellectual, Platonic luminescence represents a metaphysics of the "as if."

It goes without saying that Schelling would have desired more clarity for his fairly rhapsodic endeavor. He complains bitterly of his readers' lack of comprehension,[17] but this is partly his own fault. This is the reason why he returns to the question of metaphysics in the *Letters on Dogmatism and Criticism,* where his relation to the Spinoza-Kant-Fichte trilogy becomes clear. These letters contain the germ of his future development. As we said earlier in this paper, *Vom Ich* vacillates between the egological character (égoité) of the unconditioned and the unconditionality of the I, between intellectual intuition considered as vision and intellectual intuition considered as the self-proclamation of freedom, between Fichte in the wake of Spinoza and Spinoza in the light of Fichte.[18] The question of philosophy is understood in a radical sense. The abandonment of the Absolute, the departure from the Absolute, is the origin of all philosophizing, whether dogmatic or critical (i.e., taking the I as its point of origin). The need for philosophy, therefore, coincides with the loss of the Absolute and the acquisition of self-consciousness; the Absolute and the I have become opposed. As a result, philosophy is entirely practical in nature, born of a choice, and the case in practice is identical to the principles of the system.[19] A philosophy must be chosen not out of obligation, but freely. Why should one opt for critical philosophy? The seductive power of Spinoza has hardly abated—Spinoza having lived and breathed in his system—but the danger of contemplative intellectual intuition, namely, the risk of the annihilation of the I, is recognized and transcended. Of course, critical philosophy itself runs the risk of losing the I in its dream of a perfect reunification and an unattainable goal; but, in assigning limits to itself, it bars itself from outstripping its domain and maintains an infinite practical striving.[20] In this way the spirits of Kant and Fichte are invoked, with their unaltered works, the *Critique* and the *Science of Knowledge,* serving as a general theoretical foundation for philosophy—an interpretation laden with consequences leading one day to the break with Fichte.

It is clear that critical philosophy may perhaps result only in giving a victory to Pyrrhus, since it must continually assert itself against the appearance of dogmatism. Its freedom becomes exhausted in the activity of self-affirmation. The system of knowledge is more tentative, but in the

---

17. Plitt, 1.79 (to Hegel, July 21, 1795).
18. Criticism is "inverted" (*Fichtes Werke,* 1.294–95, 1.100–101) or "subjective" (Schiller to Goethe, October 28, 1794) Spinozism.
19. *Schellings Werke,* 1.299.   20. Ibid., 1.335.

end, as Hölderlin had foreseen,[21] the systems of action and knowledge coincide. The remainder left over by dogmatism and criticism can only be effaced with a genuine aspiration for reunification, but for the moment Fichtean unilaterality has the high ground and the system of action supersedes the theoretical (i.e., dogmatic) premise. It is considered to be an ethical creation through and through. Seen from this point of view, the passionate polemic against the faux morality of the "Kantians" at the beginning of the work appears justified. The pusillanimous Kantians who, like prestidigitators, cause a "moral God"[22] to emerge, for example, from critical philosophy are only resurrecting the old metaphysics in a new guise; their God, the guardian of a prefabricated morality, is no less an artifact and a scarecrow than that of the previous metaphysics.

Schelling's declarations in the brilliant *Letters* take us this far. In view of the development to come, we could easily turn to the *Earliest System-Programme of German Idealism*, if no doubts remained as to its authenticity as a work of Schelling. Strong arguments do tell in favor of so attributing it,[23] but they are not completely convincing. This makes it quite regrettable that the fragment fits so easily into the developing thought of the young philosopher. That "the whole of metaphysics falls under morality," that the projected philosophy should extend into the domain of physics, that the state must bow to the omnipotence of the self, that poetry and mythology will subsume and fulfill science and philosophy—these are all ideas which Schelling's ardent mind was quite capable of conceiving at the time. But it would be imprudent not to acknowledge the obscurity into which Otto Pöggeler has cast this enigmatic relic.

In any case, the writings of this period, collected under the name of *General Review*,[24] suffice to prove that Schelling, while still somewhat undecided, does not stop examining the nature, the tasks, and the construction of philosophy. The sigh that ended the tenth *Letter* was only a momentary pause, a chance to take a deep breath again.[25] The subject of these writings, which only appear incongruous on a superficial level, is the division of philosophy into parts. The new element that Schelling introduces is the philosophy of nature.

At this point, however, the presence of a critical or transcendental point of view is no longer in evidence, since the philosophy or theory of nature is subsumed under the idealist paradigm. Accordingly, the philosophy of nature takes possession of the space left vacant, so to speak,

---

21. Hölderlin, op. cit. 846–47 (Schiller, September 4, 1795).
22. *Schellings Werke*, 1.289; Plitt, 1.73 (*Briefe von und an Hegel*, ed. J. Hoffmeister, 1.17).
23. See X. Tilliette, "Schelling est-il l'auteur de l'*Ältestes Systemprogramm,*" in *L'Absolut et la Philosophie: Essais sur Schelling* (Paris: Presses Universitaires de France, 1987), pp. 26–43.
24. *Schellings Werke*, 1.343–473.   25. Ibid., 1.341.

by theoretical philosophy, while the philosophy of history serves as a counterweight; the balance is henceforth placed in equilibrium by the philosophy of art, which completes the triumvirate. Schelling expressly underlines a parallel here with the prior division of philosophy into theoretical philosophy and practical philosophy. His explications are to be found in an unfinished article that specifically examines the possibility of a philosophy of experience.[26] Experience, however, has a broad range of meaning for Schelling, and is no longer a stranger to philosophy, as this quotation indicates:

Philosophy and experience were opposed (as the name "metaphysics" already indicates) with respect to their objects. *This* opposition has vanished. The object of philosophy is the *real world* (that which is beyond the real world is *Idea*, i.e., not an object of speculation, but of *action*, and to this extent it is accordingly the object of a future experience).[27]

A distrust of metaphysics shows itself here. After the rigid dichotomies of the *Letters,* Schelling is struggling to expand and reconcile philosophy by suppressing the opposition already found in the term "metaphysics." He gives an eloquent discussion of the relation between philosophy and experience (considered in its expanded sense), followed in the path blazed by Herder, in the *Allgemeine Übersicht*. The *Letters* contain a passing reference to the "completed science."[28] Philosophy progresses along a developmental series corresponding to the self-determination of Spirit. In its self-unfolding, philosophy aims at a "common resolution of theoretical and practical philosophy,"[29] and, likewise, at the reconciliation of philosophy and experience. This is expressed elsewhere by the equation "science = universal science, into which all transcendental knowledge is resolved."[30] This transitory and reductive character of the transcendental (and the serious consequences it entails) appears very early in Schelling's thought. It aggravates his opposition to Fichte.

What goes for the development and the end, goes equally well for the origin, which represents the goal in retrospect. The division into theoretical philosophy and practical philosophy takes place under the aegis of a "higher philosophy which embraces them both, which necessarily has its point of departure in an *absolute state* of the human spirit in which there is neither theory nor practice."[31] This disunity, which is destined to become the lever of the philosophy of identity later on, refers positively to the "original autonomy of the human spirit,"[32] which is

26. Cf. *Schellings Werke*, 1.461 and 1.464–65.
27. Ibid., 1.465.
28. Ibid., 1.332n.
29. Ibid., 1.399.
30. Ibid., 1.464.
31. Ibid., 1.399.
32. Ibid., 1.398.

creative in its self-positing. But the absolute state (*Zustand* and *Gegenstand* having been opposed by Fichte and Novalis) designates also a natural, preconscious, and happy existence of the I, in which it is one with nature, and in which its productions unfold without distance. The choice between Spinoza and Fichte has not yet been decisively made.

For this reason, the question of Schelling's dependence upon Fichte becomes even more inevitable. Apart from the startling variety of ways in which they are expressed, Schelling's elucidations after the ambiguous conclusion of the *Letters* contain almost nothing that would shock Fichte: the autonomy of the I is of Fichtean origin, the parallel with Spinoza comes from Fichte, and the inclusion of theoretical within practical philosophy is the goal invoked by Fichte as the infinite task of science. Schelling's expositions, it would appear, are of an authentically Fichtean character. Nevertheless, Fichte's prophetic choice of *Foundations of the Wissenschaftslehre* as the full title of the *Wissenschaftslehre* had already betrayed these very foundations. All the evils in Schelling's relation to Fichte have their origin at this point. The still-developing and philosophically promising *Wissenschaftslehre* is from this time forward conceived of as a completed but limited system, a higher critique that is in reality searching for an adequate place in the system of philosophy as a whole.

If I am not mistaken, Schelling believed that he had found this place—one situated in "*pure* theoretical philosophy"—in the Preface to the *Ideas for a Philosophy of Nature* (1797). This passage is so relevant to our investigation that it will be worthwhile to summarize it. The "original and necessary union" of theoretical and practical philosophy is retained; there is only one science. As a result, if one, in conformity to tradition, maintains the division, it must be on a new basis. In fact, up to the present, "theoretical philosophy (under the name of metaphysics) was ... a combination of completely heterogeneous principles."[33] One part contained the universal laws of nature: metaphysics of nature, cosmology. Another part housed "metaphysical principles properly so-called, i.e., principles transcending all experience": ontology, physicotheology. "Transcending experience" is to be understood in the sense employed by the old metaphysics, or simply as "beyond all experience (up to the present)." Now the old metaphysics and "that which ... up until now was metaphysical in practical philosophy" have been destroyed—Kant having shown the way—while a (purified) theoretical philosophy only connects itself to physics; as a result, instead of being "a science ... which follows physics (metaphysics)," it is "a science which precedes physics." Nevertheless, theoretical philosophy is, according to Schel-

33. Ibid., 2.3.

ling's distinction between *pure* and *applied* philosophy, simply a form of the latter. He understands by pure theoretical philosophy, in his own words, the exploration of "the reality of our knowledge *in general*,"[34] therefore a pure theory of knowledge. This is doubtless the place where he gives his blessings to the Kantian Critique and the *Wissenschaftslehre*. There are some signs of this in the *General Review*. Reality, understood in this context, has nothing to do with realism, but instead encompasses both form and content. As we said earlier, applied theoretical philosophy is concerned with physics. It is the philosophy or theory of nature; its task consists in "deducing from general principles a *determinate* system of our knowledge (the whole of experience)."[35] This is not to say that there aren't any other possible or real principles, but this determinate system is intended to embrace the totality of knowledge, albeit without infringing upon the system of action and freedom. Practical philosophy, genuine metaphysics, is itself divided into pure and applied philosophy. Applied philosophy, according to Schelling, is the philosophy of man or of history, the possibility of which he examined in part.[36] He omits practical philosophy, possibly by oversight. In any case, it can be assumed that the important contributions of Kant and Fichte were again useful to him in this area.

The plan of the system rapidly becomes obsolete under the pressure of the philosophy of nature, although the echo of the new concept of metaphysics endures. The philosophy of art is missing, but this defect is easily corrected. The transitory nature of the schema derives from the fact that the philosophy of nature is no longer content with the status of an applied philosophy drawing its principles from some unknown source. The tacit presupposition of the Introduction to the *Ideen* is the preeminent position of the transcendental method. Shortly after the attempt to elaborate a philosophy of nature (*Ideen, Weltseele, Erster Entwurf*), Schelling reveals the fact that he is operating with principles independent of those of the I's self-positing, and especially with a conception of nature as *naturans*, active in its products and autonomous in the reciprocity of its action with the I. At first quietly, but later with pomp and fanfare, Schelling dispenses with the narrow viewpoint of the *Wissenschaftslehre*, which considers nature as an inert mass or as the mirror of the I.

The equally famous, though less brilliant, Introduction to the *System of Transcendental Idealism* (1800) attempts momentarily to lessen the impact of the impending conflict with Fichte. Nevertheless, Schelling re-

---

34. Ibid., 2.4. 35. Ibid.
36. Ibid., 1.466–73 (only the *pars destruens* has been fully edited).

serves for himself the right to a full-blown philosophy of nature which would serve as a complement and balance to transcendental philosophy or transcendental idealism. But it is noteworthy that the part is the whole, that is, that transcendental idealism subsumes the three disciplines of the developed system: theoretical philosophy, practical philosophy, and aesthetic philosophy. This new division thus cuts across the previous division of philosophy. Theoretical philosophy especially (as listed, so to speak, on the transcendental registry) represents to a certain extent the philosophy of nature. The explicit parallel drawn between nature and the I always serves to win back the resources of the philosophy of nature for the unconscious I. Indeed, Schelling tacitly confesses that the border between the philosophy of nature and theoretical (transcendental) philosophy is labile and artificial, while the major division between theoretical and practical philosophy[37] remains—a division repeating that between realism and idealism, between the philosophy of nature and idealism. Now philosophy as a whole, at least in its exposition, is a single convoluted structure, the transcendental point of view extending itself effortlessly into all regions of knowledge. Not only are theoretical and practical philosophy arranged under it, but it is completed by nature and art. But Schelling's opinion that the transcendental point of view is just that—a point of view—and is not in the first degree competent for important sections of the encyclopedia of the philosophical sciences, can already be dimly discerned. He emphasizes that only the I's self-positing yields a transcendental philosophy by which the I returns to the natural point of view.[38] This inverted theoretical world is set upright and made accessible to a philosophy of nature conceived as speculative physics or "Spinozistic physics" (this turn of phrase is very characteristic).[39] This is what is really original, and it accordingly possesses the rights of the firstborn and of precedence. In addition, nature and art are only partially reconciled in the end, as nature appears only in the limited form of purposiveness, and aesthetics serves only as a kind of prelude, notwithstanding the beauty and eloquence of the discussions that Schelling devotes to them.[40] In the end, the enigmatic light of the "absolute Identity"[41] that will soon come to dominate the system shines through the productions of history and art. In a word, the beautiful exposition of *Transcendental Idealism* only seems to hide the asymmetries and fractures that contradict its formal perfection.

37. Ibid., 3.332.
39. Ibid., 3.273.
41. Ibid., 3.603, 615.
38. Ibid., 3.535.
40. Ibid., 3.628.

The succeeding writings lead down a path from which there is no return.⁴² Schelling passes beyond transcendental idealism in a manner suiting his innate realism. He calls his realism "real-idealism" in contradistinction to "ideal-realism"⁴³—a distinction that Fichte himself did not make⁴⁴—but he is most likely already thinking of a Platonic realism of Ideas, a move that will allow him to assimilate an absolute idealism, in the *Later Essays*.⁴⁵

Philosophy, in fact, returns to its old division into physics, ethics, and aesthetics.⁴⁶ The *Wissenschaftslehre* is left completely out of the loop, and purely theoretical philosophy is subsumed from this point onwards within the philosophy of nature.⁴⁷ Fichte was doubtlessly the "perfect expositor of a point of view," and he was this with great power and remarkable energy.⁴⁸ Unfortunately for Fichte, the "true point of view," which the plucky acolyte Schelling was able to reengage, is that of nature itself.⁴⁹

We have arrived at the border of the system of identity or doctrine of unitotality. It represents for Schelling the rest of the seventh day, the Sabbath of nature and its works. The immediate result of having acquired absolute knowledge is that descriptions and construction become of primary importance, which we can see if we abstract from the polemical style dominating most of the philosophical works. The metaphysical impulse, if we understand by this a spiritual drive, abates slightly without entirely disappearing. In a philosophy that confines itself to the contemplation of the Absolute, the metaphysical question, that is, the question of the Absolute, seems to have been put in order. Nevertheless, it is evident that someone who cries to his fellow philosophers, "Come to physics and know the True,"⁵⁰ is not particularly anxious to move beyond physics. The serene and tranquil descriptions of Hen Kai Pan leave no room for the transcendental and testify to a tranquil moment in Schelling's restless thought. In fact, after as before, a splinter remains lodged in the flesh of this autarchic philosophy, or a sensitive, vulnerable spot endures, indicating the possibility and reality of the finite. Among the

---

42. "Allgemeine Deduktion des dynamischen Prozesses" (1800); "Über den wahren Begriff der Naturphilosophie" (1801); "Über das Wesen der philosophischen Kritik Überhaupt" (1802; the author is Hegel); "Über das Verhältnis der Naturphilosophie zur Philosophie Überhaupt" (1802).

43. *Schellings Werke*, 3.723.   44. *Fichtes Werke*, 1.473 (1.281).
45. *Schellings Werke*, 4.333–431; cf. esp. 408.
46. Ibid., 3.726 (Instead of aesthetics we read poetics or philosophy of art).
47. Ibid., 3.720–22.   48. Ibid., 6.80.
49. Ibid., 3.712.   50. Ibid., 3.710.

series of writings on identity, *Philosophy and Religion* (1804) therefore provides the exception, introducing as it does the Platonic and Christian schema of a fall in the azure of absolute knowledge—a forever inexplicable contingency. This writing is also the arch that, above the golden harvest of unitotality, unites the previous period with what is yet to come.

But the problem of metaphysics only returns after a period in Schelling's philosophy in which it is considered less of a problem than a designation or qualitative determination. From this point on, it was Schelling's habit to preface the exposition of his system with a brief historical consideration (which he would later enlarge on). In this historical consideration, his own philosophy is, properly understood, both standard and terminus. Metaphysics, a term synonymous with science, receives, each time it is used, an indication of the great value associated with it, and achieves in the philosophy of Schelling its true value and richness. From this arises also the weighty moral pregnancy of the concept that now reappears. It is quite noticeable, for example, in a secondary text, a work entitled "On the Essence of German Science."[51] This writing was dated incorrectly by the editor who found it in his father's papers as having been written in the year 1811. Literal correspondences with a letter (recently edited by Horst Fuhrmans) to Jacobi allow this mistake to be rectified: the correct date is 1807.[52] "German science" signifies "authentic metaphysics," and its inceptor is . . . Luther. Schelling then sketches in broad strokes the course of the German metaphysical adventure. With the Protestant Revolution of faith as passion, a genuine metaphysics appeared on the scene, but it led little by little to a fatal schism that left a gap between the positive, the finite, and the real, on the one hand, and the ideal, the negative, and the spiritual, on the other. This genuine metaphysics was reawakened by Kant, who led the "rebirth of knowledge" in the proper direction, "the first who, after much time, gave back to nature a foundation which possessed something of the divine, the incarnate, a true being."[53] The allusion to the *Critique of Judgment* is obvious. Then Fichte stopped short, just shy of the goal. In general, Germanic science is characterized by the "vitality of nature," as is demonstrated by a "host of witnesses" from Kepler to Hamann. A second characteristic of German nature is the construction of a religion "intimately connected with knowledge and grounded on science,"[54] and so Schelling, so to speak, reconnects the links between the realizations of yester-

---

51. Ibid., 8.1–18.

52. This letter (June 16, 1807), since published by Horst Fuhrmans, was shown to me in 1972 by Dr. E. Galley, the director of the Heinrich-Heine Institute in Düsseldorf, on the suggestion of Dr. Michael Brüggen.

53. *Schellings Werke*, 8.6–7.   54. Ibid., 8.8.

year and those of tomorrow. Metaphysical vocabulary is thus emphatic, it is held up as a standard, but is not the exclusive property of professional philosophers. It is present wherever grandeur and sublimity are found. True metaphysics is "of the interior," and is at bottom the "sense of totality," as the following elevated passage bears witness:

> Whatever one might say, all there is of an elevated and great nature in the world exists because of something that we can call metaphysics in the most general sense. Metaphysics is what organically creates States and fashions a heart and soul, i.e., a people, out of a mob. Metaphysics is what allows the artist and the poet to reproduce the living sensation of eternal archetypes in sensuous form.[55]

In fact, "the metaphysics of the interior" "inspires" just as much "the Statesman, the hero," as it does "the heroes of faith and science," and is equivalent to "the organic form of sensibility, of thought and action," and the "intuition and the profundity of contemplation," which are also necessary for the physicist. The most recent era had done everything in its power to thwart this true metaphysics, to the profit of a mechanistic world view or a "superficial empiricism," this being the source of the cleverness of its pedagogical and political style, for which Schelling, it goes without saying, had nothing but disdain. On the contrary, philosophy is dead if it possesses nothing of the "demonic."[56]

After this enthusiastic but covert ode to metaphysics that places the philosopher among the great enthusiasts and mystics, Schelling only once officially expressed his high regard for metaphysics. The first Lesson of the *Philosophy of Revelation* (general part) intones the old song. The entire edifice of human things is compared to the biblical dream of Nebuchadnezzer, the giant with feet of clay. Schelling continues: "If one were able to remove from the state and public life all that is to be found there of a metaphysical nature, they would unravel. True metaphysics is honor, is virtue, true metaphysics is not only religion, but also respect for the law and love of the fatherland."[57] At this point, Jaspers would seize upon the "pose" and denounce it.[58] But for Schelling these rhetorical tirades are less a hollow discourse than a muffled polemic against the conceptual rattle of Hegel's windmill.[59] He is certainly no longer the visionary of the *Weltalter;* he now exerts himself attentively, with the care

---

55. Ibid., 8. 9. There is an echo of this in the *Stuttgart Lessons* of 1810; Schelling cites his brother Karl, the doctor, in a "Dissertation on the Soul" in the *Jahrbücher für Medizin:* "The true artist in his works, the true hero in his great deeds, the philosopher in his ideas" (*Schellings Werke*, 7.473).
56. Ibid., 8.10.
57. Ibid., 13.27. Again we hear the echo of Schelling's heroic period. Falstaff's superb monologue follows immediately.
58. Karl Jaspers, *Schelling. Grösse und Verhängnis* (Munich: Piper, 1955).
59. *Schellings Werke*, 13.53.

of a watchmaker, in the effort to expose rational philosophy. However, the idea of a "manly" and "vigorous" philosophy,[60] of which morality, religion, and poetry form the heart, is retained. The subdued polemical accompaniment underlines this entirely personal pretension to an authentic metaphysics.

The context immediately suggests the proper conclusion: Schelling's true metaphysics is the invention of his later years, that is, "positive" philosophy, the content of which embraces the "positive" or the historical in the emphatic sense, reality considered as active. The exact sense of this positivity is not easy to discern, as is attested by the disagreements among present and past interpreters.[61] It is impossible to determine decisively an adequate criterion, but it is still useful to see that positive philosophy and metaphysics coincide and are mutually explicative, while they diverge from one another in the logical and negative realms. The famous division into positive and negative philosophy contributes to the accentuation of the transcendent character of metaphysics. Negative philosophy is *philosophia ascendens*, negative, and positive philosophy is *philosophia descendens*, progressive, "only the two sides together completing the circle of philosophy."[62] Schelling compares his still-undeveloped negative philosophy to the previous logic—it is a "logic of becoming"—and therefore "all that is truly metaphysics" falls on the shoulders of positive philosophy. With this, however, metaphysics is less explicated than it is invoked.

The daring appropriation of metaphysics as positive philosophy therefore effaces the problem of metaphysics, which, in any case, usually appears in Schelling rather as a spirit, an existence, an attitude, or a vocation. Or alternatively, the problematic recedes back to the line of demarcation between the two philosophies; this is the great enigma of the transition, which has so occupied and tormented the interpreters.[63] Nevertheless, Schelling is careful to discuss and explain himself by means of the tradition. We shall now examine the ultimate development of Schellingian philosophy.

Historical revision, which up to this point has only been concerned with so-called modern philosophy, extends henceforth to the "metaphysics of the past,"[64] that is, to Scholasticism. Traditionally, the metaphysics

---

60. Ibid., 9.359; Ibid., 13.11.
61. Cf. Walter Schulz's groundbreaking book, *Die Vollendung des deutschen Idealisms in der Spätphilosophie Schellings*.
62. *Schellings Werke*, 13.151n.
63. Cf. Xavier Tilliette, *Schelling. Une philosophie en devenir*, 2 vols. (Paris: J. Vrin, 1970), 2.66–70 (for the critical discussion) and 2.297–339 (for the transition).
64. *Schellings Werke*, 11.281.

of the past is called "ancient metaphysics"[65] or "the metaphysics of the School,"[66] the metaphysics of understanding.[67] However, the sense in which the term "metaphysics" is used has an almost exclusively exhortatory, eulogistic sense: it is "righteous metaphysics," the "royal science,"[68] while a despised philosophy like Hegel's represents "the absolute negation of all that is metaphysics."[69] Formerly, during the period of the *Private Stuttgart Lessons,* a reticence was evident: "A God metaphysically crammed into the beyond is worthless both for our heads and for our hearts."[70] But now metaphysics can and must vindicate the "courage of philosophy,"[71] the decisive battle (*de capite dimicatur*) for philosophy and religion.[72]

Let us return now to the subject of medieval metaphysics, which acknowledged three authorities in its attempt to accomplish its "ancient task"[73] concerning the proofs for the existence of God: common experience, understanding of universal principles, and reason or the syllogism.[74] Schelling attempts to show that modern philosophy from Descartes to Kant sacrifices this eclecticism,[75] while retaining the same object and ends. It is therefore a question of providing the ancient metaphysics with a unitary development and an organic articulation; this scheme shows that Schelling stayed faithful to himself. But this older metaphysics is itself the inheritor of metaphysics κατ' ἐξοχήν, that of Aristotle, so that the revival of philosophy returns it to its original state. Schelling chose Aristotle, the master of the West, as his last guide and mentor. Schelling's unfinished pure rational philosophy is often nothing more than a commentary on Aristotelian formulae or passages. An attentive study, one still awaiting volunteers, would furnish proof that Schelling is not an amateur Scholastic, and that he generally adapts and transposes in an appropriate way and without deformation.[76]

At the same time, however, a singular shift in emphasis occurs: the metaphysical model now dominates rational or negative philosophy. How can this be made to accord with the aforementioned statement that it is *positive* philosophy that serves as the vehicle for all that is metaphysics and metaphysical? As a matter of fact, the late Schelling affirmed both alternatives: *his* metaphysics was either the theory of potencies, or

65. Ibid., 13.82–110.
66. Ibid., 13.39 (Scholastic).
67. Ibid., 13.38–40.
68. Ibid., 13.27–28.
69. Ibid., 13.31.
70. Ibid., 7.429.
71. Ibid., 13.19.
72. Ibid., 13.32.
73. Ibid., 11.281.
74. Ibid., 11.261.
75. Ibid., 11.282.
76. Erhard Oeser, *Die antike Dialektik in der Spätphilosophie Schellings* (Überlieferung und Ausgabe, 1) (Vienna and Munich: Oldenburg, 1965); *Begriff und Systematik der Abstraktion* (Überlieferung und Aufgabe, 8) (Vienna and Munich: Oldenburg, 1969).

positive philosophy,[77] the latter in the last analysis resolving itself into the philosophy of religion. The apparent contradiction is effaced or minimized by the fact that the potencies form the logico-ontological basis or foundation of the positive or metaphysical: they are presupposed in the development of the philosophy of mythology and the philosophy of revelation. Secondly, the conception of positive philosophy, as developed before the division, still endures to such an extent that its previous ontological weight demands that it persist in applied positive philosophy in a limited form. Finally, the slight inconsistency can be resolved with the simple remark that metaphysics, for Schelling, is perhaps principally an honorific title which, in his last years, still feeds the shining glory of the philosopher by way of antonomasia.

77. Cf. Plitt, 3.135 (to Dorfmüller, April 14, 1838) and 241 (to Hubert Beckers, December 29, 1852). The span of time between the two letters, however, suggests a development or, at the very least, a change of emphasis.

PART VII
CONTRADICTION AND CONTINUITY: ESSAYS ON HEGEL'S DEVELOPMENT

PART VII

12   *Von Hegel bis Hegel:* Reflections on "The Earliest System-Programme of German Idealism"

MEROLD WESTPHAL

The brief document that has come down to us as the "Earliest System-Programme of German Idealism" has been attributed to both Schelling and Hölderlin. But it is in Hegel's handwriting, and I see no reason to challenge the arguments of Pöggeler and Harris that on the basis of the evidence now available to us we should include it among Hegel's *Jugendschriften*.[1]

But what strikes the reader from the outset is how very un-Hegelian it is. In it we encounter the notions

- that "the whole of metaphysics falls for the future within *moral theory*" rather than within Logic (510/234),
- that "a complete system of Ideas" is the same thing as the totality of "practical postulates" as Kant had begun to develop them (510/234),
- that the first Idea "is, of course, the presentation *of my self* as an absolutely free entity" (510/234),

and we are only in the second sentence of the first paragraph. Before we get to the end of the eight paragraphs that constitute this little document, we will find Hegel telling us

- that the Idea of humankind is entirely incompatible with the Idea of the state, or, more precisely, that the former "gives us no Idea of the *State*" (510/234), and

---

1. It has been printed in the works of Hegel, Hölderlin, and Schelling. See H. S. Harris, *Hegel's Development: Toward the Sunlight, 1770–1801* (Oxford: Clarendon Press, 1982), p. 510n. In my references, of the form (x/y), x = Harris's English translation (pp. 510–12) and y = the German text from Hegel's *Werke in zwanzig Bänden*, vol. 1, *Frühe Schriften*, ed. Eva Moldenhauer and Karl Markus Michel (Frankfurt: Suhrkamp, 1971). On the question of authorship, see Otto Pöggeler, "Hegel, Verfasser des ältesten Systemprogramms des deutschen Idealismus," *Hegel-Studien*, Beiheft 4 (1969):17–32, and Harris, pp. 249ff.

269

- that "the Idea that unites all the rest, the Idea of *beauty* taking the word in its higher Platonic sense ... [is] the highest act of Reason ... and that *truth and goodness only become sisters in beauty*" (511/235).

This latter theme unfolds into a primacy of the aesthetic theme that is much easier to associate with Hölderlin or even the late Heidegger than with the Hegel we have come to know and love.

Yes, love. Everybody loves Hegel. What's not to love when we can choose between at least three different ways of doing so? First, we can love him as our *hero*. We can be true believers who think that he got just about everything just about right. Second, we can love him as our *tragic hero*. We can be Hegelians without the Absolute who love his dialectical holism, while mourning the claim to totality and closure, whether at the logical or the historical level, as his tragic flaw. Or, third, we can love him as our *whipping boy*, almost as useful as Descartes or Heidegger for indirectly praising our own advanced insights. Even analytic philosophers can (and do) love Hegel in this way, though perhaps they beat up on Hegel less regularly than do their continental colleagues.

But perhaps our little text is "un-Hegelian" *only* in relation to the Hegel we have come to know and love, the "published" Hegel of the *Phenomenology, Science of Logic, Encyclopedia,* and *Philosophy of Right,* and the "unpublished" Hegel of the great Berlin lecture series on the history of philosophy, the philosophy of history, the philosophy of religion, and aesthetics. Consider the following (true) story. When he wrote the first volume of his magisterial study of Hegel's early development, Henry Harris assumed that the manuscript in Hegel's handwriting was his own copy of a text authored by Schelling or Hölderlin. Only after completing his interpretation of Hegel's development on the basis of other texts was he convinced by Pöggeler that Hegel was the author of the "System-Programme." So he appended a discussion of it to his chapter on Hegel in Berne (1793–1796), since handwriting analysis places it most likely in the summer of 1796.[2] Far from being a disruptive intrusion, the new text fit in easily and smoothly, showing a marked affinity for several of its new brothers and sisters.[3]

So we have before us a text that is wildly "un-Hegelian" by comparison with the Hegel we have come to know and love, but quintessentially Heg-

---

2. On the dating of these texts, see Gisela Schüler, "Zur Chronologie von Hegel's Jugendschriften," *Hegel-Studien* 2 (1963): 111–59. Cf. Hegel, *Werke,* 1.625–26. The chronology given by Harris (see pp. 517–27) follows Schüler (and the corresponding work of Heinz Kimmerle for the Jena writings), but not uncritically.

3. See Harris, pp. 249–57, esp. 249n2.

elian by comparison with the *Jugendschriften* to which it belongs. There is nothing new about the suggestion that there is a wide gap between the ideas of the youthful and the mature Hegel. But this text makes that point more vividly in less space than perhaps any other text. It serves as a useful reminder that the journey *von Kant bis Hegel* is also a journey *von Hegel bis Hegel*. We might almost say that in Hegel ontogeny recapitulates phylogeny, that his own *Entstehungsgeschichte* and that of the German idealism whose culmination he is often seen to be are remarkably similar in a variety of ways.

The strangeness of this text derives from its three major, "un-Hegelian" themes: the primacy of practical reason, the irrationality of the state, and the primacy of the aesthetic. We have a sandwich here, with two positives (the primacy theses) surrounding a negative. To us the two positives might seem to repel each other. Talk about the postulates of practical reason may seem to be in tension with talk about beauty as the highest act of reason. But that may very well be our problem rather than Hegel's. First, while we are inclined to read Kant's three *Critiques* as a descending arc, so far as their importance is concerned, it was quite possible in 1796 to read them as an ascending and continuous arc.

Second, and more specifically, the moral and the aesthetic, as Hegel understands them in Tübingen and Berne, are essential ingredients in any religion that could be embraced by rational individuals and a free people. By virtue of their significance for *Volksreligion*, public piety freed of all positivity, they belong essentially together. What Hegel's sandwich represents, therefore, is the affirmation of a certain moral-aesthetic-religious community over the political community to be found in the modern state. It sketches a theology for the church of which he wrote to Schelling in January 1795, "Reason and Freedom remain our password, and the Invisible Church our rallying point."[4]

To anyone who first reads Hegel's critique of Kant and Fichte as early as *Glauben und Wissen* (1802), essentially reiterated in ¶¶ 40–60 of *The Encyclopedia Logic* and in the *Lectures on the History of Philosophy*, the opening sentences of our 1796 fragment can only come as a shock. After the words "an *Ethics*" conclude an otherwise lost sentence, we read

Since the whole of metaphysics falls for the future within *moral theory*—of which Kant with his pair of practical postulates has given only an *example*, and not *exhausted* it, — this Ethics will be nothing less than *a complete system of all Ideas or of all practical postulates (which is the same thing)* [my italics].

---

4. See *Hegel: The Letters*, trans. Clark Butler and Christiane Seiler (Bloomington: Indiana University Press, 1984), p. 32.

The next sentence takes us directly from Kant to Fichte:

> The first Idea is, *of course* [my italics], the presentation *of my self* as an absolutely free entity. (510/234)

But the Hegel who wrote these words in the summer of 1796 had only the previous summer written an essay presenting Jesus as a Kantian moralist, a transcendental deduction of what Jesus must have meant (and done) regardless of what the texts we have may say.[5] Moreover, this essay is the point of departure for his next major project, begun in the late summer or fall of 1795, the much better known "Positivity of the Christian Religion."[6] There the question is how this *Jesus aus Königsberg* gave rise to a Christianity with so much positivity, meaning such offenses to rational autonomy as miracles, creeds, sacraments, and ecclesiastical authority. After writing "The method of treating the Christian religion which is in vogue today takes reason and morality as a basis for testing it," he makes it clear that he is affirming and not just reporting.

> I remark here that the general principle to be laid down as a foundation for all judgments on the varying modifications, forms, and spirit of the Christian religion is this—that the aim and essence of all true religion, our religion included, is human morality, and that all the more detailed doctrines of Christianity, all means of propagating them, and all its obligations (whether obligations to believe or obligations to perform actions in themselves otherwise arbitrary) have their worth and their sanctity appraised according to their close or distant connection with that aim.[7]

Again we get the transcendental deduction of Jesus:

> Jesus, on this view, was the teacher of a purely moral religion, not a positive one.... On this view, many ideas of his contemporaries, e.g., their expectations of a Messiah, their representation of immortality under the symbol of resurrection, their ascription of serious and incurable diseases to the agency of a powerful evil being, etc., were simply *used* by Jesus ... as contemporary ideas [*Zeitideen*] they do not belong to the content of a religion, because any such content must be eternal and unalterable.[8]

No doubt in Kant's version of this reduction of religion to ethics (as distinct, perhaps, from Lessing's), this presupposes human freedom. But Hegel's elevation of the free self to the status of First Idea, the ground

---

5. For an English translation, see "The Life of Jesus," in *Hegel: Three Essays, 1793–1795*, trans. Peter Fuss and John Dobbins (Notre Dame, Ind.: University of Notre Dame Press, 1984). Also see Harris's discussion, pp. 194ff.

6. For an English translation, see *On Christianity: Early Theological Writings*, trans. T. M. Knox (New York: Harper & Row, 1961). More precisely, it is Part 1 of this essay, the German manuscript *Man mag die widersprechendsten Betrachtungen*, that belongs to this time frame.

7. Knox, *On Christianity*, pp. 67–68; *Werke*, 1.104–5.

8. Knox, *On Christianity*, p. 71; *Werke*, 1.108–9.

and principle of any viable "complete system" of metaphysics, is so Fichtean (and ultimately Cartesian) and so foreign both to the antifoundationalism and to the unity of logic and metaphysics we find in the Hegel we have come to know and love—what are we to make of it?

It is no help to refer our document to either the Schelling or the Hölderlin we have come to know and love. For this language would be as strange from their pens as from Hegel's. But in the period just before Hegel wrote his programme, both of them were flaming Fichteans and, what is more, were sharing their enthusiasm with Hegel. Schelling had prepublication access to Fichte's 1794 *Wissenschaftslehre* and wrote a thoroughly Fichtean essay entitled *Vom Ich als Prinzip der Philosophie*, which appeared at the same book fair in the spring of 1795 as the full version of the *Wissenschaftslehre*.[9] In a letter of January 5, 1795, he writes to Hegel, "Philosophy is not yet at an end. Kant has provided the results. The premises are still missing." The result is that Kantians are stuck on the letter of the Kantian thought and do not realize its radical implications. But, on the basis of the excerpts of the *Wissenschaftslehre* he has been receiving, he writes, "*Fichte* will raise philosophy to a height at which even most of the hitherto Kantians will become giddy."[10] On February 4 he sends Hegel a summary of *Vom Ich* and its argument that only practical reason leads to the supersensible world. "Only in practical reason are we able to come upon nothing but our Absolute Self, for only the Absolute Self has circumscribed the infinite sphere. There is no other supersensible world for us than that of the Absolute Self. *God* is nothing but the Absolute Self, the Self insofar as it has annihilated everything theoretical."[11]

In between these letters Hölderlin, who was attending Fichte's lectures at Jena, had written enthusiastically to Hegel about the *Wissenschaftslehre* and *On the Vocation of the Scholar*.[12] "[Fichte's] Absolute Self, which equals Spinoza's Substance[,] contains all reality; it is everything, and outside it, is nothing."[13]

---

9. F.W.J. Schelling, *The Unconditional in Human Knowledge: Four Early Essays (1794–1796)*, trans. Fritz Marti (Lewisburg, Pa.: Bucknell University Press, 1980), p. 30. The translation of the essay is on pp. 63–149. German text in *Sämmtliche Werke*, 14 vols., ed. K.F.A. Schelling (Stuttgart and Augsburg: J. G. Cotta, 1856–1861), vol. 1. For Fichte, see *Science of Knowledge (Wissenschaftslehre) with the First and Second Introductions*, trans. Peter Heath and John Lachs (New York: Appleton-Century-Crofts, 1970). German text in *Sämmtliche Werke*, 8 vols., ed. I. H. Fichte (Berlin: Veit, 1845–1846), vol. 1.

10. Butler and Seiler, *Letters*, p. 29.   11. Ibid., p. 33.

12. An English translation of the latter is to be found in *Fichte: Early Philosophical Writings*, trans. Daniel Breazeale (Ithica, N.Y.: Cornell University Press, 1988). German text in *Sämmtliche Werke*, vol. 6.

13. Butler and Seiler, *Letters*, p. 33.

A year later both Schelling and Hölderlin would be moving away from Fichte in the direction of the Schelling and Hölderlin we have come to know and love. But in the meantime, Hegel was their convert. In an April 16 letter to Schelling he, too, speaks the language of "God as the Absolute Self" and announces his intention to study the *Wissenschaftslehre* over the summer. By August 30 he writes to Schelling that he has indeed been studying both it and Schelling's first two essays, including *Vom Ich*.[14]

In relation to the "System-Programme" there are several important features to notice about this 1795 correspondence. First, it marks Hegel's decisive (clear and, I believe, permanent) departure from theism. In his January 5 letter to Hegel, Schelling satirizes the Kantians of the letter: "It is fun to see how quickly they can get to the moral proof. Before you can turn around the *deus ex machina* springs forth, the personal individual Being who sits in Heaven above!" Fichte will put an end to all this, which Schelling identifies with "the old superstition of so-called natural religion as well as of positive religion."[15]

In his January reply, Hegel makes it clear that he has no sympathy for the Tubingen orthodoxy that wants to reestablish itself on Kantian foundations (though he holds Fichte partly responsible for this through his *Critique of All Revelation*). But just before signing off with the salute to the Invisible Church cited above, he writes, "There is one expression in your letter concerning the moral proof that I do not entirely understand: 'which they know how to manipulate so that out springs the individual, personal Being.' Do you really believe we fail to get so far?"[16] Schelling's withering reply of February 4 responds to the question

> whether I believe we cannot get to a personal Being by means of the moral proof. I confess the question has surprised me. I would not have expected it from an intimate of Lessing's. Yet you no doubt asked it only to learn whether the question has been entirely decided *in my own mind*. For you the question has surely long since been decided. For us as well [as for Lessing] the orthodox concepts of God are no more. My reply is that we get even *further* than a personal Being. I have in the interim become a Spinozist! Do not be astonished, You will soon hear how. For Spinoza the world, the object by itself in opposition to the subject, was *everything*. For me it is the *self*.[17]

There follows the summary of *Vom Ich* with its claim that "*God* is nothing but the Absolute Self" and this further commentary: "Personality arises through the unity of consciousness. Yet consciousness is not possible

---

14. Ibid., pp. 35–41.   15. Ibid., p. 29.
16. Ibid., p. 32.
17. Ibid., p. 32. This notion of Fichte as another way of being Spinoza anticipates Schelling's next essay, "Philosophical Letters on Dogmatism and Criticism." English translation in Marti, *The Unconditional*, pp. 151–220. German text in *Sämmtliche Werke*, vol. 1.

without an object. But for God—i.e., for the Absolute Self—there is no object *whatsoever;* for if there were the Absolute Self would cease to be absolute. Consequently there is no personal God, and our highest endeavor is aimed at the destruction of our personality, at passage into the absolute sphere of being; but given even eternity this passage is not *possible.* Hence only a *practical* approach toward the Absolute, hence *immortality.*"[18] Starting with the absolute freedom of the *Ich* Schelling has given consistently Fichtean transcriptions of both God and immortality.

In his letter to Hegel a week and a half earlier, Hölderlin had taken the same tack, writing, "[Fichte's] Absolute Self . . . is everything, and outside it, is nothing. There is thus no object for this Absolute Self, since otherwise all reality would not be in it. Yet a consciousness without an object is inconceivable. . . . Thus, in the Absolute Self no consciousness is conceivable."[19]

In his April reply, Hegel is fully on board, though he expects that "the idea of God as the Absolute Self" will have to remain an "esoteric philosophy." (How quickly the *Atheismusstreit* [1798] would confirm Hegel's sense that prudence and courage might be in conflict when it came to being publicly candid about these notions!) His August letter to Schelling is even more explicit. His only reservation is whether Schelling should apply the category of substance to the Absolute Self. He adds that he will "shortly send you the plan of something I am thinking to work out."[20] Could the "System-Programme" be this plan?

The second thing to notice about this correspondence is that Hegel sticks with the language of postulates as he moves from a Kantian theism to a Fichtean pantheism. This is explicit in both letters in which he shares his new Fichtean faith with Schelling. In April he writes, "After a more recent study of the postulates of practical reason I had a presentiment of what you clearly laid out for me in your last letter [the February 4 summary of *Vom Ich*], of what I found in your writing, and of what Fichte's *Foundation of the Science of Knowledge* will disclose to me completely."[21] In

---

18. Butler and Seiler, *Letters,* p. 33. The following summer, Hegel would read in the actual text of *Vom Ich* that it would leave dissatisfied "those who hastily appended a multitude of postulates of happiness to the letter of Kant" as well as

those who can believe that Kant could deem any knowledge which he thought impossible in theoretical philosophy possible in practical and thus, in practical philosophy, could again place the supersensuous world (God, etc.) as something *outside* the I, as an *object.* . . . But since we enter the supersensuous world only through the reestablishment of the absolute I, what can we expect to find there other than the I? therefore, no God as an *object,* no not-I at all, no empirical happiness, etcetera, but only pure, absolute I! (Marti, *The Unconditional,* pp. 99–100; *Sämmtliche Werke,* 1.201–2)

19. Butler and Seiler, *Letters,* p. 33.   20. Ibid., pp. 41–43.
21. Ibid., p. 35.

other words, he is moving toward a Fichtean interpretation of the postulates. And in August, after reading both Fichte and Schelling's Fichtean essays, he writes with reference to an essay he plans on the postulates: "What previously floated before my mind darkly and in undeveloped form has been illuminated by your writing in a most splendid and satisfactory manner."[22] Thus we should not be surprised to find in the "System-Programme" (Is it a sketch for the essay just mentioned?) the close juxtaposition of postulate talk with a Fichtean first principle. Nor should we be surprised that when Hegel speaks of God and immortality, he speaks of the absolute freedom "of all spirits who bear the intellectual world in themselves, and cannot seek either God or immortality outside themselves" (511/235).

Third, this is the context in which we can understand the incipient philosophy of nature in the "System-Programme." There, immediately after making the free self the first Idea, he writes:

Along with the free, self-conscious essence there stands forth—out of nothing—an entire *world*—the one true and thinkable creation out of nothing.—Here I shall descend into the realms of physics; the question is this: how must a world be constituted for a moral entity? I would like to give wings once more to our backward physics, that advances laboriously by experiments.... It does not appear that our present-day physics can satisfy a creative spirit such as ours is or ought to be. (510/234).

This sounds very much like what Hegel described to Schelling a year and a half earlier in his January letter. He wants "to determine more closely to what extent, after having fixed moral belief, we might now utilize the thus legitimated idea of God backwards ... to what extent we might take the idea of God derived from our present vantage point in moral theology [*Ethikotheologie*] with us back into physical theology [*Physikotheologie*], in order to legislate in this second field by means of that idea."[23] The morally legitimated idea of God would soon take a sharp Fichtean turn, but the idea of deriving a philosophy of nature from it remains. It would seem that Hegel is echoing the claim of the *Wissenschaftslehre*—"Only to the extent that anything is related to the practical faculty of the self, does it have independent reality"—and anticipating Fichte's later formulation of the idea that nature is nothing but the stage on which the human moral drama is played out:

The world is nothing more than our own inner acting (*qua* pure intellect), made visible to the senses in accordance with comprehensible laws of reason and limited by incomprehensible boundaries within which we simply find ourselves to be confined.... Nothing is clearer or more certain than the *meaning* of these

22. Ibid., p. 41.   23. Ibid., p. 31.

boundaries. They constitute your determinate place in the moral order of things. Whatever you perceive as a consequence of these boundaries possesses reality, the only kind of reality that pertains to you or exists for you.... Our world is the material of our duty made sensible. This is the truly real element in things, the true, basic stuff [*Grundstoff*] of all appearance.[24]

Finally, we see in this correspondence a Hegel for whom the turn to practical reason is not in the service of theoretical goals but of practical goals. Hegel's reformist zeal spills over with special clarity and force in his April letter to Schelling. When he says that he is expecting a revolution in Germany from the completion of the Kantian system, it is clear that he does not mean simply a theoretical revolution. The Fichtean notion of God as the Absolute Self may have to remain esoteric, but his conception of human freedom will not, a conception by which "man is being so greatly exalted," in which "man's capacity for freedom [is recognized], placing him in the same rank with all spirits," and in which

mankind is being presented as so worthy of respect in itself. It is proof that the aura of prestige surrounding the heads of the oppressors and gods of this earth is disappearing. The philosophers are proving the dignity of man. The peoples will learn to feel it. Not only will they demand their rights, which have been trampled in the dust, they will take them back themselves, they will appropriate them.... With the spread of how things *ought* to be, the indolence that marks people set in their ways, who always take everything the way it is, will disappear. This enlivening power of ideas ... such as the idea of the fatherland, of its constitution, and so forth—will lift hearts.[25]

This move from the *Wissenschaftslehre* to the constitution may be a bit enthymemic, but it reminds us how totally Hegel's intellectual activity at this time is in the service of his sociopolitical goals as *Volkserzieher*. Hegel would later call it a "modern folly" to try "to make a revolution without having made a reformation."[26] From the Tubingen essay on *Volksreligion* and "The Positivity of the Christian Religion" through "The Spirit of Christianity and Its Fate" to the *Verfassungsschrift*, whose latest drafts bring us into the early Jena period, Hegel is a prophetic voice seeking to accomplish both a political revolution and a religious reformation at the same time.

---

24. *Science of Knowledge*, p. 248; *Sämmtliche Werke*, 1.282. "On the Basis of Our Belief in a Divine Governance of the World," in *Introductions to the Wissenschaftslehre and Other Writings (1797–1800)*, trans. Daniel Breazeale (Indianapolis, Ind.: Hackett, 1994), pp. 149–50. German text in *Sämmtliche Werke*, 5.184–85. This latter essay triggered the *Atheismusstreit* and Fichte's dismissal from Jena.

25. Butler and Seiler, *Letters*, p. 35. Here and elsewhere I leave unchanged Hegel's use of the masculine, reminding us to be sensitive to the possibilities of gender bias. On the allergic reaction of the mature Hegel to this kind of "ought" talk, see my "Hegel's *Angst vor dem Sollen*," *Owl of Minerva* 25, no. 2 (1994).

26. ¶ 552 of the *Encyclopedia* (*Philosophy of Spirit*).

This reminds us of the second "un-Hegelian" theme of the "System-Programme": its startling hostility toward the state. The "Idea of mankind" excludes the "Idea of the *State*, since the State is a mechanical thing. . . . So we must go even beyond the State [*über den Staat hinaus*]!" (510/234).

These shocking words are a challenge to the suggestion that the "System-Programme" is quintessentially Hegelian so far as the *Jugendschriften* are concerned. For it is easy to point to numerous texts, both before and after this one, in which Hegel's attitude toward the state is positive.[27] The critique of this or that political structure or practice is directed toward a better state, not toward its elimination from the realm of reason. Thus, for example, in "The Positivity of the Christian Religion," Hegel argues that a religiously intolerant state should be replaced by a state, separated from the church, that will guarantee religious liberty for everyone.[28] Even the *Verfassungsschrift*, which includes a sharp critique of the mechanical state, begins with the lament *"Deutschland ist kein Staat mehr"* and sustains in counterpoint with this dirge the hope and the challenge for Germany to become a truly rational state.[29] The overly centralized, mechanical state to be found in contemporary France and Prussia, and in Fichte's *Naturrecht* of 1796,[30] is antithetical to freedom; but it does not exhaust the meaning of the state.

Two distinctions made in Hegel's later political thought might be helpful here. One is between the political state (*der politische Staat*) or the strictly political state (*der eigentlich politische Staat*)[31] and the state *simpliciter*. Commenting on the strangeness of the phrase "political state," Pelczynski writes:

It suggests that apart from "civil society" ("the state as the Understanding envisages it") and "the strictly political state" (which, though more adequate, is still an abstract concept) Hegel has yet another, even more complex concept of the state, "state" *sans phrase*, "state" without any qualification, "state" properly so called. It is this state . . . on which he heaps all the seemingly exaggerated superlatives for which the *Philosophy of Right* is notorious. The state in this sense means the whole population of an independent, politically and "civilly" organized coun-

27. See, e.g., Harris, p. 251.
28. Such an essentially liberal view of the state prevails in *Man mag die widersprechendsten Betrachtungen*. See note 6 above.
29. An English translation of "The German Constitution" is found in *Hegel's Political Writings*, trans. T. M. Knox (Oxford: Clarendon Press, 1964). For the lament, see p. 143; for the critique of the mechanical state, see pp. 159–64. German text in *Werke*, vol. 1.
30. Hegel may have read part of this Fichte text before writing the "System-Programme"; see Harris, pp. 251–52.
31. For these phrases, see ¶¶ 267, 273, and 276 of the *Philosophy of Right*.

try in so far as it is permeated by "ethical life" and forms an "ethical order" or "ethical community."[32]

Perhaps the clearest indication of this distinction is the fact that Hegel regularly speaks of the laws *and customs* that constitute a state. I try to make this distinction for my students by distinguishing between Washington (the city inside the Beltway) and America. There could be no America as we know it without Washington, but

> There are more things in America's cities and countrysides, Washington,
> Than are dreamt of in your beltway philosophy.

The political state is an abstraction because it is but part of a larger whole of social and cultural practices.

With regard to "the strictly political state," Hegel further distinguishes between "the external state, the state based on need, the state as the Understanding envisages it,"[33] and the truly rational political order. The former has the needy, desiring individual as its basis, and conceives community or social interaction as a means to the ends of such individuals. The state apparatus is a commodity that political consumers (there are no citizens here) are willing to pay for as long as they feel they are getting a good buy. Hegel considers this view of the state to be the conflation of civil society and the state because it both sees the state's task to be the protection of an economy based on contractual exchange and sees the state itself as the result of a contract. Thus, Hegel's sustained polemic against viewing the state as a kind of contract, with only the resources of Abstract Right at its disposal, is a critique of "the state as the Understanding envisages it."[34]

It should be clear that the repudiation of the state as a machine in the "System-Programme" is directed toward what Hegel construes to be a subrational theory and practice of "the strictly political state." There is nothing at all "un-Hegelian" about such a critique, though the focus of these critiques changes through the course of time. What is strange is that Hegel "momentarily" treats the machine conception of the state as if it exhausted the idea of the state and thus "is not interested, for the

---

32. Z. A. Pelczynski, "The Hegelian Conception of the State," in *Hegel's Political Philosophy: Problems and Perspectives*, ed. Z. A. Pelczynski (Cambridge: Cambridge University Press, 1971), p. 13.
33. *Philosophy of Right*, ¶ 183.
34. *Philosophy of Right*, ¶¶ 29, 40, 75, 113, 157–59; cf. 163. I have discussed the implications of this critique in "Hegel's Radical Idealism: Family and State as Ethical Communities," in *Hegel, Freedom, and Modernity* (Albany: State University of New York Press, 1992).

moment, in what the 'absolute freedom of all spirits' will be like on the political level."[35]

Two observations are in order. First, this moment is not quite as momentary as this formulation of Harris suggests. It may be but a moment, but it recurs, mirabile dictu, at the heart of the Hegel we have come to know and love. In Chapter 6 of the *Phenomenology*, the political state is comfortably present in Sections A and B, which trace the history of Spirit from Antigone to Robespierre. But in Section C, where Absolute Spirit makes its appearance in and as postrevolutionary modernity, the state disappears. Once again, Hegel "is not interested, for the moment, in what the 'absolute freedom of all spirits' will be like on the political level."

However difficult it may be to take seriously "the fact that it is in a setting which can only be described as anarchy that absolute Spirit comes on the scene in the *Phenomenology*,"[36] these three facts remain. (1) To repeat, at this point the political state simply disappears from Hegel's account of Spirit, not merely in name but in substance as well. (2) There is a sociological anarchy here as well, inasmuch as social roles have lost their crucial significance for human identity. (3) There is even an ethical anarchy, as conscience "is free from any content whatever; it absolves itself from any specific duty which is supposed to have the validity of law. In the strength of its own self-assurance it possesses the majesty of absolute autarky, to bind and to loose."[37] The triadic structure of the anarchistic setting in which Spirit finally emerges as Absolute in the *Phenomenology* makes it clear that the absence of the state is no accidental oversight.

This is not to say that Hegel has become a radical individualist. But the community constituted by conscience and forgiveness does not compromise any of Hegel's three anarchies, which leads to my second observation. Later on Hegel might have called the transpolitical community he here affirms the state *sans phrase*. But he does not do so in either the "System-Programme" or in the *Phenomenology*, and this fact must be correlated, whether as cause or as effect, with the fact that in both texts the political state shows up only in forms that must be repudiated. To be more precise, these forms must be repudiated not because the political state as such is abstract and must always be *Aufgehoben* in a larger, richer social totality, but because they are not rationally adequate even for the limited role the political state is called upon to play.

35. Harris, pp. 251–52.
36. See my *History and Truth in Hegel's "Phenomenology,"* 3rd ed. (Bloomington: Indiana University Press, 1988), p. 176. For the analysis that follows, see pp. 175–81 and "Verzeihung und Anarchie," *Hegel Jahrbuch* (1972): 105–9.
37. *Phenomenology of Spirit*, trans. A. V. Miller (Oxford: Clarendon Press, 1977), p. 393; *Phänomenologie des Geistes*, ed. J. Hoffmeister (Hamburg: Felix Meiner, 1952), s. 456.

We could put the point in Habermasian terms. From start to finish Hegel is committed to the view that to be rational the political state must be "lifeworld" and not merely "system." But on at least two occasions, in 1796 and a decade later in 1806, he "momentarily" holds the view that the political state can only be a system that threatens to colonize the lifeworld, thereby depriving its citizens of their true freedom. It is not surprising that the first of these moments has received scant attention. But it is scandalous that Hegel scholarship has retained such a thoroughgoing lack of curiosity about the second. The question about the relation of the *Phenomenology* to the System has always been posed in terms of its role as an introduction to the Logic. But for those who find Hegel's aspirations for Absolute Knowledge to be an unfortunate Cartesian hangover, the question of the political relation of the early, mature Hegel to the late, mature Hegel should be at least as important.

I turn now to the third "un-Hegelian" thesis of the "System-Programme," the one I have labeled the primacy of the aesthetic. Five of the eight paragraphs of our fragment are devoted to it. In addition to the ideas cited at the beginning of this essay, we find

- that "the philosophy of the spirit is an aesthetic philosophy"
- that poetry is to become "at the end once more, what she was in the beginning—the *teacher of mankind*"
- that not only the mob but the philosopher "must have a *religion of the senses* . . . a polytheism of the imagination and of art"
- that "we must have a new mythology . . . in the service of the Ideas, it must be a mythology of *Reason*"
- that "until we express the Ideas aesthetically, i.e., mythologically, they have no interest for the *people*," but, when mythology becomes philosophical and philosophy becomes mythological, "universal freedom and equality of spirits will reign!" (511–12/235–36)

Many of these themes were already present in the Tubingen essay of 1793.[38] A *Volksreligion*, an essential ingredient in the life of any free people, must be subjective and not merely objective. That is to say, it must be a matter of the heart and not merely of the understanding. We cannot live by the *Ideen* of pure reason alone, for the link between our cognitive faculties and our heart is not very direct. "In a folk-religion particularly, it is of the greatest moment, that heart and fancy [*Phantasie*]

---

38. Harris translates this important essay, *Religion ist eine*, in the same appendix that includes his translation of the "System-Programme" and three other fragments (pp. 481–507). It will be cited in the same x/y format as the "System-Programme." See note 1 above.

should not go unsatisfied, that fancy should be fulfilled with great and pure images [*Bilder*], and that the more beneficent feelings should be aroused in the heart" (497/30–31). For this reason the first canon of *Volksreligion*, that "its doctrines must be grounded on universal Reason," is immediately followed by a second, that "fancy, heart, and sensibility [*Phantasie, Herz, und Sinnlichkeit*] must not thereby go empty away" (499/33). Since "we are generally too much men of Reason and of words to love beautiful images," it would be a good idea "to link myths with the religion itself from the start," providing fancy with "a beautiful path for it to strew with flowers" (502/37–38).

It is not surprising that when Schiller published his letters *On the Aesthetic Education of Man* in 1795, Hegel read them immediately and described them to Schelling as "a masterpiece."[39] Schiller's goal, like Hegel's, is essentially political and he turns to "follow the path of aesthetics, since it is through Beauty that we arrive at Freedom."[40] The current state, a "clockwork" mechanism "based on need," is "rotten and tottering," but it must be repaired while it is still running. For this reason we need to "search for some support for the continuation of society, to make it independent of the actual State which we want to abolish."[41] A truly free state would socialize us from sensuous nature to moral and rational freedom, but the condition for its creation cannot be either nature, which we need to surpass, nor morality, which we have not yet attained. The character needed to create the politics that would nourish the cultivation of rational, moral freedom can only come from the arts. The aesthetic is the only possible bridge from sensuous nature to reason and morality.[42] Beauty is the savior that can redeem us from the savagery in which feelings rule our principles and the barbarity in which our principles destroy our feelings.[43] This is why it is "no mere poetic license, but also philosophical truth, to call Beauty our second creator."[44]

---

39. In the same letter of April 16, 1795 (Butler and Seiler, *Letters*, p. 36) in which he announced his intention to study the *Wissenschaftslehre* over the summer. Hegel comes to Fichte immersed in Schiller, who, though he cites both the *Wissenschaftslehre* and *On the Vocation of the Scholar*, is tackling the problem of human freedom from a very different direction.

40. Friedrich Schiller, *On the Aesthetic Education of Man: In a Series of Letters*, trans. Reginald Snell (New York: Frederick Ungar, 1965), p. 27. German text in *Werke in drei Bänden*, ed. Herbert G. Göpfert (Munich: Carl Hanser Verlag, 1966), 2.447.

41. Schiller, *Aesthetic Education*, pp. 28–30, 35; cf. p. 46. *Werke*, 2.448–49, 452; cf. 459.

42. Schiller, *Aesthetic Education*, pp. 29, 50–51, 108–10. *Werke*, 2.448–49, 462, 499–501.

43. Schiller, *Aesthetic Education*, pp. 34, 55. *Werke*, 2.451–52, 465. It is in the concept of barbarism that Schiller's critique of Kantian ethics surfaces.

44. Schiller, *Aesthetic Education*, p. 102. *Werke*, 2.495.

As Hegel echoes these themes from Schiller, he anticipates the aesthetic turn Schelling will take (this time following Hegel, and, no doubt, Hölderlin) as he turns away from Fichte. In his *System of Transcendental Idealism* Schelling summarizes the special relationship between art and philosophy by making the philosophy of art the "organon" and "keystone" of philosophy; this means that there are only two paths beyond ordinary reality to the ideal world: poetry and philosophy.[45] It entails two fundamental parallels. Subjectively, genius is to the aesthetic what the ego is to philosophy, which is to say, aesthetic intuition is the equivalent of intellectual intuition. Objectively, beauty is the artist's presentation of the infinite in a finite mode, which is to say, the Greek myths, for example, are symbols of the Ideas.[46]

Although Schelling had moved from transcendental idealism and the philosophy of nature to identity philosophy by the time he gave his lectures on the philosophy of art, the central theme of art as metaphysically revelatory remains. When art moves beyond "sensual stimulation" (today we would say beyond "entertainment") it takes on a sacred character and becomes "a proclaimer of divine mysteries, the unveiler of the ideas . . . [a] phenomenon emanating directly from the absolute."[47] This means that "absolute beauty is the truth of the ideas" and that "the gods of any mythology are nothing other than the ideas of philosophy intuited objectively or concretely."[48]

To this Schelling adds an idea that I believe is not found in the *System of Transcendental Idealism*, "the possibility of a future mythology." As distinct from Greece, modernity sees the world as history, as morality, in short, as antithesis rather than as harmony.

Its gods are gods of history. *They* will not be able to become truly gods, living, independent, and poetic, until they have taken possession of nature, or until they have become nature gods. One must not seek to force the realistic mythology of the Greeks onto Christian culture; one must rather, in quite the reverse fashion, seek to plant its idealistic deities into nature itself, just as the Greeks place their realistic gods into history. This seems to me to be the final destiny of all modern poesy. . . . Neither do I hide my conviction that in the philosophy of

---

45. *System of Transcendental Idealism (1800)*, trans. Peter Heath (Charlottesville: University of Virginia Press, 1978), pp. 12–14. *Sämmtliche Werke*, 3.349–51.

46. *Transcendental Idealism*, pp. 224–29; *Sämmtliche Werke*, 3.619–25.

47. *The Philosophy of Art*, trans. Douglas W. Scott (Minneapolis: University of Minnesota Press, 1989), p. 4. *Sämmtliche Werke*, 5.345. Cf. p. 19; 5.372.

48. *The Philosophy of Art*, pp. 7, 17; *Sämmtliche Werke*, 5.352, 370. Cf. p. 35; 5.390–91— "*These same syntheses of the universal and particular that viewed in themselves are ideas, that is, images of the divine, are, if viewed on the plane of the real, the* gods. . . . What ideas are for philosophy, the gods are for art, and vice versa."

nature, as it has developed from the idealistic principle, the first, distant foundation has been laid for that future symbolism and mythology that will be created not by an individual but rather by the entire age.

It is not *we* who want to give the idealist culture its gods through *physics*. We rather await its gods.[49]

We probably cannot fully appreciate the degree to which pre-Kantian European civilization was grounded in metaphysics. After Kant destroyed the foundations, what could the righteous do? How could contact with the Infinite and Absolute be reestablished, once the path of metaphysical speculation had been blocked? Hegel's ultimate answer to this question is bold: through metaphysical speculation. But in order for this to be possible it must go beyond the fixity and finitude of the Understanding and the antinomic dialectic of Reason (which was as far as Kant was able to go) to the synthetic, speculative side of Reason which a new Logic can unfold.[50]

Between Kant and the Hegel who prescribes more and better metaphysical speculation as the cure for the speculative illnesses Kant diagnosed, we find a series of rather different proposals for regaining contact with an Ultimate Source of meaning. Kant and Fichte point us to moral experience; Schleiermacher points us to religious experience; while Hölderlin and the S-men (Schiller, the Schlegels, Schelling, and eventually Schopenhauer) point us to aesthetic experience. These are not sharply distinct and tend to fuse in various combinations, moral-religious, moral-aesthetic, and religious-aesthetic. But they share an important commitment. We could replace the language of experience with the discourse of practice and speak of moral, religious, and aesthetic practices. But whether we speak of experience or praxis, it is most definitely not theory that is our foundational link with God. We could speak here of a shared commitment to the primacy of practical reason, if that phrase were not already associated with one specific variety of this wider phenomenon. Or, returning to the language of experience, we could speak of a new empiricism, if that term were not still so tightly linked to narrow, Anglo-American forms of the appeal to experience from Locke to logical positivism.

This antitheory theme, or, to be more precise, this Kantian sense that theory cannot ground itself, might suggest that the path from the First *Critique* to the *Phenomenology of Spirit* is paved with precocious postmodernists or "proto-pomos." But if we look more closely we will see the ambiguity of this description. For while the proposals and positions in

---

49. *The Philosophy of Art*, pp. 76–77; *Sämmtliche Werke*, 5.448–49.
50. See ¶¶ 79–82 of the *Encyclopedia (Logic)*.

question may well presuppose, on essentially Kantian grounds, the fall of the logocentric foundations of Western culture (*das zugrunde Gehen des Grundes*), each is clearly and self-consciously the pursuit of the metaphysics of presence by other means. So the Hegelian return to the primacy and autonomy of theory is perhaps less radical than it might seem, since it is means rather than ends that are at issue. (This remains true whether the end is itself practical, as for Schiller and the Hegel of this period, or theoretical, as for Fichte and Schelling.) Neither the metaphysical foundations of political freedom, in the former case, nor the metaphysical foundations of speculative theory, in the latter case, can be found in speculative theory.

In the present context, however, the point to notice is that the early Hegel belongs, temporarily but unambiguously, among those post-Kantian Germans for whom the Concept is not our link to the Eternal.[51] Already in the Tubingen essay of 1793, *Religion ist eine*, he insists that religion is "not mere science of God ... not a merely historical or rational knowledge" but "a concern of the heart."[52] Sounding very much like Kierkegaard, he distinguishes subjective from objective religion, or religion from theology. He associates the latter with understanding, memory, evidences, and doctrines, but for the latter he abstracts "absolutely from all scientific or, more precisely, metaphysical knowledge of God" in order to focus on the heart. "Subjective religion is alive, it is effective in the inwardness of our being, and active in our outward behaviour."[53]

This explains why, when Harris speaks of the "prophetic enthusiasm" Hegel exhibits in the "System-Programme," when he subsumes all the projects of the eighteenth-century Hegel under the megaproject of *Volkserzieher*, and when he sums up these projects in terms of Hegel's longing for a "way back to intervention in the life of men," we meet a rather Marxian Hegel.[54] By that I mean we meet a thinker who is not yet a philosopher in the Hegelian sense, "committed to understanding the world, rather than to changing it."[55] The young Hegel was an intellectual

---

51. In spite of their essentially speculative, even onto-theological goals, I think this formulation fits Fichte and Schelling both (1) because of the role of intellectual intuition in their conception of philosophy and (2) because of the dependence of philosophy itself on either moral or aesthetic experience.

52. This passage is found in Harris, p. 482; *Werke*, 1.11.

53. Harris, pp. 484–86; *Werke*, 1.13–17. For an even more uncompromising assault on the primacy of the Concept, see "Eleusis," the poem Hegel sent to Hölderlin not long after he wrote the "System-Programme." English translation in Butler and Seiler, *Letters*, pp. 45–48; *Werke*, 1.230–33.

54. See Harris, p. 257, Prelude and Coda, and chap. 5, esp. p. 416, which identifies the chapter title about intervention as coming from a letter to Schelling in November 1800. For that passage in context, see Butler and Seiler, *Letters*, p. 64.

55. Harris, p. xxxii.

activist who most definitely wanted to change the world; and either he was too naïve or he lived too early to know, as we (who live after knowledge as well as after virtue) are privileged to know, that in seeking to change the world one must choose between Kierkegaard and Marx, that inwardness and community are mutually exclusive.

How do we get from this very "un-Hegelian" Hegel to the Hegel who will introduce the Owl of Minerva with these words, "One word about giving instruction as to what the world ought to be. Philosophy in any case always comes on the scene too late to give it"?[56] Harris tells us that Hegel's Jena turn to philosophy as understanding rather than changing the world resulted from the failure of his project of reform, from the fact that his ideal "did not avail against the stubbornness of actual life." And he insists that this is not a tragic defeat, since it opens the door to Hegelian philosophy as we have come to know and love it.[57]

I would like to conclude these reflections with three thoughts on this way of telling the story. First, I disagree radically with the claim that this is not a tragic defeat. That the machine state has prevailed over moral goodness and aesthetic beauty in the modern world, that community based on shared ideals has succumbed to social interactions construed as instrumental vis-à-vis the consumerist goals of possessive individuals—these facts signify, in my view, nothing less than the tragedy of modernity, a tragedy for which no speculative grandeur can compensate.[58]

Second, whether we speak of tragedy or not, I believe we are indebted to Harris for pointing out how deeply rooted in resignation is the Hegel we have come to know and love. Hegelianism is one of the many forms of stoicism that has shaped our world, from Spinoza to Sartre, or rather, from Descartes to Derrida. If we keep this in mind we will not glide over passages in which Hegel speaks of "reason as the rose in the cross of the present"[59] without hearing the anguish they express. Listen, for example, to the conclusion of his *Lectures on the Philosophy of Religion*, where the reconciliation of reason and religion is

merely a partial one without universality. Philosophy forms in this connection a sanctuary apart, and those who serve in it constitute an isolated order of priests, who must not mix with the world. . . . How the actual present-day world is to find its way out of this state of disruption, and what form it is to take, are questions

56. *Philosophy of Right*, trans. T. M. Knox (Oxford: Clarendon Press, 1942), p. 12. *Werke*, 7.27–28. See note 25 above.

57. Harris, p. xv.

58. The attempt to ground community on ideals that are both immoral and ugly is hardly any solution. I am thinking of National Socialism.

59. *Philosophy of Right*, p. 12. Note (re note 56 above) the close juxtaposition of this language with Hegel's repudiation of ought talk. *Werke*, 7.26.

which must be left to itself to settle, and to deal with them is not the immediate practical business and concern of philosophy.[60]

The Hegelian celebration of modernity has a coda attached to it that takes a lot of the wind out of its sails.

Finally, disillusionment and resignation are not by themselves sufficient to account for Hegel's turn to philosophy, in the Hegelian sense. Why not, for example, pursue the standpoint of "Eleusis," the poem he sent to Hölderlin shortly after the "System-Programme," and join his poetic friend on the path to a nonpolitical aestheticism?[61] An important part of the answer to this question, I believe, is that the Jena Hegel, culminating in the *Phenomenology*, is under the spell of a quest for certainty that is as Cartesian in substance as it is anti-Cartesian in method. Hegel comes to operate under an epistemological mandate that is conspicuous by its absence throughout his brief and private (unpublished) career as *Volkserzieher*. I shall not trace the emergence of the assumption we must know with certainty and that we must do so via clear and distinct ideas, that is, that we must have discursive, conceptual knowledge, not just intuition, even intellectual intuition. Nor shall I try to explain this change from the strange, "un-Hegel" of the eighteenth century to the Hegel we have come to know and love. I shall only note its coincidence with Hegel's despair over possibilities of changing the world and ask whether there is a link. Nietzsche writes that

the Dionysian man resembles Hamlet: both have once looked truly into the essence of things, they have *gained knowledge*, and nausea inhibits action; for their action could not change anything in the eternal nature of things; they feel it to be ridiculous or humiliating that they should be asked to set right a world that is out of joint. Knowledge kills action.[62]

My question is whether it might (also) be the other way around. Is it the (perceived) impossibility of meaningful action that gives rise to the demand for Knowledge? There is, of course, a third alternative, the path of sophistry and cynicism. But I was not asked to speak about the present age.

---

60. *Lectures on the Philosophy of Religion*, 3 vols., trans. E. B. Speirs and J. Burton Sanderson (New York: Humanities Press, 1962), 3.151; *Werke*, 17.343–44. For a slightly more succinct version, see *Lectures on the Philosophy of Religion*, 3 vols., ed. Peter C. Hodgson (Berkeley and Los Angeles: University of California Press, 1985), 3.162; *Vorlesungen über die Philosophy der Religion*, 3 vols., ed. Walter Jaeschke (Hamburg: Felix Meiner, 1984), 3.96–97.
61. See note 52 above.   62. *The Birth of Tragedy*, section 7.

13   Hegel on Absolute Knowing
MARTIN J. DE NYS

During the last half of the 1790s Hegel considered a problem and reflected on the work of a particular figure in connection with that problem. The problem he considered was that of the conditions under which religion, and specifically Christianity, might exercise an integrating role in public and personal life. The figure on whose work he reflected was Kant. Varying assessments of the merit of Hegel's considerations and reflections during this period are certainly possible. But within the larger compass of Hegel's philosophical endeavors they do not stand in isolation. They lead to a focus on the issue of the nature of self-consciousness, understood with reference to the Kantian distinction of spontaneity and receptivity, that receives treatment—and for Hegel resolution—in the 1807 *Phenomenology of Spirit* and in the doctrine of absolute knowing that completes that work.

In this paper, I want first to examine some of the considerations and reflections that Hegel develops in the later years of the 1790s and that lead to an issue that drives his philosophy forward. Then, I want to discuss some texts in the First *Critique* that locate that issue, and that for Hegel both represent Kant's greatest achievement and indicate the necessity of critical advance. Finally, I want to discuss the doctrine of absolute knowing in the 1807 *Phenomenology*, in the light of the issue that comes into focus in the 1790s and of Kant's position on that issue. This discussion will consider the critical appropriation of Kant that belongs to the doctrine of absolute knowing, and allude to the conception of metaphysical thinking that emerges specifically in Hegel's version of absolute idealism.

I

The presence of Kant in Hegel's understanding of religion in 1795 is unmistakable. In "The Positivity of the Christian Religion" he maintained that "the aim and essence of all true religion, our religion included, is human morality, and that all the more detailed doctrines of Christianity . . . have their worth and sanctity appraised according to their close or distant connection with that aim."[1] Morality, in turn, has as the condition of its possibility self-legislating reason, understood in Kantian terms; it belongs in its authentic form to those "who have felt themselves able to give themselves a moral law which arises from freedom."[2] In the reconstruction of the Sermon on the Mount that belongs to Hegel's 1795 essay "The Life of Jesus," Hegel's Jesus proclaims that " 'To act on a maxim that you can will as a universal law among all men, binding for you as well'—this is the fundamental law of all morality, the substance of all moral legislation and the sacred books of all people."[3] Earlier in the same reconstruction he announces, "You have been told to love your friends and country, although you may hate your enemies and foreigners. But I say, if you cannot love your enemies, at least respect the humanity in them."[4] Respect for humanity and for the moral law is the moral motive that reason itself brings about; it "can be aroused only in a subject in whom the law itself is the legislator, from whose consciousness this law proceeds."[5] Respect for the moral law surpasses and must "prevail over the inclinations [*Neigungen*] and even over the love of life itself," and over "every impulse[*jede Regung*]."[6] Morality requires avoidance of external wrongs and resistance of the propensity thereto, and surpasses gratification even of impulses that do not "violate the letter of the law."[7] Respect for the moral law also surpasses an understanding of moral precepts as "statutory commands," and of the conformity of persons to the moral law as a "slavish obedience to laws not laid down by themselves."[8] These understandings "make reason a purely receptive faculty, instead of a legislative one,"[9] and this contravenes the very condition of the possibility of morality. Indeed, "any precept is capable of becoming positive, since anything can be proclaimed in a forcible way with a suppression of freedom."[10] One achieves the moral standpoint by surpassing the givenness of merely sensible impulses and wholly positive precepts through practical and rational autonomy.

1. Hegel, "Positivity of the Christian Religion," in *Friedrich Hegel: Early Theological Writings*, trans. T. M. Knox and Richard Kroner (New York: Harper, 1961), p. 68; hereafter cited as *ETW. Hegels Theologische Jugendschriften*, ed. Herman Nohl (Tübingen: J.C.B. Mohr, 1907), p. 153; hereafter cited as Nohl.
2. *ETW,* p. 142; Nohl, p. 210.
3. Hegel, "The Life of Jesus," in *Hegel: Three Essays, 1793–1795*, ed. and trans. Peter Fuss and John Dobbins (Notre Dame, Ind.: University of Notre Dame Press, 1984), pp. 115–16, translation modified; hereafter cited as *Three Essays*. Nohl, p. 87.
4. *Three Essays*, p. 112; Nohl, p. 87.   5. *ETW,* p. 144; Nohl, p. 212.
6. *Three Essays*, pp. 128, 129; Nohl, pp. 99, 100.
7. *Three Essays*, p. 112; Nohl, p. 83.   8. *ETW,* pp. 68, 69; Nohl, p. 153.
9. *ETW,* p. 85; Nohl, p. 165.   10. *ETW,* pp. 171–72; Nohl, p. 143.

The foregoing remarks may easily suggest that Hegel's appropriation of Kant's moral philosophy, such as it was in 1795, at least, was thoroughgoing and uncritical. But this suggestion would be misleading. As will be seen, its correction is important for understanding the way in which Hegel comes to address Kant's theoretical philosophy as well.

In the reconstruction of the conversation with Nicodemus in "The Life of Jesus," Hegel's Jesus responds to the question about being born again by saying:

> "Man as man ... is not an altogether sensuous being; he is not by nature just confined to pleasure-seeking impulses ... as a rational being he has received as his inheritance a spark of the divine essence ... this autonomous and immutable power makes its presence known to you from within. But just how this power is linked with the rest, with our changeable human sensibility—this we do not know."[11]

A little later he adds, "Reason does not condemn the natural impulses, but governs and refines them, and whoever does not listen to it ... passes judgment on himself. ... Such a man shrinks away from reason's light, for it imposes morality as a matter of duty."[12] These statements distinguish sensible impulses and practical reason, assert the autonomy of reason, and stress the necessity that reason be ascendent over sensible impulses. They also express doubt as to the correct understanding of the relation between reason and sensibility, maintain that reason must transform sensible impulses by refining them, and assert that it is in the absence of that refinement that morality is a matter of duty alone.

Further, in the version of the Sermon on the Mount this essay presents, Hegel's Jesus says, "A sure sign of growth in moral perfection is the increase of brotherly love in you and your readiness to forgive ... if the light of the soul, the light of reason grows dim, how are our drives and inclinations supposed to obtain their proper bearing?"[13] Sensible drives and inclinations, which are to be distinguished from reason, can nonetheless assume a direction or bearing in the light of reason, and their assumption of this bearing is a moral necessity. Hegel clearly insists, in a passage in the "Positivity" essay, that charity (*Wohltätikeit*), a duty that morality demands, follows from the arousal of my sympathy (*mein Mitleiden*), given myself as a pathological being, endowed with sympathetic impulses (*mich as pathologisches Wesen* [*mit sympathetischen Neigungen begabtes*]).[14]

One finds, then, in Hegel's work in 1795, as Adrian Peperzak notes with reference to "The Life of Jesus,"[15] two positions about the relation

---

11. *Three Essays*, p. 108; Nohl, p. 79.
12. *Three Essays*, p. 108; Nohl, p. 80.
13. *Three Essays*, p. 114; Nohl, p. 85.
14. See *ETW*, p. 96; Nohl, p. 174.
15. See Adriaan T. B. Peperzak, *Le jeune Hegel et la vision morale du monde* (The Hague: Martinus Nijhoff, 1960), p. 71.

of moral reason to the inclinations of inner nature. Both assert the autonomy of practical reason. Both assert that practical reason resists inclinations toward actions that are contrary to or only in accord with the letter of the moral law. One opposes reason and sensible inclinations. The other maintains that reason can transform sensible inclinations by giving direction to them, and that the transformed exercise of sensible inclinations is a moral necessity.

Complexities also belong to Hegel's early position on the relation of self-legislating reason to moral precepts that occur as givens in public and cultural institutions. The moral standpoint that self-legislating reason defines excludes conformity to precepts whose status is determined wholly by external authority and that are "positive" in that sense. Moral autonomy excludes heteronomy and receptivity of that sort. However, the positivity of a belief or precept depends on whether it presents itself "as something given throughout or as something given qua free and freely received."[16] Moral autonomy does not exclude receptivity in relation to beliefs or precepts that are freely appropriable by a subject. Moreover, the state needs citizens who conform to the requirements of law and morality as well, but cannot, Hegel maintains, of itself or directly require that citizens be moral.[17] The state needs institutions that cultivate the moral standpoint in citizens, on the basis of the trust that those institutions inspire. Religious institutions, in what Hegel takes to be their authentic form, best accomplish this task.[18] Authentic religious institutions present beliefs and precepts, a faith, that one can receive and recognize as one's own,[19] and that dispose individuals toward moral requirements and ideals. Religious institutions ideally express the beliefs and precepts that they promulgate through imagery linked to the history and culture of a people, just because that imagery arouses trust and renders beliefs and precepts more readily appropriable by a people.[20]

Once again, in 1795, Hegel maintains two positions about the relation between self-legislating reason and precepts that occur as givens in the public and cultural domain. Both exclude conformity to precepts supported wholly by authority from the moral standpoint. The first sharply distinguishes between autonomy and receptivity, and fails to qualify receptivity. The second does qualify receptivity, includes it within the moral standpoint, and suggests that it is necessary for the cultivation of the moral standpoint.

The conception of morality, then, with which Hegel's early considerations of religion stand in essential connection, makes use of Kantian dis-

16. *ETW*, p. 174; Nohl, p. 145.
17. *ETW*, p. 98; Nohl, p. 175.
18. See ibid.
19. *ETW*, p. 121; Nohl, p. 194.
20. See *ETW*, pp. 145–51; Nohl, pp. 214–19.

tinctions, while maintaining that autonomous practical reason takes up into itself both inclinations given in inner nature and externally given precepts. Hegel tried to resolve the ambiguities ingredient in this position in "The Spirit of Christianity and Its Fate," an essay he began in 1798, and especially through the notion of "love" that belongs to that essay.

The consciousness to which love responds has as its basis the "most prodigious disbelief in nature" (*ungeheuerste Unglaube an die Natur*).[21] This consciousness conceives of divine reality as beyond and opposed to the world and as a master of the world. Divinity masters outer nature by imposing lawful limits on its elements. On humans, it imposes laws in the form of commandments, thus mastering inner nature. Humans participate in the mastery that the divine master of the world exercises through their dominion over other living creatures. Action that exercises this dominion and that conforms to divine commandments occurs in a situation in which humans stand opposed to their own inner nature and to external natural realities and external divine reality.

Love responds to this situation, and to the consciousness that defines it, as a dynamism of reconciliation. It is completed by authentic religious practice, which is "the most holy, the most beautiful of all things; it is our endeavor to unify the discords necessitated by our development and our attempt to exhibit the unification in the *ideal* as fully *existent*, as no longer opposed to reality, and to express and confirm it in a deed."[22] With respect to the relation of the human subject to inner nature, "The opposition of duty to inclination has found its unification in the modifications of love, i.e. [,] in the virtues."[23] With respect to the relation of the human subject to outer reality, natural and divine, love in its religious completion effects unification or reconciliation insofar as the imagination generates from natural elements an image of the divine that gives focus and stability to felt devotion.[24] In each case, love and its religious completion comprise a vital dynamism that both determines and is determined by inner inclinations and external realities. This dynamism neither masters the realities it determines, nor is it mastered by the realities that determine it. Rather, it unifies oppositions in a reconciliation to which the concepts of mastery and being mastered no longer apply.

These observations help one to see how, in the essay begun in 1798, Hegel tries to deal with the problem in the position held in his writings of 1795. In the 1795 essays, Hegel opposes reason to inner inclinations

---

21. *ETW*, p. 182; Nohl, p. 244.   22. *ETW*, p. 206; Nohl, p. 262.
23. *ETW*, p. 225; Nohl, p. 277. See also *ETW*, p. 214, and Nohl, p. 268, where Hegel is especially critical of Kant.
24. See *ETW*, pp. 251–52; Nohl, p. 300. See also *ETW*, p. 289; Nohl, p. 332.

and external precepts, and also qualifies that opposition. In "The Spirit of Christianity," Hegel expressly holds that "Opposition is the possibility of reunification."[25] The oppositions he focuses on there obtain for the subject of moral action, between duty and inclination, and between self-determining action and natural and divine reality, which threaten and command action. Love, especially in its religious embodiment, accomplishes the unification of the terms that belong to these oppositions, and thus reconciles these oppositions. This reconciliation occurs insofar as love is the ultimate ground of a situation in which it both determines and is determined by the realities of inner inclinations and external nature and divinity. That is, love reconciles oppositions between the terms on which it focuses insofar as it reconciles a fundamental opposition within itself.

One must note, as H. S. Harris does, that in 1798 Hegel did not assert the primacy of love over rational thought. Rather, "he believed, like Plato and Kant, in the natural authority of reason, and he believed, like Plato, that love is itself the most important manifestation of reason as a living force."[26] In bringing about the reconciliations that it effects, love exhibits the truth, the rational truth, of the terms it unifies and of their unifications. It does this, as already noted, by integrating the moments of determining and being determined, or, to use Kantian terms, the moments of spontaneity and receptivity, in a situation of which it is itself the dynamic ground. But to claim that a process that integrates these moments exhibits the rational truth of things presupposes that these moments can in principle be integrated. And it implies that that integration can be an achievement of reason as such.

In "The Spirit of Christianity," Hegel was critically unable to probe either this presupposition or this implication. While he maintained that love, as such and in its religious form, was a rational power, he also identified reason with reflective thinking that mirrors given realities and fixes distinctions and oppositions. He could not conceive of a process in which rational thought examines its presuppositions for the sake of surpassing them by justifying them, and for the sake of showing the necessity of the integrations whose achievements mark its own most radical possibilities. The concept of that process of examination, when Hegel does arrive at it, is the concept of the science that he calls "phenomenology." Phenomenology concludes in the standpoint he calls "absolute knowing," and, according to Hegel, "'Absolute knowledge,' the highest conception of all, develops out of the conception of 'love' and the self-

25. *ETW*, p. 232; Nohl, p. 282.
26. H. S. Harris, *Hegel's Development: Toward the Sunlight, 1770–1801* (Oxford: Clarendon Press, 1972), p. 326.

consciousness of 'life,' and hence as the reconciliation of thought (or 'reflection') with existence."[27] In arriving at the conception of absolute knowing that continues his critical advance beyond Kant's practical philosophy, Hegel gives further critical consideration to a most fundamental Kantian distinction, that between spontaneity and receptivity, as it occurs in Kant's theoretical philosophy. He does this by arguing for a conception of self-consciousness that both preserves and surpasses the understanding of self-consciousness maintained by Kant. It is important now to turn to texts in the First *Critique* that present Kant's understandings of the distinction between spontaneity and receptivity and of self-consciousness, as further background for a consideration of Hegel's doctrine of absolute knowing.

2.

In the "Transcendental Deduction" of the B edition of the First *Critique*, Kant maintains that

an *object* is that in the concept of which the manifold of a given intuition is *united*. Now all unification of representations demands a unity of consciousness in the synthesis of them. Consequently it is the unity of consciousness that alone constitutes the relation of representations to an object, and therefore their objective validity and the fact that they are modes of knowledge, and upon it therefore rests the very possibility of the understanding.[28]

These statements presuppose an analysis of the unity of apperception that appeals to a distinction between the receptivity of sensible intuition, and the spontaneity of the understanding through which combination (*Verbindung*) comes about.[29] Insofar as representations are given as a manifold, they can be given in sensible intuition, through which the subject is affected and to which nothing but receptivity belongs. Combination, however, cannot derive from the senses or belong as such to the pure forms of sensibility. It is "an act of spontaneity of the faculty of representation,"[30] an act of the understanding that is in general terms a "synthesis."

There belong to the concept of combination, moreover, the manifold and its synthesis, and also its unity as a synthetic unity. Insofar as combination involves this unity, the principle of combination is "the 'I think,'"

27. Ibid., p. 391.
28. Kant, *Critique of Pure Reason*, trans. Norman Kemp Smith (New York and Toronto: Macmillan and St. Martin's, 1929), p. 156 [B137]; hereafter cited as *Critique*. *Kritik der reinen Vernunft* (Frankfurt: Suhrkamp, 1968), p. 139.
29. See *Critique*, B129–30.   30. Ibid.

which must be able "to accompany all my representations."[31] The "I think" is the principle of unity in the manifold through an "act of spontaneity"[32] that cannot belong to sensibility. Apperception here is pure, as contrasted with empirical. It is original, because it is "that self-consciousness which, while generating the representation *'I think'* (a representation which must be capable of accompanying all other representations, and which in all consciousness is one and the same), cannot itself be accompanied by any further representation."[33] And its unity is a transcendental unity, a condition of a priori knowledge.

The "thoroughgoing identity" or unity that does belong to pure, original, transcendental apperception can belong to apperception "only insofar as I *conjoin* one representation with another, and am conscious of the synthesis of them."[34] Transcendental self-consciousness, as opposed to empirical self-consciousness, has to do with the identity of the subject. This identity is capable of being represented only insofar as it is possible to unite in one consciousness the manifold of representations that are given. This means that the unity of apperception is originally a synthetic unity. It is as a synthetic unity that apperception stands as the principle of combination in the manifold, insofar as combination here involves synthesis and unity as well.

The foregoing remarks do in part presuppose a sharp distinction between the receptivity of sensible intuition, in which a manifold is given, and the spontaneity of the understanding, that accounts for unity through that "upon which all the rest of its employment is based,"[35] the synthetic unity of apperception. They are consistent with an insistence on there being "different sources of our knowledge,"[36] and with the position that the understanding is a faculty that "by itself knows nothing whatever, but merely combines and arranges the material of knowledge, that is, the intuitions, which must be given to it by its object."[37] But the foregoing arguments also surpass and in their own way problematize a sharp distinction between receptivity and spontaneity.

To begin with, one may note, with de Vleeschauwer, that Kant differentiates between apperception and its unity.[38] Synthetic unity must belong to apperception as the principle of unity in the manifold. At the same time, Kant needs to give an account of the synthetic unity of apper-

31. *Critique*, B131.
32. *Critique*, B132.
33. Ibid.
34. *Critique*, B133.
35. *Critique*, B137.
36. *Critique*, A260/B316.
37. *Critique*, B144.
38. H. J. de Vleeschauwer, *La déduction transcendentale dans l'oeuvre de Kant*, 3 vols. (Paris: Librairie Ernest Leroux, 1937), 3.103. See *Critique*, B133.

ception. According to that account, it is the possibility of uniting the manifold of given representations in one consciousness that allows one to represent the unity of the "I think" as a synthetic unity. This means that the unity that must belong to apperception does belong to apperception only in virtue of that of which it is the principle, that is, unity in the manifold.[39] It is hard to avoid concluding that apperception, to which spontaneity belongs, is nonetheless affected with regard to its unity by that whose principle of unity it is. One could maintain that, according to Kant's position, "The subject therefore synthesizes itself in the act of synthesizing the object,"[40] or of bringing about unity in the manifold. But even on these terms apperception brings about unity in the manifold as the ground of its own synthetic unity. Apperception both accounts for unity in the manifold of representations, and receives from the unity whose account it is its own unity. What seems to be a sharp distinction between spontaneity and receptivity is nuanced in that the "I think" is arguably receptive in terms of its own unity.[41]

The distinction between spontaneity and receptivity is further nuanced by remarks about the manifold and its combination. Kant begins the B Deduction, one may recall, by maintaining that one accounts for a manifold of representations through reference to sensibility, and for synthesis and unity only through the understanding, and ultimately through the "I think." Synthesis and unity "can never come to us through the senses, and cannot, therefore, be already contained in the pure forms of sensible intuition."[42] But Kant also maintains that "only insofar as I can grasp the manifold of the representations in one con-

---

39. *Critique*, B135. Kant concludes his first discussion of the synthetic unity of apperception in the B Deduction by saying that "This amounts to saying, that I am conscious to myself *a priori* of *a necessary synthesis of representations — to be entitled the original synthetic unity of apperception*—under which all representations that are given to me must stand, but under which they first also have to be brought by means of synthesis" (my emphasis).

40. Robert Stern, *Hegel, Kant, and the Structure of the Object* (London and New York: Routledge, 1990), p. 29.

41. See H. J. Paton, *Kant's Metaphysic of Experience*, 2 vols. (London and New York: Allen & Unwin and Humanities Press, 1936), 1.512, 513, 515. Paton says that

> The unity of apperception is itself impossible apart from the synthesis of the given manifold, and consciousness of this synthesis. As always in Kant, the unity of apperception and the unity of the manifold mutually condition one another, if indeed they are not to be regarded as identical with one another.... It is only because I can combine the manifold of ideas in *one* consciousness that I can represent to myself the identity of consciousness in these ideas.... The conclusion of the whole matter is that the synthetic unity of apperception is the ground of the necessary synthetic unity of the manifold, and *vice versa*.

But Paton does not see in these remarks a problem regarding the distinction between spontaneity and receptivity.

42. *Critique*, B130.

sciousness do I call them *mine*."⁴³ In other words, the manifold of given representations is intelligible only if subsumed in its givenness under the principle that accounts for combination. Or, the manifold of representations necessarily involves combination as well as multiplicity, not as given, but in its givenness.

The complexity that this statement indicates deepens if one examines, even briefly, the doctrine of the transcendental synthesis of the imagination in the B Deduction. Kant distinguishes the synthesis that the categories represent in themselves and in abstraction from specifically human sensibility, from the capacity of the understanding "to detemine inner sense through the manifold of given representations in accordance with the synthetic unity of apperception."⁴⁴ The latter synthesis is entitled "the transcendental synthesis of the imagination," in that it has to do with sensibility but involves the spontaneity of the understanding in its first action on sensibility.⁴⁵ According to Kant, "Inner sense . . . contains the mere form of intuition, but without combination of the manifold in it . . . which is possible only through consciousness of the determination of the manifold by the transcendental imagination."⁴⁶ He later notes, however, that "space and time are represented *a priori* not merely as *forms* of sensible intuition, but themselves as intuitions which contain a manifold [of their own], and therefore are represented with the determination of the *unity* of the manifold. . . . [T]his *unity of the synthesis* of the manifold, without or within us, and consequently also a combination to which everything that is represented as determined in space and time must conform, is given *a priori* . . .—not indeed in, but with these intuitions [*schon mit (nicht in) diesen Anschauungen*]."⁴⁷ This is to say not only that the manifold of representations involves synthesis and unity in its givenness, even if not as given, but also and primordially that the forms of sensibility involve a manifold and the combination of that manifold in their givenness, even if not as given, to which combination "everything that is represented as determined in space and time must conform." On these terms it is not quite fair to say that combination is given *with* but not *in* intuition. What is given *in* intuition is the synthesis and unity of the manifold of representations, even if synthesis and unity are attributable not to the givenness of the given, but to its subordination to the activity of the understanding, and ultimately to apperception.

Kant believes that he demonstrates the cooperation between understanding and sensible intuition that is necessary for any possible experi-

---

43. *Critique*, B134.
44. *Critique*, B150.
45. See *Critique*, B151–52.
46. *Critique*, B154.
47. *Critique*, B160–61.

ence, that is, knowledge of objects. But he does this through arguments that attribute a certain receptivity to apperception, in that synthetic unity belongs to apperception in virtue of the unity of the manifold that has apperception as its principle; and that attribute combination to the manifold of representations in its givenness, while holding that intuition accounts only for the manifold as such. As Robert Pippin notes, Kant argues that

> if all unification rules were derived from experience, there could not be a unity of apperception. He also wants to prove that such conditions determine the possibility of an intuited manifold.... To the later idealists, that must have looked like a serious blurring of the distinction between concept and intuition.... He appears to be trying to argue that objects "in their very givenness" conform to the categories. But if he is successful in doing this, then he has shown that what counts as given in experience is also determined by conceptual conditions, by the spontaneity of the subject. And this would render problematic the whole distinction between spontaneity and receptivity.[48]

An implication of the "problematic" aspect of the distinction between spontaneity and receptivity that Pippin notes, one that will be important for Hegel, appears in comments in the A Deduction about the transcendental object. There, Kant observes that an object that corresponds to and is thus distinct from our knowledge "must be thought of only as something in general = x, since outside of our knowledge we have nothing which we could set over against this knowledge as corresponding to it."[49] But further, the object is that which requires that our bits of knowledge agree among themselves, or "possess the unity which constitutes the concept of an object."[50] Kant insists that this "unity which the object makes necessary can be nothing else than the formal unity of consciousness in the synthesis of the manifold of representations."[51] He goes on to identify and also to distinguish the necessary identity of self-consciousness and the unity of a synthesis of appearances that makes them reproducible and that determines an object for their intuition.[52]

Insofar as appearances are only representations, their object cannot occur in intuition and can only be called a nonempirical, transcendental something in general. But insofar as our empirical concepts have "objective reality," this is because of "The pure concept of this transcendental object," which refers just "to that unity which must be met with in any manifold of knowledge which stands in relation to an object" (*die in*

---

48. Robert Pippin, *Hegel's Idealism: The Satisfactions of Self-Consciousness* (Cambridge: Cambridge University Press, 1989), pp. 29–30.
49. *Critique*, A104.
50. *Critique*, A104–5.
51. *Critique*, A105.
52. See *Critique*, A108.

einem Manigfaltigen der Erkenntnis angetroffen muss, so fern es in Beziehung auf einem Gegenstand stet).[53] Now this implies that, while access to an object that corresponds to by being simply distinct from our knowledge is denied, a distinction between the object known and our knowledge of the object nonetheless falls within knowing itself. The object, determined as such by unity, is something to which the manifold of knowledge "stands in relation" and which it meets. The unity of the manifold of representations that determines the same with respect to objectivity both belongs to that manifold and distinguishes itself from it when representations count as modes of knowledge. The conditions of the unity of apperception are the conditions of the unity that determines the object, and these are nonetheless distinguishable unities.

Kant's arguments about apperception or self-consciousness, then, both support and surpass a sharp distinction between spontaneity and receptivity. And, while denying in one sense access to a distinct object that corresponds to our knowledge, they also locate a distinction between our knowledge and an object corresponding to our knowledge within knowledge itself. According to Hegel, Kant's doctrine of self-consciousness "goes beyond the mere *representation* of the relation in which the *I* stands to the *understanding*, or concepts stand to a thing and its properties and accidents," and advances to "the *thought* of that relation."[54] This achievement, which one should note establishes the thought of two relations, makes possible recognition that "the *comprehension* of an object consists in nothing else than that the ego makes it *its own*, pervades it and brings it into *its own form*, that is, into the *universality* that is immediately a *determinateness*, or a determinateness that is immediately a universality."[55] Given this recognition, apperception grounds a synthesis "in which a duality in unity could be cognized, a cognition, therefore, of what is required for truth."[56] The argument that establishes that duality in unity belongs to the *Phenomenology of Spirit*. It proceeds by examining forms of the distinction between the object of our knowledge and knowledge of the same that fall within knowing, and concludes, in the doctrine of absolute knowing, with a conception of self-consciousness that surpasses the sharp distinction between spontaneity and receptivity by interrelating them and at the same time maintaining that they are distinct.

---

53. *Critique*, A109.
54. G.W.F. Hegel, *Science of Logic*, trans. A. V. Miller (London and New York: Allen & Unwin and Humanities Press, 1969), p. 584, translation modified; hereafter cited as *Logic*. *Wissenschaft der Logik*, ed. Moldenhauer u. Michel (Frankfurt: Suhrkamp, 1969), p. 254; hereafter cited as *Logik*.
55. *Logic*, pp. 584–85; *Logik*, p. 255.   56. *Logic*, p. 594; *Logik*, p. 267.

3.

The discussion of absolute knowing that concludes the *Phenomenology of Spirit* is complex, by itself and because one must consider it in relation to the work as a whole. The science that Hegel calls "phenomenology" is precisely defined with regard to its task and subject matter. The task is not only to present "natural consciousness" or the prephilosophical individual with a conception of the standpoint of philosophical knowing or science, that is, absolute knowing, but to "provide him with a ladder to this standpoint" and to "show him this standpoint within himself."[57] The subject matter is the epistemic relationship of certainty and truth. Phenomenology examines claims to certain knowledge of the truth by examining different figures or shapes of the experience of consciousness in which such claims are ingredient. It observes these diverse shapes of the experience of consciousness as they follow upon one another with immanent necessity, and it deserves to be called "science" because it detects this necessity and thus is self-determining in the development of its observations.[58]

The mode of cognition that Hegelian phenomenology claims to demonstrate in its conclusion receives at least three interrelated characterizations. It involves a "reconciliation of consciousness with self-consciousness."[59] It exhibits a warranted coincidence of certainty and truth.[60] And it involves the "transformation ... of Substance into Subject," the appropriation of what Hegel calls "substance" by self-consciousness knowing.[61]

It will be essential for our purposes to center discussion on the first of these characterizations. Genuinely philosophical or absolute knowing, defined by a reconciliation of consciousness and self-consciousness, follows from a "surmounting [*Überwindung*] of the object of consciousness."[62] This, Hegel insists, does not only entail that the object surpasses externality in its relation to the activities of self-consciousness. It also entails that the activities in question comprise "the externalization of self-consciousness that posits the thinghood [of the object]."[63] This in

---

57. G.W.F. Hegel, *Phenomenology of Spirit*, trans. A. V. Miller (Oxford: Clarendon Press, 1977), pp. 14, 15; hereafter cited as *Phenomenology*. Hegel, *Phänomenologie des Geistes*, ed. Moldenhauer u. Michel (Frankfurt: Suhrkamp, 1970), p. 29; hereafter cited as *Phänomenologie*.
58. *Phenomenology*, p. 56; *Phänomenologie*, p. 80.
59. *Phenomenology*, p. 482; *Phänomenologie*, p. 579.
60. *Phenomenology*, p. 485; *Phänomenologie*, pp. 582–83.
61. *Phenomenology*, p. 488; *Phänomenologie*, p. 584.
62. *Phenomenology*, p. 479; *Phänomenologie*, p. 575.
63. Ibid.

turn has two meanings. It means that the object belongs to the unity of self-consciousness with itself. And it means that the unity of self-consciousness with itself preserves and does not annul objectivity, "so that self-consciousness is in communion with itself in *its* otherness as such."[64]

In making sense of these comments, it is important to recognize the way in which absolute knowing emerges from the experience of consciousness. Absolute knowing comes about at the conclusion of phenomenology through a recollection (*Erinnerung*)[65] of the diverse forms of the experience of consciousness that have presented themselves in that science. This recollection involves a gathering together (*Versammlung*)[66] of achievements that belong to shapes of the experience of consciousness.

Shapes of the experience of consciousness are structures defined by conceptions of the object of consciousness, consciousness itself, and the relation between them. Within these structures, there falls a distinction between two interrelated terms: "the moment of knowledge," and that which is known and which "is also outside of this relationship [i.e., the knowledge relationship] or exists *in itself:* the moment of truth."[67] Within shapes of the experience of consciousness, that is to say, there falls a distinction that repeats the distinction between our knowledge and the object corresponding to our knowledge, already mentioned in connection with Kant's doctrine of the transcendental object. Phenomenology investigates conscious knowing; in Hegel's terms, "'being-for-another' and 'being-in-itself' both fall *within* the knowledge we are investigating."[68] That which presents itself in conscious knowing as something in-itself, something corresponding to our knowledge, has four characteristics. It is a determinacy. It is something given. It is a unity that integrates a multiplicity of differences. And it is "the standard which consciousness itself sets up by which to measure what it knows."[69] A shape of the experience of consciousness is a determinate structure in which consciousness takes a given determinacy and sets it up as a standard for assessing the legitimacy of knowledge claims.

As shapes of the experience of consciousness succeed each other with immanent necessity, there appear within the experience of consciousness fundamental determinations of what is supposed to count as being-in-itself for consciousness, on account of revisions of the definition of the given, unified, and integrating determinacy that consciousness sets

64. Ibid.
66. *Phänomenologie*, p. 582.
67. *Phenomenology*, p. 53; *Phänomenologie*, p. 77.
68. Ibid.

65. *Phänomenologie*, pp. 590–91.

69. Ibid.

up as its standard. These determinations are, in Hegel's terminology, immediate being, or individuality; being-for-another, or determinateness; and essence, or the universal. They appear in shapes of the experience of consciousness because of transformations that the object undergoes within those shapes, and because of the activities of consciousness within those shapes. Thus, in the first three chapters of the *Phenomenology*, the object shows itself to be an immediate individual thing that nonetheless exhibits its determinateness to another—in this case, to perception—and that finally discloses its intelligibility in universal terms to the understanding.[70] In later phenomenological developments that consider reason and spirit, consciousness defines itself in terms of or in relation to an immediate thing through scientific observation; defines things in terms of their utility for itself as cultivated consciousness; and finally defines its own universal, moral knowledge as radically essential for the intelligibility of the world.[71]

Recollection retrieves these determinations from determinate shapes of the experience of consciousness, gathers them together, and exhibits their unity. It is also the case, however, that the unity of these determinations itself appears in a determinate way in the science of the experience of consciousness. Indeed, this unity appears in phenomenology in a determinate way twice: in the discussion of the community of conscientious selves that concludes the phenomenological consideration of morality, and in the consideration of revealed religion.[72]

This is not the occasion to consider in any detail the arguments that belong to these divisions of Hegel's phenomenology.[73] Suffice it to say that the contexts of experience that belong to the conscientious community and revealed religion exhibit, each in a different way, the unification of individuality, being-for-another, and essential universality. Recollection integrates these determinate unifications of these determinations. This integration shows that awareness of the world refers consciousness back to its own activities as the source of the intelligibility of the world, and that awareness of its own activity focuses consciousness on the world and on the ultimate dimension of the world whose intelligibility it discloses. Consciousness relates itself to the many different and interrelated domains of the world, and relates that world to itself, so as to think through and grasp the intelligibility of reality or the world through its

70. *Phenomenology*, p. 480; *Phänomenologie*, p. 576.
71. *Phenomenology*, pp. 480–82; *Phänomenologie*, pp. 576–78.
72. See *Phenomenology*, p. 483; *Phänomenologie*, p. 580.
73. I have briefly discussed these arguments, with reference to the issue now in view, in "The Substance of Knowing Is History: Absolute Knowing and History in Hegel's *Phenomenology*," in *Reason in History: Proceedings of the American Catholic Philosophical Association* 68 (1994): 135–44.

own activities. This defines the reconciliation of consciousness with self-consciousness, and exhibits thinking as an activity that attains a warranted coincidence of certitude with truth in its comprehension of the rational structure of reality.

At just this point one must recognize why absolute knowing, characterized by the reconciliation of consciousness with self-consciousness, is not another shape or figure of the experience of consciousness. Figures of consciousness are determinate structures that presuppose given determinacies that define being-in-itself. Recollection, in retrieving determinations from those structures and unifying them, also releases those determinations from those structures. Recollection absolves this conception of knowing from any dependence on determinate structures of consciousness, and from any specific determinacy that serves as a standard for the legitimacy of knowledge claims. It demonstrates that knowing is an autonomous dynamic that grasps realities of any determinate character and cognizes their essential intelligibility. This occurs as self-consciousness thinks through the differences belonging to determinate realities so as to realize the identities that integrate and preserve those differences.

The image of absolving with reference to absolute knowing is borrowed from Heidegger. He correctly says that

> the term *absolute* means initially "not relative." . . . For knowledge to be qualitatively other than relative knowledge . . . it must not remain bound but must liberate and absolve itself from what it knows and yet as so absolved, as absolute, still be a knowledge. To be absolved from what is known does not mean "abandoning" it, but "preserving it by elevating it."[74]

He later adds, "What is known absolutely can only be that which knowledge knowingly lets emerge and which, only as emerging thus, stands in knowledge; it is not an object, but an emergence."[75] Without the philosophical standpoint cognition involves, in Hegel's own words, "a disclosure or revelation [*Offenbarkeit*] which is in fact concealment [*Verborgenheit*],"[76] since in presupposing some given determinacy as a standard consciousness conceals from itself both the autonomy of knowing and the range of intelligibilities grasped through autonomous knowing. Absolute knowing discloses thought as the power of disclosure, the power that allows what is known to emerge or present itself in and through the activity of knowing.

---

74. Martin Heidegger, *Hegel's Phenomenology of Spirit*, trans. Parvis Emad and Kenneth Maly (Bloomington: Indiana University Press, 1980), pp. 14, 15.
75. Ibid., p. 110.
76. *Phenomenology*, p. 487; *Phänomenologie*, p. 584.

This surpassing of dependence upon the givenness of what presents itself through any specific determinacy as being-in-itself does not annul determinacy as such, or the distinction between what is known and our knowledge of the same, or the distinction between that which is in-itself and that which is for knowledge. It rather entails that thought "knowingly lets emerge" that which is in-itself, and gives itself in its determinacy and is known. The spontaneity of thinking, to use Kant's term, takes up into itself or receives that which is in-itself by allowing the intelligibility of the same to emerge in and through its own activities. Self-consciousness is, in its self-relatedness, the ground of the intelligibility of its other.

Hegel extends these remarks by maintaining that the absolute standpoint exhibits knowing as the power "which empties itself of itself and sinks into its substance, and also, as Subject, has gone out of that substance into itself, making that substance into an object and a content at the same time as it annuls the difference between objectivity and content."[77] "Substance," in this setting, names the circumambient context of natural realities and of social practices, institutions, and norms that situates the lives of individual and interrelated selves, and that is given in historical experience and in the phenomenologically disciplined experience of consciousness. Thought may, in a warranted manner, comprehend the intelligibility of the world that situates consciousness and discloses itself in thinking. At the same time, the world that knowing comprehends is a "substance" into which thinking "empties" itself. It immerses itself in, "sinks into," considerations of actualities as they present themselves in interpreted experience, in order to grasp their intelligibility through its own self-determined considerations. In accomplishing these considerations, the "I" does not "cling to itself in the form of self-consciousness, as if it were afraid of the externalization of itself."[78] It is rather the case that self-consciousness establishes its identity just through that "externalization" whereby it reenacts the intelligibility of the world: "the 'I' is not merely the self, but the *identity of the self with itself;* but this identity is complete or immediate oneness with Self, or this *Subject* is just as much *Substance.*"[79] Self-consciousness establishes the "identity of the Self with itself" insofar as it relates itself to its other and overcomes the externality of its own other, its own substance, by determining its intelligibility through its own activities. The identity that belongs to self-consciousness comes about as a relation to itself achieved through its relation to its other.

77. *Phenomenology,* p. 490; *Phänomenologie,* pp. 587–88.
78. *Phenomenology,* p. 490; *Phänomenologie,* p. 588.
79. *Phenomenology,* p. 489; *Phänomenologie,* p. 587.

These comments attempt, in part, to show the unity that belongs to the three characterizations of absolute knowing previously mentioned. Hegel maintains that the standpoint of absolute knowing to which phenomenology concludes, and the conception of self-consciousness ingredient in that standpoint, represents a critical advance beyond Kant. At the same time, Hegel's notions of absolute knowing and self-consciousness, at least as described in these pages, are surprisingly Kantian. Hegel claims to show that the identity of self-consciousness is the ultimate ground of the intelligibility of that which occurs in experience and is known. He maintains that self-consciousness achieves its identity through relating itself to that which is known. He maintains that a distinction between what corresponds to our knowledge and our knowledge of the same falls within the stages of consciousness that phenomenology organizes, and in another but no less genuine way falls within the knowing that he entitles absolute. He maintains that what corresponds to our knowledge presents itself as a unity that integrates differences, and that knowledge involves referring those differences to the unity that integrates and preserves them, and that is established through their integration and preservation.

What Hegel does claim to surpass in the critical philosophy is Kant's treatment of the distinction between spontaneity and receptivity, and Kant's treatment of the distinction between the object to which knowledge refers and the object considered apart from its subsumption under the conditions of knowledge, as terminal and irreconcilable distinctions. As suggested above, arguments in which Kant makes use of and in that sense preserves the first of these distinctions also surpass it. Hegel claims to show, given the cognitive standpoint that he calls "absolute," that the activities of self-consciousness are of course not simply receptive, but neither are they simply spontaneous. The activities of self-consciousness involve a spontaneous receptivity; they are activities that belong to self-consciousness and through which self-consciousness allows that which presents itself to exhibit itself in its own intelligibility. By showing this, Hegel claims to show that the reality of that which presents itself in self-consciousness corresponds to the intelligibility that it exhibits in and through the activities of self-consciousness. Things exhibit the intelligibility that belongs to them in themselves insofar as they are subsumed under the ultimate principle of knowledge and intelligibility, the identity of self-consciousness. This position retains the distinction between our knowledge and that which corresponds to our knowledge, and entails that the concept of things considered in abstraction from their subsumption under the conditions of knowledge is an empty concept.

By surpassing the critical philosophy in these ways, Hegel resolves the problems that confronted him and that he could not resolve in the 1790s. By concluding through phenomenology to the standpoint of absolute knowing, Hegel claims to show the legitimacy of a conception of self-consciousness as the ultimate ground of a process in which its activities both determine and are determined by things that are known. The integration of spontaneity and receptivity in this process of which self-consciousness is the ultimate ground is just that which allows it to be a process that determines and discloses the rational truth of things. The determination and the disclosure of the rational truth of things occurs insofar as the activities of self-consciousness show that and how differences and oppositions reconcile themselves in unities that integrate and preserve them. The conception of absolute knowing that belongs to Hegel's 1807 *Phenomenology* radicalizes in rational form and is the successor to the notions of love, love's religious fulfillment, and love's imaginative embodiment that belong to his earlier work.

At the same time, the conception of absolute knowing that Hegel claims to demonstrate in 1807, through phenomenology and through a critical appropriation of Kant, is not only a reformulation of notions and a resolution of problems that occupied him earlier. In demonstrating, as he at least believed, the legitimacy and the necessity of the standpoint of absolute knowing, Hegel claimed to demonstrate, as already noted, a proposition about the intelligible reality of things and a proposition about the essential power of self-conscious thinking. He claimed to show that the intelligible reality of things themselves exhibits itself in the disclosive activities of rational self-consciousness. And he claimed to show that the rational activities of self-consciousness are disclosive processes that allow the intelligible reality of things to appear just insofar as they are subsumed under them. If so, then a determination of the most essential and radical conditions or necessities of thinking understood as the power of disclosure entails a determination of the most essential and radical conditions or necessities ingredient in the reality of things. For Hegel, as for Kant, the most essential and radical conditions or necessities that determine thinking are categorial. Categories define modes of identifying, distinguishing, and interrelating. A systematic articulation of the categories that progressively define the activities of identifying, distinguishing, and interrelating that belong to thinking is at once a systematic articulation of categories that grasp the identities, distinctions, and interrelations that determine the reality of things.

The science that articulates these categories is, according to Hegel, of course, logic, and he asserts that "*Logic . . . coincides with Metaphysics, the science of things set and held in thoughts*—thoughts accredited able to express the essential reality of things."[80] But the warranted coincidence of logic and metaphysics that Hegel claims follows from and requires a demonstration of the two propositions about things and about thinking just mentioned. One could say, then, that Hegel could have entitled his 1807 work the *Prolegomena to Any Future Metaphysics*. Phenomenology is the Hegelian science that provides a demonstration of those propositions about things and about thinking in the conception of absolute knowing to which it concludes.

80. G.W.F. Hegel, *The Logic of Hegel*, trans. William Wallace (Oxford: Oxford University Press, 1904), p. 45. Hegel, *Enzyklopädie der philosophischen Wissenschaften*, 3 vols., ed. Moldenhauer u. Michel (Frankfurt: Suhrkamp, 1970), vol. 1, p. 24.

Appendix One: The Earliest System-Programme of German Idealism (1796 or 1797)
Translated by Daniel O. Dahlstrom

... *an Ethics*. Since the whole of metaphysics in the future falls under *morality* (of which Kant with his two practical postulates has given us merely one *example* and not by any means *exhausted*), this ethics will be nothing else but a complete system of all ideas or, what is the same, all practical postulates. The first idea is naturally the representation *of me myself* as an absolutely free entity. With this free, self-conscious entity, there emerges at the same time an entire *world*—out of nothing—the only true and thinkable *creation out of nothing*. Here I shall descend to the fields of physics; the question is this: How must a world be constituted for a moral entity? I would like to give wings again to our physics that plods so slowly and with such difficulty by experiments.

Then, if philosophy provides the ideas and experience the data, we can finally have in outline the physics that I expect from later ages. It does not appear that the current physics could satisfy a creative spirit such as ours is or should be.

From nature I come to the *work of human beings*. Assuming the idea of humanity, I want to show that there is no idea of the *state*, since the state is something *mechanical*, just as little as there is an idea of a *machine*. Only what is an object of *freedom*, is called an *"idea."* Hence, we must move beyond the state!—For every state must treat free human beings as cogs in a machine and it should not do that and, therefore, it must *cease*. You see for yourselves that here all the ideas of eternal peace and so forth are only ideas *subordinate* to a higher idea. At the same time I want to lay down here the principles for a *history of humanity* and to strip naked and expose the entire miserable human production of the state, constitution, government, legislation. Finally come the ideas of a moral world, divinity, immortality—overthrow of all superstition; pursuit, by means of reason itself, of the priesthood that nowadays puts on airs of being reasonable.—Absolute freedom of all spirits who bear the intellectual world within themselves and do not permit themselves to look for either God or immortality *outside themselves*.

Finally, the idea that unites everything, the idea of *beauty*, in the higher Platonic sense of the word. I am now convinced that the highest act of reason, the act in which it encompasses all ideas, is an aesthetic act and that *truth and goodness* are rendered sisters *only in beauty*. The philosopher must possess as much aesthetic power as the poet. Human beings without aesthetic sense are only philosophers of the letter. The philosophy of spirit is an aesthetic philosophy. One cannot be rich in spirit about anything, one cannot even reason about history in a spiritually rich way—without aesthetic sense. Here it should be apparent what is really missing in human beings who do not understand any ideas and confess honestly enough that everything is obscure to them as soon as matters move beyond indexes and tables of contents.

Poesy receives thereby a higher dignity; she becomes again in the end what she was at the beginning—*the teacher of mankind.* For there is no longer any philosophy, any history. The art of poetry alone will survive all other sciences and arts.

At the same time we often hear that the great masses must have a *sensuous religion.* Not only the great masses, even the philosopher is in need of it. Monotheism of reason and heart, polytheism of imagination and art, this is what we need.

Here I will speak first of an idea that, as far as I know, has not yet occurred to any human being. We must have a new mythology, but this mythology must be in the service of ideas. It must be a mythology of *reason.*

Until we render the ideas aesthetic, that is to say, mythological, they are of no interest to the *people* and, vice versa, until the mythology is rational, the philosopher has to be ashamed of it. Thus, in the end, enlightened and unenlightened must extend their hands to one another; the mythology must become philosophical and the people rational, while the philosophy must become mythological, in order to make philosophers sensuous. Everlasting unity will then prevail among us. Never more that contemptuous look, never more the people's blind quivering in the face of its wisemen and priests. Only then does the *equal* development of *all* powers await us, the powers of each individual separately as well as of all of them together. No power will be suppressed any more. Universal freedom and equality of all spirits will prevail!—A higher spirit, sent from heaven, has to found this new religion among us; it will be the last, greatest work of mankind.

Appendix Two: Chronology of a Selection of Some Central Works in the Historical Transition from Transcendental Philosophy to German Idealism: 1781–1807

1781	Kant, Immanuel. *Kritik der reinen Vernunft*. 1st ed.
1783	———. *Prolegomena zu einer jeden künftigen Metaphysik, die als Wissenschaft wird auftreten können.*
1784–1791	Herder, Johann Gottfried. *Ideen zur Philosophie der Geschichte der Menschheit.*
1785	Kant, Immanuel. *Grundlegung zur Metaphysik der Sitten.*
	Jacobi, Friedrich Heinrich. *Über die Lehre des Spinoza, in Briefen an Herrn Moses Mendelssohn.*
1786	Hamann, Johann Georg. *Entkleidung und Verklärung, ein fliegender Brief.*
1786/1787	Reinhold, Karl Leonhard. *Briefe über die Kantische Philosophie.*
1787	Herder, Johann Gottfried. *Gott, einige Gespräche.*
	Kant, Immanuel. *Kritik der reinen Vernunft.* 2d rev. ed.
	Jacobi, Friedrich Heinrich. *David Hume über den Glauben, oder Idealismus und Realismus.*
	Rehberg, August Wilhelm. *Über das Verhältnis der Metaphysik zu der Religion.*
1788	Kant, Immanuel. *Kritik der praktischen Vernunft.*
	Schiller, Friedrich. *Die Götter Griechenlands/Die Künstler.*
1789	Reinhold, Karl Leonhard. *Versuch einer neuen Theorie des menschlichen Vorstellungsvermögens.*
1790	Kant, Immanuel. *Kritik der Urteilskraft.*
	Maimon, Salomon. *Versuch über die Transzendentalphilosophie.*
1790/1792	Reinhold, Karl Leonhard. *Briefe über die Kantische Philosophie.* (reproduction of 1786/1787 entry)
1792	Fichte, Johann Gottlieb. *Versuch einer Kritik aller Offenbarung.*
	Hölderlin, Friedrich. *Hymnen an die Ideale der Menschheit.*
	Schulze, Gottlob Ernst. *Aenesidemus, oder über die Fundamente der von Herrn Prof. Reinhold in Jena gelieferten Elementar-Philosophie.*
1792/1794	Reinhold, Karl Leonhard. *Ausführliche Darstellung des negativen Dogmatismus oder des metaphysischen Skeptizismus.*
1793	Beck, Jakob Sigismund. *Erläuternder Auszug den Kritischen Schriften*

des Herrn Prof. Kant, auf Anraten desselben. Vol. 1, Erster Band, welcher die Kritik der spekulativen und praktischen Vernunft enthält.
Kant, Immanuel. *Die Religion innerhalb der Grenzen der bloßen Vernunft.*
Maimon, Salomon. *Streifereien im Gebiete der Philosophie.*
Schiller, Friedrich. *Über Anmut und Würde.*
Storr, Gottlob Christian. *Annotationes theologicae ad philosophicam Kantii de religione doctrinam.*

1793/1794   Fichte, Johann Gottlieb. *Eigne Meditationen über Elementarphilosophie.*
1793–1797   Herder, Johann Gottfried. *Briefe zur Beförderung der Humanität.*
1794   Beck, Jakob Sigismund. *Erläuternder Auszug den Kritischen Schriften des Herrn Prof. Kant, auf Anraten desselben. Vol. 2, Zweiter Band, welcher die Kritik der Urteilskraft und die metaphysischen Anfangsgründe der Naturwissenschaft enthält.*
Fichte, Johann Gottlieb. *Grundlage der gesamten Wissenschaftslehre.*
———. [Rezension:] *Aenesidemus, oder...*
———. *Über den Begriff der Wissenschaftslehre oder der sogenannten Philosophie, als Einleitungsschrift zu seinen Vorlesungen über diese Wissenschaft.*
Hölderlin, Friedrich. *Fragment von Hyperion.*
Maimon, Salomon. *Versuch einer neuen Logik oder Theorie des Denkens.*
Schelling, Friedrich Wilhelm Joseph von. *Über die Möglichkeit einer Form der Philosophie.*

1794/1795   Fichte, Johann Gottlieb. *Grundlage der gesamten Wissenschaftslehre, als Handschrift für seine Zuhörer.*

1795   Fichte, Johann Gottlieb. *Grundriß des Eigentümlichen der Wissenschaftslehre.*
Kant, Immanuel. *Zum ewigen Frieden.*
Reinhold, Karl Leonhard. *Versuch einer neuen Theorie des menschlichen Vorstellungsvermögens.* 2d ed.
Schelling, Friedrich Wilhelm Joseph von. *Vom Ich als dem Prinzip der Philosophie.*
Schiller, Friedrich. *Briefe über die ästhetische Erziehung des Menschen.*

1795/1796   Goethe, Johann Wolfgang. *Wilhelm Meisters Lehrjahre.*
1796   Beck, Jakob Sigismund. *Erläuternder Auszug den Kritischen Schriften des Herrn Prof. Kant, auf Anraten desselben. Vol. 3, Dritter Band, welcher den Standpunkt dartstellt aus welchem die Kritische Philosophie zu beurteilen ist: Einzig möglicher Standpunkt, aus welchem die Kritische Philosophie beurteilt werden muss.*
———. *Grundriß der Kritischen Philosophie.*
Hegel, Georg Wilhelm Friedrich [though Hegel's authorship is disputed by some]. *Das älteste Systemprogramm des deutschen Idealismus.*
Schelling, Friedrich Wilhelm Joseph von. *Philosophische Briefe über Dogmatismus und Kritizismus.*
Schiller, Friedrich. *Über naive und sentimentalische Dichtung.*

1796/1797   Fichte, Johann Gottlieb. *Die Grundlage des Naturrechts nach den Prinzipien der Wissenschaftslehre.*

1797	Fichte, Johann Gottlieb. *Erste Einleitung in die Wissenschaftslehre.*
	Maimon, Salomon. *Kritische Untersuchungen über den menschlichen Geist oder das höhere Erkenntniss- und Willensvermögen.*
	Bardili, Christoph Gottfried. *Briefe über den Ursprung der Metaphysik.*
	Kant, Immanuel. *Die Metaphysik der Sitten.*
	Schelling, Friedrich Wilhelm Joseph von. *Ideen zu einer Philosophie der Natur.*
1797/1798	Fichte, Johann Gottlieb. *Versuch einer neuen Darstellung der Wissenschaftslehre. Einleitung. Zweite Einleitung für Leser, die schon ein philosophisches System haben.*
1797–1799	Hölderlin, Friedrich. *Hyperion oder Der Eremit in Deutschland.*
	———. *Empedokles—Fragmente.*
1798	Fichte, Johann Gottlieb. *Das System der Sittenlehre nach den Principien der Wissenschaftslehre.*
	———. *Zweite Einleitung in die Wissenschaftslehre.*
	Kant, Immanuel. *Der Streit der Fakultäten.*
	———. *Die Anthropologie in pragmatischer Hinsicht.*
	Schelling, Friedrich Wilhelm Joseph von. *Von der Weltseele, eine Hypothese der höheren Physik.*
1799	Fichte, Johann Gottlieb. *Apellation an das Publikum.*
	Herder, Johann Gottfried. *Verstand und Erfahrung, Vernunft und Sprache, eine Metakritik zur Kritik der reinen Vernunft.*
	Novalis (von Hardenberg, Friedrich). *Die Christenheit oder Europa.*
	Schelling, Friedrich Wilhelm Joseph von. *Erster Entwurf eines Systems der Naturphilosophie.*
	Schlegel, August Wilhelm von. *Fragmente im "Athenäum."*
	Schleiermacher, Friedrich. *Reden über die Religion an die Gebildeten unter ihren Verächtern.*
1800	Bardili, Christoph Gottfried. *Grundriß der ersten Logik.*
	Fichte, Johann Gottlieb. *Der geschlossene Handelsstaat.*
	———. *Die Bestimmung des Menschen.*
	Herder, Johann Gottfried. *Kalligone.*
	Hamann, Johann Georg. *Golgatha und Schlebimini, Metakritik über den Purismum der reinen Vernunft.*
	Schelling, Friedrich Wilhelm Joseph von. *System des transzendentalen Idealismus.*
	Schleiermacher, Friedrich. *Monologen.*
1800–1802	Hegel, Georg Wilhelm Friedrich. *Die Verfassung Deutschlands.*
1801	Jacobi, Friederich Heinrich. *Über das Unternehmen des Kritizismus.*
	Schelling, Friedrich Wilhelm Joseph von. *Darstellung meines Systems der Philosophie.*
	———. *Über den wahren Begriff der Naturphilosophie.*
	Hegel, Georg Wilhelm Friedrich. *De Orbitis Planetarum.*
	———. *Differenz des Fichteschen und Schellingschen Systems der Philosophie.*
	Schulze, Gottlob Ernst. *Kritik der theoretischen Philosophie.*
1802	Hegel, Georg Wilhelm Friedrich. "Glauben und Wissen." *Kritisches Journal der Philosophie.*

———. "Über das Wesen in der philosophischer Kritik." (Introduction for) *Kritisches Journal der Philosophie.*
———. "Verhältnis des Skeptizismus zur Philosophie." *Kritisches Journal der Philosophie.*
———. "Wie der gemeine Menschenverstand die Philosophie nehme—dargestellt an den Werken des Herrn Krugs." *Kritisches Journal der Philosophie.*
Schelling, Friedrich Wilhelm Joseph von. *Bruno, oder über das göttliche und natürliche Prinzip der Dinge.*

1803   Hegel, Georg Wilhelm Friedrich. "Über die wissenschaftlichen Behandlungsarten des Naturrechts." *Kritisches Journal der Philosophie.*
Schleiermacher, Friedrich. *Kritik der bisherigen Sittenlehre.*
Fries, Jakob Friedrich. *Reinhold, Fichte und Schelling.*
Krause, Karl Christian Friedrich. *Grundlage des Naturrechts, oder philosophischer Grundriß des Ideals des Rechts.*
———. *Grundriß der historischen Logik.*

1804   Bardilis und Reinholds Briefwechsel.
Schelling, Friedrich Wilhelm Joseph von. *Philosophie und Religion.*
Krause, Karl Christian Friedrich. *Entwurf des Systems der Philosophie, I. Abteilung.*

1805   Fries, Jakob Friedrich. *Wissen, Glaube und Ahndung.*

1806   Fichte, Johann Gottlieb. *Anweisung zum seligen Leben.*
———. *Grundzüge des gegenwärtigen Zeitalters.*
Schelling, Friedrich Wilhelm Joseph von. *Verhältnis des Idealen und Realen in der Natur.*
Herbart, Johann Friedrich. *Hauptpunkte der Metaphysik* (vol. 1).

1807   Hegel, Georg Wilhelm Friedrich. *Phänomenologie des Geistes.*
Fries, Jakob Friedrich. *Neue Kritik der reinen Vernunft.*

Contributors

Karl Ameriks was born in Munich and studied at Yale (B.A., Ph.D.). He has had grants (Fulbright, ACLS, NEH, von Humboldt) to research German Idealism in Tübingen, Köln, Münster, Freiburg, Marburg, and Berlin. He is professor of philosophy at the University of Notre Dame. A former president of the North American Kant Society, he has authored *Kant's Theory of Mind* (Oxford), co-edited (with Dieter Sturma) *The Modern Subject: Conceptions of the Self in Classical German Philosophy* (SUNY), co-edited and co-translated *Lectures on Metaphysics/Immanuel Kant* (Cambridge), and co-translated Husserl's *Experience and Judgment* (Northwestern). He is editing a Cambridge Companion to German Idealism, serves as co-editor of the series *Cambridge Texts in the History of Philosophy*, and is completing a work on the reception of Kant's philosophy.

Hans Michael Baumgartner was born in Munich in 1933 and received his doctorate (1962) and his Habilitation (1971) from the University of Munich. He is currently Professor of Philosophy at the University of Bonn. A member of the Schelling Commission of the Bavarian Academy of Science, he is also the director of Görres-Gesellschaft Institute for Interdisciplinary Research and serves as the head of the Institute's philosophy department. From 1986 to 1992 he was president of the International Schelling Society. His publications include the following: *Die Unbedingtheit des Sittlichen. Eine Auseinandersetzung mit Nicolai Hartmann* (1962), *Kontinuität und Geschichte. Zur Kritik und Metakritik der historischen Vernunft* (1972), *Philosophie in Deutschland 1945–1975* (co–author) (1978), *Kants "Kritik der reinen Vernunft". Eine Anleitung zur Lektüre selbst* (1991). He has served as editor of the following publications: *Historisch-Kritische Schelling-Ausgabe* (1976 ff.), *J.G. Fichte-Bibliographie* (1968), *Handbuch Philosophischer Grundbegriffe* (1973–1974), *Zeitschrift für Philosophische Forschung* (1978–1988), *Philosophisches Jahrbuch* (1989 ff.).

Michael Baur, Assistant Professor of Philosophy at Fordham University, holds a Ph.D. in philosophy from the University of Toronto and a J. D. from Harvard Law School. He has been a Fulbright researcher at the

University of Heidelberg, Germany, and is currently at work on a translation of J. G. Fichte's *Foundations of Natural Right*. He is co-editor (with John Russon) of *Hegel and the Tradition: Essays in Honour of H. S. Harris* (University of Toronto Press), and author of several articles and book chapters on Kant, Fichte, Hegel, Heidegger, and Gadamer. He is also currently Secretary of the Hegel Society of America.

Daniel Breazeale was born in Houston, Texas in 1945, received his Ph.D. from Yale University in 1971, and is currently Chair and Professor of Philosophy at the University of Kentucky. He is co-founder of the North American Fichte Society and has published numerous articles on German philosophy from Kant to Nietzsche, with a focus upon J. G. Fichte and other early post-Kantians. Breazeale is also the editor and translator of three volumes of Fichte's writings, including *Fichte: Early Philosophical Writings* (Cornell, 1988), *Foundations of Transcendental Philosophy (Wissenschaftslehre) novo methodo* (Cornell, 1992), and *Introductions to the Wissenschaftslehre and Other Writings* (Hackett, 1994).

Daniel O. Dahlstrom, currently Professor of Philosophy at Boston University, is the author of numerous articles on the history of modern European philosophy, from the eighteenth through the twentieth century. His more recent publications include *Das Logische Vorurteil: Untersuchungen zur Wahrheitstheorie des frühen Heidegger* (1994), "Kant and Jacobi" in *Proceedings of the Eight International Kant Congress* (1995), "Ethik, Recht und Billigheit" in *Jahrbuch fur Recht und Ethik* (1997), and an entry on "Edmund Husserl" in *Encyclopedia of Aesthetics* (1998). He has also translated and edited Friedrich Schiller's *Essays* (1993) and Moses Mendelssohn's *Philosophical Writings* (1997).

Martin J. De Nys holds a Ph.D. in philosophy from Loyola University of Chicago. He is Associate Professor of Philosophy at George Mason University in Fairfax, VA. He specializes in nineteenth and twentieth century continental philosophy, with special focus on the philosophy of religion, political philosophy, and metaphysics.

Klaus Düsing was born in 1940 and studied at the universities of Zürich and Köln. He received his doctorate from Köln in 1967 and his Habilitation from the University of Bochum in 1975. He has been a professor at Bochum (1977), at Siegen (1980) and at the University of Köln (since 1983), where he is currently Chair of the Philosophy Department and Director of the Husserl Archives. His publications include the following: *Die Teleologie in Kants Weltbegriff* (1986), *Das Problem der Subjektivität in Hegels Logik* (1995), *Hegel und die Geschichte der Philosophie* (1983), *Schellings und Hegels erste absolute Metaphysik* (1988), and *Selbstbewusstseinsmodelle* (1997).

Karsten Harries was born in Jena, Germany and is a professor of philosophy at Yale University. He has published and lectured widely on Heidegger, early modern philosophy, and the philosophy of art and architecture. He is author of more than 130 articles and reviews and of four books: *The Meaning of Modern Art* (Evanston: Northwestern, 1968), *The Bavarian Rococo Church: Between Faith and Aestheticism* (New Haven: Yale, 1983), *The Broken Frame: Three Lectures* (Washington, D.C.: CUA Press, 1990), and *The Ethical Function of Architecture* (Cambridge, Mass.: MIT, 1997). With Christoph Jamme he has edited *Martin Heidegger: Kunst, Politik, Technik* (1992), which appeared in an English version as *Martin Heidegger: Politics, Art, and Technology* (1994).

John McCumber received his B.A. from Pomona College and his M.A. and Ph.D. (in Philosophy and Classics) from the University of Toronto. He has taught at the University of Toronto, the University of Michigan at Dearborn, the Graduate Faculty of the New School for Social Research, and Northwestern University, where he is currently a Professor of German. He is the author of three books and numerous articles on Hegel, Heidegger, contemporary continental philosophy, and the history of philosophy.

Kenneth L. Schmitz is professor emeritus at the University of Toronto and a Fellow of Trinity College, as well as the director of the S.T.D. Program at the John Paul II Institute, Washington, D.C. He is the author of *The Gift: Creation* and *At the Center of the Human Drama*. His most recent of many articles is "Gnostizismus im Denken der deutschen Aufklärung", in *Internationale Katholische Zeitschrift Communio*, no. 6 (November–December, 1997).

Xavier Tilliette was born in Corbie (France) on July 23, 1921 and entered the novitiate of the Society of Jesus at Laval on September 26, 1938. After completing his doctorate in 1970, he taught at the Catholic Institute of Paris (1969–1988) and at the Pontifical University Gregoriana in Rome (1972–1996). He has been guest-professor in Lima, Ponce (Puerto-Rico), Notre Dame (South Bend), Turin, Naples, Genova, Triest, among other institutions. His chief publications include: *Schelling, une Philosophie en Devenir* (2 vols. 1970), *Karl Jaspers* (1960), *Schelling im Spiegel seiner Zeitgenossen* (4 vols. 1974–1996), *Le Christ de la Philosophie*

(1990), *Le Christ des Philosophes* (1993), *L'intuition Intellectuelle de Kant à Hegel* (1995), and *Schelling, une Biographie* (1999).

Alexander von Schönborn was born in Prague in 1938. He received his doctorate from Tulane University in 1971 and has been on the faculties of Fordham University, the University of Texas at Austin and the University of Missouri-Columbia. He has been the recipient of numerous research grants from these institutions as well as from external agencies such as DAAD and Max-Planck. His research has centered on the history of German philosophy, notably Kant, Hegel and Heidegger. He began to work on K. L. Reinhold when he became aware not only how issues arising relative to the thought of the thinkers just mentioned come together in Reinhold's work, but also that he is an acute philosopher in his own right. Professor von Schönborn has published an annotated bibliography and several articles specifically on Reinhold and is currently translating a work of the latter concerning the foundations of Kantian ethics.

Merold Westphal is Distinguished Professor of Philosophy at Fordham University. He has served as President of the Hegel Society of America and the Søren Kierkegaard Society and as Executive Co-Director of the Society for Phenomenology and Existential Philosophy. He is the author of *History and Truth in Hegel's Phenomenology; Hegel, Freedom, and Modernity; Kierkegaard's Critique of Reason and Society; Becoming a Self: A Reading of Kierkegaard's Concluding Unscientific Postscript; God, Guilt, and Death: An Existential Phenomenology of Religion;* and *Suspicion and Faith: The Religious Uses of Modern Atheism.* Much of his current work concerns either Levinas or the religious significance of postmodern philosophy, especially in Heidegger and Derrida.

Bibliography

Allison, Henry. *Kant's Theory of Freedom*. Cambridge and New York: Cambridge University Press, 1990.
———. *Kant's Transcendental Idealism*. New Haven: Yale University Press, 1983.
Ameriks, Karl. "Kant and Guyer on Apperception." *Archiv für Geschichte der Philosophie* 65 (1983): 174–86.
———. "Kant and Hegel on Freedom: Two New Interpretations." *Inquiry* 35 (1992): 219–32.
———. "Kant, Fichte, and Short Arguments to Idealism." *Archiv für Geschichte der Philosophie* 72 (1990): 63–85.
Ameriks, Karl, and Dieter Sturma, eds. *The Modern Subject: Conceptions of the Self in Classical German Philosophy*. Albany: State University of New York Press, 1995.
Asveld, Paul. *La pensée religieuse du jeune Hegel*. Louvain: Publications universitaires de Louvain, 1953.
Baggesen, K., and A. Baggesen, eds. *Aus Jens Baggesen's Briefwechsel mit Karl Leonhard Reinhold und Friedrich Heinrich Jacobi*. Leipzig: F. A. Brockhaus, 1831.
Bardili, C. G. *Grundriß der Ersten Logik, gereiniget von den Irrthümern bisheriger Logiken überhaupt, der Kantischen insbesondere; Keine Kritik sondern eine Medicina mentis, brauchbar hauptsächlich für Deutschlands Kritische Philosophie*. Stuttgart: Franz Christian Löflund, 1800.
Baumgartner, Hans Michael, ed. *Schelling: Einführung in seine Philosophie*. Freiburg and Munich: Karl Alber, 1975.
Beck, Lewis White. *A Commentary on Kant's "Critique of Practical Reason."* Chicago: University of Chicago Press, 1960.
Beiser, Frederick. *The Fate of Reason: German Philosophy from Kant to Fichte*. Cambridge, Mass.: Harvard University Press, 1987.
Best, Otto F., and Hans-Jürgen Schmitt, eds. *Die deutsche Literatur: Ein Abriss in Text und Darstellung: Romantik I*. Stuttgart: Reclam, 1976.
Böhm, W. "Hölderlin als Verfasser des 'Ältesten Systemprogramms des deutschen Idealismus.'" *Deutsche Vierteljahrsschrift* 4 (1926): 339–426.
Bondeli, Martin. *Das Anfangsproblem bei Karl Leonhard Reinhold: Eine systematische und entwicklungsgeschichtliche Untersuchung zur Philosophie Reinholds in der Zeit von 1789 bis 1803*. Frankfurt am Main: Vittorio Klostermann, 1995.
Breazeale, Daniel. "Between Kant and Fichte: Karl Leonhard Reinhold's 'Elementary Philosophy.'" *Review of Metaphysics* 35 (1982): 785–821.
———. "Why Fichte Now?" *Journal of Philosophy* 88 (1991): 524–31.
Breazeale, Daniel, and Tom Rockmore, eds. *Fichte: Historical Contexts/Contemporary Controversies*. Atlantic Highlands, N.J.: Humanities Press, 1994.
Brehier, Emile. *The Nineteenth Century: Period of Systems 1800–1850*. Translated by Wade Baskin. Vol. 6 of *The History of Philosophy*. Chicago: University of Chicago Press, 1968.

Brenner, Anton. *Schellings Verhältnis zu Leibniz: Ein Beitrag zur Geschichte des Wiedererwachens der echten Leibnizschen Philosophie (nach der Herrschaft der Wolffschen Schule) und zur Entwicklung der Schellingschen Philosophie.* Augsburg: Schoder, 1937.
Bubner, Rüdiger, ed. *Das älteste Systemprogramm: Studien zur Frühgeschichte des deutschen Idealismus.* Hegel-Studien 9. Bonn: Bouvier, 1973.
Butler, Eliza Marian. *The Tyranny of Greece over Germany.* Boston: Beacon Press, 1958.
Cassirer, Ernst. *Das Erkenntnisproblem in der Philosophie und Wissenschaft der neueren Zeit.* Berlin: Bruno Cassirer, 1922.
———. *Idee und Gestalt.* Berlin: Bruno Cassirer, 1929.
Christensen, Darrell E., ed. *Hegel and the Philosophy of Religion.* The Hague: Martinus Nijhoff, 1970.
Claesges, Ulrich. *Geschichte des Selbstbewußtseins: Der Ursprung des spekulativen Problems in Fichtes Wissenschaftslehre von 1794–95.* The Hague: Martinus Nijhoff, 1974.
de Vleeschauwer, Herman-Jean. *La déduction transcendentale dans l'oevre de Kant.* Paris: Librairie Ernest Leroux, 1937; English edition, New York: Garland: 1976.
———. *The Development of Kantian Thought.* London: Thomas Nelson and Sons, 1962.
Desmond, William. *Art and the Absolute: A Study of Hegel's Aesthetics.* Albany: State University of New York Press, 1986.
di Giovanni, George, and H. S. Harris, eds. and trans. *Between Kant and Hegel: Texts in the Development of Post-Kantian Idealism.* Albany: State University of New York Press, 1985. Soon to be republished by Hackett Publishing Company.
Druet, Pierre-Phillippe. "'L'Anstoss' fichtéen: Essai d'élucidation d'une métaphor." *Revue philosophique de Louvain* 70 (1972): 384–92.
Düsing, Klaus. "Das problem des höchsten Gutes in Kants praktischer Philosophie." *Kant-Studien* 62 (1971): 5–42.
———. "Die Rezeption der Kantischen Postulatenlehre in den frühen philosophischen Entwürfen Schellings und Hegels." In *Das älteste Systemprogramm: Studien zur Frühgeschichte des deutschen Idealismus*, Hegel-Studien 9, edited by Rüdiger Bubner. Bonn: Bouvier, 1973.
———. *Die Teleologie in Kants Weltbegriff.* Second, expanded edition. Bonn: Bouvier, 1986.
———. "Hegels 'Phänomenologie' und die idealistische Geschichte des Selbstbewußtseins." *Hegel-Studien* 28(1993): 103–126.
Düsing, Wolfgang. *Friedrich Schiller. Über die ästhetischen Erziehung des Menschen in einer Reihe von Briefen: Text, Materialen, Kommentar.* Munich: C. Hanser, 1981.
Fichte, Johann Gottlieb. *Attempt at a Critique of All Revelation.* Translated by Garrett Green. Cambridge and New York: Cambridge University Press, 1978.
———. *Briefwechsel.* Edited by Hans Schulz. Hildesheim: G. Olms, 1967.
———. *Fichte: Early Philosophical Writings.* Translated by Daniel Breazeale. Ithaca, N.Y.: Cornell University Press, 1988.
———. *Fichte: Foundations of Transcendental Philosophy — Wissenschaftslehre (novo methodo).* Translated by Daniel Breazeale. Ithaca, N.Y.: Cornell University Press, 1992.
———. *Grundlage des Naturrechts nach Principien der Wissenschaftlehre.* Vol. 1.3–4, *J. G. Fichte — Gesammtausgabe der Bayrischen Akademie der Wissenschaften.* Edited

by Reinhard Lauth and Hans Gliwitzki. Stuttgart-Bad Cannstatt: Frommann-Holzboog, 1966.

———. *Introductions to the "Wissenschaftslehre" and Other Writings (1797–1800)*. Translated by Daniel Breazeale. Indianapolis, Ind.: Hackett, 1994.

———. *J. G. Fichte — Gesammtausgabe der Bayrischen Akademie der Wissenschaften*. Edited by Reinhard Lauth and Hans Gliwitzki. Stuttgart-Bad Cannstatt: Frommann-Holzboog, 1964– .

———. *Johann Gottlieb Fichtes sämmtliche Werke*. 8 vols. Edited by I. H. Fichte. Berlin: Veit, 1845–1846.

———. "On the Foundation of Our Belief in a Divine Government of the Universe." Translated by Paul Edwards. In *Nineteenth Century Philosophy*, edited by Patrick Gardiner. New York: Free Press, 1969.

———. *The Science of Knowledge (Wissenschaftslehre) with the First and Second Introductions*. Translated by Peter Heath and John Lachs. Cambridge: Cambridge University Press, 1982.

———. *Über den Begriff der Wissenschaftslehre oder der sogennanten Philosophie, als Einladungsschrift zu seinen Vorlesungen über diese Wissenschaft*. Weimar: Verlag des Industrie-Comptoirs, 1794.

———. *Wissenschaftslehre novo methodo*. Edited by Erich Fuchs. Hamburg: Felix Meiner, 1982.

Fischer, Kuno. *Geschichte der neuern Philosophie*. Heidelberg: Carl Winter, 1890.

Fischer, Michael W. *Die Aufklärung und ihr Gegenteil: Die Rolle der Geheimbünde in Wissenschaft und Politik*. Berlin: Dunker und Humblot, 1982.

Flatt, J. F. *Beiträge zur christlichen Dogmatik und Moral und zur Geschichte derselben*. Tübingen: Heerbrandt, 1792.

———. *Briefe über den moralischen Erkenntnisgrund der Religion überhaupt und besonders in Beziehung auf die Kantische Philosophie*. Tubingen, 1789.

Forster, Michael. *Hegel and Skepticism*. Cambridge, Mass.: Harvard University Press, 1989.

Frank, Manfred. *Die Unhintergehbarkeit von Individualität*. Frankfurt am Main: Suhrkamp, 1986.

———. "Intellektuelle Anschauung." In *Die Aktualität der Frühromantik*, edited by E. Behler and J. Hörisch. Paderborn: Schöningh, 1987.

———. *Selbstbewußtsein und Selbsterkenntnis*. Stuttgart: Reclam, 1991.

———. *Selbstbewußtseinstheorien von Fichte bis Sartre*. Frankfurt am Main: Suhrkamp, 1991.

Funke, Gerhard, ed. *Akten des 4. internationalen Kant-Kongresses Mainz. 6.–10. April 1974*. Berlin: Walter de Gruyter, 1974.

Görland, Ingtraud. *Die Entwicklung der Frühphilosophie Schellings in der Auseinandersetzung mit Fichte*. Frankfurt am Main: Vittorio Klostermann, 1973.

Guéroult, M. "Les 'déplecements' (*Verstellungen*) de la conscience morale Kantienne selon Hegel." In *Hommage à Jean Hyppolite*, edited by Suzanne Bachelard. Paris: Presses universitaires de France, 1971.

Guyer, Paul. *Kant and the Claims of Taste*. Cambridge: Harvard University Press, 1979.

Haering, Theodor. *Hegel. Sein Wollen und sein Werk*. Leipzig and Berlin: B. G. Teubner, 1929.

Harries, Karsten. "The Root of All Evil: Lessons of an Epigram." *International Journal of Philosophical Studies* 1 (1993): 1–20.

Harries, Karsten, and Christoph Jamme, eds. *Martin Heidegger: Politics, Art, and Technology.* New York: Holmes and Meier, 1994.
Harris, H. S. *Hegel's Development: Night Thoughts (1801–1806).* Oxford: Clarendon Press, 1983.
———. *Hegel's Development: Toward the Sunlight (1770–1801).* Oxford: Clarendon Press, 1972.
———. "The Young Hegel and the Postulates of Practical Reason." In *Hegel and the Philosophy of Religion,* edited by Darrell E. Christensen. The Hague: Martinus Nijhoff, 1970.
Hegel, G.W.F. *Aesthetics.* Translated by T. M. Knox. Oxford: Oxford University Press, 1975.
———. *Ästhetik.* Edited by Friedrich Bassenge. Frankfurt am Main: Europäische Verlagsanstalt, 1966.
———. *Differenz des Fichte'schen und Schelling'schen Systems der Philosophie.* Hamburg: Felix Meiner, 1962.
———. *Enzyklopädie der philosophischen Wissenschaften im Grundrisse.* 3d ed. Heidelberg: Osswald (C. F. Winter), 1830.
———. *Enzyklopädie der philosophischen Wissenschaften im Grundrisse (1830).* Hamburg: Felix Meiner, 1959.
———. *Friedrich Hegel: Early Theological Writings.* Translated by T. M. Knox and Richard Kroner. New York: Harper, 1961.
———. *Gesammelte Werke.* Edited under the direction of the German Research Council. Hamburg: Felix Meiner, 1968ff.
———. *Hegel: The Letters.* Translated by Clarke Butler and Christiane Seiler. Bloomington: Indiana University Press, 1984.
———. *Hegel: Three Essays.* Translated by Peter Fuss and John Dobbins. Notre Dame, Ind.: University of Notre Dame Press, 1984.
———. *Hegel's Logic: Being Part One of the Encyclopaedia of the Philosophical Sciences (1830).* Translated by William Wallace. Oxford: Clarendon Press, 1975.
———. *Hegel's Phenomenology of Spirit.* Translated by A. V. Miller. Oxford: Oxford University Press, 1977.
———. *Hegel's Political Writings.* Translated by T. M. Knox. Oxford: Clarendon Press, 1964.
———. *Hegel's Science of Logic.* Translated by A. V. Miller. London and New York: George Allen and Unwin and Humanities Press, 1969.
———. *Hegels theologische Jugendschriften.* Edited by Herman Nohl. Tübingen: J.C.B. Mohr, 1907.
———. *Lectures on the Philosophy of Religion.* Edited by Peter C. Hodgson. Berkeley and Los Angeles: University of California Press, 1985.
———. *Lectures on the Philosophy of Religion.* Translated by E. B. Speirs and J. Burton Sanderson. New York: Humanities Press, 1962.
———. *The Logic of Hegel.* Translated by William Wallace. Oxford: Oxford University Press, 1904.
———. *On Christianity: Early Theological Writings.* Translated by T. M. Knox. New York: Harper & Row, 1961.
———. *Phänomenologie des Geistes.* Edited by Johannes Hoffmeister. Hamburg: Felix Meiner, 1952.
———. *Philosophy of Right.* Translated by T. M. Knox. Oxford: Oxford University Press, 1967.

———. *Sämtliche Werke*. Edited by Johannes Hoffmeister. Hamburg: Felix Meiner, 1952.
———. *Sämtliche Werke*. Edited by Georg Lasson. Leipzig: Felix Meiner, 1923–1932.
———. *Vorlesungen über die Philosophie der Religion*. Edited by Walter Jaeschke. Hamburg: Felix Meiner, 1984.
———. *Werke in zwanzig Bänden*. Edited by Eva Moldenauer and Karl Markus Michel. Frankfurt am Main: Suhrkamp, 1969–1971.
———. *Wissenschaft der Logik*. Edited by Georg Lasson. Lepizig: Felix Meiner, 1951.
Heidegger, Martin. *Erläuterungen zu Hölderlins Dichtung*. Vol. 4 of the *Gesamtausgabe*. Frankfurt am Main: Vittorio Klostermann, 1981.
———. *Hegel's Phenomenology of Spirit*. Translated by Parvis Emad and Kenneth Maly. Bloomington: Indiana University Press, 1980.
———. *Hölderlin's Hymnen "Germanien" und "Der Rhein."* Vol. 39 of the *Gesamtausgabe*. Frankfurt am Main: Vittorio Klostermann, 1980.
———. *Schellings Abhandlung über das Wesen der menschlichen Freiheit 1809*. Edited by Hildegard Feick. Tübingen: Max Niemeyer, 1971.
———. *Sein und Zeit*. Tübingen: Max Niemeyer, 1977.
Heine, Heinrich. *The Romantic School and Other Essays*. Edited by Jost Hermand and Robert C. Holub. New York: Continuum, 1985.
Hemmerle, Klaus. *Gott und das Denken nach Schellings Spätphilosophie*. Freiburg: Herder, 1968.
Henrich, Dieter. *Fichtes ursprüngliche Einsicht*. Frankfurt am Main: Vittorio Klostermann, 1967.
———. "Hölderlin über Urteil und Sein." *Hölderlin-Jahrbuch* 14 (1965–1966): 73–96.
———. *Identität und Objectivität*. Heidelberg: Carl Winter, 1976.
———. "The Identity of the Subject in the Transcendental Deduction." In *Reading Kant*, edited by E. Schaper and W. Vossenkuhl. Oxford: Blackwell, 1989.
———. *Konstellationen: Probleme und Debatten am Ursprung der idealistischen Philosophie*. Stuttgart: Klett-Cotta, 1991.
———. "Some Historical Presuppositions of Hegel's System." In *Hegel and the Philosophy of Religion*, edited by Darrell E. Christensen. The Hague: Martinus Nijhoff, 1970.
Hermelink, H. *Geschichte der evangelischen Kirche in Württemburg von der Reformation bis zur Gegenwart*. Stuttgart and Tübingen: R. Wunderlich, 1949.
Hersche, Peter. *Der Spätjansenismus in Österreich*. Vienna: Verlag der Österreichischen Akademie der Wissenschaften, 1977.
Hiltscher, Reinhard. "Stellt Fichtes Theorie von 'Ich' in der WL von 1794/95 eine Produktionstheorie des 'Ich' dar?" *Fichte-Studien* 5 (1993): 107–16.
Hinske, Norbert, Erhard Lange, and Horst Schröpfer, eds. *Der Aufbruch in den Kantianismus: Der Frühkantianismus an der Universität Jena 1785–1800 und seine Vorgeschichte*. Stuttgart-Bad Cannstatt: Frommann-Holzboog, 1995.
Hoffheimer, Michael. "The Influence of Schiller's Philosophy of Nature on Hegel's Philosophical Development." *Journal of the History of Ideas* 46 (1985): 213–44.
Hoffmeister, Johannes, ed. *Briefe von und an Hegel*. Hamburg: Felix Meiner, 1952.
———, ed. *Dokumente zu Hegels Entwicklung*. Stuttgart: Frommann, 1936.

Hohler, Thomas P. "Fichte and the Problem of Finitude." *Southwestern Journal of Philosophy* 7 (1976): 15–33.
——. *Imagination and Reflection: Intersubjectivity. Fichte's Grundlage of 1794*. The Hague: Martinus Nijhoff, 1982.
Hölderlin, Friedrich. *Hölderlin: Sämtliche Werke und Briefe*. 2 vols. Edited by Günther Mieth. Munich: Hanser, 1973.
——. *Hölderlin: Werke und Briefe*. Edited by Friedrich Beissner and Jochen Schmidt. Frankfurt am Main: Insel Verlag, 1968.
——. *Poems and Fragments*. Translated by Michael Hamburger. London: Routledge and Keegan Paul, 1961.
——. *Sämtliche Werke*. Edited by Paul Stapf. Berlin and Darmstadt: Tempel, 1960.
Hollerbach, Alexander. *Der Rechtsgedanke bei Schelling*. Frankfurt am Main: Vittorio Klostermann, 1957.
Holz, Harald. "Die Struktur der Dialektik in den Frühschriften von Fichte und Schelling." *Archiv für die Geschichte der Philosophie* 52 (1970): 71–90.
——. *Spekulation und Faktizität. Zum Freiheitsbegriff des mittleren und späten Schelling*. Bonn: Bouvier, 1970.
Honeth, Axel, ed. *Zwischenbetrachtungen: Im Prozess der Aufklärung*. Frankfurt am Main: Suhrkamp, 1989.
Hyppolite, Jean. "L'idée fichtéene de la doctrine de la science et le projet husserlien." In *Figures de la pensée philosophique*, vol. 1. Paris: Presses universitaires de France, 1971.
Jacobi, Friedrich Heinrich. *David Hume über den Glauben, oder Idealismus und Realismus, ein Gespräch*. Vol. 2 of the *Werke*. Edited by F. H. Jacobi and F. Köppen. Leipzig: Fleischer, 1812.
——. *Werke*. Six volumes. Edited by F. H. Jacobi and F. Köppen. Leipzig: Fleischer, 1812–1825.
Jamme, Christoph. *"Ein ungelehrtes Buch. Die philosophische Gemeinschaft zwischen Hölderlin und Hegel in Frankfurt 1791–1800."* *Hegel-Studien* 23. Bonn: Bouvier, 1983.
Jaspers, Karl. *Schelling. Grösse und Verhängnis*. Munich: Piper, 1955.
Kain, Philip J. *Schiller, Hegel, and Marx: State, Society, and the Aesthetic Ideal of Ancient Greece*. Kingston, Ontario, Canada: McGill-Queen's University Press, 1982.
Kant, Immanuel. *Critique of Pure Reason*. Translated by Norman Kemp Smith. New York: St. Martin's Press, 1965.
——. *Grundlegung der Metaphysik der Sitten*. Vol. 4 of *Kants gesammelte Schriften*. Edited by the Royal Prussian Academy of Sciences and Its Successors. Berlin: Reimer; later Berlin and New York: Walter de Gruyter, 1903.
——. *Kants gesammelte Schriften*. Edited by the Royal Prussian Academy of Sciences and Its Successors. Berlin: Reimer; later Berlin and New York: Walter de Gruyter, 1902–1938, 1968.
——. *Kritik der praktischen Vernunft*. Vol. 5 of *Kants gesammelte Schriften*. Edited by the Royal Prussian Academy of Sciences and Its Successors. Berlin: Reimer; later, Berlin and New York: Walter de Gruyter, 1908, 1968.
——. *Kritik der reinen Vernunft*. Vol. 3 of *Kants gesammelte Schriften*. Edited by the Royal Prussian Academy of Sciences and Its Successors. Berlin: Reimer; later Berlin and New York: Walter de Gruyter, 1904.
——. *Kritik der reinen Vernunft*. Edited by Raymund Schmidt. Hamburg: Meiner, 1971.

———. *Kritik der Urteilskraft*. Vol. 5 of *Kants gesammelte Schriften*. Edited by the Royal Prussian Academy of Sciences and Its Successors. Berlin: Reimer; later Berlin and New York: Walter de Gruyter, 1908, 1968.
———. *Prolegomena to Any Future Metaphysics*. Translated by Paul Carus. Revised by James W. Wellington. Indianapolis, Ind.: Hackett, 1977.
———. *Religion innerhalb der Grenzen der blossen Vernunft*. 2d ed. Konigsberg: Friedrich Nicolovius, 1794.
———. *Sämmtliche Werke*. 14 volumes. Edited by Karl Rosenkranz and Friedrich Wilhelm Schubert. Leipzig: Leopold Voss, 1840.
———. *Werke*. 11 volumes. Edited by Ernst Cassirer. Berlin: Bruno Cassirer, 1922.
———. *Werke in sechs Bänden*. Edited by Wilhelm Weischedel. Wiesbaden: Insel Verlag, 1960.
Kelly, George Armstrong. *Hegel's Retreat from Eleusis*. Princeton, N.J.: Princeton University Press, 1978.
Klemm, David E., and Günter Zöller, eds. *Figuring the Self: Subject, Absolute, and Others in Classical German Philosophy*. Albany: State University of New York Press, 1997.
Klemmt, Alfred. *Karl Leonhard Reinholds Elementarphilosophie: Eine Studie über den Ursprung des spekulativen deutschen Idealismus*. Hamburg: Felix Meiner, 1958.
Koselleck, Reinhard. *Kritik und Krise: Ein Beitrag zur Pathogenese der bürgerlichen Welt*. Freiburg and Munich: Karl Alber, 1959.
Krug, Wilhelm Traugott. *Allgemeines Handwörterbuch der philosophischen Wissenschaften, nebst ihrer Literatur und Geschichte*. Leipzig: F. A. Brockhaus, 1833.
Lauth, Reinhard. "Das Problem der Interpersonalität bei Fichte." In *Transzendentale Entwicklungslinien von Descartes biz zu Marx und Dostojewski*. Hamburg: Felix Meiner, 1989.
———. "Der Ursprung der Dialektik in Fichtes Philosophie." In *Transzendentale Entwicklungslinien von Descartes biz zu Marx und Dostojewski*. Hamburg: Felix Meiner, 1989.
———. *Die Entstehung von Schellings Identitätsphilosophie in der Auseinandersetzung mit Fichtes Wissenschaftslehre*. Freiburg and Munich: Karl Alber, 1975.
———. "Die erste philosophische Auseinandersetzung zwischen Fichte und Schelling 1795–1797." *Zeitschrift für philosophische Forschung* 21 (1967): 341–67.
———, ed. *Philosophie aus einem Prinzip: Karl Leonhard Reinhold*. Bonn: Bouvier-Grundmann, 1974.
Lauth, Reinhard, Eberhard Heller, and Kurt Hiller, eds. *Karl Leonhard Reinhold: Korrespondenzausgabe der österreichischen Akademie der Wissenschaften*. Stuttgart-Bad Cannstatt: Frommann-Holzboog, 1983.
Lessing, K. G., ed. *Gotthold Ephraim Lessings Leben, nebst seinem übrigen litterarischen Nachlasse*. Berlin: Voss, 1793.
Liebmann, Otto. *Kant und die Epigonen: Eine kritische Abhandlung*. Berlin: Reuther and Reichard, 1912.
Maimon, Salomon. *Gesammelte Werke*. 7 volumes. Edited by Valerio Verra. Hildesheim: G. Olms, 1965–1976.
Makkreel, Rudolph A. *Imagination and Interpretation in Kant: The Hermeneutical Import of the "Critique of Judgment."* Chicago: University of Chicago Press, 1990.
McCumber, John. *The Company of Words: Hegel, Language, and Systematic Philosophy*. Evanston, Ill.: Northwestern University Press, 1989.
———. *Poetic Interaction*. Chicago: University of Chicago Press, 1989.

Meier, F. *Die Idee der Transzendentalphilosophie beim jungen Schelling.* Winterthur: P. G. Keller, 1961.
Metzger, Wilhelm. *Die Epochen der Schellingschen Philosophie von 1795 bis 1802.* Heidelberg: C. Winter, 1911.
Minor, Jakob, August Sauer, and Richard Maria Werner, eds. *Beiträge zur Geschichte der deutschen Literatur und des geistigen Lebens in Österreich.* Vienna: Carl Konegen, 1883.
Neuhouser, Frederick. *Fichte's Theory of Subjectivity.* Cambridge: Cambridge University Press, 1990.
Novalis. *Schriften.* Edited by Paul Kluckhohn and Richard Samuel. Stuttgart: Kohlhammer, 1960.
Oeser, Erhard. *Begriff und Systematik der Abstraktion. Die Aristoteles-interpretation bei Thomas von Aquin, Hegel und Schelling als Grundlegung der philosophischen Erkenntnislehre.* Vienna and Munich: Oldenburg, 1969.
―――. *Die antike Dialektik in der Spätphilosophie Schellings.* Vienna and Munich: Oldenburg, 1965.
O'Neill, Onora. *Constructions of Reason.* Cambridge and New York: Cambridge University Press, 1989.
Paton, Herbert James. *Kant's Metaphysic of Experience.* London and New York: George Allen and Unwin and Humanities Press, 1936.
Pelczynski, Z. A., ed. *Hegel's Political Philosophy: Problems and Perspectives.* Cambridge: Cambridge University Press, 1971.
Peperzak, Adriaan T. *Le jeune Hegel et la vision morale du monde.* The Hague: Martinus Nijhoff, 1960.
Perrinjaquet, Alain. "Some Remarks Concerning the Circularity of Philosophy and the Evidence of Its First Principle in the Jena *Wissenschaftslehre.*" In *Fichte: Historical Contexts/ Contemporary Controversies,* edited by Daniel Breazeale and Tom Rockmore. Atlantic Highlands, N.J.: Humanities Press, 1994.
Philonenko, Alexis. *La liberté humaine dans la philosophie de Fichte.* Paris: J. Vrin, 1966.
Pinkard, Terry. *Hegel's Dialectic.* Philadelphia: Temple University Press, 1988.
Pippin, Robert. *Hegel's Idealism: The Satisfactions of Self-Consciousness.* Cambridge and New York: Cambridge University Press, 1989.
Platner, Ernst. *Philosophische Aphorismen.* Leipzig: Sigwart, 1784.
Plitt, G. L., ed. *Aus Schellings Leben: In Briefen.* 3 vols. Leipzig: S. Hirzel, 1869.
Pöggeler, Otto. "Hegel, der Verfasser des ältesten Systemprogramms des deutschen Idealismus." *Hegel-Studien* 4. Bonn: Bouvier, 1969.
―――. *Hegels Idee einer Phänomenologie des Geistes.* Freiburg: Karl Alber, 1993.
―――. *Hegels Jugendschriften und die Idee einer Phänomenologie des Geistes.* Unpublished Habilitation, University of Heidelberg, 1966.
Porter, Roy, and Mikulás Teich, eds. *The Enlightenment in National Context.* Cambridge and New York: Cambridge University Press, 1981.
Prauss, Gerold. *Die Welt und wir.* Stuttgart: Metzler, 1990.
―――. *Kant über die Freiheit als Autonomie.* Frankfurt am Main: Vittorio Klostermann, 1983.
Pupi, Angelo. *La formazione della filosofia di K. L. Reinhold 1784–1794.* Milan: Società Editrice Vita e Pensiero, 1966.
Reinhold, Ernst. *Karl Leonhard Reinhold's Leben und litterarisches Wirken, nebst einer Auswahl von Briefen Kant's, Fichte's, Jacobi's und andrer philosophirender Zeitgenossen an ihn.* Jena: Friedrich Frommann, 1825.

Reinhold, Karl Leonhard. *Anleitung zur Kenntniß und Beurtheilung der Philosophie in ihren sämmtlichen Lehrgebäuden.* Vienna: J. V. Degen, 1805.
———. *Beyträge zur Berichtigung bisheriger Missverständnisse der Philosophen.* Jena: Johann Michael Mauke, 1790.
———. *Beyträge zur leichtern Übersicht des Zustandes der Philosophie beym Anfange des 19. Jahrhunderts.* Hamburg: Friedrich Perthes, 1803.
———. *Briefe über die Kantische Philosophie.* Edited by Raymund Schmidt. Leipzig: Reclam, 1923.
———. *Das menschliche Erkenntnisvermögen, aus dem Gesichtspunkte des durch die Wortsprache vermittelten Zusammenhangs zwischen der Sinnlichkeit und dem Denkvermögen.* Kiel: im Verlage der akademischen Buchhandlung, 1816.
———. *Die alte Frage: Was ist die Wahrheit? bey den erneuerten Streitigkeiten über die göttliche Offenbarung und die menschliche Vernunft, in nähere Erwägung gezogen.* Altona: Johann Friedrich Hammerich, 1820.
———. *Grundlegung einer Synonymik für den allgemeinen Sprachgebrauch in den philosophischen Wissenschaften.* Kiel: August Schmidt, 1812.
———. *Schriften zur Religionskritik und Aufklärung, 1782–1784.* Bremen: Jacobi-Verlag, 1977.
———. *Über das Fundament des philosophischen Wissens nebst einigen Erläuterungen über die Theorie des Vorstellungsvermögens.* Jena: Johann Michael Mauke, 1791.
———. *Über die Paradoxeien der neuesten Philosophie.* Hamburg: Friedrich Perthes, 1799.
———. *Verhandlungen über die Grundbegriffe und Grundsätze der Moralität aus dem Gesichtspunkte des gemeinen und gesunden Verstandes, zum Behuf der Beurtheilung der sittlichen, rechtlichen, politischen und religiösen Angelegenheiten.* Lubeck and Leipzig: Friedrich Bohn, 1798.
———. *Versuch einer neuen Theorie des menschlichen Vorstellungsvermögens.* Prague and Jena: C. Widtmann and J. M. Mauke, 1789.
Robson-Scott, William Douglas. *The Literary Background of the Gothic Revival in Germany.* Oxford: Clarendon Press, 1965.
Roehr, Sabine. *A Primer on German Enlightenment: With a Translation of Karl Leonhard Reinhold's "The Fundamental Concepts and Principles of Ethics."* Columbia: University of Missouri Press, 1995.
Rosenkranz, Karl. *Hegels Leben.* Berlin: Duncker und Humblot, 1844.
Röttgers, Kurt. *Kritik und Praxis: Zur Geschichte des Kritikbegriffs von Kant bis Marx.* Berlin: Walter de Gruyter, 1975.
Royce, Josiah. *The Spirit of Modern Philosophy.* Boston: Houghton, Mifflin, 1892.
Sauer, Werner. *Osterreichische Philosophie zwischen Aufklärung und Restauration: Beiträge zur Geschichte des Frühkantianismus in der Donaumonarchie.* Amsterdam: Rodopi, 1982.
Schelling, F.W.J. *Briefe und Dokumente.* Edited by Horst Fuhrmans. Bonn: Bouvier, 1962.
———. *The Philosophy of Art.* Translated by Douglas W. Scott. Minneapolis: University of Minnesota Press, 1989.
———. *Sämmtliche Werke.* 14 volumes. Edited by Karl Friedrich August Schelling. Stuttgart and Augsburg: J. G. Cotta, 1856–1861.
———. *Schellings Werke.* 6 volumes. Edited by Manfred Schröter. Munich: C. H. Beck, 1958.
———. *System of Transcendental Idealism.* Translated by Peter Heath. Charlottesville: University of Virginia Press, 1978.

———. *Über das Verhältnis der bildenden Künste zu der Natur.* Edited by Lucia Sziborsky. Hamburg: Felix Meiner, 1983.
———. *The Unconditional in Human Knowledge.* Translated by Fritz Marti. Lewisburg, Pa.: Bucknell University Press, 1980.
Schiller, Friedrich. *Friedrich Schiller: Essays.* Edited by Walter Hinderer and Daniel Dahlstrom. New York: Continuum, 1993.
———. "On the Naïve and the Sentimental in Literature." In *Friedrich Schiller: Essays.* Edited by Walter Hinderer and Daniel O. Dahlstrom. New York: Continuum, 1993.
———. *On the Aesthetic Education of Man: In a Series of Letters.* Translated by Reginald Snell. New York: Frederick Ungar, 1965.
———. *On the Aesthetic Education of Man in a Series of Letters.* Translated and edited by Elizabeth M. Wilkinson and L. A. Willoughy. Oxford: Clarendon Press, 1967.
———. *Schillers Werke.* Edited by Axel Gellhaus. Weimar: Hermann Böhlauys Nachfolger, 1984.
———. *Werke in drei Bänden.* Munich: C. Hanser, 1966.
———. *Werke, Nationalausgabe. Historisch-Kritische Ausgabe.* 42 volumes. Edited by Julius Petersen and Freidrick Beißnen/Lieselotte Blumenthal and Benno von Wiese/Norbert Oellers. Weimar: Böhlau, 1943–1996.
Schlegel, August Wilhelm. *Vorlesungen über dramatische Kunst und Literatur.* Stuttgart, Berlin, Cologne, Mainz: Kohlhammer, 1966.
Schmidt, Jochen. *Hölderlins geschichtsphilosophische Hymnen: "Friedensfeier" — "Der Einzige" — "Patmos."* Darmstadt: Wissenschaftliche Buchgesellschaft, 1990.
———, ed. *Dichter über Hölderlin.* Frankfurt am Main: Insel, 1969.
Schroll-Fleischer, Niels Otto. *Der Gottesgedanke in der Philosophie Kants.* Odense: Odense University Press, 1981.
Schröter, Manfred. "Der Ausgangspunkt der Metaphysik Schellings." In *Kritische Studien: Über Schelling und zur Kulturphilosophie.* Munich: R. Oldenbourg, 1971.
Schüler, Gisela. "Zur Chronologie von Hegels Jugendschriften." *Hegel-Studien* 2 (1963): 111–59.
Schulz, Walter. *Die Vollendung des deutschen Idealismus in der Spätphilosophie Schellings.* Stuttgart: W. Kohlhammer, 1955.
———. "Introduction" to *System des transzendentalen Idealismus,* by F.W.J. Schelling. 2d ed. Edited by Ruth-Eva Schulz. Hamburg: Felix Meiner, 1962.
———, ed. *Fichte-Schelling Briefwechsel.* Frankfurt am Main: Suhrkamp, 1968.
Schulze, Gottlob Ernst. *Aenesidemus oder über die Fundamente der von dem Herrn Professor Reinhold in Jena gelieferten Elementarphilosophie.* Edited by Arthur Liebert. Berlin: Reuther and Reichhard, 1911. Reprinted in *Aeteas Kantiana.* Brussels: Culture et Civilisation, 1969.
Schurr, Adolf. *Philosophie als System bei Fichte, Schelling, und Hegel.* Stuttgart-Bad Cannstatt: Frommann-Holzboog, 1974.
Shikaya, Takako. "Hölderlin, Dichter jenseits des Idealismus." In *Idealismus mit Folgen. Die Epochenschwelle um 1800 in Kunst und Geisteswissenschaften.* Munich: Fink, 1994.
Stern, Robert. *Hegel, Kant, and the Structure of the Object.* London and New York: Routledge, 1990.
Stolzenberg, Jürgen. *Fichtes Begriff der intellektuellen Anschauung.* Stuttgart: Klett-Cotta, 1986.

Strauß, L. "Hölderlins Anteil an Schellings frühem Systemprogramm." *Deutsche Vierteljarhschrift für Literaturwissenschaft und Geistesgeschichte* 5 (1927): 710–13.
Teichner, Wilhelm. *Rekonstruction oder Reproduktion des Grundes: Die Begründung der Philosophie als Wissenschaft durch Kant und Reinhold.* Bonn: Bouvier-Grundmann, 1976.
Tilliette, Xavier. *Schelling: Une philosophie en devenir.* Paris: J. Vrin, 1970.
Tittel, Gottlob August. *Kantische Denkformen oder Kategorien.* Frankfurt: Gebhardt, 1787.
van Dülmen, Richard. *Der Geheimbund der Illuminaten: Darstellung, Analyse, Dokumentation.* Stuttgart-Bad Cannstatt: Frommann-Holzboog, 1975.
Velkley, Richard L. *Freedom and the End of Reason: On the Moral Foundation of Kant's Critical Philosophy.* Chicago: University of Chicago Press, 1989.
Verra, Valerio. *Dopo Kant. Il criticismo nell'età preromantica.* Turin: Edizioni di Filosofia, 1957.
von Hartmann, Eduard. *Schellings philosophisches System.* Leipzig: Hermann Hacke, 1897.
von Schönborn, Alexander. *Karl Leonhard Reinhold: Eine annotierte Bibliographie.* Stuttgart-Bad Canstatt: Frommann-Holzboog, 1991.
Wackenroder, Wilhelm Heinrich. *Sämtliche Werke und Briefe: Historisch-kritische Ausgabe.* Edited by Silvio Vietta and Richard Littlejohns. Heidelberg: C. Winter, 1991.
Weishaupt, Adam. *Über die Gründe und Gewissheit der menschlichen Erkenntnis: Zur Prüfung der kantischen Critic der reinen Vernunft.* Nuremberg: Gratenau, 1788. Reprinted in *Aeteas Kantiana.* Brussels: Culture et Civilisation, 1969.
Westphal, Merold. *Hegel, Freedom, and Modernity.* Albany: State University of New York Press, 1992.
———. "Hegel's Angst vor dem Sollen." *Owl of Minerva* 25 (1994): 187–94.
———. *History and Truth in Hegel's Phenomenology.* Atlantic Highlands, N.J.: Humanities Press, 1979.
White, Alan. *Absolute Knowledge: Hegel and the Problem of Metaphysics.* Athens: Ohio University Press, 1983.
Wieland, W. "Die Anfänge der Philosophie Schellings und die Frage nach der Natur." In *Natur und Geschichte: Karl Löwith zum 70. Geburtstag.* Stuttgart: Kohlhammer, 1967.
Wild, Christoph. *Reflexion und Erfahrung: Eine Interpretation der Früh- und Spätphilosophie Schellings.* Freiburg and Munich: Karl Alber, 1968.
Wilm, Emil Carl. *The Philosophy of Schiller in Its Historical Relations.* Boston: John W. Luce, 1912.
Winckelmann, Johann Joachim. *Geschichte der Kunst des Altertums.* Darmstadt: Wissenschaftliche Buchgesellschaft, 1972.
Wood, Allen. "Fichte's Philosophical Revolution." *Philosophical Topics* 19 (1991): 1–28.
———. *Kant's Moral Religion.* Ithaca, N.Y.: Cornell University Press, 1970.
Yovel, Yirmiahu. *Kant and the Philosophy of History.* Princeton, N.J.: Princeton University Press, 1980.

Name Index

The authors would like to thank Anthony Giampietro for his work on this index.

Aenesidemus, 75–77, 241
Allison, Henry E., 45
Ameriks, Karl, 4–5, 116
Antigone, 280
Aquinas, Thomas. *See* Thomas Aquinas
Aristotle, Aristotelian, 13, 24, 62, 74, 144, 189–191, 195, 265
Arnim, Achim von, 148, 181, 196
Arnim, Bettina von, 148
Asveld, Paul 216–17

Baggesen, Jens, 42, 50
Bardili, Christoph Gottfried, 38, 40–41, 44, 50, 62
Baumgartner, Hans Michael, 7, 241
Baur, Michael, 1, 3, 63, 130
Beck, Lewis White, 19
Beckett, Samuel, 43
Beethoven, Ludwig von, 181
Beiser, Frederick C., 45
Bengel, Johann Albrecht, 166
Berkeley, George, 113
Blumauer, Aloys, 47
Böhm, Wilhelm, 152, 228.
Bondeli, Martin, 36, 41, 44–45, 58, 60
Born, Ignaz von, 48
Bouterwek, F. L., 44
Braun, Hermann, 245
Breazeale, Daniel, 4, 75, 77, 81, 95, 117, 128–30
Brecht, Martin, 204, 217
Brehier, Emile, 95
Brenner, Anton, 233
Brentano, Clemens von, 148, 181, 196
Brüggen, Michael, 262
Butler, Eliza Marian, 147, 273, 275, 277, 282, 285

Cassirer, Ernst, 37, 138–39, 142
Cesa, Claudio, 104
Christ, Jesus. *See* Jesus Christ

Claesges, Ulrich, 249
Copleston, Frederick, 33, 42, 186, 188

Dahlstrom, Daniel O., 1, 13, 130, 309
Dawson, Christopher, 184
De Nys, Martin, 9, 288
Derrida, Jacques, 286
Descartes, René, 183–84, 265, 270, 273, 281, 286–87
Desmond, William, 153, 160, 183
de Vleeschauwer, Herman-J., 36, 295
Dietz, Carl Immanuel, 57, 204
Dilthey, Wilhelm, 251
Dionysus, 153, 156, 159
Diotima, 164, 166, 168, 170
Döderlein, Johann Ludwig, 204
Don Martinus, 46
Druet, Pierre-Philippe, 96
Düsing, Klaus, 7, 9, 22, 201, 210, 245
Düsing, Wolfgang, 146

Eberhard, Johann August, 44
Eichendorff, Joseph von, 181
Endymion, 163
Erdmann, Johann Eduard, 42
Erhard, Johann Benjamin, 57

Fichte, I. H. (*son of* Johann Gottlieb Fichte), 96
Fichte, Johann Gottlieb, 3–5, 8, 13; and *abstract realism*, 95–115; and *aesthetics*, 136, 138–39; and (Kant's) *doctrine of postulates*, 201, 203, 208, 210, 213, 217, 220–21, 224–27, 231–32; and the *"Earliest System-Programme of German Idealism,"* 271–78, 282–85; and *metaphysics*, 252–59, 261–62; and *the primacy of the practical*, 116–30; and the influence of (Karl Leonhard) *Reinhold*, 33–41, 44–45, 50–51, 58, 60–63; and *religion*, 147–48, 152, 173; and (German) *Romanticism*, 177,

NAME INDEX

Fichte, Johann Gottlieb (*continued*)
 181–82, 185–88, 191, 193, 195–96; and *skepticism*, 64, 74–90; and the *unconditioned in knowing*, 241–50
Fischer, Kuno, 42
Fischer, Michael W., 49
Flatt, J. F., 44, 77, 206, 209, 216
Forster, Michael, 63
Frank, Manfred, 101, 116, 127
Fries, Jakob Friedrich, 44
Fuhrmans, Horst, 253, 262

Galley, Eberhard, 262
Garve, Christian, 34, 69
George, Stefan, 149
Gilson, Etienne, 190
Girndt, Helmut, 39
Gliwitzky, Hans, 48
Goethe, Johann Wolfgang von, 153, 178, 184
Gontard, Susette, 164
Görland, Ingtraud, 245–46
Görres, Joseph, 181
Grimm, *The Brothers*, 96, 181, 196
Guéroult, Martial, 236, 252

Habermas, Jürgen, 281
Haering, Theodor, 216, 219, 221
Hamann, Johann Georg, 184, 262
Hamburger, Michael, 155, 162, 167–68
Harries, Karsten, 5–6, 9, 147
Harris, H. S., 178, 216, 225, 269–70, 278, 280–81, 285–86, 293
Harris, James, 44
Hartmann, Eduard von, 251
Haydn, Franz Josef, 48
Hegel, Georg Wilhelm Friedrich, 1, 3, 5–9; and *absolute knowing*, 288–307; and (Fichte's) *abstract realism*, 95, 102, 113, 115; and *aesthetics*, 133–46; and (Kant's) *doctrine of postulates*, 201, 203–5, 208, 210, 215–31, 233–37; and the *"Earliest System-Programme of German Idealism,"* 269–87; and *Hölderlin/religion*, 147–75; and *metaphysics*, 253, 263, 265; and the influence of (Karl Leonhard) *Reinhold*, 33, 35–42, 45, 51, 58, 60–61; and (German) *Romanticism*, 176–80, 182, 185, 187–91, 193–95; and *skepticism*, 63–65, 67, 74–75, 82, 85–91; and the *unity of Kant's critical philosophy*, 13, 24
Heidegger, Martin, 21, 148–50, 167, 251, 270, 303
Heine, Heinrich, 179
Helios, 154
Heller, Eberhard, 43

Hellingrath, Norbert von, 149
Hemmerle, Klaus, 251
Henrich, Dieter, 45, 57, 95, 101, 108, 116, 148, 204, 216
Heracles, 156, 159
Herbart, Johann Friedrich, 44
Herder, Johann Gottfried von, 34, 44, 51, 160, 184, 219, 232, 257
Hermelink, Heinrich, 204, 208
Hermias, 75
Hersche, Peter, 47
Heydenreich, Karl Heinrich, 44
Hiller, Kurt, 43
Hiltscher, Reinhard, 109
Hoffheimer, Michael, 140
Hoffmann, E. T. A., 196
Hohler, Thomas, 104, 109
Hölderlin, Friedrich, 5–6, 9; and (Kant's) *doctrine of postulates*, 203–4, 223, 227–28, 235; and the *"Earliest System-Programme of German Idealism,"* 269–70, 273–74, 283–85, 287; and *Hegel/religion*, 147–75; and *metaphysics*, 253, 256; and (German) *Romanticism*, 178
Hollerbach, Alexander, 211
Holz, Harald, 248–49, 251
Humboldt, Wilhelm von, 133, 138, 146
Hume, David, 3, 47, 63, 68–70, 75, 90–91
Hyppolite, Jean, 113

Jachmann, Reinhold Bernhard, 37
Jacob, L. H., 44
Jacobi, Friedrich Heinrich, 34–35, 38, 46, 52–53, 60–61, 68, 112, 119, 208, 215, 226, 231, 252, 262
Jacobs, Wilhelm G., 242, 247
Jamme, Christoph, 148, 152
Jaspers, Karl, 263
Jauss, Hans Robert, 179
Jenisch, Daniel, 54, 55
Jesus Christ, 6, 53, 153–58, 160, 164–65, 167, 169, 171–72, 174, 203–4, 208, 262, 272, 289–90
John (the Evangelist), 164, 166–69

Kain, Philip J., 136
Kant, Immanuel, 1–2, 4, 7–9; and *absolute knowing*, 288–99, 301, 304–6, 309; and (Fichte's) *abstract realism*, 108; and *aesthetics*, 134–35, 137–39, 141–45; and his *doctrine of postulates*, 201–37; and the *"Earliest System-Programme of German Idealism,"* 269, 271–75, 277, 284–85; and *metaphysics*, 252–56, 258–59, 262, 265; and (Fichte's) *primacy of the practical*, 116–26, 129, 133; and (Karl Leonhard)

Reinhold, 33–38, 41, 43–45, 48, 51–56, 58–62; and *religion*, 147–48, 160; and (German) *Romanticism*, 182–85, 187–96; and *skepticism*, 63–74, 77, 82, 84; and the *unconditioned in knowing*, 241, 243–46, 249–50; and the *unity* of his *critical philosophy*, 13–29
Keil, Robert, 46
Kelly, George Armstrong, 135
Kennington, Richard, 28
Kepler, Johannes, 262
Kierkegaard, Søren, 285, 286
Kiesewetter, Johann Gottfried Christian, 44
Kimmerle, Heinz, 270
Kleist, Heinrich von, 196
Klemmt, Alfred, 44
Klopstock, Friedrich Gottlieb, 173–74, 184
Knox, T. M., 272
Koselleck, Reinhard, 48–49
Kroner, Richard, 42
Krug, Wilhelm Traugott, 41–42, 44
Kutscher, Arthur, 134

Lauth, Reinhard, 39, 45- 46, 48, 50, 104, 114, 245, 252
Lavater, Johann Kaspar, 44, 49
Leibniz, Gottfried Wilhelm, 16, 47, 62, 184, 232–33, 241
Léon, Xavier, 252
Lessing, Gotthold Ephraim, 178, 208, 223, 226, 272, 274
Liebmann, Otto, 37
Locke, John, 55, 284
Luna, 163
Luther, Martin, 262

Maimon, Salomon, 34–35, 67–69, 71–72, 241
Makkreel, Rudolph A., 187
Malebranche, Nicolas, 184
Marcel, Gabriel, 187
Mark (the Evangelist), 171
Martinus, Don, 46
Marx, Karl, 13, 285–86
Matthew (the Evangelist), 171
McCumber, John, 5, 133
Medicus, Fritz, 252
Meier, F., 211
Mendelssohn, Moses, 28, 53
Metzger, Wilhelm, 211, 253
Michelet, Karl Ludwig, 42
Mill, John Stuart, 38
Moore, George Edward, 38
Mozart, Wolfgang Amadeus, 48

Nebuchadnezzer, 263
Neuffer, Christian Ludwig, 148
Neuhouser, Frederick, 76, 109, 116, 122, 128
Newton, Isaac, 26
Nicodemus, 290
Nicolai, Friedrich, 47
Niethammer, F. I., 109, 206, 210, 232
Nietzsche, Friedrich, 147, 287
Nohl, Herman, 149, 289
Novalis, 6, 179, 185, 258

Ockham, 190
Oeser, Erhard, 265
Oetinger, Friedrich Christoph, 147

Pareyson, Luigi, 109
Paton, Herbert James, 296
Paul, Saint, 157
Pelczynski, Z. A., 278–79
Pepermann, Don Paulus, 33
Peperzak, Adriaan, 203, 217–18, 221, 225, 290
Perrinjaquet, Alain, 104, 126–28
Philonenko, Alexis, 104, 109
Pippin, Robert, 116, 298
Platner, Ernst, 68–70
Plato, 24, 62, 144, 148–49, 151, 189, 254–55, 261–62, 293
Plitt, G. L., 253, 255, 256, 266
Pöggeler, Otto, 148, 152, 220, 228, 256, 269–70
Prauss, Gerold, 45, 116
Pupi, Angelo, 45

Rehberg, August Wilhelm, 215
Reid, Thomas, 112
Reimarus, Hermann Samuel, 173
Reinhold, Karl Leonhard, 1, 2, 3, 33–62; and *skepticism*, 70, 72–78, 84; 184, 216, 225, 233, 241, 243
Rilke, Rainer Maria, 149
Robespierre, Maximilien, 280
Robson-Scott, William Douglas, 184
Roehr, Sabine, 44, 49–50
Rosenkranz, Karl, 42
Rosenstrauch-Königsberg, Edith, 47,49
Rosenzweig, Franz, 152, 211, 228, 231
Röttgers, Kurt, 50
Rousseau, Jean-Jacques, 148, 184, 197, 216–18, 232
Royce, Josiah, 113
Russell, Bertrand, 38

Sandberger, Jörg, 204, 217
Sartorius, 217, 223

Sartre, Jean-Paul, 103, 115, 286
Sauer, Werner, 44, 48, 51–53, 55
Schelling, Friedrich Wilhelm Joseph von, 3, 6–8, 13; and (Fichte's) *abstract realism*, 113; and *aesthetics*, 134, 136; and (Kant's) *doctrine of postulates*, 201, 203–16, 220–21, 223–36; and the *"Earliest System-Programme of German Idealism,"* 269–71, 273, 274–77, 282–83, 285; and *intellectual intuition*, 125; and *metaphysics*, 251–66; and (Karl Leonhard) *Reinhold*, 36, 38–41, 44–45, 51, 58, 61; and *religion*, 147–50, 152, 157, 160; and (German) *Romanticism*, 178, 180, 182–83, 185–91, 193, 195; and *skepticism*, 64; and the *unconditioned in knowing*, 241–50
Schelling, Karl, 263
Schiller, Friedrich, 5, 51; and *aesthetics*, 133–46; and the *"Earliest System-Programme of German Idealism,"* 282–85; and *religion*, 151–54, 160–61; and (German) *Romanticism*, 182, 187
Schlegel, August Wilhelm, 6, 183, 189, 284
Schlegel, Friedrich, 176–77, 179, 181, 186, 195, 284
Schleiermacher, Friedrich, 178, 284
Schmid, K. C. E., 44
Schmidt, Jochen, 147, 156–58, 166, 173
Schmidt, Raymund, 37
Schmitt, Hans-Jürgen, 180
Schmitz, Kenneth L., 6–7, 176
Schopenhauer, Arthur, 34–35, 284
Schröter, Manfred, 246, 251
Schüler, Gisela, 270
Schulz, Walter, 246, 248, 251, 264
Schulze, Gottlob Ernst, 3, 44, 68–69, 75–78, 85, 119, 241
Schürmann, Reiner, 162
Schurr, Adolf, 246
Schütz, Christian Gottfried, 54
Schwab, Gustav, 148
Seiler, Christiane, 273, 275, 277, 282, 285
Shaftesbury, Anthony Ashley Cooper, 218
Shikaya, Takako, 148–49
Sinclair, Isaak von, 178
Socrates, 67, 150, 161
Sokolowski, Robert, 28
Solger, Karl Wilhelm Ferdinand, 6, 177
Sonnenfels, Josef von, 48
Sophocles, 161–62
Spinoza, Benedict, 8, 52, 148, 178, 184, 194, 206; and the *"Earliest System-Programme of German Idealism,"* 273–74, 286; and *ethics*, 208–12, 214–15, 226–27, 231; and *metaphysics*, 252–55, 258, 260; and the *unconditioned in knowing*, 243–44
Stamm, Marcelo, 41, 58
Steffens, H., 253
Stern, Robert, 296
Stolzenberg, Jürgen, 122
Storr, Gottlob Christian, 203, 209, 217, 220, 223
Strauß, Ludwig, 152, 211, 227–28, 231–32
Süskind, Friedrich Gottlieb, 203–4, 209, 217, 220, 223

Tatarkewicz, 188
Teichner, Wilhelm, 45
Tetens, Johann Nicolaus, 28
Thomas Aquinas, 189
Tieck, Ludwig, 177, 181, 196
Tilliette, Xavier, 8–9, 251, 264
Tittel, Gottlob August, 69

van Dülmen, Richard, 49
Vasari, Giorgio, 188
Velkley, Richard L., 13, 118
Verra, Valerio, 252
Vleeschauwer, Herman-J. *See* de Vleeschauwer
Voigt, Christian Gottlob von, 52
von Schönborn, Alexander, 2, 33, 43

Wackenroder, Wilhelm Heinrich, 6, 186, 196
Wangermann, Ernst, 47
Weishaupt, Adam, 48–49, 69
Westphal, Merold, 8–9, 269
Wieland, Christoph Martin, 51, 184
Wild, Christoph, 248, 269
Wilm, Emil, 134, 141
Winckelman, Johann Joachim, 153–54, 160
Wittgenstein, Ludwig, 146
Wizenmann, Thomas, 53
Wolff, Christian, 16, 55, 253
Wollner, J. C. von, 49
Wood, Allen, 19, 117, 129
Wundt, Max, 252

Yovel, Yirmiahu, 13, 19

Zahn, M., 43, 44, 45

www.ingramcontent.com/pod-product-compliance
Lightning Source LLC
Chambersburg PA
CBHW032302300426
44110CB00033B/273